Kaplan Publishing are constantly finding new ways to make a difference to your studies and our exciting online resources really do offer something different to students looking for exam success.

This book comes with free MyKaplan online resources so that you can study anytime, anywhere. **This free online resource is not sold separately and is included in the price of the book.**

Having purchased this book, you have access to the following online study materials:

CONTENT	ACCA (including FBT, FMA, FFA)		FIA (excluding FBT, FMA, FFA)	
	Text	Kit	Text	Kit
Electronic version of the book	✓	✓	✓	✓
Knowledge checks with instant answers	✓		✓	
Material updates	✓	✓	✓	✓
Latest official ACCA exam questions*		✓		
Pocket Notes (digital copy)	✓		✓	
Study Planner	✓			
Progress Test including questions and answers	✓		✓	
Syllabus recap Videos		✓		✓
Revision Planner		✓		✓
Question Debrief and Walkthrough Videos		✓		
Mock Exam including questions and answers		✓		

* Excludes BT, MA, FA, FBT, FMA, FFA; for all other papers includes a selection of questions, as released by ACCA

How to access your online resources

Received this book as part of your Kaplan course?
If you have a MyKaplan account, your full online resources will be added automatically, in line with the information in your course confirmation email. If you've not used MyKaplan before, you'll be sent an activation email once your resources are ready.

Bought your book from Kaplan?
We'll automatically add your online resources to your MyKaplan account. If you've not used MyKaplan before, you'll be sent an activation email.

Bought your book from elsewhere?
Go to **www.mykaplan.co.uk/add-online-resources**
Enter the ISBN number found on the title page and back cover of this book.
Add the unique pass key number contained in the scratch panel below.
You may be required to enter additional information during this process to set up or confirm your account details.

This code can only be used once for the registration of this book online. This registration and your online content will expire when the examinations covered by this book have taken place. Please allow one hour from the time you submit your book details for us to process your request.

Please scratch the film to access your unique code.

Please be aware that this code is case-sensitive and you will need to include the dashes within the passcode, but not when entering the ISBN.

AF891392

PUBLISHING

ACCA Award in Financial Management
(RQF Level 4)

FFM

Foundations in Financial Management

STUDY TEXT

KAPLAN PUBLISHING'S STATEMENT OF PRINCIPLES

LINGUISTIC DIVERSITY, EQUALITY AND INCLUSION

We are committed to diversity, equality and inclusion and strive to deliver content that all users can relate to.

We are here to make a difference to the success of every learner.

Clarity, accessibility and ease of use for our learners are key to our approach.

We will use contemporary examples that are rich, engaging and representative of a diverse workplace.

We will include a representative mix of race and gender at the various levels of seniority within the businesses in our examples to support all our learners in aspiring to achieve their potential within their chosen careers.

Roles played by characters in our examples will demonstrate richness and diversity by the use of different names, backgrounds, ethnicity and gender, with a mix of sexuality, relationships and beliefs where these are relevant to the syllabus.

It must always be obvious who is being referred to in each stage of any example so that we do not detract from clarity and ease of use for each of our learners.

We will actively seek feedback from our learners on our approach and keep our policy under continuous review. If you would like to provide any feedback on our linguistic approach, please use this form (you will need to enter the link below into your browser).

https://docs.google.com/forms/d/1Vc4mltBPrfViy8AhfyKcJMHQKBmLaLPoa_WPqFNf4MI/edit

We will seek to devise simple measures that can be used by independent assessors to randomly check our success in the implementation of our Linguistic Equality, Diversity and Inclusion Policy.

British Library Cataloguing-in-Publication Data

A catalogue record for this book is available from the British Library.

Published by:

Kaplan Publishing UK
179 - 191 Borough High Street,
London,
SE1 1HR

ISBN: 978-1-83735-240-1

Printed and bound in Great Britain.

Acknowledgments

We are grateful to the Association of Chartered Certified Accountants for permission to reproduce past examination questions. The answers have been prepared by Kaplan Publishing.

CONTENTS

Quality and accuracy are of the utmost importance to us so if you spot an error in any of our products, please send an email to mykaplanreporting@kaplan.com with full details, or follow the link to the feedback form in MyKaplan. Our Quality Coordinator will work with our technical team to verify the error and take action to ensure it is corrected in future editions.

INTRODUCTION

This is the new edition of the study text for FFM – **Foundations in Financial Management**, approved by the ACCA and fully updated and revised according to the examiner's comments.

This study text has been written specifically for ACCA Foundation students and has been reviewed by the ACCA. A clear and comprehensive style, numerous examples and highlighted key terms help you to acquire the information easily. Plenty of activities and self-test questions enable you to practise what you have learnt.

At the end of most of the chapters you will find practice questions. Many of these are exam-style questions and will give you a good idea of the way you will be tested. To give you some more invaluable practice at exam style questions (including many real past-exam questions), you should also buy the Kaplan Exam Kit for FFM.

ACCA SUPPORT

For additional support with your studies please also refer to the ACCA Global website.

SYLLABUS AND STUDY GUIDE

Position of the subject in the overall syllabus

FFM will build on the knowledge of the main receipts and payments that an organisation has and the methods of recording these receipts and payments, developed in the compulsory FIA exams.

However, there will not be a presumption of any prior knowledge from the other Options exams.

Foundations in Financial Management (FFM)

This syllabus and study guide is designed to help with teaching and learning and is intended to provide detailed information on what could be assessed in any examination session.

GUIDE TO EXAMINATION ASSESSMENT

ACCA reserves the right to examine anything contained within any study guide at any examination session. This includes knowledge, techniques, principles, theories, and concepts as specified.

For the financial accounting, audit and tax exams, except where indicated otherwise, ACCA will publish **examinable documents** once a year to indicate exactly what regulations and legislation could potentially be assessed within identified examination sessions.

Examinations regulation **issued** or legislation **passed** on or before 31st August annually, will be assessed from September 1st of the following year to August 31st of the year after. Please refer to the examinable documents for the exam (where relevant) for further information.

Regulation issued or legislation passed in accordance with the above dates may be examinable even if the **effective** date is in the future. The term issued or passed relates to when regulation or legislation has been formally approved.

The term effective relates to when regulation or legislation must be applied to entity transactions and business practices.

The study guide offers more detailed guidance on the depth and level at which the examinable documents will be examined. The study guide should therefore be read in conjunction with the examinable documents list.

Qualification structure

The Certified Accounting Technician (CAT) Qualification consists of nine exams which include seven of the FIA examination exams, at all three levels, plus two examinations from three of the specialist options exams. The CAT qualification also requires the completion of the Foundations in Professionalism (FiP) module and 12 months relevant work experience, including the demonstration of 10 work based competence areas. Exemptions can be claimed from a maximum of the first four FIA exams for relevant work experience.

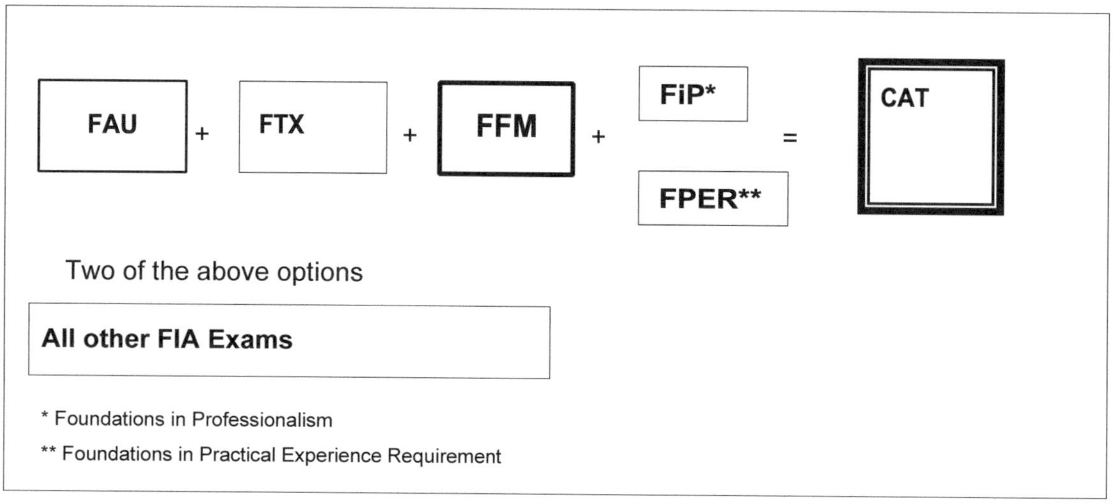

Syllabus structure

The CAT syllabus is designed at three discrete levels. To be awarded the CAT qualification students must either pass or be exempted from all nine examinations including two specialist options exams. Exemptions based on relevant work experience can be claimed from up to the first four FIA exams.

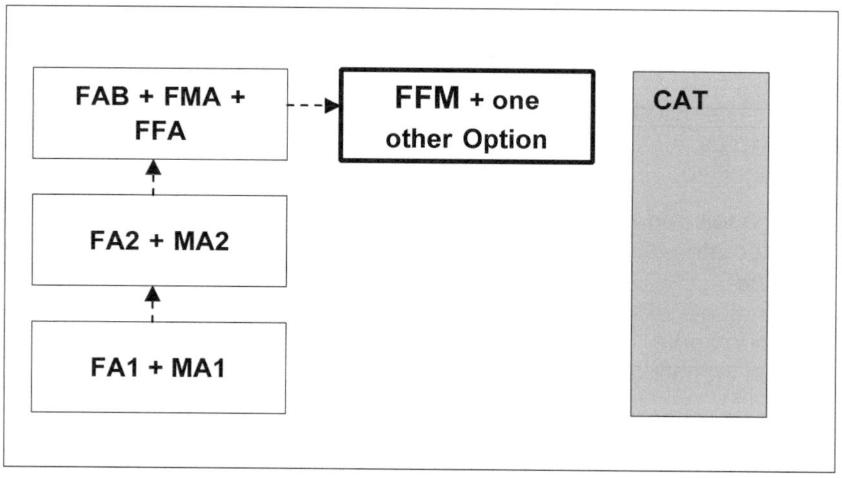

Syllabus

AIM

To develop knowledge and understanding of ways organisations finance their operations, plan and control cash flows, optimise their use of working capital and allocate resources to long term investment projects.

RATIONALE

The syllabus for FFM, Foundations in Financial Management, introduces students to different ways of managing finance within an organisation with the aim of enhancing business performance. This includes planning and controlling of cash flow in both the short and long term, how to manage capital investment decisions and managing trade credit for an efficient flow of cash.

The syllabus starts by introducing the principles of effective working capital management, and the impact working capital has on an organisation's cash flow. It then looks at the techniques for forecasting cash to aid an organisation in planning its cash needs.

The next area of the syllabus looks at the different ways of managing cash in the short, medium and long term, including investing funds in capital projects. It then looks at procedures for effective credit management to maximise flow of cash to the business.

The syllabus finally considers the digital and employability skills in preparing for and taking the FFM exams. This includes being able to interact with different question item types, manage information presented in digital format and being able to use the relevant functionality and technology to prepare and present response options in a professional manner. These skills are specifically developed by practising and preparing for the FFM examination, using the learning support content for computer-based examinations available via the practice platform and the ACCA website and will need to be demonstrated during the live examinations.

MAIN CAPABILITIES

On successful completion of this exam, candidates should be able to:

A Explain and apply the principles of working capital management

B Apply a range of accounting techniques used to forecast cash within the organisation

C Describe methods and procedures for managing cash balances

D Explain principles in making medium to long term financing decisions

E Explain and apply principles in making capital investment decisions

F Describe credit management methods and procedures

G Demonstrate employability and technology skills

DETAILED SYLLABUS

A Working capital management

1 Working capital management cycle

2 Inventory control

3 Accounts payables and receivables control

B Cash budgeting

1 Nature and sources of cash

2 Cash budgeting and forecasting

C Managing cash balances

1 Treasury function

2 Overview of financial markets

3 Managing deficit cash balances

4 Managing surplus cash balances

D Financing decisions

1 Money in the economy

2 Medium term financing

3 Long term financing

4 Financing for small and medium sized enterprises

E Investment decisions

1 Financing concepts

2 Capital budgeting

3 Capital investment appraisal

F Credit management

1 Legal issues

2 Credit granting

3 Monitoring accounts receivables

4 Debt collection

G Employability and technology

1 Use computer technology to efficiently access and manipulate relevant information

2 Work on relevant response options, using available functions and technology as would be required in the workplace

3 Navigate windows and computer screens to create and amend responses to exam requirements, using the appropriate tools

4 Present data and information effectively, using the appropriate tools

APPROACH TO EXAMINING THE SYLLABUS

The syllabus is assessed by a two hour computer based examination. Questions will assess all parts of the syllabus and will include both computational and non-computational elements.

The examination will consist of two sections structured as follows:

Section A	**Marks**
Fifteen compulsory multiple choice questions each worth 2 marks	30
Section B	
Seven compulsory questions	
Q1 (20 marks)	20
Q2, 3, 4 and 5 (5 marks each)	20
Q6 and 7 (15 marks each)	30
Total	100

Study Guide

WORKING CAPITAL MANAGEMENT

1 Working capital management cycle

(a) Define working capital.[k]

(b) Explain why working capital management is important.[k]

(c) Explain the relationship between cash flows and the working capital cycle.[s]

(d) Demonstrate the calculation of the working capital cycle (also known as the cash operating cycle).[s]

(e) Outline the possible relationships between inventory levels and sales.[s]

(f) Define and explain over-trading and over-capitalisation.[s]

(g) Identify and calculate over-trading and over-capitalisation financial indicators.[s]

2 Inventory control

(a) Discuss the key considerations when developing an inventory ordering and storage policy.[s]

(b) Define and explain work in progress.[k]

(c) Define economic order quantity (EOQ).[k]

(d) Apply the EOQ model.[s]

(e) Discuss the effects of just-in-time on inventory control.[s]

(**Note:** Economic Batch Quantities, where all items in a batch do not arrive simultaneously, will not be examined.)

3 Accounts payable and receivables control

(a) Explain the role of accounts payables in the working capital cycle.[k]

(b) Explain the role of accounts receivables in the working capital cycle.[k]

(c) Explain the need to monitor accounts payables.[s]

(d) Explain accounts payables control operations and the importance of accounts payables management.[s]

(e) Describe the various types and form of accounts payables.[k]

(f) Describe the various accounts payables payment methods and procedures (for example, direct debit, cheque).[s]

(g) Evaluate and demonstrate the issues involved with early payment and settlement discounts.[s]

(h) Identify the risks of taking increased credit and buying under extended credit terms.[s]

B CASH BUDGETING

1 Nature and sources of cash

(a) Define cash, cash flow and funds.[k]

(b) Explain the importance of cash flow management and its impact on liquidity and company survival.[s]

(c) Outline the various sources and applications of finance.[k]

(i) Regular revenue receipts and payments

(ii) Capital receipts and payments

(iii) Drawings or dividends and disbursements

(iv) Exceptional receipts and payments

(d) Distinguish between the cash flow patterns of different types of organisations.[s]

(e) Explain the importance of cash flow for sustainable growth of such organisations.[s]

(f) Define 'cash accounting' and 'accruals accounting'.[k]

(g) Explain the difference between cash accounting and accruals accounting.[k]

(h) Reconcile cash flow to profit.[s]

2 Cash budgeting and forecasting

(a) Explain the objectives of a cash budget.[k]

(b) Explain and illustrate statistical techniques used in forecasting cash flows.[s]

(c) Explain inflation and the impact on cash flow and profit.[k]

(d) Prepare a cash budget, including adjustments for timing of receipts and payments.[s]

(e) Discuss and illustrate how cash budgets can be used as a mechanism for monitoring and control.[s]

(f) Carry out simple sensitivity analysis on a cash budget or forecast.[s]

(g) Prepare a simple cleared funds forecast.[s]

C MANAGING CASH BALANCES

1 Treasury function

(a) Outline the basic treasury functions.[k]

(b) Discuss the advantages and disadvantages of a centralised treasury function.[k]

(c) Discuss the advantages and disadvantages of centralised cash control.[k]

(d) Describe cash handling procedures (including recording practises.[k]

(e) Describe the issues to be considered when attempting to hold optimal cash balances.[s]

(f) Outline the statutory and the other regulations relating to the management of cash.[k]

2 Overview of financial markets

(a) Explain the role and functions of various types of banks (including the structure of the banking system).[k]

(b) Identify the major financial intermediaries.[k]

(c) Outline the general roles of financial intermediaries.[k]

(d) Outline the key benefits of financial intermediation.[k]

(e) Outline the relationships between financial institutions.[k]

(f) Explain the purpose and main features of:[s]

- (i) Bank deposits
- (ii) Certificates of deposit
- (iii) Government stocks
- (iv) Local authority bonds
- (v) Bills of exchange

(g) Explain the purpose and main features of:[s]

- (i) Equity
- (ii) Preferred shares
- (iii) Debentures
- (iv) Unsecured loan stock
- (v) Convertible and redeemable debts
- (vi) Warrants

(h) Explain the basic nature of a money market.[k]

(i) Describe the way in which a stock market (both main and second tier) operates.[k]

(j) Discuss ways in which a company may obtain a stock market listing and the advantages and disadvantages of having a stock market listing.[s]

3 Managing deficit cash balances

(a) Discuss situations where it may be appropriate to raise short-term finance.[s]

(b) Describe the different forms of bank loans and overdrafts, their terms and conditions.[s]

(c) Explain the legal relationship between bank and customer.[k]

(d) Explain the nature of trade credit and its use as a short-term source of finance.[s]

(e) Evaluate the risks associated with increasing the amount of short-term finance in an organisation.[s]

(f) Discuss the relative merits and limitations of short term finance.[s]

4 Managing surplus cash balances

(a) Define what is meant by 'surplus funds'.[k]

(b) Explain how surplus funds may arise.[k]

(c) Discuss the objectives to be considered in the investment of surplus funds.[s]

(d) Invest surplus funds according to organisational policy and within defined financial authorisation limits.[s]

(e) Define the risk-return trade-off.[k]

(f) Outline what is meant by risk of default, systematic risk and unsystematic risk.[k]

(g) Outline how the Baumol cash management model works. (**Note:** Calculations are not required.)[k]

(h) Discuss the limitations of the Baumol cash management model.[k]

(i) Suggest appropriate liquidity levels for a range of different organisations.[s]

D FINANCING DECISIONS

1 Money in the economy

(a) Define what is meant by 'money supply' in an economic context.[k]

(b) Outline how money supply may be controlled in an economy.[k]

(c) Outline the basic relationship between the demand for money and interest rates.[k]

(d) Explain briefly and illustrate the interaction between inflation and interest rates.[s]

(e) Discuss the possible consequences of inflation in an economy and its effect on organisations in general.[k]

(f) Describe how the application of different monetary policies can affect the economy.[k]

2 Medium term financing

(a) Discuss situations where it may be appropriate to raise medium-term finance.[s]

(b) Describe the main features of hire purchase, and leases.[k]

(c) Compare and contrast the main features of hire purchase, and leases (NB – lease or buy decisions are not examinable).[s]

(d) Discuss the relative merits and limitations of medium term finance.[s]

3 Long term financing

(a) Discuss situations where it may be appropriate to raise long-term finance.[s]

(b) Describe the key factors to be considered when deciding on an appropriate source of long term finance (debt or equity).[s]

(c) Calculate relative gearing and earnings per share under different financial structures.[s]

(d) Discuss the relative merits and limitations of long term finance.[s]

(e) Describe the key factors that should be considered in deciding the mix of short/medium/long term finance in an organisation.[s]

(f) Discuss the nature and importance of internally generated funds.[k]

(g) Outline the major sources of government funds e.g. grants, regional and national schemes.[k]

4 Financing for small and medium sized enterprises

(a) Outline the requirements for finance of SMEs (purpose, how much, how long).[k]

(b) Describe the nature of the financing problem for SMEs in terms of the funding gap, maturity gap and inadequate security.[s]

(c) Discuss the contribution of lack of information in SMEs to help explain the problems of SME financing.[k]

(d) Describe and discuss the response of government agencies and financial institutions to the SME financing problem.[s]

(e) Describe the main features of venture capital.[k]

(f) Describe the key areas of concern to venture capitalists when evaluating an application for funding.[s]

(g) Explain how the use of such measures as credit suppliers, hire purchase, factoring and second tier listing can help to ease the financial problems of SMEs.[s]

(h) Outline appropriate sources of finance for SMEs.[s]

E INVESTMENT DECISIONS

1 Financing concepts

(a) Explain the differences between simple and compound interest.[k]

(b) Calculate future values.[s]

(c) Discuss the concept of time value of money.[s]

(d) Discuss the concept of discounting.[s]

(e) Calculate present values, making use of present value tables to establish discount factors.[s]

2 Capital budgeting

(a) Discuss the importance of capital investment planning and control.[k]

(b) Outline the issues to consider and the steps involved in the preparation of a capital expenditure budget.[s]

(c) Define and distinguish between capital and revenue expenditure.[k]

(d) Compare and contrast investment in non-current assets and investment in working capital.[k]

(e) Describe capital investment procedures (authorisation and monitoring).[k]

3 Capital investment appraisal

(a) Calculate the payback and discounted payback of a project and assess its usefulness as a method of investment appraisal.[s]

(b) Calculate the accounting rate of return of a project and assess its usefulness as a method of investment appraisal.[s]

(c) Discuss the concept of relevant cash flows for decision making.[k]

(d) Identify and evaluate relevant cash flows for individual investment decisions.[s]

(e) Explain the concept of net present value and how it can be used for project appraisal.[k]

(f) Calculate net present value and interpret the results.[s]

(**Note:** NPV calculations will not include adjustments for inflation, tax or working capital.)

(g) Outline the concept of internal rate of return and how it can be used for project appraisal.[k]

(h) Calculate internal rate of return and interpret the results.[s]

(i) Discuss the relative merits of NPV and IRR, including mutually exclusive projects and multiple yields.[k]

(j) Explain the superiority of DCF methods over payback and accounting rate of return.[k]

F CREDIT MANAGEMENT

1 Legal issues

(a) Explain the key elements of a basic contract (offer, acceptance, remedies for breach of contract etc.).[k]

(b) Briefly outline specific terms and conditions that may be included in contracts with credit customers (e.g. length of credit period, amount of interest on late payments, retention of title.[s]

(c) Outline the basic legal procedures for the collection of debts.[k]

(d) Identify the main data protection issues that should be considered when dealing with accounts receivables records.[k]

(e) Explain bankruptcy and insolvency.[k]

2 Credit granting

(a) Explain the importance of credit management, including the level of trade credit, the role of the credit control function and the activities of the credit control function.[k]

(b) Explain the need to establish a credit policy and outline the steps involved, including setting maximum credit amounts and periods and total credit levels.[s]

(c) Explain the key categories that should be considered when assessing the credit-worthiness of a customer.[k]

(d) Outline the various internal sources of information that may be used in assessing the credit-worthiness of a customer.[s]

(e) Outline the various external sources of information that may be used in assessing the credit-worthiness of a customer.[s]

(f) Define and explain credit scoring.[k]

(g) Identify possible reasons for rejecting an application for credit or extending credit.[s]

(h) Describe how the financial statements of a customer can be used to assess the credit-worthiness of a customer.[s]

(i) Identify and apply the common ratios that may be used to analyse the financial statements of a customer in order to assess their credit-worthiness.[s]

(j) Evaluate the usefulness and limitations of ratio analysis in assessing credit-worthiness.[s]

3 Monitoring accounts receivables

(a) Identify the main contents of accounts receivables records.[s]

(b) Describe the main internal sources that may be used to monitor accounts receivables (including aged trade receivables analysis, average periods of credit, incidence of bad debts).[s]

Note: You may be required to prepare an aged accounts receivables analysis.

(c) Describe the main external sources that may be used to monitor accounts receivables (including credit rating agencies, industry sources, financial reports, press coverage, official publications, bank or supplier reference).[s]

4 Debt collection

(a) Identify the main methods used to identify potential problems with credit customers meeting their payment obligations.[k]

(b) Describe ways in which credit customers could be encouraged to pay promptly including effects of offering discounts.[s]

(c) Describe the main techniques and methods that may be used to assist in the collection of overdue debts.[s]

(d) Identify debt recovery methods appropriate to individual customers.[s]

(e) Explain procedures for writing off debts (double entry recording is excluded).[k]

(f) Describe how factoring works and the main types of service provided by factors.[s]

(g) Define invoice discounting and outline how this form of factoring works.[s]

(h) Calculate the cost of factoring arrangements, invoice discounting and changes in credit policy.[s]

G EMPLOYABILITY AND TECHNOLOGY

(a) Use computer technology to efficiently access and manipulate relevant information.

(b) Work on relevant response option, using available functions and technology, as would be required in the workplace.

(c) Navigate windows and computer screens to create and amend responses to exam requirements, using the appropriate tools.

(d) Present data and information effectively using the appropriate tools.

SUMMARY OF CHANGES TO FFM

ACCA periodically reviews its qualification syllabuses so that they fully meet the needs of stakeholders including employers, students, regulatory and advisory bodies and learning providers.

There have been no amendments to the FFM syllabus and study guide.

THE EXAMINATION

Format of the examination

The examination is a two-hour computer based exam.

		Number of marks
Section A:	15 multiple choice questions, worth 2 marks each	30
Section B:	7 written questions worth 5–20 marks each	
	Q1 20 marks	20
	Q2, 3, 4 and 5 (5 marks each)	20
	Q6 and 7 (15 marks each)	30
		100

Examination tips – Computer Based Exam (CBE)

In addition to reading the tips contained here, we recommend that you review the resources available on the ACCA Global Website before sitting the CBE. Here you will find guidance documents, videos and a link to the CBE question practice platform.

Before the exam starts – You will be given 10 minutes to read the introductory page and the four pages of instructions. These will be the same for each FFM exam and therefore it is important that you familiarise yourself with these (using the ACCA practice exams) during your revision. The exam time (2 hours) will start automatically at the end of the 10 minutes or earlier if requested by you.

Plan your strategy before you go in; allocating 36 minutes to Section A, and then 1.8 minutes per mark for each of the questions in Section B.

Answering the questions

Section A: Multiple choice questions: Read the question and try to answer it without referring to the answers. When you have an answer, compare it to the choices given and (hopefully) pick the correct one. If your answer does not match any of the choices given, try to rework your answer.

You will not have marks deducted for putting the wrong answer, so always make a guess if you cannot get the correct answer.

Section B: Constructed response questions: Start by reading the detail of the question, and the specific requirements.

Decide on the use of a word processing format, a spreadsheet format or both.

For calculations, use a logical and well laid out structure. Calculations should be labelled and referenced in to any relevant discussion. For discursive answers use bold headings and sub-headings and professional language.

Ensure all aspects of the requirement are covered in a sensible and balanced way. It is vital that you relate your answer to the specific circumstances given.

If you get completely stuck with a question return to it later.

If you do not understand what a question is asking, state your assumptions. Even if you do not answer in precisely the way the examiner hoped, you should be given some credit, if your assumptions are reasonable.

Some questions ask you to present your answer in the form of a report or a memo or other document. Use the correct format – there could be easy marks to gain here.

STUDY SKILLS AND REVISION GUIDANCE

Preparing to study

Set your objectives

Before starting to study decide what you want to achieve – the type of pass you wish to obtain.

This will decide the level of commitment and time you need to dedicate to your studies.

Devise a study plan

Determine when you will study.

Split these times into study sessions.

Put the sessions onto a study plan making sure you cover the course, course assignments and revision.

Stick to your plan!

Effective study techniques

Use the **SQR3** method

Survey the chapter – look at the headings and read the introduction, summary and objectives. Get an overview of what the text deals with.

Question – during the survey, ask yourself the questions that you hope the chapter will answer for you.

Read through the chapter thoroughly, answering the questions and meeting the objectives. Attempt the exercises and activities, and work through all the examples.

Recall – at the end of the chapter, try to recall the main ideas of the chapter without referring to the text. Do this a few minutes after the reading stage.

Review – check that your recall notes are correct.

Use the **MURDER** method

Mood – set the right mood.

Understand – issues covered and make note of any uncertain bits.

Recall – stop and put what you have learned into your own words.

Digest – go back and reconsider the information.

Expand – read relevant articles and newspapers.

Review – go over the material you covered to consolidate the knowledge.

MATHEMATICAL TABLES

Formula

Economic order quantity

$$= \sqrt{\frac{2C_0D}{C_h}}$$

Present Value and Annuity Tables follow on the next page.

Present value table

Present value of 1 i.e. $(1+r)^{-n}$

where r = discount rate

n = number of periods until payment

Periods (n)	1%	2%	3%	4%	5%	6%	7%	8%	9%	10%	
1	0.990	0.980	0.971	0.962	0.952	0.943	0.935	0.926	0.917	0.909	1
2	0.980	0.961	0.943	0.925	0.907	0.890	0.873	0.857	0.842	0.826	2
3	0.971	0.942	0.915	0.889	0.864	0.840	0.816	0.794	0.772	0.751	3
4	0.961	0.924	0.888	0.855	0.823	0.792	0.763	0.735	0.708	0.683	4
5	0.951	0.906	0.863	0.822	0.784	0.747	0.713	0.681	0.650	0.621	5
6	0.942	0.888	0.837	0.790	0.746	0.705	0.666	0.630	0.596	0.564	6
7	0.933	0.871	0.813	0.760	0.711	0.665	0.623	0.583	0.547	0.513	7
8	0.923	0.853	0.789	0.731	0.677	0.627	0.582	0.540	0.502	0.467	8
9	0.914	0.837	0.766	0.703	0.645	0.592	0.544	0.500	0.460	0.424	9
10	0.905	0.820	0.744	0.676	0.614	0.558	0.508	0.463	0.422	0.386	10
11	0.896	0.804	0.722	0.650	0.585	0.527	0.475	0.429	0.388	0.350	11
12	0.887	0.788	0.701	0.625	0.557	0.497	0.444	0.397	0.356	0.319	12
13	0.879	0.773	0.681	0.601	0.530	0.469	0.415	0.368	0.326	0.290	13
14	0.870	0.758	0.661	0.577	0.505	0.442	0.388	0.340	0.299	0.263	14
15	0.861	0.743	0.642	0.555	0.481	0.417	0.362	0.315	0.275	0.239	15

(n)	11%	12%	13%	14%	15%	16%	17%	18%	19%	20%	
1	0.901	0.893	0.885	0.877	0.870	0.862	0.855	0.847	0.840	0.833	1
2	0.812	0.797	0.783	0.769	0.756	0.743	0.731	0.718	0.706	0.694	2
3	0.731	0.712	0.693	0.675	0.658	0.641	0.624	0.609	0.593	0.579	3
4	0.659	0.636	0.613	0.592	0.572	0.552	0.534	0.516	0.499	0.482	4
5	0.593	0.567	0.543	0.519	0.497	0.476	0.456	0.437	0.419	0.402	5
6	0.535	0.507	0.480	0.456	0.432	0.410	0.390	0.370	0.352	0.335	6
7	0.482	0.452	0.425	0.400	0.376	0.354	0.333	0.314	0.296	0.279	7
8	0.434	0.404	0.376	0.351	0.327	0.305	0.285	0.266	0.249	0.233	8
9	0.391	0.361	0.333	0.308	0.284	0.263	0.243	0.225	0.209	0.194	9
10	0.352	0.322	0.295	0.270	0.247	0.227	0.208	0.191	0.176	0.162	10
11	0.317	0.287	0.261	0.237	0.215	0.195	0.178	0.162	0.148	0.135	11
12	0.286	0.257	0.231	0.208	0.187	0.168	0.152	0.137	0.124	0.112	12
13	0.258	0.229	0.204	0.182	0.163	0.145	0.130	0.116	0.104	0.093	13
14	0.232	0.205	0.181	0.160	0.141	0.125	0.111	0.099	0.088	0.078	14
15	0.209	0.183	0.160	0.140	0.123	0.108	0.095	0.084	0.074	0.065	15

Annuity table

Present value of an annuity of 1 i.e. $\frac{1-(1+r)^{-n}}{r}$

where r = discount rate

n = number of periods

Periods (n)	1%	2%	3%	4%	5%	6%	7%	8%	9%	10%	
1	0.990	0.980	0.971	0.962	0.952	0.943	0.935	0.926	0.917	0.909	1
2	1.970	1.942	1.913	1.886	1.859	1.833	1.808	1.783	1.759	1.736	2
3	2.941	2.884	20829	2.775	2.723	2.673	2.624	2.577	2.531	2.487	3
4	3.902	3.808	3.717	3.630	3.546	3.465	3.387	3.312	3.240	3.170	4
5	4.853	4.713	4.580	4.452	4.329	4.212	4.100	3.993	3.890	3.791	5
6	5.795	5.601	5.417	5.242	5.076	4.917	4.767	4.623	4.486	4.355	6
7	6.728	6.472	6.230	6.002	5.786	5.582	5.389	5.206	5.033	4.868	7
8	7.652	7.325	7.020	6.733	6.463	6.210	5.971	5.747	5.535	5.335	8
9	8.566	8.162	7.786	7.435	7.108	6.802	6.515	6.247	5.995	5.759	9
10	9.471	8.983	8.530	8.111	7.722	7.360	7.024	6.710	6.418	6.145	10
11	10.37	9.787	9.253	8.760	8.306	7.887	7.499	7.139	6.805	6.495	11
12	11.26	10.58	9.954	9.385	8.863	8.384	7.943	7.536	7.161	6.814	12
13	12.13	11.35	10.63	9.986	9.394	8.853	8.358	7.904	7.487	7.103	13
14	13.00	12.11	11.30	10.56	9.899	9.295	8.745	8.244	7.786	7.367	14
15	13.87	12.85	11.94	11.12	10.38	9.712	9.108	8.559	8.061	7.606	15

(n)	11%	12%	13%	14%	15%	16%	17%	18%	19%	20%	
1	0.901	0.893	0.885	0.877	0.870	0.862	0.855	0.847	0.840	0.833	1
2	1.713	1.690	1.668	1.647	1.626	1.605	1.585	1.566	1.547	1.528	2
3	2.444	2.402	2.361	2.322	2.283	2.246	2.210	2.174	2.140	2.106	3
4	3.102	3.037	2.974	2.914	2.855	2.798	2.743	2.690	2.639	2.589	4
5	3.696	3.605	3.517	3.433	3.352	3.274	3.199	3.127	3.058	2.991	5
6	4.231	4.111	3.998	3.889	3.784	3.685	3.589	3.498	3.410	3.326	6
7	4.712	4.564	4.423	4.288	4.160	4.039	3.922	3.812	3.706	3.605	7
8	5.146	4.968	4.799	4.639	4.487	4.344	4.207	4.078	3.954	3.837	8
9	5.537	5.328	5.132	4.946	4.772	4.607	4.451	4.303	4.163	4.031	9
10	5.889	5.650	5.426	5.216	5.019	4.833	4.659	4.494	4.339	4.192	10
11	6.207	5.938	5.687	5.453	5.234	5.029	4.836	4.656	4.486	4.327	11
12	6.492	6.194	5.918	5.660	5.421	5.197	4.988	4.793	4.611	4.439	12
13	6.750	6.424	6.122	5.842	5.583	5.342	5.118	4.910	4.715	4.533	13
14	6.982	6.628	6.302	6.002	5.724	5.468	5.229	5.008	4.802	4.611	14
15	7.191	6.811	6.462	6.142	5.847	5.575	5.324	5.092	4.876	4.675	15

Chapter 1

CASH AND CASH FLOWS

Businesses exist to make profit, but they cannot survive without cash. This chapter explains the nature of cash receipts and payments in a business, and considers the importance of cash flow and liquidity. Cash flow is compared with profitability. The elements of cash management are explained, and the relationship between cash management and credit control is introduced.

This chapter covers Syllabus part B1.

CONTENTS

LEARNING OUTCOMES

At the end of this chapter you should be able to:

- Define cash, cash flow and funds
- Explain the importance of cash flow management and its impact on liquidity and company survival
- Outline the various sources and applications of finance
  - (i) regular revenue receipts and payments
  - (ii) capital receipts and payments
  - (iii) drawings or dividends and disbursements
  - (iv) exceptional receipts and payments
- Distinguish between the cash flow patterns of different types of organisations
- Explain the importance of cash flow for sustainable growth of such organisations
- Define 'cash accounting' and 'accruals accounting'
- Explain the difference between cash accounting and accruals accounting
- Reconcile cash flow to profit.

1 THE NATURE OF CASH AND CASH FLOWS

1.1 RELEVANT DEFINITIONS

The first requirement in this syllabus is for you to be able to define cash, cash flows and funds.

Cash can be defined as money, in the form of notes and coins. It is the most liquid of assets and represents the lifeblood for growth and investment. Cash includes:

- coins and notes
- current accounts and short-term deposits
- bank overdrafts and short-term loans
- foreign currency and deposits that can be quickly converted to your currency.

It does not include:

- long-term deposits
- long-term borrowing
- money owed by customers
- inventory (stock).

It is important not to confuse cash with profit. Profit is the difference between the total amount a business earns and all of its costs, usually assessed over a year or other trading period. A business may be able to forecast a good profit for the year, yet still face times when it is strapped for cash.

Cash flow is a term for receipts and payments of cash. Cash flow shows the money flowing into a business from sales, interest payments received, and any borrowings and the amount of money flowing out of a business through paying for wages, rent, interest owing, paying back loans, buying raw materials, tax and so on.

Cash flow can be described as a cycle: a business uses cash to acquire resources. The resources are put to work and goods and services produced. These are then sold to customers, the business then collects and deposits the cash from the sales and so the cycle repeats.

Net cash flow is the difference between the cash received in a period and the cash paid out in the same period.

On any single day, or in any week or month, cash receipts can exceed cash payments, in which case the cash flow is positive. Equally, cash payments can exceed cash receipts, and the cash flow is negative. Over time, a business should expect cash receipts to exceed cash payments, or at least that cash payments should not exceed cash receipts.

Funds can be defined as any arrangement that enables goods or services to be bought. It therefore usually means money (i.e. cash or bank balances) or credit (i.e. lending or borrowing). Every transaction that a business makes can be interpreted in terms of a source of funds and use of funds, which must be equal in total.

Managing cash in a business is basically similar to the management of cash by an individual. An individual might receive cash every month in the form of a salary and pay out money on a variety of expenses, such as food and drink, travel, rent and so on. Some spending is likely to be on credit (using a credit card, perhaps), just as businesses take credit for most of their purchases, but credit card bills have to be paid eventually. Individuals have to make sure that they have enough cash coming in each month to make all the payments that have to be made. An individual might have a bank overdraft facility, but the bank will not let the overdraft exceed the agreed limit.

Businesses have the same concerns. They can buy on credit, but suppliers eventually have to be paid. They can borrow and negotiate an overdraft facility, but there are limits to borrowing. Consequently, cash has to be managed, to make sure that there is always enough money to keep the business going.

1.2 CASH CYCLE AND OPERATING CYCLE

The cash flow cycle, in its simplest form, revolves around the company's trading cycle. The process involves purchasing inventory (stock), converting it to cash or accounts receivable via sales, collecting those accounts receivable, and paying suppliers who extended trade credit.

Cash cycle and operating cycle

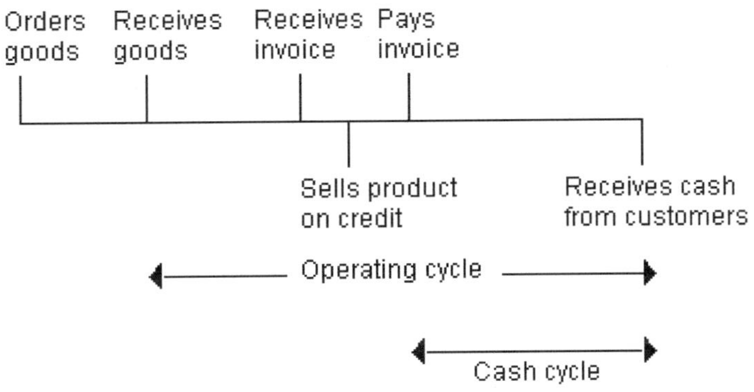

The cash flow cycle is the period of time required for an organisation to receive invested funds back in the form of cash. The full cash flow cycle can be divided into two distinct cycles:

1 The **operating cycle** – the time period between acquiring inventory from suppliers and the actual cash collection from receivables (debtors) for goods sold.

2 The **cash cycle** – the time period between the cash payment for inventory and the cash collection of accounts receivables generated in the sale of the final product.

The cash conversion period measures the amount of time it takes to convert the organisation's product or service into cash inflows. It is calculated by:

+ The number of days that cash is locked up as inventory or work in progress

+ The number of days that cash is locked up in receivables

– Days that cash is free because the business has not paid its bills

2 THE SOURCES AND APPLICATIONS OF FINANCE

2.1 SOURCES AND USES OF CASH

Sources and uses of cash cover three activities in an enterprise:

1. **Operating activities** are activities that create revenue or expense in the entity's major line of business. The largest cash inflow from operations is the collection of cash from customers. Operating activities that create cash outflows include payments to suppliers, payments to employees, interest payments, payment of income taxes and other operating cash payments.

2. **Investing activities** include lending money and collecting on those loans, buying and selling productive assets that are expected to generate revenues over long periods, and buying and selling securities not classified as cash equivalents. Cash inflows generated by investing activities include sales of long-lived assets such as property, plant and equipment, sales of debt or equity instruments and the collection of loans.

3. **Financing activities** include borrowing and repaying money from payables (creditors), obtaining resources from owners and providing both a return on their investment and a return of their investment. The return on investment is provided in the form of dividends.

Sources of cash	Uses of cash
Obtaining finance:	Paying payables or stockholders:
• Increase in long-term debt	• Decrease in long-term debt
• Increase in equity	• Decrease in equity
• Increase in current liabilities	• Decrease in current liabilities
Selling assets	Buying assets
• Decrease in current assets	• Increase in current assets
• Decrease in fixed assets (non-current assets)	• Increase in fixed assets (non-current assets)

Fixed assets (which are also known as non-current assets), as you know, are assets that are used by the business on a continuing basis. Current assets are items which are either cash already or which the business intends to turn into cash. Current liabilities are debts that the business has to pay in the near future – which we take to mean debts due for payment within the next year.

Working capital is the net difference between current assets and current liabilities.

ACTIVITY 1

Working capital is the third different meaning given to the word 'capital' in accounting terms.

Required:

Can you explain the three meanings?

For a suggested answer, see the 'Answers' section at the end of the book.

2.2 MAIN TYPES OF CASH RECEIPTS AND PAYMENTS

The cash receipts for a business come from a variety of sources, and there are various reasons for making cash payments. Cash receipts and payments can be categorised into the following types:

- revenue receipts and payments
- capital receipts and payments
- drawings/dividends and disbursements
- exceptional receipts and payments.

All of these types of cash receipt and payment affect the cash flows of a business, and cash management involves making sure that the total amount of cash received from these sources is always enough to make all the necessary cash payments.

Revenue receipts and payments are cash receipts and payments arising from the normal course of business. Revenue receipts are cash receipts from:

- cash sales, and
- payments by trade receivables.

Revenue payments are payments in the normal course of business, and include payments:

- to trade payables
- to employees for salaries and wages (and to the tax authorities for income tax deductions)
- for business expenses such as office rental payments, telephone bills, payments out of petty cash, and so on.

Capital receipts are receipts of long-term funds or cash from the sale of non-current assets or long-term investments. The owners of a business put new capital into the business in the form of new cash. For example, the shareholders in a company might agree to put more cash into the business by subscribing for a new issue of shares. Similarly, a sole trader might decide to put some extra money into the business by transferring cash from a personal bank account to a business bank account.

Capital payments are payments for capital expenditure, such as the purchase of new non-current assets (equipment, motor vehicles and so on).

Occasionally, a business might raise new cash by obtaining a long-term loan. A loan from a bank is a liability, but long-term (non-current) liabilities can be thought of as a 'capital receipt'. Similarly, the repayment of a loan might be thought of as a 'capital payment'.

Drawings/dividends and disbursements

When a business makes profits, it usually pays out some of those profits to its owners.

- Payments out of profits to a sole trader or partners in a partnership are known as drawings.
- Payments out of profits to the shareholders of a company are known as dividends.

Businesses can pay drawings or dividends whenever they want to. However, many companies pay dividends to shareholders twice each year. One dividend payment is an interim dividend, paid in the middle of the year when the profits for the first six months are known. The second dividend payment is a final dividend, which is paid after the end of the year when the profits for the full year are known.

In practice, this means that during any financial year, a company might pay out in dividends to its shareholders:

- a final dividend for the previous financial year, and
- an interim dividend for the current financial year.

The term 'disbursement' simply means a payment. The term could be used, however, to mean payments of:

- interest on loans and overdrafts, and on other debts for which interest is payable (such as loan stock or 'bonds' in the case of companies)
- income tax payable by a company out of its profits (corporation tax in the UK).

EXCEPTIONAL RECEIPTS AND PAYMENTS

The foregoing are all relatively routine transactions. They are known and they can be planned for. There is always the possibility that there will be a significant movement because of an unusual or 'exceptional' transaction that does not fall into any of the categories described above. An example would be the costs of closing down part of a business.

2.3 CASH FLOW PATTERNS IN DIFFERENT BUSINESSES

The 'dynamics' or patterns of revenue receipts and payments vary greatly between different types of business. Many businesses have regular expenditure patterns, such as constant monthly salary costs and regular monthly accommodation costs. However, patterns of cash receipts vary enormously, as the following examples might suggest.

- A retail business with a chain of shops or stores buys goods for resale, often obtaining credit of 30 to 60 days from suppliers. It might hope to re-sell many of the items fairly quickly, typically for cash. As we have already noted, many retail businesses are therefore able to receive cash from selling their goods even before they have had to pay their suppliers. Cash receipts are also daily, or at least every day that the shops are open.

- A hat manufacturer has a seasonal business, with most sales in the spring and early summer. Its sales are likely to be on credit to retailers and other distributors, on 30 to 60 days' credit. It produces hats continually throughout the year, so has fairly constant monthly cash expenditures.

- A large contracting business might have to spend a lot of cash in bidding to win a large construction contract. Some companies, for example, have spent several years in bidding for government contracts to build schools, hospitals or roads. If they win a new contract, they are likely to have to spend heavily on hiring labour and buying or renting equipment. Cash receipts from the customer are likely to be in the form of progress payments, which are usually occasional large amounts.

- A training college or university is likely to receive most of its income at the start of its courses, mainly at the beginning of the academic year. Its costs and cash expenditures occur over the duration of the course. It should therefore expect a large cash surplus at the start of the academic year, which then gradually reduces as the year progresses.

You might be aware of other businesses with different cash flow patterns from these.

3 CASH FLOW AND PROFIT

For a business to survive, over the longer term it has to be profitable. In the short term, however, cash flow is more important than profit. If a business cannot make an essential payment, it could be faced with insolvency and payables could take action to recover the money owing to them. In the short term:

- a business can make a loss but still have enough cash to survive, receiving more cash than it pays

- a business can be profitable but run out of cash, spending more cash than it receives.

In the short term, profits and cash flow are different. There are several reasons for this.

- Some items of cash spending and cash receipt do not affect profits at all. In particular capital receipts and capital payments do not affect profits. A business could earn a profit but spend large sums of money on capital expenditure, so that it makes a profit but has a negative cash flow.

- Profits are calculated after deducting depreciation charges on non-current assets. Depreciation is a notional charge, and does not affect cash flow at all. It is an accounting device for spreading the cost of a non-current asset over its useful life.

- Cash flow is affected by the need to invest in operational working capital. Operational working capital is defined as the working capital a business needs to carry on its day-to-day business operations. It consists of its inventory (stock) plus its trade receivables minus its trade payables.

Investing in working capital affects cash flow, and when the total amount of working capital of a business changes, the profits earned in the period will differ from the operational cash flows. It might not seem obvious why this should be the case.

- **Inventory (stock).** A business buys raw materials or supplies and uses these to manufacture goods or provide services. Materials and supplies are bought before goods can be produced or services can be provided, which means that a business has to pay for its inventory before it earns anything from sales.
- **Receivables (debtors).** When businesses sell goods or services on credit, they make a profit when the sale occurs, but they do not get any cash receipts until the customer pays. A business therefore incurs the costs of making a sale, and spends cash in advance of receiving the cash income.
- **Payables (creditors).** On the other hand, if a business buys goods and services on credit, it benefits by not having to pay for them until sometime after they have been received.

We can compare the gross profit from trading with the operating cash flows from trading in a company that buys and resells goods.

The statement of profit or loss reports the total value of sales and the cost of goods sold in a year and shows:

Sales revenue – Cost of sales = Profit

However, if goods are sold on credit the cash receipts will differ from the value of sales, as receivables will pay after the year-end. The cost of goods sold will also differ as some goods are purchased on credit and some may remain in inventory at the year-end.

The operational cash flow is reported as cash in (Sales + Opening receivables – Closing receivables) – Cash out (Purchases + Opening payables – Closing payables).

ACTIVITY 2

Calculate the profit and the operational cash flow resulting from the year's trading figures for ABC given below:

Sales revenue	$240,000
Cost of sales	$204,000
Opening inventory	$14,400
Payables at start of year	$13,200
Receivables at start of year	$18,000
Closing inventory	$25,200
Payables at end of year	$16,800
Receivables at end of year	$28,800

For a suggested answer, see the 'Answers' section at the end of the book.

The following example illustrates how the profits of a business and its cash flows in the same period are different because of working capital.

Example

In September 20X4 Peter entered into a contract with QAZ Co, a manufacturer of electrical equipment. Under the terms of the contract, Peter will repair any electrical items failing within their warranty period that are returned to QAZ for repair by its dissatisfied customers. He will invoice QAZ as follows:

Labour	$25 per hour
Materials	Cost + 40%

Peter will receive payment from QAZ against a sales invoice, sent at the end of each month, with payment to be made 60 days after the invoice date.

Peter pays wages of $10 per hour, paying his employees at the end of each week. Payments to suppliers for materials are made one month after receipt from the supplier.

Let's suppose that Peter opens a separate bank account for receipts and payments for this contract with QAZ.

The following transaction details relate to October, November and December 20X4:

	October	**November**	**December**
	$	$	$
Wages cost	400	500	700
Material cost	600	800	1,000
Sales invoiced	1,840	2,370	3,150

The contract is profitable, because the sales exceed the combined cost of wages and materials.

	October	**November**	**December**
	$	$	$
Sales	1,840	2,370	3,150
Costs:			
Wages cost	400	500	700
Material cost	600	800	1,000
Total costs	1,000	1,300	1,700
Profit	840	1,070	1,450

However, Peter's cash flows in the first few months of the contract are a cause for concern.

	October	**November**	**December**
	$	$	$
Receipts:			
Paid sales invoices	0	0	1,840
Payments			
Wages	400	500	700
Materials	0	600	800
Total payments	400	1,100	1,500
Cash surplus/(deficit) for the month	(400)	(1,100)	340
Opening cash balance	0	(400)	(1,500)
Closing cash balance	(400)	(1,500)	(1,160)

Peter has to be able to fund the wage costs and material costs for the first two months before any money is received from QAZ for the work done. He will therefore have to find $1,500 in cash, or borrow to meet these cash requirements, even though the contract is profitable from the first month onwards.

Every month, the difference between profit and cash flow forces Peter to invest more in working capital. There is no inventory, and working capital is therefore total receivables minus total payables.

	End of October	**End of November**	**End of December**
	$	$	$
Receivables			
Unpaid sales in October	1,840	1,840	–
Unpaid sales in November	–	2,370	2,370
Unpaid sales in December	–	–	3,150
Total receivables	1,840	4,210	5,520
Payables for materials	600	800	1,000
Working capital	1,240	3,410	4,520
Increase/(decrease) in working capital in the month	1,240	2,170	1,110

So profits and cash flows each month can be reconciled by adjusting for the working capital movement as follows:

Profit in the month	840	1,070	1,450
Increase/(decrease) in working capital in the month	1,240	2,170	1,110
Net cash flow in the month	(400)	(1,100)	340

We could do this calculation for any company, although it would become very much more complicated if the company had more than one contract in progress or had a more complicated set of transactions to analyse.

3.1 CASH FLOW AND BUSINESS SURVIVAL

In the short run, a loss-making business can survive, provided that it has enough cash or access to new borrowings. A profitable business might not survive if it has negative cash flows, unless it has enough cash in the bank to cover the deficit or unless it has access to new borrowings. In the past, there have been many examples of apparently successful businesses collapsing because they ran out of cash.

3.2 CASH FLOW AND BUSINESS GROWTH

Cash flow is the lifeblood of a business. Cash is absolutely critical in the growth and wellbeing of a business.

Cash flow analysis shows whether the enterprise's daily operations generate enough cash to meet their business obligations. It also indicates how major cash outflows relate to major cash inflows. Early identification of cash-related problems will facilitate better control of cash flows and will allow adequate time to plan and prepare for the sustained growth of the business.

A successful business that is trying to grow can also run into cash flow difficulties. As it increases its sales, a business might have to take on more employees, and buy more equipment and other non-current assets. It might have to buy larger quantities of inventory, and give its customers longer credit periods. To avoid cash flow problems, a business should therefore plan its sales growth, and make sure that it will have the liquidity (cash or new debt) to finance its growth.

3.3 LIQUIDITY

Liquid assets consist of both cash and items that could or will be converted into cash within a short time, with little or no loss. They include some investments, for example:

- deposits with banks or building societies where a minimum notice period for withdrawal is required.
- investments in government securities, which in the UK are called gilt-edged stocks (or 'gilts').

Other liquid assets are trade receivables and, possibly, inventory.

- Trade receivables should be expected to pay what they owe within a fairly short time, so receivables are often considered a liquid asset for a business.
- In some businesses, such as retailing, inventory will be used or re-sold within a short time, to create sales for the business and cash income. Inventory is less liquid than receivables.

A business has liquidity if it has access to enough liquid assets to meet its essential payment obligations when they fall due. This means that a business is extremely liquid if it has a large amount of cash, plus investments in gilts and funds in notice accounts with a building society, plus a large amount of trade receivables and inventory.

Liquidity is also boosted if a business has an unused overdraft facility, so that it could go into overdraft with its bank if it needed to.

A business that has good liquidity is unlikely to have serious cash flow problems. For all businesses, it is important to make revenue payments when they fall due. Trade payables and employees should all be paid on time. When a liquid business has to make a cash payment, it should be able to obtain the money from somewhere to do it. Normally, the cash to pay suppliers and employees comes from the cash received from trade receivables.

The liquidity of a business, particularly its operational activities, is therefore related to its working capital, and in particular its inventory, receivables and short-term payables.

Conclusions so far

- Cash flow and profit are not the same.
- One reason for the difference is changes in operational working capital. Operational working capital consists of inventory plus trade receivables minus trade payables.
- To survive in the short term a business must have liquidity. Liquidity means cash or ready access to sources of cash, such as new borrowing.
- A business that has reached its borrowing limits needs to have positive cash flow to survive.
- Cash flow management should ensure survival and promote sustainable growth in the business.

ACTIVITY 3

What separates cash from profits? Explain why lots of sales might not mean lots of cash.

For a suggested answer, see the 'Answers' section at the end of the book.

3.4 RECONCILING CASH AND PROFITS

It is often useful to reconcile a firm's profit figure to its cash inflow from operating activities. The main reconciling items are:

- non-cash items that affect profit, such as depreciation and profits/losses on disposals of asset
- movements in inventories, payables and receivables.

Therefore, the standard layout for a reconciliation would be:

Operating profit	X
Add: Depreciation charges	X
Add: Loss on sale of non-current assets (or deduct profit on sale)	X
Add: Decrease in inventory (or deduct increase)	X
Add: Decrease in trade receivables (or deduct increase)	X
Add: Increase in trade payables (or deduct decrease)	X
Net cash inflow from operating activities	X

Example

Wild Co made an operating profit of $27,000 last year. Depreciation was $6,000 in the year, and assets with a book value of $40,000 were sold for $35,000. Extracts from the statement of financial position at the start and the end of the year show the following:

	Start of year	**End of year**
Inventory	$10,000	$14,500
Receivables	$21,000	$20,000
Payables	$13,100	$14,050

The net cash inflow for the year can be found from the following reconciliation:

	$
Operating profit	27,000
Add: Depreciation charges	6,000
Add: Loss on sale of non-current assets	5,000
Deduct: increase in inventory	(4,500)
Add: Decrease in trade receivables	1,000
Add: Increase in trade payables	950
Net cash inflow from operating activities	35,450

ACTIVITY 4

Muchacho Co generated $44,500 of cash from its operating activities last year.

Extracts from the statement of financial position at the start and the end of the year show the following:

	Start of year	**End of year**
Inventory	$17,000	$12,500
Receivables	$34,000	$29,000
Payables	$36,000	$32,500

Depreciation was $25,000 in the year, and assets with a book value of $10,000 were sold for $25,000.

Required:

Calculate the profit made by Muchacho last year.

For a suggested answer, see the 'Answers' section at the end of the book.

4 CASH ACCOUNTING AND ACCRUALS ACCOUNTING

Profit does not necessarily equal cash. Cash flow includes cash items other than those associated with trading, for example receipt of shareholders' capital, and expenditure on non-current assets. Also, trading or operational transactions are not all converted into cash within the accounting period; they may be held as accounts payable, inventory and accounts receivable, until a subsequent accounting period.

Since businesses need liquidity and positive cash flows to survive, it might be asked why it is usual to focus on profitability rather than cash flow. Traditionally, business performance has been measured by profit using a system of accounting known as **accruals accounting**. In a system of accruals accounting, revenues and costs are reported in the period where the sale occurs, even if the cash flows for the sale and costs of sale occur in different periods, whereas a system of cash accounting records cash payments and cash receipts as they occur within an accounting period.

Definition The **accruals concept** in accounting has been defined as follows. 'Revenues and costs are accrued (that is, recognised as they are earned or incurred, not as money is received or paid), matched with one another so far as their relationship can be established or justifiably assumed, and dealt with in the statement of profit or loss of the period to which they relate.'

Accruals accounting is recognised by law, and businesses are required to use it to measure their profitability for the purpose of external financial reporting.

Definition **Cash accounting** is an alternative to accruals accounting. It is a system of accounting for costs and income on the basis of cash payments and cash receipts.

It is an accounting method where receipts are recorded during the period they are received, and the expenses in the period in which they are actually paid. Basically, when the cash is received for a sale, it is recorded in the accounting books as a sale. This is in contrast with accruals accounting, where revenue and expenses are recorded when they are earned or incurred.

However, cash accounting is not generally accepted as good accounting practice because businesses enter into transactions that are legally enforceable prior to the exchange of cash, but the use of cash accounting does not reflect any transactions which have taken place but are not yet paid for.

For example, a business has received $50,000 in cash sales during the year. It has spent $40,000 in cash on expenses. It has receivables owing $10,000 at 30 June. It owes suppliers $7,000 for goods and services received. On a cash accounting basis, the net profit of the business would be $10,000 (i.e. $50,000 less $40,000). On an accruals accounting basis, the net profit would be $13,000 (i.e. $50,000 + $10,000 – $40,000 – $37,000).

Although cash accounting is not used for measuring profitability, cash flow management is a vital aspect of business. Businesses should:

- forecast what their cash flows are likely to be in the future, so that they can take measures to ensure that they will have enough cash/liquidity. Cash flow forecasts might be prepared as cash budgets
- monitor actual cash flows, to make sure that these are in line with expectation (for example, by comparing them with the cash budget) and that the business still has enough cash to meet its requirements.

4.1 ACCRUALS ACCOUNTING

The accruals concept, or matching concept, requires that revenue and costs are:

- recognised as they are earned or incurred
- 'matched' with one another in the period to which they relate
- dealt with in the statement of profit or loss of the period to which they relate, irrespective of the period of receipt or payment

Accruals – it may be that an expense has been incurred within an accounting period, for which an invoice may or may not have been received. Such charges must be matched to the accounting period to which they relate and therefore an estimate of the cost (an accrual) must be made and included as an accounting adjustment in the accounts for that period.

Prepayment – it may be that an expense has been incurred within an accounting period that related to future period(s). As with accruals, these costs are not necessarily related to sales and cannot be matched with sales. Such charges must also be matched to the period to which they relate and therefore the proportion of the charges that relate to future periods (a prepayment) must be calculated and included as an adjustment in the accounts for that period.

Revenues are included in the period in which the sale takes place rather than when cash is received. It is therefore appropriate to 'match' the costs or expenses incurred in generating this income in the same period. The operating profit determined in this way is supposed to indicate how efficiently the resources of the business have been utilised.

For example, cost of goods sold is included in the statement of profit or loss in the same year that the sale of the goods generates income.

	$
Sale made 28 December 20X8	5,000
Money received from customer 1 February 20X9	5,000
Cost of goods sold	3,300

For the year ended 31 December 20X8 the statement of profit or loss extract would be as follows:

	$
Sales	5,000
Cost of sales	(3,300)

Although the cash is received the year after the actual sale took place (20X9), it is recognised in the statement of profit or loss for the year ended 31 December 20X8. In accordance with the accruals concept the cost of those goods must also be included in that year.

Although in the main the accruals concept is easy to apply, there are circumstances which cause problems, the most common being the purchase of non-current assets.

A non-current asset will incur a cost in one year, the year of purchase, but will generate income over many years. The solution is to spread the cost over the period the asset will generate income, so matching income and expense. The method used to achieve this is depreciation.

CONCLUSION

This chapter provided an introduction to cash and credit management. We also discussed the types of cash flow and their different patterns. Some cash flows will be regular, but others will be less frequent, or unpredictable, and these can be a major influence on an enterprise's cash position.

Cash management is absolutely crucial to the smooth running of the company, and possibly even to its survival. A key to successful cash management is accurate cash forecasting and cash budgeting. This is described in the next chapter.

KEY TERMS

Cash flow – receipts and payments of cash.

Revenue receipts – cash receipts from cash sales and payments by credit customers.

Revenue payments – payments for operating expenses incurred in the normal course of business (payments to suppliers, employees and so on).

Capital receipts – receipts of cash as new long-term finance or from the sale of non-current assets or long-term investments.

Capital payments – cash payments for the purchase of fixed assets and other long-term investments.

Liquid assets – cash and other assets that can be cashed easily (short-term investments) or will turn into cash fairly soon (e.g. receivables).

Liquidity – liquid assets and access to new sources of short-term finance (e.g. overdraft facility).

SELF-TEST QUESTIONS

		Paragraph
1	Define cash.	1.1
2	Define cash flow.	1.1
3	What are the main types of cash flow for a business?	2.2
4	State some of the reasons why the profit in a period is different from the net cash flow.	3
5	What are liquid assets?	3.3
6	Define liquidity.	3.3
7	Explain 'cash accounting'.	4
8	Explain 'accruals accounting'.	4.1

Chapter 2

CASH BUDGETS

Cash budgets are a very important tool used by managers to ensure that they do not run out of cash. This chapter discusses the purpose of cash budgets and explains how they should be constructed.

This chapter covers Syllabus part B2.

CONTENTS

LEARNING OUTCOMES

At the end of this chapter you should be able to:

- Explain the objectives of a cash budget
- Explain and illustrate statistical techniques used in forecasting cash flows
- Explain inflation and the impact on cash flow and profit
- Prepare a cash budget, including adjustments for timing of receipts and payments
- Discuss how cash budgets can be used as a mechanism for monitoring and control
- Carry out simple sensitivity analysis on a cash budget or forecast
- Prepare a simple cleared funds forecast.

1 OBJECTIVES OF A CASH BUDGET AND TYPES OF CASH BUDGET

1.1 CASH BUDGETS AND CASH FORECASTS

Definition A **cash budget** (or cash flow budget) is a detailed forecast of cash inflows and outflows for a future time period, incorporating revenue and capital items and other cash flow items.

Some businesses prepare cash budgets on a month-by-month basis over a longer budget period. For example, a business might include a cash budget in its annual budget, and the cash budget might be for each month over the one-year budget period.

Some businesses prepare cash budgets or cash flow forecasts much more frequently, because it is essential to forecast and plan cash flows in detail on a week-by-week, or even a day-by-day basis.

A cash budget is a management plan for the most important factor of a company's viability – its cash position. A company's cash position determines how suppliers will be paid, how a banker will respond to a loan request, how fast a company can grow, as well as directly influencing dividends, increases to owner's equity and profitability.

1.2 OBJECTIVES OF A CASH BUDGET

Cash budgets have two main objectives.

1. A cash budget is used to estimate or plan future cash shortages/surpluses and allow time to make plans for dealing with them. If the forecast is for a large cash surplus, management can plan in advance what it intends to do with the money. If the forecast is for a cash deficit, management can make arrangements in advance to have access to additional funds, for example an overdraft facility. Alternatively, it can devise ways of trying to improve cash flows, so that the cash position will be better than forecast.

2. A cash budget can be used as a reference point for monitoring actual cash flows. Actual cash flows can be compared with budgeted cash flows. This comparison can help to identify weaknesses in cash management, such as inadequate procedures for collecting money from receivables. It can also help to review forecasts of cash flows, and decide whether the business will still have enough cash or whether new sources of borrowing will be necessary.

Cash forecasting may also be used as an aid for some, or all, of the following:

- To set borrowing limits and minimise cost of funds. The knowledge that funds are required in advance gives the cash manager time to ensure adequate funds and borrowing limits are available, to look for surpluses from other parts of the group that can be used via inter-company loans to fund the shortages or to look for the cheapest source of funds from the financial markets. Having to provide liquidity at short notice, or even immediately if a deficit occurs, often means paying a premium as there may not be time to put the most appropriate borrowing facilities in place or identify the cheapest sources of funds.

- To maximise interest earnings. This is a similar exercise to minimising the cost of funds; knowing that a surplus will occur in advance enables the cash manager to look for the most effective ways to invest funds.

- For liquidity management. Forecasts provide an early warning of liquidity problems by estimating: the amount of cash required; the period when it is required; the length of time it will be required for; and whether it will be available from anticipated sources. Cash flow management steps can be taken to ensure that the gaps are closed, or at least narrowed, when they are predicted early. These steps might include lowering the organisation's investment in accounts receivable or inventory, or looking to outside sources of cash, such as a short-term loan, to fill the cash flow gaps.
- For foreign exchange risk management. Some companies require their business units to produce both local currency (home currency to the unit) and foreign currency cash forecasts. This enables treasury to identify the size and timings of currency flows and either 'match' them against opposite flows within the company, or hedge them in the currency markets.
- For financial control. Cash forecasting can often be used to model payables and receivables against known sales and purchases. This type of forecasting identifies mismatches between credit periods granted to customers and the amount of credit actually taken. It can also enable comparison with credit taken from suppliers and hence to identify working capital financing.
- To monitor and set strategic objectives. Various corporate strategies and objectives can be planned using cash forecasting and reviewed or monitored by comparing actual cash flows relating to specific products, projects or business units, against those planned.
- For budgeting for capital expenditure and project appraisal. This type of cash flow projection will often be carried out by companies to ascertain that they are generating sufficient cash, not only to finance normal operating needs but also to finance the acquisition of new capital goods (e.g. machinery). It is also often requested by banks or finance companies to ensure that potential borrowers are generating sufficient cash to enable them to make loan and interest payments without jeopardising the other activities of the business.
- As a tool for working capital management. Increasingly cash forecasting techniques are being linked to working capital management. In this respect concepts such as 'just-in-time' delivery of raw materials can be refined and linked with 'just-in-time' payments and cash management. As raw materials are ordered, paid for and consumed, and inventory of finished goods are warehoused or sold, the cash forecasts can be continually refined so that they become both a detailed cash planning tool and a method for managing actual and predicted cash flows and account balances.

1.3 ESTIMATING FUTURE CASH FLOWS

To be useful for management, cash budgets must be reasonably reliable. This means that they have to be based on realistic assumptions. Cash budgets depend on estimates or assumptions about:

- budgeted sales and costs of sales
- assumptions about lagged receipts and payments, for example how long will it take for receivables to pay what they owe, and how much credit will be taken from payables.

There are two important methods of checking the reasonableness of cash forecasts.

- Individuals who are in a good position to **verify the accuracy of forecasts or estimates** should be consulted. These individuals should also be in a position to identify any exceptional items of cash receipt or payment that the person preparing the budget is unaware of.

- The **assumptions in the budget should be checked for reasonableness**. For example, if the sales budget provides for a 10% increase in sales but the cash budget provides for a reduction in cash, the reasons for this apparent inconsistency should be checked.

1.4 BUDGETING A CASH DEFICIT: MEASURES THAT CAN BE TAKEN

When a cash budget is prepared and a cash deficit is predicted in any month, it will be essential to make sure that the problem can be overcome and that the business will not face collapse due to a lack of funds.

A cash deficit can be dealt with in any of the following ways:

- The business might have liquid assets that can be sold off quickly to raise cash when the need arises. For example, a business might have invested money in short-term financial investments. If so, plans can be made to convert these investments into cash in time to avoid the cash deficit.

- If the business does not already have arrangements to borrow the cash it needs, it should take steps to try and borrow. Many small businesses rely on a bank overdraft. A practical solution might therefore be to approach the bank with a request for an overdraft facility that is large enough to cover any anticipated cash deficit.

- It might be possible to defer some cash spending and so some cash payments, so that a short-term cash deficit is avoided. For example, if a business is planning capital expenditures, it could be decided to defer capital spending, and only allow capital expenditures to resume after the period of cash shortage has ended.

- Measures could be taken to improve collections of outstanding debts. For example, if there are customers who do not pay on time, and take longer periods of credit than they should, improved debt collection procedures could succeed in speeding up receipts of cash, and help to improve cash flows.

- It might also be possible to ask major suppliers to agree to more generous credit terms, and allow the business longer to pay for its purchases. If more credit can be obtained from suppliers, cash flows will improve.

- It might be possible to improve cash flows by cutting day-to-day expenditures. For example, a temporary ban on overtime could be imposed, and restrictions placed on using casual labour.

1.5 TYPES OF CASH BUDGET

There are two types of cash budget:

(a) **Receipts and payments budget.** This is a forecast of cash receipts and payments based on predictions of sales and cost of sales and the timings of the cash flows relating to these items.

(b) **Statement of financial position forecast.** This is a forecast derived from predictions of future statements of financial position. Predictions are made of all items excepting cash, which is then derived as a balancing figure.

Receipts and payments budgets are much more detailed than statement of financial position forecasts.

2 CASH FORECAST BASED ON THE STATEMENT OF PROFIT OR LOSS AND THE STATEMENT OF FINANCIAL POSITION

Statement of profit or loss

In the previous chapter, we saw how the firm's profit figure can be reconciled to its cash generated from operating activities. Using the same method, a forecast of cash generated can be created by adjusting forecasted operating profit for non-cash items and movements in inventory, payables and receivables.

Example

Smother Co forecasts that it will make an operating profit of $87,000 next year. Depreciation will be $26,000 in the year, and assets with a book value of $30,000 are expected to be sold for $25,000. Extracts from the statement of financial position at the start and the end of the year show the following:

	Start of year (current figures)	**End of year (forecast)**
Inventory	$110,000	$113,500
Receivables	$226,000	$220,000
Payables	$133,000	$144,500

The forecast net cash inflow for the year can be found from the following reconciliation:

	$
Operating profit	87,000
Add: Depreciation charges	26,000
Add: Loss on sale of non-current assets	5,000
Deduct: increase in inventory	(3,500)
Add: Decrease in trade receivables	6,000
Add: Increase in trade payables	11,500
Net cash inflow from operating activities	132,000

Statement of financial position

A statement of financial position based forecast is an estimate of the enterprise's statement of financial position at a future date. It is used to identify either the funding shortfall or the cash surplus in the statement of financial position at the forecast date.

The technique involves constructing the expected statement of financial position as at the end of the forecast or budget period. If every item in the statement of financial position can be predicted except for the cash balance, the cash balance will be the 'balancing figure'.

Typically this may require forecasts of:

- changes to non-current assets (acquisitions and disposals)
- future inventory levels
- future receivables levels
- future payables levels
- changes to share capital and other long-term funding (e.g. bank loans)
- changes to retained profits.

Example

Zed has the following statement of financial position at 30 June 20X3:

	$	$
Non-current assets		
Plant and machinery		192,000
Current assets		
Inventory	16,000	
Trade receivables	80,000	
Bank	2,000	
		98,000
Total assets		290,000
Issued share capital		216,000
Accumulated profits		34,000
Shareholders' funds		250,000
Current liabilities		
Trade payables	10,000	
Dividend payable	30,000	
		40,000
Total equity and liabilities		290,000

The company expects to acquire further plant and machinery costing $8,000 during the year to 30 June 20X4.

(a) The levels of inventory and trade receivables are expected to increase by 5% and 10% respectively by 30 June 20X4 due to business growth.

(b) Trade payables and dividend liabilities are expected to be the same at 30 June 20X4.

(c) No share issue is planned, and accumulated profits for the year to 30 June 20X4 are expected to be $42,000.

(d) Plant and machinery is depreciated on a reducing balance basis at the rate of 20% per annum for all assets held at the statement of financial position date.

Produce a statement of financial position forecast as at 30 June 20X4, and predict what the cash balance or bank overdraft will be at that date.

Solution

Zed
Statement of financial position at 30 June 20X4

	$	$
Non-current assets		
Plant and machinery		160,000
[(192,000 + 8,000) × 80%]		
Current assets		
Inventory [16,000 × 105%]	16,800	
Trade receivables [80,000 × 110%]	88,000	
Bank	67,200	
		172,000
Total assets		332,000
Issued share capital		216,000
Accumulated profits [34,000 + 42,000]		76,000
Shareholders' funds		292,000
Current liabilities		
Trade payables	10,000	
Dividend payable	30,000	
		40,000
		332,000

The forecast is that the bank balance will increase by $65,200 (i.e. $67,200 – $2,000). This can be reconciled as follows:

	$	$
Accumulated profit		42,000
Add: Depreciation (20% of ($192,000 + $8,000))		40,000
		82,000
Less: Plant and machinery acquired		(8,000)
		74,000
Increase in inventory	800	
Increase in trade receivables	8,000	
		(8,800)
Increase in cash balance		65,200

3 CASH BUDGETS IN RECEIPTS AND PAYMENTS FORMAT

Cash flow based forecasts (receipts and payments) are forecasts of the timing and amount of cash receipts and payments, net cash flows and changes in cash balances. A cash budget (or cash flow budget) covers a planning period, and is sub-divided into shorter individual time periods, which could be quarters, months, weeks or even days. For each individual time period, the budget shows:

- the opening cash balance at the start of the time period (which is just the closing balance brought forward from the previous period)
- the expected cash receipts, itemised and in total
- the expected cash payments, itemised and in total
- the net cash flow for the period, which is the difference between total cash receipts and total cash payments
- the closing cash balance, which is calculated from the opening balance and the net cash flow for the period.

A typical receipts and payments cash budget format is as follows, with illustrative figures included. This example covers four months but in an exam question, you may have to deal with a different number of months or periods.

Cash budget for (period)

	January	**February**	**March**	**April**
Cash receipts	$	$	$	$
Cash from receivables	54,000	63,000	58,000	54,000
Cash sales	3,000	4,000	2,000	1,000
Cash from sale of non-current assets	–	1,000	–	500
Total receipts	57,000	68,000	60,000	55,500
Cash payments				
Payments to suppliers	24,000	29,000	24,000	27,000
Payments of wages and salaries	26,000	28,000	26,000	28,000
Payments for non-current asset purchases	4,000	14,000	–	3,000
Payment of dividend	–	5,000	–	–
Total payments	54,000	76,000	50,000	58,000
Net cash flow	3,000	(8,000)	10,000	(2,500)
Opening cash balance	6,000	9,000	1,000	11,000
Closing cash balance	9,000	1,000	11,000	8,500

It is important to include all expected items of cash receipt and cash payment, including exceptional payments and receipts.

3.1 LAGGED RECEIPTS AND PAYMENTS

A receipts and payments budget is often based on a statement of profit or loss forecast. The starting point is therefore to estimate sales and the cost of sales for the period. To forecast the cash flows from sales and costs of sales, we must then allow for the fact that receipts from credit sales occur sometime after the sale has taken place, and payments to suppliers take place sometime after the purchase. In other words, receipts and payments lag behind the sale and cost of sale.

The task in preparing a receipts and payments cash budget is largely to forecast when the cash receipts and cash payments will take place, given forecasts for:

- sales and purchases, and
- assumptions about the length of the time lag between (a) sale and receipt and (b) purchase and payment.

4 PREPARING A CASH BUDGET

To prepare a cash budget based on receipts and payments, you need to take each item of cash receipt and cash payment in turn, and work out the expected cash flow in each time period. The most complex calculations are normally those for receipts from sales and payments to suppliers.

4.1 RECEIPTS FROM SALES

A business might have some cash sales, but most businesses sell mainly on credit. To prepare a cash budget, assumptions have to be made about:

- when customers will pay
- the level of bad (irrecoverable) debts.

For example, it might be estimated that for credit sales, 50% of customers will pay in the month following sale, 30% two months after sale, 15% three months after sale and bad (irrecoverable) debts will be 5% of credit sales.

You can then take sales for each time period in turn, and estimate when the money will actually be received as cash.

Example

A business has estimated that 10% of its sales will be cash sales, and the remainder credit sales. It is also estimated that 50% of credit customers will pay in the month following sale, 30% two months after sale, 15% three months after sale and bad (irrecoverable) debts will be 5% of credit sales.

Total sales figures are as follows:

Month	$
October	80,000
November	60,000
December	40,000
January	50,000
February	60,000
March	90,000

Required:

Prepare a month-by-month budget of cash receipts from sales for the months January to March.

Solution

Credit customers take up to three months to pay so, in the first month of the budget period, January, the business should expect some cash receipts for credit sales three months earlier, in October. It might be useful to prepare a table for workings, as follows:

Sales month	Total sales	Cash receipts January	Cash receipts February	Cash receipts March
	$	$	$	$
October	80,000	10,800	–	–
November	60,000	16,200	8,100	–
December	40,000	18,000	10,800	5,400
January	50,000	5,000	22,500	13,500
February	60,000	–	6,000	27,000
March	90,000	–	–	9,000
Total receipts		50,000	47,400	54,900

For example, October sales were $80,000 and 90% of these ($72,000) were credit sales. Of these 15% are expected to pay three months later in January, so the cash receipts in January from October sales are expected to be $10,800 (15% of $72,000).

Similarly, November sales were $60,000 in total and of these $54,000 were credit sales. Of the credit sales, 30% will pay two months later in January and 15% three months later in February.

January sales are expected to total $50,000, of which $5,000 will be cash sales and $45,000 credit sales. Of the credit sales, there should be receipts from 50% ($22,500) in February and 30% ($13,500) in March.

Make sure that you can see how all the figures in this workings table have been calculated.

In this table receipts from cash sales and receipts from credit sales are combined into a single figure for receipts from sales for the month. The receipts from cash sales and receipts from credit sales could be calculated separately if required.

ACTIVITY 1

A business is preparing a cash budget for the period July to September. Sales are as follows:

Month	Cash sales	Credit sales
	$	$
April (actual)	4,500	60,000
May (actual)	3,700	64,000
June (actual)	2,100	50,000
July (budget)	4,500	60,000
August (budget)	4,500	65,000
September (budget)	5,000	75,000

It is estimated that 60% of credit customers will pay in the month following sale, 30% two months after sale and 10% three months after sale. No bad (irrecoverable) debts are expected.

Required:

Prepare a month-by-month cash receipts budget, showing:

- receipts from cash sales
- receipts from credit sales
- total receipts.

For a suggested answer, see the 'Answers' section at the end of the book.

4.2 PAYMENTS TO SUPPLIERS AND FOR WAGES AND SALARIES

Budgeted payments to suppliers for purchases can be calculated in a similar way to calculating budgeted sales receipts. You need figures for:

- purchases in each time period, analysed between credit purchases and (if any) cash purchases
- estimates for the amount of credit taken from suppliers (for example, one month or two months).

Payments for materials purchases

An added complication with payments for material purchases could be that in order to calculate purchase quantities in each time period, you must first calculate the quantities used and then allow for any planned increase or decrease in inventory levels in the period to work out purchase quantities.

Example

A manufacturing business makes and sells widgets. Each widget requires two units of raw materials, which cost $3 each. Production and sales quantities of widgets each month are as follows:

Month	**Sales and production units**
December (actual)	50,000
January (budget)	55,000
February (budget)	60,000
March (budget)	65,000

In the past, the business has maintained its inventory of raw materials at 100,000 units. However, it plans to increase raw material inventory to 110,000 units at the end of January and 120,000 units at the end of February. The business takes one month's credit from its suppliers.

Required:

Calculate the budgeted payments to suppliers each month for raw material purchases.

Solution

When raw materials inventory levels are increased, the quantities purchased will exceed the quantities consumed in the period. Purchase quantities and the cost of purchases are therefore as follows. Figures for December are shown because December purchases will be paid for in January, which is in the budget period.

		Purchases of raw materials for production and for increase in inventory levels			
	Units of widgets produced	**December**	**January**	**February**	**March**
		Units	**Units**	**Units**	**Units**
December	50,000	100,000			
January	55,000		110,000		
February	60,000			120,000	
March	65,000				130,000
Increase in inventory		–	10,000	10,000	–
Total purchase quantities		100,000	120,000	130,000	130,000
Purchase cost (at $3 per unit)		$300,000	$360,000	$390,000	$390,000

Having established the purchases each month, we can go on to budget the amount of cash payments to suppliers each month. Here, the business will take one month's credit.

	January	**February**	**March**
	$	$	$
Payments to suppliers	300,000	360,000	390,000

At the end of March, there will be unpaid purchase from suppliers of $390,000 for raw materials, and these suppliers will be paid in April.

Payments of wages and salaries

Wages and salaries are usually paid in arrears, at the end of the week or month. This means, however, that employees who are paid a monthly salary will receive their money at the end of the month to which the salary cost relates. It is therefore usual to assume that salaries are paid for in the same month as they are incurred.

A similar assumption is often made for wages. However, each organisation can establish its own assumptions for cash budgeting, and you should apply whatever assumptions are required.

Payments for overheads expenses

You might be required to calculate the budgeted cash payments for overheads expenses. Overheads expenses might be variable or fixed.

- Total variable overhead costs vary with the volume of production or sales.
- Fixed overheads are a fixed amount for the period. Unless there is any information to the contrary, you should assume that fixed overhead costs are an equal amount every time period. However, this might not be the case and you should check carefully the information available.

Most overhead costs are expenses that are paid in cash, and the business might take credit from its suppliers of overhead cost items. However, depreciation is an overhead expense, but is not a cash flow item. If there are any depreciation charges in total overhead costs, these must be deducted to calculate a 'cash expenses' figure for overheads.

Example

A manufacturing company makes product WSX, for which the variable overhead cost is $2 per unit. Fixed costs are budgeted at $450,000 for the year, of which $130,000 are depreciation charges. The remaining fixed costs are incurred at a constant rate every month, with the exception of factory rental costs, which are $80,000 each year, payable 50% in December and 50% in June.

With the exception of rental costs, 10% of overhead expenses are paid for in the month they occur and the remaining 90% are paid in the following month.

The budgeted production quantities of product WSX are:

	Units
September	40,000
October	60,000
November	50,000
December	30,000

Required:

Prepare a month-by-month cash budget for overhead payments in the period October – December.

Solution

Workings: Fixed overheads

	$
Annual fixed overheads	450,000
Deduct depreciation	130,000
Cash expenses	320,000
Deduct annual factory rental	80,000
Regular monthly cash expenses for the year	240,000
Regular cash expenses each month	20,000

These expenses will be paid for as follows: $2,000 in the month incurred and $18,000 in the following month. However, total cash spending on these regular fixed cost items will be $20,000 in every month. An additional $40,000 is paid in June and December, for rent.

Workings: Variable overheads

	Units	Variable overhead costs	Payment in		
			October	November	December
		$	$	$	$
September	40,000	80,000	72,000	–	–
October	60,000	120,000	12,000	108,000	–
November	50,000	100,000	–	10,000	90,000
December	30,000	60,000	–	–	6,000
Total payments			84,000	118,000	96,000

An overhead cash payments budget can now be prepared.

	October	November	December
	$	$	$
Variable overheads	84,000	118,000	96,000
Fixed overheads	20,000	20,000	60,000
Total payments	104,000	138,000	156,000

ACTIVITY 2

You are given the following budgeted information about an organisation.

	Jan	Feb	March
Opening inventory in units	100	150	120
Closing inventory in units	150	120	180
Sales in units	400	450	420

The cost of materials is $2 per unit and 40% of purchases are for cash whilst 60% are on credit and are paid two months after the purchase.

Required:

Calculate the budgeted purchases payments for March.

For a suggested answer, see the 'Answers' section at the end of the book.

4.3 MARK UPS AND MARGINS

In some cash budget questions, you will be expected to manipulate mark ups and margins to derive the sales figure from the cost figure or vice versa.

Mark ups

A mark up is a profit expressed as a percentage of cost. So for example if the cost of an item is $200 and the mark up on cost is 10%, the selling price is $220 (being the cost of $200 plus the mark up of 10%).

Margins

A margin is a percentage expressed as a percentage of selling price. So for example if the selling price is $500 and the margin is 20%, the cost is $400 (being 80% of the selling price – if profit margin is 20% of selling price, cost must be the other 80%).

4.4 OTHER RECEIPTS AND PAYMENTS

For most cash budgets, the most time-consuming tasks are calculating the budgeted cash receipts from sales and the cash payments for operating costs. Once you have done this, you should then obtain forecasts for other receipts and payments, such as:

- payments for non-current asset purchases
- receipts from non-current asset disposals
- payments of tax
- payments of dividends (or drawings, in the case of a sole trader business or a partnership)
- interest, for example, a business might have a bank loan on which it has to pay interest.

These should be included in the cash budget, using the format shown earlier.

4.5 A COMPREHENSIVE EXAMPLE

A comprehensive example will now be used to show how a simple cash receipts and payments budget is constructed.

The following budgeted statement of profit or loss has been prepared for Q for the four months January to April 20X1:

	January	**February**	**March**	**April**
	$000	$000	$000	$000
Sales revenue	60.0	50.0	70.0	60.0
Cost of production	50.0	55.0	32.5	50.0
(Increase)/decrease in inventory	(5.0)	(17.5)	20.0	(5.0)
Cost of sales	45.0	37.5	52.0	45.0
Gross profit	15.0	12.5	17.5	15.0
Administration and selling overhead	8.0	7.5	8.5	8.0
Net profit before interest	7.0	5.0	9.0	7.0

The working papers provide the following additional information:

1. 40% of the production cost relates to direct materials. Materials are bought in the month prior to the month in which they are used. 50% of purchases are paid for in the month of purchase. The remainder are paid for one month later.

2. 30% of the production cost relates to direct labour which is paid for when it is used.

3. The remainder of the production cost is production overhead. $5,000 per month is a fixed cost, which includes $3,000 depreciation. Fixed production overhead costs are paid monthly in arrears. The remaining overhead is variable. The variable production overhead is paid 40% in the month of usage and the balance one month later.

4 The administration and selling costs are paid quarterly in advance on 1 January, 1 April, 1 July and 1 October. The amount payable is $15,000 per quarter.

5 Payables on 1 January 20X1 are expected to be:

Direct materials $10,000

Production overheads $11,000

6 All sales are on credit. 20% of credit customers are expected to pay in the month of sale and 80% in the following month. Unpaid receivables at the start of January were $44,000.

7 The company intends to purchase capital equipment costing $30,000 in February which will be payable in March.

8 The bank balance on 1 January 20X1 is expected to be $5,000 overdrawn.

Required:

Prepare a cash budget for each of the months January to March 20X1 for Q, showing clearly the bank balance at the beginning and end of each month.

Solution

We can take each item of cash flow in turn, and use workings tables to calculate what the monthly cash flows are.

Working 1: Cash from sales

	Total sales	**Cash receipts**		
		January	**February**	**March**
	$	$	$	$
Opening receivables		44,000	–	–
January	60,000	12,000	48,000	–
February	50,000	–	10,000	40,000
March	70,000	–	–	14,000
Total receipts		56,000	58,000	54,000

Working 2: Payments for materials purchases

Material purchases are made in the month prior to the month in which they are used, so the starting point for working out materials purchases and payments for the purchases is the production costs in each month.

	January	**February**	**March**	**April**
	$	$	$	$
Total cost of production	50,000	55,000	32,500	50,000
Material costs of production (40%)	20,000	22,000	13,000	20,000
Purchases in the month	22,000	13,000	20,000	unknown

Payments are made 50% in the month of purchase and 50% in the following month. The payables at 1 January will all pay in January, since these represent 50% of material purchases in December.

	Purchases	Cash payments to suppliers		
		January	February	March
	$	$	$	$
Opening payables for materials		10,000		
January	22,000	11,000	11,000	–
February	13,000	–	6,500	6,500
March	20,000	–	–	10,000
Total payments		21,000	17,500	16,500

Working 3: Payments for overheads

In this example, we have to separate fixed and variable overheads. Total overhead costs are 30% of production costs (100% – 40% direct materials – 30% direct labour).

	January	February	March
	$	$	$
Total cost of production	50,000	55,000	32,500
Overhead costs of production (30%)	15,000	16,500	9,750
Fixed costs	5,000	5,000	5,000
Variable overhead costs	10,000	11,500	4,750

Of the monthly fixed overhead costs of $5,000, $3,000 is depreciation which is not a cash expenditure. Monthly fixed cost cash expenditure is therefore $2,000.

The opening balance of unpaid overhead costs at the beginning of January must consist of $2,000 fixed overheads and $9,000 (the balance) variable overheads. All these costs should be paid for in January. Variable overheads are paid 40% in the month of expenditure and 60% the following month.

	Cost	Cash payments to suppliers		
		January	February	March
	$	$	$	$
Fixed overheads				
Opening payables for fixed production overheads		2,000		
January cash fixed overheads	2,000	–	2,000	–
February cash fixed overheads	2,000	–	–	2,000
March cash fixed overheads	2,000	–	–	–
Total payments for fixed overheads		2,000	2,000	2,000
Variable overheads				
Opening payables for variable production overheads		9,000		
January variable overheads	10,000	4,000	6,000	
February variable overheads	11,500	–	4,600	6,900
March variable overheads	4,750	–	–	1,900
Total payments for variable overheads		13,000	10,600	8,800

The other items of cash flow are straightforward, although it is important to notice that the payments for administration and selling overheads are paid quarterly, and the cash payment ($15,000) is not the same as the total overhead cost for the quarter. Presumably there are depreciation charges within the total costs given.

Payments for direct labour are 30% of direct labour costs (= 30% of production costs) in the month.

The cash budget can be prepared as follows:

	January	February	March
	$	$	$
Receipts			
From sales	56,000	58,000	54,000
Payments			
Capital expenditure	–	–	30,000
For direct materials	21,000	17,500	16,500
For direct labour	15,000	16,500	9,750
For fixed production overheads	2,000	2,000	2,000
For variable production overheads	13,000	10,600	8,800
For admin/selling overhead	15,000	–	–
Total payments	66,000	46,600	67,050
Receipts less payments	(10,000)	11,400	(13,050)
Opening cash balance	(5,000)	(15,000)	(3,600)
Closing cash balance	(15,000)	(3,600)	(16,650)

The company will be overdrawn throughout the three-month period; therefore it is essential that it should have access to borrowings to cover the shortfall. The bank might already have agreed an overdraft facility, but this should be at least $16,650 and ideally higher, to allow for the possibility that actual cash flows will be even worse than budgeted.

ACTIVITY 3

The following data and estimates are available for ABC for June, July and August:

	June	July	August
	$	$	$
Sales	45,000	50,000	60,000
Wages	12,000	13,000	14,500
Overheads	8,500	9,500	9,000

The following information is available regarding direct materials:

	June	July	August	September
	$	$	$	$
Opening inventory	5,000	3,500	6,000	4,000
Material usage	8,000	9,000	10,000	

Notes:

1 10% of sales are for cash, the balance is received the following month. The amount received in June for May's sales is $29,500.

2 Wages are paid in the month they are incurred.

3 Overheads include $1,500 per month for depreciation. Overheads are settled the month following. $6,500 is to be paid in June for May's overheads.

4 Purchases of direct materials are paid for in the month purchased.

5 The opening cash balance in June is $11,750.

6 A tax bill of $25,000 is to be paid in July.

Required:

(a) Calculate the amount of direct material purchases in EACH of the months of June, July and August.

(b) Prepare a cash budget for June, July and August.

For a suggested answer, see the 'Answers' section at the end of the book.

4.6 A COMPREHENSIVE SIX-MONTH CASH BUDGET EXAMPLE

Whiteadder started in business on 1 January 20X5 with capital of $20,000 which was paid into the company's bank. A machine costing $120,000 and sundry fixtures and fittings costing $6,000 were purchased.

The fixtures and fittings were fully paid for on 3 January. The payment terms for the machine were 75% on delivery on 5 January and the remaining 25% one month later.

The company will manufacture Stone Roses, which have the following standard costs based upon a budgeted production of 72,900 Stone Roses over the coming six months.

	$	$
Selling price		10.00
Variable costs		
Labour	2.50	
Material	1.75	
Variable overhead	0.75	
Fixed production overhead	2.00	(7.00)
Profit		3.00

The fixed production overhead is:

- 50% due to factory rent and rates
- 45% due to light and power; and
- 5% due to depreciation of the machine.

It is company policy not to depreciate fixtures and fittings.

Rent and rates are paid monthly on the last day of the month to which they relate. Light and power is paid quarterly on the last day of the quarter.

Expected sales of Stone Roses in units are as follows:

January	February	March	April	May	June	July
$10,000	$12,000	$14,000	$16,000	$11,000	$9,000	$9,000

Company policy will be to maintain inventory of 10% of the following month's sales. Inventory of finished goods will be valued on a marginal cost basis.

No inventory of raw material is required.

Half of the sales will be for cash and half on credit. Of the credit sales it has been decided to offer a 2% discount to credit customers who pay in the month following the month of sale; it is anticipated that 75% of credit customers will take up the discount, and the remainder will pay one month later.

All purchases of direct material are from one supplier who extends a one-month credit period.

Advertising costs of $1,000 will be paid in February. Variable overheads and direct labour are paid in the month incurred.

The bank charges 2% interest per month on overdrafts based on the balance at the end of the month. Interest is taken from the bank account on the first day of the following month.

Required:

Prepare a budgeted cash flow statement for the six months to 30 June 20X6, showing each month separately.

Solution

The cash budget can be prepared as follows:

Whiteadder Budgeted cash flow for the six months ending 30 June 20X5

	January $	**February** $	**March** $	**April** $	**May** $	**June** $
Income						
Capital	20,000					
Cash sales	50,000	60,000	70,000	80,000	55,000	45,000
Credit sales		36,750	56,600	66,450	76,300	60,425
	70,000	96,750	126,600	146,450	131,300	105,425
Expenditure						
Fixtures and fittings	6,000					
Machine	90,000	30,000				
Labour	28,000	30,500	35,500	38,750	27,000	22,500
Variable o/head	8,400	9,150	10,650	11,625	8,100	6,750
Material		19,600	21,350	24,850	27,125	18,900
Rent and rates	12,150	12,150	12,150	12,150	12,150	12,150
Light and power			32,805			32,805
Advertising		1,000				
Interest		1,491	1,634	1,384	230	
	144,550	103,891	114,089	88,759	74,605	93,105
Balance b/f		(74,550)	(81,691)	(69,180)	(11,489)	45,206
Net cash flow	(74,550)	(7,141)	12,511	57,691	56,695	12,320
Balance c/f	(74,550)	(81,691)	(69,180)	(11,489)	45,206	57,526

Workings:

1 Budgeted production (units)

	January $	**February** $	**March** $	**April** $	**May** $	**June** $
Sales	10,000	12,000	14,000	16,000	11,000	9,000
Closing inventory	1,200	1,400	1,600	1,100	900	900
Opening inventory		(1,200)	(1,400)	(1,600)	(1,100)	(900)
Production	11,200	12,200	14,200	15,500	10,800	9,000
Labour (@$2.50)	28,000	30,500	35,500	38,750	27,000	22,500
Paid	January	February	March	April	May	June
V/overhead (@$0.75)	8,400	9,150	10,650	11,625	8,100	6,750
Paid	January	February	March	April	May	June
Material (@$1.75)	19,600	21,350	24,850	27,125	18,900	15,750
Paid	February	March	April	May	June	July

2 Cash received from credit sales

	January $	**February** $	**March** $	**April** $	**May** $	**June** $
Credit sales	50,000	60,000	70,000	80,000	55,000	45,000
January		36,750	12,500			
February			44,100	15,000		
March				51,450	17,500	
April					58,800	20,000
May						40,425
		36,750	56,600	66,450	76,300	60,425

	January $	**February** $	**March** $	**April** $	**May** $	**June** $
Discount		750	900	1,050	1,200	825
Total discount $4,725						

3 Fixed production overhead

	$
Total fixed overhead ($2.00 × 72,900)	145,800
Made up as follows:	
Rent and rates (50%)	72,900
Light and power (45%)	65,610
Depreciation (5%)	7,290
	145,800

Cash flow

Rent and rates $12,150 monthly.

Light and power $32,805 on 31 March and 30 June.

Depreciation has no cash impact.

5 SENSITIVITY ANALYSIS

When budgets are prepared, there are a very large number of assumptions and estimates, for example the estimated sales each month, the estimates of costs, assumptions about when customers will pay and when suppliers will be paid, and so on. Any of these estimates and assumptions could turn out to be inaccurate.

Sensitivity analysis is a modelling and risk assessment procedure in which changes are made to significant variables in order to determine the effect of these changes on the planned outcome. Longer-term forecasts need to be subjected to sensitivity analysis as things can change from year to year. The sensitivity used will vary depending on the type of situation being modelled, but may make allowances for currency fluctuations; interest movements; changes in rates of inflation; economic influences; changes in the market place and competitor strategies.

Therefore, companies using sensitivity analysis may produce several cash forecasts based on a number of 'what if' scenarios.

5.1 COPING WITH UNCERTAINTY IN THE CASH BUDGET

One way to cope with cash budgeting uncertainty is to prepare several cash budgets based on several forecasted scenarios e.g. pessimistic, most likely and optimistic. From this range of cash flows, the financial manager can determine the amount of financing necessary to cover the most adverse situation. This method will also provide a sense of the risk attached to alternatives.

The most common items for which sensitivity analysis is done are:

- sales
- cost of goods sold and gross profit
- operating expenses
- interest rates

- accounts receivable days
- stockholding days
- accounts payable days on hand
- major non-current asset purchases or reductions.

With sensitivity analysis, we can look at the consequences of what might happen if things turn out differently. For example, what if sales are 10% less than predicted, or what if capital expenditure is double the amount forecast? By changing the value of different variables in the model, a number of different scenarios may be produced, allowing a full picture to emerge of how the achievement of planning targets would be affected by different values for each variable, e.g. wages, introduction of new machinery or sales price.

Depending on what the results of the analysis show, management might decide to take action to reduce the potential risks.

As a simple example we can show the budgeted sales for an organisation as follows:

	January	**February**	**March**	**April**
	$	$	$	$
Sales	6,000	8,000	4,000	5,000

All sales are on credit and credit customers tend to pay in the following pattern:

In month of sale	10%
In month after sale	40%
Two months after sale	45%

The organisation expects a bad (irrecoverable) debt rate of 5%.

Using these figures we can calculate the budgeted cash receipts from customers in April as $5,700.

April sales: 10% × $5,000	$500
March sales: 40% × $4,000	$1,600
February sales: 45% × $8,000	$3,600
Total	$5,700

Using sensitivity analysis on these figures we can show the effect on the cash receipts from credit customers in April with higher or lower than anticipated receipts:

Cash from:	**What if bad (irrecoverable) debt rate was 10%?**	**What if sales were 10% less than expected?**	**What if sales were 10% more than expected?**
Apr sales:	10% × $5,000 = $500	10% × $4,500 = $450	10% × $5,500 = $550
Mar sales:	40% × $4,000 = $1,600	40% × $3,600 = $1,440	40% × $4,400 = $1,760
Feb sales:	40% × $8,000 =$3200	45% × $7,200 = $3,240	45% × $8,800 = $3,960
Total	$5,300	$5,130	$6,270

5.2 USING A COMPUTER TO FORECAST CASH FLOW

With the aid of a computer and suitable software, a mathematical model can be used to reduce the tedium of carrying out numerous repetitive calculations and simplify the alteration of assumptions and the presentation of results. A computer-based model can be constructed using a spreadsheet or acquired as a stand-alone package.

A cash flow model can be used to compile forecasts, assess possible funding requirements and explore the likely financial consequences of alternative strategies. Used effectively, a model can help prevent major planning errors, anticipate problems, and identify opportunities to improve cash flow or provide a basis for negotiating short-term funding from a bank.

Generally, when seeking external funding, the time horizon covered by a set of projections should be equal to or greater than the period for which the funding is needed. The greater the amount of funding required and the longer the period of exposure for the provider of these funds, the more comprehensive must be the supporting projections and plan.

Analytical models used in spreadsheet decision support include: what-if analysis, goal-seeking analysis and optimisation analysis.

What if analysis involves the changing of a single variable or multiple variables to determine its/their effect on the model as a whole e.g. What if:

- 40% of customers are one month in arrears?
- 50% of customers are two months in arrears?
- 10% of customers are three months in arrears?
- What if we spend more on buying non-current assets?
- What if sales growth is only 1% a month?

Goal seeking is the reverse of What if analysis where you made changes and saw what resulted. In 'goal seeking', you know the result you want and make changes until you get that result e.g. how many products to sell in order to generate $200,000 profit.

Optimisation analysis involves finding the optimum value from a model by changing certain variables given certain constraints e.g. measuring the effect on the profitability of capital investment under different assumptions of rates of interest, market growth rates or inflation rates. Assumptions and figures can be changed and the spreadsheet automatically recalculates the results.

5.3 FORECASTING USING TIME SERIES ANALYSIS

Some variables can be analysed as a time series i.e. a set of values that follows a repetitive pattern over time. For example, the temperature at noon every day in a particular location would behave as a time series – high temperatures in summer and lower temperatures in winter, in a repeating pattern over time.

Analysis of a time series in the past can enable us to predict the likely value of the series in the future. This can be useful for predicting sales or costs of a business.

Historic movements in a time series are separated into four elements:

- The trend – perhaps sales in the past have exhibited a steady upward pattern. This upward movement would be called the trend and would be expected to continue in the future.

- Seasonal variation – many businesses sell more items in the quarter leading up to Christmas. Therefore, the expectation in future would be that this pattern would continue.

- Random variations – occasionally there might be an unexpected blip when analysing an historic set of data. For example, an unusually small sales figure one month, when the business had to be closed due to a fire in the factory. Random variations would be ignored when forecasting future values, because they are not expected to recur.

- Cyclical variations – these are fluctuations over very long periods of time. Usually we aren't able to analyse enough data over a sufficiently long period to be able to identify significant cyclical variations.

Therefore, when forecasting using time series analysis, the trend and seasonal variations are identified from historic patterns and then forecasts are made on the assumption that these patterns continue.

5.4 STRENGTHS AND WEAKNESSES OF SENSITIVITY ANALYSIS

Strengths	Weaknesses
• No complicated theory to understand. • Information presented to management in a form that facilitates subjective judgement to decide the likelihood of the various possible outcomes considered.	• It assumes that changes to variables can be made independently, e.g. material prices will change independently of other variables. • It only identifies how far a variable needs to change; it does not look at the probability of such a change. • It only provides information on the basis of which decisions can be made. It does not point to the correct decision directly.

6 FORECASTING WITH INFLATION

6.1 INFLATION AND INDEX NUMBERS

Inflation is the process whereby the price of commodities steadily rises over time. The result of inflation is that a given sum of money will buy fewer and fewer goods over time, i.e. money has less and less purchasing power. In periods of severe inflation, price rises take place at an increasing rate. This makes it very difficult for governments, businesses and individuals to plan ahead. Inflation reduces the value of money so that savings in particular become less attractive, and people on fixed incomes such as pensioners find that their purchasing power is reduced. Whilst a high rate of inflation is undesirable, regular and predictable price rises over a period of time are seen as positive since they encourage economic growth.

Inflation often makes information difficult to interpret. If data simply shows, for example, the cost of raw materials used, it may be difficult to assess changes in quantities used when the prices of the raw materials are subject to inflation. If management wishes to interpret changes in quantities of materials used, they must first adjust the expenditure figures for price changes.

An **index number** shows the rate of change of a variable from one specified time to another. A price index measures the change in the money value of a group of items over a period of time. In the UK, the inflation rate is calculated from the prices of a range of different goods and services selected to represent average spending patterns. The different items in the 'basket' of goods and services are given different weights, so that things we spend more on, such as housing, motoring and food, are given more importance. The best known is probably the retail price index (RPI), which measures changes in the prices of goods and services supplied to retail customers. This index is often thought of as a 'cost of living' index.

Inflation is usually measured as a percentage increase in the RPI. If the rate of inflation is 10% a year, for example, $50,000 worth of purchases last year will, on average, cost $55,000 this year. At the same inflation rate, those purchases will cost $60,500 next year, and their cost will double after only seven years.

Index numbers may also measure quantity changes (e.g. volumes of production or trade) or changes in values (e.g. retail sales, value of exports). Most accountants acknowledge that the accounts of businesses are distorted when no allowance is made for the effects of inflation. The use of index numbers is often required for the preparation of inflation-adjusted accounts.

6.2 INDEX NUMBERS – PRICE AND QUANTITY PERCENTAGE RELATIVES

Price and quantity percentage relatives (also called percentage relatives) are based on a single item. There are two types: price relatives and quantity relatives.

A **price relative** shows changes in the price of an item over time.

A **quantity relative** shows changes in quantities over time.

The formulae for calculating these relatives are as follows:

$$\text{Simple price index} = \frac{p_1}{p_0} \times 100$$

$$\text{Simple quantity index} = \frac{q_1}{q_0} \times 100$$

Where:

p_0 is the price at time 0

p_1 is the price at time 1

q_0 is the quantity at time 0

q_1 is the quantity at time 1

The concept of time 0, time 1 and so on is simply a scale counting from any given point in time. Thus, for example, if the scale started on 1 January 20X0 it would be as follows:

1 Jan 20X0	1 Jan 20X1	1 Jan 20X2	1 Jan 20X3
Time 0 (base year)	Time 1	Time 2	Time 3

The starting point is chosen to be most convenient for the problem under consideration.

Example

If a commodity costs $2.60 in 20X4 and $3.68 in 20X5, calculate the simple price index for 20X5, using 20X4 as base year (i.e. time 0).

Solution

$$\text{Simple price index} = \frac{p_1}{p_0} \times 100 = \frac{3.68}{2.60} \times 100 = 141.5$$

This means that the price has increased by 41.5% of its base year value, i.e. its 20X4 value.

Example

6,500 items were sold in 20X8 compared with 6,000 in 20X7. Calculate the simple quantity index for 20X8 using 20X7 as base year.

Solution

$$\text{Simple quantity index} = \frac{q_1}{q_0} \times 100 = \frac{6{,}500}{6{,}000} \times 100 = 108.3$$

This means that the quantity sold has increased by 8.3% of its 20X7 figure.

Usually, an index number is required to show the variation in a number of items at once rather than just one as in the examples above. The RPI is such an index and consists of a list of items as diverse as the price of bread, the cost of watch repairs, car repairs and cinema tickets.

By using appropriate weights, price relatives can be combined to give a multi-item price index. To determine the weighting, we need information about the relative importance of each item.

ACTIVITY 4

A product that cost $12.50 in 20X0, cost $13.65 in 20X1. Calculate the simple price index for 20X1 based on 20X0.

For a suggested answer, see the 'Answers' section at the end of the book.

6.3 SELECTING WEIGHTS

The weights applied to price relatives should, in general, reflect the amount spent or total value of each item purchased, rather than simply the quantities purchased (however standardised). The reason is that this eliminates the effect of a relatively low-priced item having a very high price relative from only a small price rise.

Example

The price of peas and bread, and the amount consumed in both years, is as follows:

Item	**20X5 price**	**20X6 price**	**Units consumed (both years)**
Peas	2 cents	3 cents	2
Bread	15 cents	16 cents	5

Required:

(a) Construct a price-relative index using:

(i) quantity weights

(ii) value weights.

(b) Explain why the value weighted price relative is the more useful.

Solution

(a) (i) **Using quantity weights**

Item	**20X5 p_0 cents**	**20X6 p_1 cents**	**q***	**Quantity weight only $W_A (= q)$**	**Value weight W_B $(= p_0 \times q)$**
Peas	2	3	2	2	2 × 2 = 4
Bread	15	16	5	5	15 × 5 = 75
				7	79
				ΣW_A	ΣW_B

*Same consumption pattern for both years

Item	$\frac{p_1}{p_0} \times 100$	$W_A \times \frac{p_1}{p_0} \times 100$	$W_B \times \frac{p_1}{p_0} \times 100$
Peas	150.0	300.0	600.0
Bread	106.7	533.5	8,002.5
		833.5	8,602.5
		$\Sigma\left[WA \times \frac{p^1}{p^0} \times 100\right]$	$\Sigma\left[WB \times \frac{p^1}{p^0} \times 100\right]$

Therefore, using quantity weights only, the index is as follows:

$$\frac{\Sigma\left[W_A\left(\frac{p_1}{p_0} \times 100\right)\right]}{\Sigma W_A} = \frac{833.5}{7} = 119.1$$

(This would imply an average increase in prices of 19.1%.)

(ii) **Using value weights, the index is:**

$$\frac{\sum\left[W_B\left(\frac{p_1}{p_0}\times 100\right)\right]}{\sum W_B} = \frac{8{,}602.5}{79} = 108.9$$

(This implies an average increase of 8.9%.)

(b) The fact that the value weighted average of price relatives is the more realistic can be shown by considering total expenditure:

Item	**Expenditure 20X5**		**Expenditure 20X6**		**% increase**
		cents		cents	
Peas	2 × 2	4	2 × 3	6	50%
Bread	5 × 15	75	5 × 16	80	6.7%
		——		——	——
Total budget		79		86	8.86%

Thus, an equal **money** price rise for two items will cause a higher percentage price rise for the lower-priced item which is compensated for when the weights used are the value or expenditure on each item, since this reduces the importance of the lower priced item.

Algebraically, as $W = q \times p_0$ then the weighted average of price relatives, which is:

$$\frac{\sum\left[W\left(\frac{p_1}{p_0}\times 100\right)\right]}{\sum W}, \text{ becomes } \frac{\sum\left[qp_0 \times \frac{p_1}{p_0}\right]}{\sum qp_0}\times 100 = \frac{\sum qp_1}{\sum qp_0}\times 100$$

ACTIVITY 5

A production process uses 10 sacks of product A and 30 of product B per year. The costs are as follows:

Item	**20X1**	**20X2**
Product A	$6.50	$6.90
Product B	$2.20	$2.50

Construct a price relative index using:

(a) quantity weights

(b) value weights.

For a suggested answer, see the 'Answers' section at the end of the book.

6.4 THE IMPACT OF INFLATION ON CASH FLOW AND PROFITS

As we have already noted, inflation can be defined as a general increase in prices. This can also be described as a general decline in the real value of money. The main impact on an organisation's forecasts is that they can become out of date very quickly.

When inflation is very high the value of financial assets e.g. debt declines. Organisations will try to collect their debts quickly so that the cash can be reinvested. By delaying payments to suppliers, the underlying value of the debt can be reduced.

In periods of increasing inflation lenders will require an increasing return i.e. interest rates may be very high, so in the short term a treasurer will invest surplus cash on short-term deposit.

Index numbers are used to predict future cash inflows and outflows, estimating the future price index and giving management a better idea of the amount of sales in cash or the likely size of cash payments. They can also be used in forecasting borrowing limits, which might be fixed in monetary terms. Different indices can be used for items, such as capital goods or various types of revenue, which may be subject to differing rates of inflation.

7 CLEARED FUNDS

Cleared funds can be defined as:

'Sums that have been transferred through a payment clearing system, debited to the originator of the transfer, credited to the recipient and are available to earn interest.'

When a business pays money into its bank account, it can take up to three days for the payment to 'clear'. Until funds have been cleared, they are not available for making payments.

Example

A company with no money in its bank account pays a cheque for $20,000 into the account on Monday, and the payment is not cleared until Thursday. The company asks the bank to make an immediate transfer payment of $15,000 to a supplier on the Wednesday.

Since there is no money in the account until the funds are cleared on Thursday, the payment on Wednesday will put the company into overdraft by $15,000 (for one day).

7.1 CLEARED FUNDS FORECASTS

A cleared funds forecast shows the actual cash available to a company in its bank accounts. If cleared funds are negative, the company has an overdraft for this amount, on which interest will be charged.

At any one time, there will usually be uncleared funds (also referred to as the 'float'). These are funds that have been credited to a beneficiary's account but which are not yet available for withdrawal. Such cash may be tied up for a variety of reasons. First, there may be a transmission delay, i.e. a delay between sending and receiving a payment (through the post). Second, there may be a delay between when a payment is received and when it is actually paid into the receiver's bank account. Third, the payment has to go through the bank's clearing system. This can take a number of days. The advantage of electronic payments, of course, is that they are only subject to the third of these delays. The time at which they will become cleared funds can therefore be anticipated with much more accuracy.

For some businesses, it is important to know what the value of its cleared funds will be on any day, so that it can manage its bank overdraft and overnight borrowing. For others the business may be in a cash surplus position. If this is the case then there may be large sums of money sitting in their current account that could be invested, thereby earning interest. If it is left in a current account for even a few days, thousands of pounds of potential interest may be lost. By preparing a cleared funds forecast management can decide whether to put cash on an overnight deposit, or a one week deposit, or even longer.

A business might therefore prepare cleared funds forecasts on a daily basis, over a short-term planning period of a few days.

Computerised treasury management systems are available from banks. These can be used to monitor when cleared funds will become available to the account. The information available from a treasury management system can be used to prepare day-by-day cleared funds forecasts.

7.2 PREPARING A CLEARED FUNDS FORECAST

The forecast can be prepared using a combination of the following three methods:

1 obtaining information from the organisation's bank(s)

2 by bank reconciliation – forecasting for other receipts and payments that have taken place but not yet lodged with a bank

3 adapting the cash budget by adjusting the cash book payments and receipts for float times.

There are four main parts to a cleared funds forecast:

1 receipts

2 payments (for supplies, wages, salaries, etc.)

3 cleared excess receipts over payments (i.e. the net amount of your receipts and payments). In this section, you should also show your cleared balance brought forward each day and your cleared balance carried forward each day

4 uncleared funds float – you should show the total uncleared receipts and payments each day.

The bottom line of the forecast should then be the total book balance carried forward each day.

A cleared funds forecast might be constructed as follows:

			Day		
	Monday	**Tuesday**	**Wednesday**	**Thursday**	**Friday**
	$	$	$	$	$
Receipts					
Payments					
Change in cleared funds					
Opening balance of cleared funds					
Closing balance of cleared funds					
Uncleared funds float					
Receipts					
Payments					
Total book balance c/f					

WORKED EXAMPLE

The simplest way to demonstrate how to prepare a cleared funds forecast is to go through a question.

Weed Care Co

Weed Care Co is a manufacturing company producing and selling a range of weed killers to wholesale customers. It has three suppliers and two customers.

Weed Care Co relies on its cleared funds forecast to manage its cash.

Table 1: Receipts from customers

Customer name	Credit terms	Payment method	7 November 20X5 sales	7 October 20X5 sales
P Co	1 calendar month	BACS	$300,000	$260,000
Q Co	None	Cheque	$360,000	$320,000

P Co always makes its payments exactly one month after purchasing goods. Receipt of money by BACS is instantaneous.

Q Co's cheque will be paid into Weed Care Co's bank account on the same day as the sale is made and will clear on the fourth day following this (excluding day of payment).

Table 2: Payments to suppliers

Supplier name	Credit terms	Payment method	7 November 20X5 purchases	7 October 20X5 purchases	7 September 20X5 purchases
Grass Co	1 calendar month	Direct debit	$130,000	$110,000	$90,000
Roots Co	2 calendar months	Cheque	$170,000	$160,000	$150,000
Soil Co	None	Cheque	$190,000	$180,000	$170,000

Payments to Grass Co are made by direct debit on the 7th day of each month for the previous month's purchases.

Weed Care Co will send out, by post, cheques to Roots Co and Soil Co on 7 November. The amounts will leave its bank account on the third day following this (excluding the day of posting).

Table 3: Wages and salaries

	November 20X5	October 20X5
Weekly wages	$26,000	$36,000
Monthly salaries	$130,000	$120,000

Factory workers are paid cash wages (weekly). They will be paid one week's wages, on 11 November, for the last week's work done in October.

All the office workers are paid salaries (monthly) by BACS. Salaries for October will be paid on 11 November.

Other miscellaneous payments

Every Monday morning, the petty cashier withdraws $500 from the company bank account for the petty cash tin. The money leaves Weed Care's bank account straight away.

New office furniture will be ordered by telephone on 7 November at a total cost of $1,250. The company's debit card will be used and the amount will therefore leave Weed Care Co's bank account on the next day.

Other information

The balance on Weed Care's bank account will be $350,000 on 7 November 20X5. This represents both the book balance and cleared funds.

You have been asked to prepare a cleared funds forecast for the period Monday 7 November to Friday 11 November 20X5 inclusive using the information provided. Show clearly the uncleared funds float each day.

Answer approach

You should tackle the question as follows:

Set out the pro forma for your answer. Once the pro forma has been laid out, the rest of the question is quite straightforward. Candidates sometimes do poorly in these types of questions because they walk into the exam hall without knowing the pro forma.

Since you are preparing the forecast over five days, you will need six columns – one for each day plus the first column for your narrative. There are four main parts to a cleared funds forecast:

- receipts (from P Co and Q Co)
- payments (for supplies, wages, salaries, petty cash and office furniture)
- cleared excess receipts over payments (i.e. the net amount of your receipts and payments). In this section, you should also show your cleared balance brought forward each day and your cleared balance carried forward each day
- uncleared funds float – you should show the total uncleared receipts and payments each day.

The bottom line of the forecast should then be the total book balance carried forward each day.

You should then begin filling in the numbers by working methodically through the information. The following points should be noted in relation to the question:

When calculating the daily receipts from customers and the payments to suppliers, be sure to carefully note the credit terms. If you fail to do this, you will be using the wrong receipts figure and losing easy marks. The payment method is obviously very important too. BACS payments, standing orders and direct debits will generally leave the company's bank account on the date stated. If the payment is a cheque, you will have to read the additional information carefully in order to establish the date when the funds will clear.

Similarly, it is essential to read the information carefully for wages and salaries because, as is the case in this question, workers will usually 'work in hand', i.e. work for some time before being paid and often always have wages owing. This practice discourages workers from leaving jobs without giving adequate notice to their employers.

You should finish the question by completing the following:

Cleared excess receipts over payments. This line is simply the receipts less the payments each day. You must then, for each day, add the cleared balance brought forward to this figure. Don't forget to insert the opening balance b/f at the beginning of the week ($350,000). Your closing balance each day will then be your opening balance for the next day, just as in a monthly cash budget.

Uncleared funds float. At the end of each day there may be receipts, for example, that have been paid into the company's account but will not have cleared yet. These are your uncleared funds float receipts. Similarly, cheques may have been sent out, which you know have not been received by the payee yet. These are your uncleared funds float payments. Net the receipts and payments off against each other.

Total book balance c/f. This is the bottom line of your cleared funds forecast and shows the total of the cleared and uncleared receipts and payments.

Your final answer should look like this:

	7 Nov	**8 Nov**	**9 Nov**	**10 Nov**	**11 Nov**
	$	$	$	$	$
Receipts					
P Co	260,000				
Q Co					360,000
	260,000	**0**	**0**	**0**	**360,000**
Payments					
Grass Co	110,000				
Roots Co				150,000	
Soil Co				190,000	
Wages					36,000
Salaries					120,000
Petty cash	500				
Office furniture		1,250			
	110,500	1,250	0	340,000	156,000
Cleared excess receipts over payments	149,500	(1,250)	0	(340,000)	204,000
Cleared balance b/f	350,000	499,500	498,250	498,250	158,250
Cleared balance c/f	499,500	498,250	498,250	158,250	362,250
Uncleared funds float					
Receipts	360,000	360,000	360,000	360,000	0
Payments	(341,250)	(340,000)	(340,000)	0	0
	18,750	20,000	20,000	360,000	0
Total book balance c/f	518,250	518,250	518,250	518,250	362,250

ACTIVITY 6

Goyte Co is a manufacturing company producing and selling a range of products to wholesale customers. It has two suppliers and three customers.

Goyte Co relies on its cleared funds forecast to manage its cash.

Table 1: Receipts from customers

Customer name	Credit terms	Payment method	18 June sales	18 May sales	18 April sales
Owen Co	1 calendar month	BACS	$6,000	$10,000	$4,000
Hughes Co	None	Cheque	$12,000	$20,000	$5,000
Betjeman Co	2 calendar months	BACS	$8,000	$6,000	$7,000

Owen Co and Betjeman Co always make their payments exactly in line with their credit terms. Receipt of money by BACS is instantaneous.

Hughes Co's cheque will be paid into Goyte Co's bank account on the same day as the sale is made and will clear on the third day following this (excluding day of payment).

Table 2: Payments to suppliers

Supplier name	Credit terms	Payment method	18 June purchases	18 May purchases	18 April purchases
Hooting Co	1 calendar month	Direct debit	$20,000	$10,000	$9,000
Howling Co	2 calendar months	Cheque	$17,000	$16,000	$10,000

Payments to Hooting Co are made by direct debit on the 18th day of each month for the previous month's purchases.

Goyte Co will write and post out a cheque to Howling Co 18 June. The amount will leave its bank account on the third day following this (excluding the day of posting).

Table 3: Wages and salaries

	June	May
Weekly wages	$22,000	$25,000
Monthly salaries	$90,000	$88,000

Semi-skilled manual workers are paid cash wages (weekly). They will be paid one week's wages, on 19 June, for the last week's work done in May.

Skilled manual workers are paid salaries (monthly) by BACS. Salaries for May will be paid on 20 June.

Other miscellaneous payments

On 20 June, the petty cashier expects to withdraw $800 in cash from the company bank account for the petty cash tin.

A new machine was ordered on 17 June and the payment of $14,000 is to be made by cheque. The cheque will be written and posted on 18 June so the money should leave Goyte Co's bank account on the third day following this (excluding the day of posting).

Other information

The balance on Goyte Co's bank account was $226,000 at the end of 17 June. This represents both the book balance and cleared funds.

Required:

Prepare a cleared funds forecast for the period 18 June to 21 June inclusive using the information provided. Show clearly the uncleared funds float each day.

For a suggested answer, see the 'Answers' section at the end of the book.

8 CASH BUDGETS AS A MECHANISM FOR MONITORING AND CONTROL

8.1 CONSULTING STAFF ABOUT FUTURE CASH FLOWS

Cash budgets are prepared by accountants, but operational managers are responsible for earning income and for spending. When a cash budget is drafted, appropriate individuals (operational managers) should be consulted, to check:

- that they agree with the assumptions in the cash budget about income and expenditure, and receipts and payments
- whether there are any other exceptional items of receipt or payment that have been overlooked and so are missing from the draft cash budget.

As a general approach to reviewing cash budgets, you should think about:

- whether there is a noticeable trend in sales, and whether this seems reasonable
- whether the trend in variable costs is consistent with the trend in sales
- whether there are any changes in payment patterns, in receipts from customers or payments to suppliers
- whether all items of cash receipt and payment have been considered, including capital expenditures and any exceptional items
- whether inflation in costs and any planned sales price increases have been taken into account.

These points might seem sensible and straightforward. Attempt the following activity to check that you understand them.

ACTIVITY 7

You have been given the following budgeted information for your company for the period January to April.

	December (actual)	January	February	March	April
	$	$	$	$	$
Sales	20,000	21,000	22,000	23,000	24,000
Cost of production and sales					
Direct materials	10,000	10,000	10,000	11,000	11,000
Direct labour	3,000	3,000	3,000	3,000	3,200
Overheads	5,000	5,000	5,000	5,000	5,000
Total costs	18,000	18,000	18,000	19,000	19,200
Profit	2,000	3,000	4,000	4,000	4,800

At 1 January, unpaid suppliers for materials purchased totalled $10,000 and unpaid overheads were $4,000. Overheads are all fixed and include $1,000 of depreciation charges each month.

All sales are on credit. Until this budget period, customers have all paid in the month following sale. However, from January sales onwards, 50% of customers will pay one month following the month of sale and 50% two months after sale.

A draft cash budget prepared from this information is shown below.

	January	February	March	April
	$	$	$	$
Cash receipts from customers	20,000	10,500	21,500	22,500
Cash payments				
For direct materials	10,000	10,000	10,000	11,000
For direct labour	3,000	3,000	3,000	3,200
For overhead expenses	4,000	4,000	4,000	4,000
	17,000	17,000	17,000	18,200
Receipts less payments	3,000	(6,500)	4,500	4,300
Opening cash balance	500	3,500	(3,000)	1,500
Closing cash balance	3,500	(3,000)	1,500	5,800

(a) Write a memo to your supervisor, Tom Harris, setting out any criticisms of the cash budget that has been prepared. If you think that any aspects of the forecast should be checked, suggest which staff might be consulted.

(b) Suppose that your company does not have an overdraft facility with its bank. Suggest what action might be taken in view of the budgeted cash deficit in February.

For a suggested answer, see the 'Answers' section at the end of the book.

8.2 MONITORING ACTUAL CASH FLOWS

One of the objectives of a cash budget is to provide a basis or reference point against which actual cash flows can be monitored. Comparing actual cash flows with the budget can help with:

- identifying whether cash flows are much better or worse than expected
- predicting what cash flows are now likely to be in the future, and in particular whether the business will have enough cash (or liquidity) to survive
- the reasons for any significant differences between actual and budgeted cash flows.

The forecast might differ from the actual due to poor forecasting techniques or to unpredictable events or developments such as the loss of a major customer, changes in interest rates or inflation, which can affect costs and revenues differently.

Monitoring against the cash flow forecast can take place over different timescales, depending upon:

- the nature of the business
- the scale of the cash flowing into and out of the business
- whether forecast assumptions require additional funding.

Just as cash flows can highlight shortfalls in funding within a business, so too can they highlight whether surplus funds are being generated. This would allow the business to invest those surplus funds to its benefit.

The benefit from preparing timely cash flow forecasts is that you have early indications of both good and not so good events. This allows you to take early action to avoid possible problems and to maximise returns on cash generated within the business.

8.3 CASH FLOW CONTROL REPORTS

Regular reporting of actual budgeted cash flows compared with budgeted cash flows should be carried out on a daily, weekly or monthly basis, depending on the size of the business and the frequency and value of its cash receipts and payments.

In common with all management reports, the purpose of a cash flow report is to provide a basis for management decision making. For this reason the report needs to be addressed to the manager who can control the cash flows.

Cash receipts

There are normally two main types of cash receipt to monitor: receipts from customers and investment income (e.g. interest).

Cash receipts from customers depend on:

- the volume and value of sales, and
- the time taken by customers to pay.

It is important to identify the cause of any difference in cash flow between budget and actual because the control action required will differ in each case.

If budgeted and actual cash receipts differ because budgeted and actual sales volumes are different, it should be remembered that the difference in volume should affect expenditures and cash payments too. The implications for cash flow should therefore be considered in terms of net cash flows – in other words the difference in cash receipts less the difference in cash payments.

If budgeted and actual cash receipts differ because customers are taking more or less time to pay what they owe, action should be taken either to amend the budget or to take measures to speed up customer payments.

Cash payments

Payments can be divided into three categories:

- payments of a routine, recurring nature which are unrelated to activity level (e.g. rent, senior management salaries)
- payments of a routine nature which are related to activity level (e.g. payments to suppliers for purchases/expenses, wage payments, payments to sales staff of sales commissions)
- payments of a non-recurring nature (e.g. taxation, dividends, major capital expenditures).

Some payments will be committed and uncontrollable. Others might be reduced or deferred to improve cash flow.

Revising the cash budget or preparing a new cash forecast

It is important that comparisons of actual cash flows should be against meaningful targets. From time to time it may therefore be necessary to revise the cash budget or prepare a new cash flow forecast. This should take account of the cash flows that have actually occurred and what future cash flows are now expected to be, in the light of revised estimates and management measures to deal with some of the problems. Such revised budgets, in the light of extra information coming to light, are known as rolling forecasts.

CONCLUSION

Cash budgets are important because they help a business to plan its cash flows, and manage the risk. Constructing a cash budget is a fairly straightforward exercise, although it can involve a large amount of number crunching. You should try to gain as much practice as you can in preparing cash budgets, particularly receipts and payments budgets.

Cash flow is vital to the survival of a business, and the cash budget and cash flow reports are important sources of information for monitoring and managing the cash position.

Sensitivity analysis or 'what if' investigations allow you to alter assumptions and figures and see what happens. The ability to ask 'what if' questions using a spreadsheet is of considerable benefit to managers. This is mainly because they can analyse the effect of changes in any of the variables in a very short time, without any elaborate recalculations.

KEY TERMS

Cash budget – a detailed forecast of cash inflows and outflows for a future time period, incorporating revenue and capital items and other cash flow items.

Cash flow forecast – used to describe the preparation of future cash flow estimates.

Cash budget – a forecast that is adopted as a formal plan or target.

Lagged receipts and payments – receipts from credit sales occur sometime after the sale has taken place, and payments to suppliers take place sometime after the purchase.

SELF-TEST QUESTIONS

		Paragraph
1	What measures might be taken to reduce or avoid a cash deficit predicted by a cash budget?	1.4
2	What are the two types of cash budget or cash forecast?	1.5
3	What are the main cash receipts itemised in the cash budget?	3
4	What are lagged receipts?	3.1
5	Describe one of the ways of coping with uncertainty in the cash budget.	5.1
6	What are the two types of relatives?	6.2
7	Cash flow reports are used to monitor actual cash flows. How often should they be produced?	8.3

PRACTICE QUESTION 1

ANN DREW

You have been provided with the following cash flow report, comparing actual cash flows with the cash budget for the period January to March:

	January		**February**		**March**	
	Budget	**Actual**	**Budget**	**Actual**	**Budget**	**Actual**
	$	$	$	$	$	$
Cash receipts						
Cash sales	6,000	4,500	6,000	5,900	8,000	7,500
Cash from credit customers	29,000	28,500	30,000	28,000	32,000	29,000
Total receipts	35,000	33,000	36,000	33,900	40,000	36,500
Cash payments						
Payments for materials	15,000	15,500	18,000	18,000	20,000	19,500
Wages and salaries	8,000	8,600	9,000	8,800	10,000	9,800
Overhead expenses paid	7,000	7,200	8,000	7,900	8,000	8,000
Capital expenditure	–	1,000	2,000	2,400	–	2,000
Interest on loan	–	–	–	–	4,000	4,000
Total payments	30,000	32,300	37,000	37,100	42,000	43,300
Cash receipts less payments	5,000	700	(1,000)	(3,200)	(2,000)	(6,800)
Opening cash balance	6,000	6,000	11,000	6,700	10,000	3,500
Closing cash balance	11,000	6,700	10,000	3,500	8,000	(3,300)

Your company currently has a bank overdraft limit with its bank of $5,000.

Required:

Prepare a memo for your supervisor, Ann Drew, identifying the problems that appear to have arisen with cash flows, in comparison with the budget, and suggest any suitable measures that should be taken. **(10 marks)**

For a suggested answer, see the 'Answers' section at the end of the book.

PRACTICE QUESTION 2 – NOTE THAT THIS QUESTION IS LONGER THAN A TYPICAL EXAM QUESTION BUT IS INCLUDED HERE TO COVER SEVERAL KEY TOPICS

CHASE

Chase, a distributor, is preparing a cash budget for the six months to 30 June 20X5. The following information could be relevant.

1 Sales are expected to be $70,000 each month in January to March, $80,000 each month in April to June and $75,000 each month in July to September. 20% of total sales are paid for in the month of sale, 50% in the following month and 30% in the month after that.

2 Receivables at the end of December were $80,000. Of these, $60,000 are expected to pay in January and 2% will be bad (irrecoverable) debts. The remainder will pay in February.

3 The gross profit is 25%.

4 Purchases are made two months before the month of sale, and 30 days' credit is taken from suppliers.

5 Administration and distribution expenses are expected to be $8,500 each month. Of these $500 each month consists of depreciation charges and $2,000 comprise rental charges. The rental charges are paid half-yearly with the period ended 30 June due in June. The remaining expenses are paid for at an even rate each month.

6 The company plans to make a share issue of 50,000 $1 shares in May, at a premium of $0.60 per share.

7 The company intends to place a special advertisement in a trade magazine in May, but this will not be paid for until July. The cost of the advertisement will be $1,500.

8 Opening inventory is $105,000 at the start of January and is expected to be $112,500 at the end of June. This information is provided for the purpose of the reconciliation of the budgeted profit to the budgeted cash position only.

9 The company has an overdraft balance of $108,000 at 1 January.

10 Interest is charged at 1% per month on an overdraft. The interest is calculated on the closing balance at the end of each month, and paid on the first day of the following month.

11 No non-current asset purchases are planned in the period January to June, and no taxation payments are due.

Required:

(a) Prepare a monthly cash budget for the period January to June 20X5. **(20 marks)**

(b) Prepare a budgeted statement of profit or loss for the six-month period January to June 20X5. **(8 marks)**

(c) Prepare a statement reconciling the budgeted profit for the period with the change in the budgeted cash position between the beginning of January and the end of June. **(12 marks)**

(Total: 40 marks)

For a suggested answer, see the 'Answers' section at the end of the book.

Chapter 3

CASH MANAGEMENT

A business should manage its cash balances and ensure that it has adequate liquidity. This involves keeping liquidity under continual review. In this chapter we consider how companies can optimise their cash positions by using cash management models and trying to reduce float. In many large organisations a specialised treasury department will be responsible for managing cash balances.

This chapter covers Syllabus parts C1 and C4.

CONTENTS

LEARNING OUTCOMES

At the end of this chapter you should be able to:

- Outline how the Baumol cash management model works (**Note:** Calculations are not required)
- Discuss the limitations of the Baumol cash management model
- Suggest appropriate liquidity levels for a range of different organisations
- Outline the basic treasury functions
- Discuss the advantages and disadvantages of a centralised treasury function
- Discuss the advantages and disadvantages of centralised cash control
- Describe cash handling procedures (including recording practices)
- Outline the issues to be considered when attempting to hold optimal cash balances
- Outline the statutory and the other regulations relating to the management of cash.

1 MANAGING CASH AND CASH BALANCES

Cash is the most liquid asset of all and is vital for the existence of any business. Its efficient management is crucial to the solvency of the business because, as we all know, cash is the focal point of the funds flows in a business.

It can be understood in two senses – one is the actual cash held by the firm and deposits that can be withdrawn on demand, and the other includes marketable securities (gilts, bills and certificates of deposit) which can be converted into cash immediately.

Cash in current accounts must be held so that bills are paid on time (transactions balance), for emergencies such as strikes, weather disruptions, etc. (precautionary balance), bank requirements for loans or other services provided (compensating balance), and for taking advantage of bargains (speculative balance).

Cash management refers to the practices and techniques designed to accelerate and control collections, ensure prompt deposit of receipts, improve control over payment methods, and eliminate idle cash balances. The goal of cash management is to reduce the amount of cash that is being used within the firm so as to increase profitability, but without reducing business activities or exposing the firm to undue risk in its financial obligations.

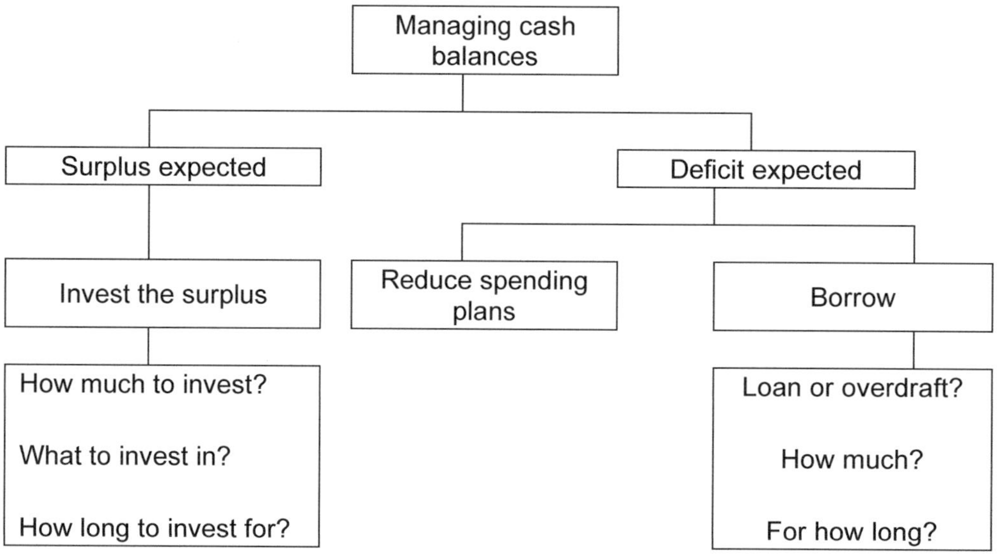

Managing cash usually involves the following issues:

- the preparation and use of cash budgets
- managing the collection and payment of cash
- the management of short-term cash investments
- the management of overdrafts and bank loans
- the use of cash management models
- evaluating whether to use a centralised treasury department.

1.1 CASH BUDGETS

The objectives of cash budgets are as follows:

- To integrate and appraise the effect of operating budgets on the firm's cash resources.
- To anticipate cash shortages and surpluses, and to allow time to plan how to deal with them.
- To provide a basis for comparison with actual in order to identify unplanned occurrences.

A **cash budget** is essential for **control of day-to-day cash balances** and to allow efficient forward planning of the options for dealing with **short-term deficits and surpluses**.

Relationship of cash forecasts with cash budgets

The cash budget reflects the impact on cash resources of budgeted sales, costs and changes in asset structure, and is also confirmation that plans are financially viable.

It is important to distinguish between a budget and a forecast.

- A **cash forecast** is an estimate of cash receipts and payments for a future period under existing conditions before taking account of possible actions to modify cash flows, raise new capital or invest surplus funds.
- A **cash budget** is a commitment to a plan for cash receipts and payments for a future period after taking any action necessary to bring the preliminary cash forecast into conformity with the overall plan of the business. It is an integral part of the master budget of the business and confirms that plans are financially viable.

1.2 MANAGING THE COLLECTION AND PAYMENT OF CASH

Two conditions would allow an enterprise to operate for extended periods with cash balances either near or at zero:

- a completely accurate forecast of net cash flows over the planning horizon
- a perfect matching of cash receipts and payments.

Unfortunately, this is rarely the case and the cash manager is challenged by the variable nature of cash flows. Cash flows can be:

- **Mistimed** – outflows often precede inflows.
- **Mismatched** – inflows may not entirely cover outflows.
- **Irregular** – inflows may be uneven. Many seasonal businesses (e.g. retailers and the tourism industry) face extra challenges in managing their cash. Inflows are concentrated during peak months of activity but operating expenses continue throughout the year.
- **Unpredictable** – cash flows can be difficult to forecast. Bills may be presented earlier than anticipated or the collection of funds may take longer than forecast. The unpredictability factor increases significantly in cross-border business.

The objective in cash collection is to reduce the lag between the time the customer pays and the time cheques clear. The objective of cash payment is to slow down payments and increase the time when cheques are written and received. In other words collect early, pay late. Of course the delays that help the payer hurt the recipient. Recipients, speeding up collections try to reduce delays to get available cash sooner. Payers, slowing down payments, prefer delays to be able to use their cash longer.

What can be done to speed up cash collections and slow down cash outflows?

To **accelerate** collection procedures the enterprise can try to reduce float or offer discounts to customers for early payment.

We have already mentioned float in uncleared balances in the previous chapter but it can be described as the time from when a cheque is written until the actual recipient can draw upon or use the funds.

Float management involves controlling the collection and payment of cash. Types of float include:

- **Mail float** – when cheques are trapped in the postal system from the moment a customer sends a remittance cheque until the enterprise begins to process it.
- **Processing float** – the time it takes for the receiver to process the cheque for deposit in the bank.
- **Availability (or transit) float** – the time that it takes the bank to clear the cheque and adjust the company's account.

Payment float – availability of funds in the enterprise's bank account during the time the payment cheque is clearing through the banking system.

Methods of accelerating collection include:

- ensuring that cheques received are presented to the bank on the day of receipt
- collecting cheques from local customers' premises
- requesting payment through the Bank Giro system
- persuading regular customers to use standing orders, direct debits or BACS, which is an electronic transfer of funds between banks
- using CHAPS (Clearing House Automated Payments System) for large corporate customers to make immediate transfers of funds.

Alternatively, there are ways of **delaying** payment such as holding payment for several days after postmarked in office or calling the supplier to verify statement accuracy for large amounts. However, none of these methods are recommended.

The financial benefit of float reduction can be calculated with the following formula:

Sales per day × Days of float reduction × Assumed yield

where Sales per day = Annual revenues/Days in year.

ACTIVITY 1

If a company has daily sales of $69,594,521, could invest in marketable securities to yield 6% annually and could eliminate four days of float, what would its savings be?

For a suggested answer, see the 'Answers' section at the end of the book.

1.3 SHORT-TERM CASH INVESTMENTS

Short-term investment opportunities present themselves when cash surpluses arise. Companies may hold cash not only for transaction motives, but also for precautionary and speculative motives.

- **Transactions motive**: the need to hold cash to meet day-to-day operational requirements.
- **Precautionary motive**: the need to hold extra cash to cover unexpected business requirements.
- **Speculative motive**: cash may be held to exploit unanticipated business or investment opportunities. The company's attitude to risk and working capital management will determine the planned cash holdings.

Firms with an aggressive working capital policy will plan to minimise funds held, and borrow whenever cash is needed.

Firms with a defensive policy will set aside cash in an investment portfolio, which can be drawn upon when the need arises.

We will be discussing short-term cash investments in more detail in the next chapter.

1.4 BORROWING FROM THE BANK

When a business decides that it needs to borrow money from its bank, it has to consider whether a loan or an overdraft, or a combination of the two, would be appropriate.

The factors to consider are as follows:

Purpose of the borrowing. A bank usually provides an overdraft to cover temporary cash shortages in the customer's current account, due to the timing of receipts and payments. In contrast, a bank will be more willing to consider a bank loan when a business needs money to pay for a long-term asset that will earn profits over a period of time. It would not be appropriate, for example, to pay for the cost of a large item of capital equipment with a bank overdraft.

The duration of the borrowing. If a business needs to borrow for a fairly long term, it should try to obtain a loan. In contrast, if the money is needed to cover temporary cash shortages that will arise from time to time, an overdraft makes more sense. With an overdraft, the borrower pays an arrangement fee, but then pays interest only when the current account is overdrawn. In contrast, interest on a loan is payable throughout the term of the loan, regardless of whether or not the borrower actually needs the money all the time.

Interest rates. There could be a fairly big difference between the interest rate payable on an overdraft and the interest on a medium-term loan, with overdraft rates usually being higher. A borrower should prefer the borrowing option that minimises the cost.

Security. A bank might insist on taking security for a loan, but might be more willing to provide an unsecured overdraft facility. If so, the borrower might prefer an overdraft.

As a general rule, a bank will agree to a bank overdraft to finance short-term cash shortages that arise because funds are tied up in inventory and receivables. A bank is more likely to suggest a loan for the purchase of long-term assets.

Bank overdrafts – these are mainly provided by the clearing banks and represent permission by the bank to write cheques even though the firm has insufficient funds deposited in the account to meet the cheques.

An overdraft limit will be placed on this facility, but provided the limit is not exceeded, the firm is free to make as much or as little use of the overdraft as it desires.

The bank charges interest on amounts outstanding at any one time, and the bank may also require repayment of an overdraft at any time.

The **advantages of overdrafts** are as follows:

- Flexibility – they can be used as required.
- Cheap – interest is usually 2–5% above base rate (and all loan interest is a tax deductible expense).

The **disadvantages of overdrafts** are as follows:

- Overdrafts are legally repayable on demand. Normally, however, the bank will give customers assurances that they can rely on the facility for a certain time period, say six months.
- Security is usually required by way of fixed or floating charges on assets or sometimes, in private companies and partnerships, by personal guarantees from owners.
- Interest costs vary with bank base rates.

Overall, bank overdrafts are one of the most important sources of short-term finance.

Bank loan – this represents a formal agreement between the bank and the borrower, that the bank will lend a specific sum for a specific period (one to seven years being the most common). Interest must be paid on the whole of this sum for the duration of the loan.

A bank loan is liable to be more expensive than the overdraft and is less flexible but, on the other hand, there is no danger that the source will be withdrawn before the expiry of the loan period. Interest rates and requirements for security will be similar to overdraft lending.

1.5 GETTING THE BEST TERMS FROM THE BANK

It is important to remember that, when a business discusses borrowing terms with its bank, although it will try to obtain a favourable interest rate, the cost of interest is by no means the only issue to consider.

As well as discussing the interest cost, a cash manager will need to make sure that:

- the borrowing limit is high enough to meet the foreseeable needs of the business
- the borrowing is available for long enough to meet the needs of the business
- the bank does not have the right to call in the debt at short notice and demand immediate repayment (which would be the case with an uncommitted overdraft facility)
- the relationship between the bank and the business is open, honest and friendly. A bank is more likely to continue supporting a business whose managers it trusts to keep it properly informed about its affairs.

ACTIVITY 2

The cash budget for your business for the next three months is as follows:

	July	August	September
	$	$	$
Receipts less payments	(25,000)	(37,000)	3,000
Opening cash balance	10,000	(15,000)	(52,000)
Closing cash balance	(15,000)	(52,000)	(49,000)

Your business banks with North Bank, and currently has an overdraft facility with a limit of $25,000. The excess of payments over receipts in July is due to seasonal factors, but in August it is due largely to budgeted capital expenditure of $20,000. The cash position is expected to improve from September.

The business does not have any short-term investments that it could cash in.

The manager of South Bank has indicated in a telephone conversation with the chief accountant of your business that, if the business were to switch its account to South Bank, it would be given an overdraft facility with a limit of up to $50,000.

Required:

Write a memo to your chief accountant explaining the liquidity problems faced by the business in the next three months, and suggesting with reasons what the most appropriate steps might be to deal with the problems you foresee.

For a suggested answer, see the 'Answers' section at the end of the book.

2 CASH MANAGEMENT MODELS

2.1 RISK AND EXPOSURE

Risk refers to the possibility that actual events or outcomes will turn out differently from what was expected. Generally, we associate risk with the possibility that actual outcomes will turn out worse than forecast.

In the context of cash flows and liquidity, the following risks have to be managed:

- the risk that cash receipts will be lower than expected or that cash payments will be higher than expected, so that actual cash balances turn out to be much less than forecast
- the risk that when the business is faced with a cash shortage, it is unable to borrow the money it needs, or unable to raise more cash by selling off some of its assets
- the risk that when surplus cash is invested, the interest earned on the investment turns out to be much lower than it could have been or the risk of lost deposits through bank failure.

When a business is faced with these risks, it is said to have an exposure to risk. The role of the cash manager is to monitor and control these risks, and to prevent them from threatening the survival of the business or having a significant impact on profitability.

2.2 LIQUIDITY LEVELS FOR A RANGE OF DIFFERENT ORGANISATIONS

Liquidity refers to having cash or ready access to funds. A business has adequate liquidity if:

- it has enough cash to make payments when required, or
- it can turn other assets into cash readily to obtain the money to make payments when required, or
- it can borrow money to make payments when required.

Liquidity measures are based on the notion that a business cannot operate if it is unable to pay its bills. A sufficient amount of cash and other short-term assets must be available when needed. On the other hand, because most short-term assets do not produce any return, a strong liquidity position will be damaging to profits. Therefore, management must try to keep the firm's liquidity as low as possible whilst ensuring that short-term obligations will be met.

Some assets are more liquid than others. Cash is a highly liquid asset while accounts receivable and inventory are somewhat less liquid.

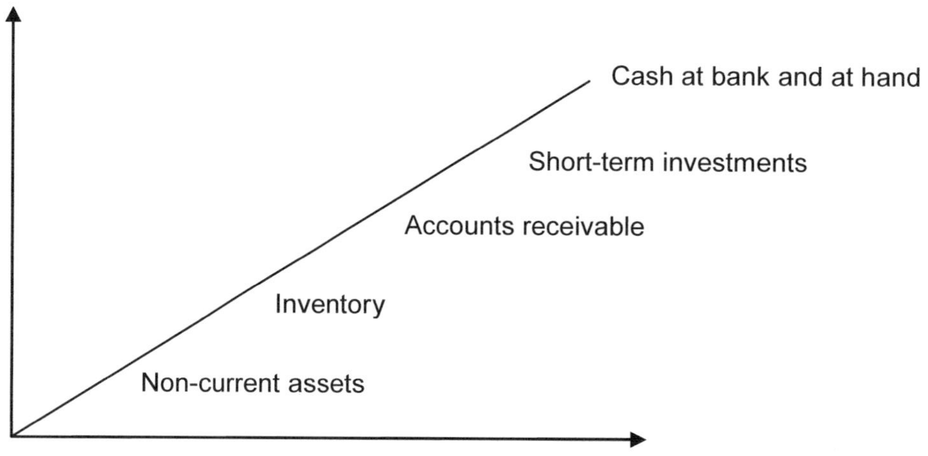

Levels of liquidity

In Chapter 1 we illustrated the connection between the operating, cash, trade and accounting cycles. The usual pattern is for cash outflows to precede inflows. The purchase of raw materials leads to additional, ongoing expenses associated with the conversion process. A sale does not necessarily result in an immediate cash inflow. A company will need sufficient liquidity to finance the operations until funds are actually collected. Each industry will have its own pattern of cash and liquidity levels. For example, a restaurant buys fresh produce in the morning, transforms the ingredients into meals, which are then sold and paid for during the day. The time between when the cash payments are made and the cash is collected is less than a day; the business has an 18–24-hour cash flow cycle and high levels of liquidity. At the other end of the spectrum, the aircraft industry has a considerably longer operating and cash flow cycle and low levels of liquidity. Years are spent on design and development and contract negotiations for the purchase of raw materials. This is followed by a protracted manufacturing and testing phase, after which a sale is concluded, usually, on a long-term lease basis.

There are also industries with a reverse cash flow cycle, although these are the exception rather than the rule. For example, in the insurance business, policyholders pay premiums in advance, and claims are paid long after the cash inflow has been received.

To decide whether there is adequate liquidity, cash managers must continually look forward, and assess the cash requirements of the business by preparing new cash forecasts. If a cash shortage is anticipated, the business should prepare to:

- sell any liquid assets that it owns
- arrange to borrow the funds required.

When planning liquidity, it usually makes sense to provide for a 'safety margin', in case actual cash flows turn out worse than expected.

Example

A company has prepared a cash budget and has forecast an overdraft in month 1 of $20,000. However, in month 3 it expects to have a cash surplus of $100,000, which will last for six months.

When planning how to manage the cash balances, it is important to ensure that the company has access to an overdraft facility of at least $20,000. Ideally, the overdraft limit should be higher than $20,000, just in case cash flows are worse than budgeted.

If the business has investments that it can sell off to raise cash, its overdraft requirements can be reduced.

The company should start to consider what to do with the cash surplus from month 3. No final decision has to be taken yet, and the cash position should be reviewed nearer to the beginning of month 3. The surplus could be invested, but the amount available might turn out to be less than $100,000 and the surplus might last for less than six months. If the business invests too much for too long, what arrangements are in place to ensure that liquidity remains adequate. For example, could the company use an overdraft facility if it found itself unexpectedly short of cash and unable to sell off its investments in good time?

ACTIVITY 3

A company has prepared the following cash budget for the first six months of next year.

	January	**February**	**March**	**April**	**May**	**June**
	$000	$000	$000	$000	$000	$000
Receipts less payments	12	(14)	(50)	120	7	(15)
Opening cash balance	35	47	23	(27)	93	100
Closing cash balance	47	23	(27)	93	100	85

Required:

Prepare a memo to your supervisor in which you suggest what measures might be taken in the six-month period to manage cash in order to maintain adequate liquidity.

For a suggested answer, see the 'Answers' section at the end of the book.

2.3 ISSUES ASSOCIATED WITH ATTEMPTING TO HOLD OPTIMAL CASH BALANCES

One of the objectives of cash flow management is to hold the right amount of cash. If we hold too much cash, we lose the opportunity to earn a return on idle cash. If we hold too little cash, we run the risk of not making timely payments to suppliers, banks and other parties. We want to have an optimal cash balance that is neither excessive nor deficient. The optimal amount of cash (sometimes called target cash balance) for a firm to hold involves a trade-off between the opportunity costs of holding too much cash and the trading costs of holding too little.

A number of different models have been developed for managing cash balances and providing rough guidelines for determining the optimal cash position. However, we will only be looking at the Baumol model.

All models assume that a business will have a certain amount of ready cash available, in a bank current account, for day-to-day transactions. In addition, an amount of buffer funds will be invested in deposit accounts, marketable securities, etc. and these can be used to top up the current account or absorb short-term surpluses from it, as appropriate.

The points addressed by the models are as follows:

- At what point should cash move between the current account and the buffer funds?
- How much cash should be moved?

There are conflicting costs.

- Each time cash is moved in or out of the buffer funds, transaction costs will be incurred – these are often fixed.
- Any cash held within the current account has an opportunity cost associated with it, represented by the difference between the interest earned in the current account (if any) and that earned in the buffer funds.

Cash management models attempt to **minimise the total costs** associated with cash movements between a current account and short-term investments – the 'opportunity' cost of lost interest plus transaction costs – by determining when, and how much, cash should be transferred each time.

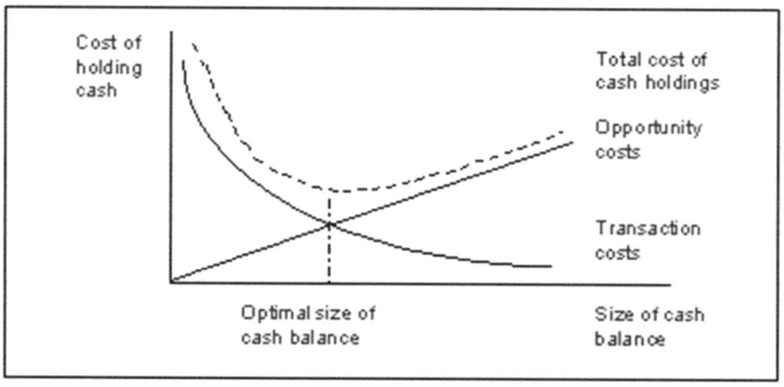

If the balances held in the current account are kept as low as possible by frequent movements of cash in and out, in order to minimise the holding costs, this may lead to excessive transaction costs.

The models attempt to find an optimal cash management strategy that will minimise the total of these costs.

2.4 THE BAUMOL MODEL

William Baumol first noted that cash balances are, in many respects, similar to inventories, and that the EOQ inventory model, which will be covered later in this study text, can be used to establish a target cash balance.

The Baumol model assumes the cash manager invests excess funds in interest bearing securities and liquidates them to meet the firm's demand for cash.

As investment returns increase, the opportunity cost of holding cash increases and the cash manager decreases cash balances. As transaction costs (cost of liquidating short-term investments) increase, the cash manager decreases the number of times he or she liquidates securities, leading to higher cash balances.

Managing the cash/short-term investments mix involves determining the optimal frequency for replenishing cash and the amount of securities to liquidate. Liquidating short-term investments is costly.

Costs include the brokerage fees, delivery costs (such as the cost of a bonded courier), telephone charges, the opportunity cost of redirected managerial effort and, possibly, a liquidity discount on the securities the firm sells. A liquidity discount is the difference between a dealer's quote and the price the firm would receive if it could wait for a buyer willing to pay full market value.

2.5 LIMITATIONS OF BAUMOL'S MODEL

The major limitations of cash management models are in their underlying assumptions.

Assumptions of Baumol's model

- The firm is able to forecast its cash need with certainty.
- The firm's cash payments occur uniformly over a period of time whereas in reality cash outflows occur at different times, different due dates, etc.
- It assumes no cash receipts during the projected period; obviously cash is coming in and out on a frequent basis.
- It does not allow for safety cash reserves.
- The opportunity cost of holding cash is known and it does not change over a period of time.
- The firm will incur the same transaction cost whenever it converts its securities to cash.

Limitations of Baumol's model

It does not allow the cash flows to fluctuate. Firms in practice do not use their cash balance uniformly nor are they able to predict daily cash inflows and outflows.

2.6 HOW BAUMOL'S CASH MANAGEMENT MODEL WORKS

The EOQ model can be applied to cash management if you view cash as an operating asset, just like inventory. In this view, cash has a carrying cost, which is the opportunity cost for investing the funds, and an order cost, which is the cost per transaction of liquidating marketable securities and transferring the money to a current bank account.

If a company's cash resources are steadily used up by a constant daily demand for cash, the model could be applied to the situation so that the optimum regular cash injection, x, into the current account can be calculated:

$$x = \sqrt{\frac{2 \times \text{Annual cash disbursements} \times \text{Cost per sale of securities}}{\text{Interest rate}}}$$

where x = the optimum regular cash injection into the current account.

Example

A company faces a constant demand for cash totalling $200,000 pa. It replenishes its current account (which pays no interest) by selling constant amounts of gilts, which are held as an investment earning 6% pa. The cost per sale of gilts is a fixed $15 per sale.

The optimum amount of gilts sold, x, for each cash injection into the current account will be:

$$x = \sqrt{\frac{2 \times 200{,}000 \times 15}{0.06}}$$

= $10,000

Baumol's model suggests that, when interest rates are high, the cash balance held without earning interest should be low, which seems sensible.

The problem with the model of course is its unrealistic assumption that firms face a constant demand for cash. In practice cash will be a net receipt one week and a net payment another week.

3 TREASURY MANAGEMENT

Treasury management covers activities concerned with **managing the liquidity of a business**, the importance of which to the survival and growth of a business cannot be over-emphasised

The term 'treasurer', and therefore 'treasury department', is an old one that has been resurrected in a modern context. It essentially covers the following activities:

- banking and exchange
- cash and currency management (including foreign currency)
- investment in short-term assets
- risk and insurance
- raising finance.

Although the treasury function is not usually responsible for credit control and collecting debts, it should work closely with the credit control function.

3.1 WHY HAVE A TREASURY DEPARTMENT?

The functions carried out by the treasurer have always existed, but have been absorbed historically within other finance functions. A number of reasons may be identified for the modern development of separate treasury departments:

- Size and internationalisation of companies. These factors add to both the scale and the complexity of the treasury functions.
- Size and internationalisation of currency, debt and security markets. These make the operations of raising finance, handling transactions in multiple currencies and investing much more complex. They also present opportunities for greater gains.
- Sophistication of business practice. This process has been aided by modern communications, and as a result the treasurer is expected to take advantage of opportunities for making profits or minimising costs, which did not exist a few years ago.

For these reasons, most large international corporations have moved towards setting up a separate treasury department.

3.2 TREASURY RESPONSIBILITIES

Treasury departments are not large, since they are not involved in the detailed recording of transactions. The treasurer will typically be responsible for cash management, overseeing bank relationships, including bank borrowing (short and long term), liquidity management, foreign exchange, risk management, corporate finance, and the management of pension assets.

He or she will generally:

- report to the finance director (financial manager), with a specific emphasis on borrowing and cash and currency management
- have a direct input into the finance director's management of debt capacity, debt and equity structure, resource allocation, equity strategy and currency strategy
- be involved in investment appraisal, and the finance director will often consult the treasurer in matters relating to the review of acquisitions and divestments, dividend policy and defence from takeover.

3.3 ADVANTAGES AND DISADVANTAGES OF A CENTRALISED TREASURY FUNCTION

There is no such thing as a 'typical' organisation. Each company will evolve a structure that is appropriate to its size, business and priorities. In larger companies, it is usual to see a greater segregation of responsibilities than in smaller companies, where separation of duties is not always economically possible. However, one emerging organisational development that appears to be present in most global companies is the centralisation of treasury and finance, to concentrate expertise and bank contact in a single location.

Should treasury activities in a large international group be centralised or decentralised?

Advantages of centralisation are as follows:

- Improved co-ordination.
- Location of functions close to financial markets.
- Greater economies of scale – no need for treasury skills to be duplicated throughout the organisation.
- Better short term investment opportunities. The centralised treasury will have more cash available to invest so will be able to negotiate better returns on investments.
- One highly trained central department can assemble a highly skilled team, with knowledge of dealing in futures, options, forward contracts, swaps and Eurocurrency markets, etc. and offer skills that could not be available if every company had their own treasury.
- The group's foreign currency risk can be managed much more effectively from a centralised treasury since only the treasury department can appreciate the total exposure situation. A total hedging policy is more efficiently carried out by head office rather than each company doing its own hedging.

Centralised treasury management often results in a highly skilled team, cheaper borrowing, lower bank charges and more effective hedging of currency risk, but some motivational and local knowledge benefits may be lost.

Advantages of decentralisation include:

- Greater autonomy leads to greater motivation. Individual companies will manage their cash balances more attentively if they are responsible for them rather than simply remitting them up to head office.
- Local operating units should have a better feel for local conditions than head office and can respond more quickly to local developments.

If they are **decentralised**, each operating company must appoint an officer responsible for that company's own treasury operations.

3.4 ADVANTAGES AND DISADVANTAGES OF CENTRALISED CASH CONTROL

There are several different methods of centralising a company's cash. Below are some of these options:

1. **Centralise in the country of currency** – this refers to when sterling is kept in the UK, Swiss francs are kept in Switzerland, etc. This is the cheapest method of centralising and the most efficient for cash flow management. It provides the lowest costs for payments and collections while allowing access to the best possible services.
2. **Centralise in the country of domicile** – if you have a French subsidiary making a dollar payment it would use a dollar account in France. This can be an expensive approach because it constantly creates cross-border payments. This method offers a company the advantage of the convenience of being able to deal with its home bank.

3 **Centralise in the country of the functional currency** – some companies are now moving to the third model, which is an enhancement of the first model. While keeping transaction accounts in-country, companies concentrate all their cash in the country where they have their euro concentration account. This model offers the best of both worlds – it keeps the benefit from the first option of having low cost payments, while substantially improving liquidity management across currencies.

The advantages of centralised cash control include the following:

- It allows the enterprise to assemble many of the accounting and reporting responsibilities into a single location, or company, where payments, writing cheques or taking requisitions for subsidiary companies can be applied. A full audit trail is provided across all companies/divisions. This approach allows the reduction of duplicate effort and training from location to location, and maintains the inter-company balances between the subsidiary and the central companies, for full reporting and tracking at the transaction level.

- If they are **centralised**, each operating company/division holds only the minimum cash balance required for day-to-day operations, remitting the surplus to the centre for overall management. This process is sometimes known as **cash pooling**, the pool usually being held in a major financial centre or a tax haven country.

- One company/division does not borrow at high rates while another has idle cash. Borrowing requirements can be reduced by offsetting the borrowing needs of one account against the positive cash position of others.

- Maximisation of liquidity and minimisation of external borrowing. Necessary borrowings can be arranged in bulk, at keener interest rates than for smaller amounts. Similarly, by consolidating balances, bulk deposits of surplus funds will attract higher rates of interest than smaller amounts.

- Transfer prices can be established to minimise the overall group tax bill.

- Funds can be quickly returned to a company/division requiring cash via direct transfers.

- It offers more reliable cash flow forecasting.

- Each division's daily participation in the centralised cash control system can be monitored and management can receive timely corporate-wide balance information.

The disadvantages of centralised cash control include the following:

- It is more difficult for sources of finance to be diversified and to match local assets.

- Subsidiaries and divisions cannot be given more autonomy to be more responsive to their individual needs.

- There are limited opportunities to invest cash balances on a short-term basis.

4 PROCEDURES, AUTHORISATION AND SECURITY

4.1 AUTHORISATION LIMITS FOR INVESTING

Cash management is a day-to-day concern, and decisions about whether to invest surplus cash have to be taken quickly. Similarly, it might be necessary to decide quickly to cash in existing investments in order to raise cash to meet an unexpected cash shortage.

Decisions about investing and cashing in investments therefore cannot be taken easily by senior management, and the task is likely to be delegated to an authorised individual. This individual is likely to be someone in the accounts section or, in larger companies, in the treasury section.

However, this individual should be given a limit to the total amount he or she can invest without approval by senior management, and to the amount that he or she can invest in a particular form of security. For example, a company might allow a designated individual in the accounts department to invest surplus cash of up to $250,000, but no more than $100,000 should be invested in Certificates of Deposit and no more than $100,000 in government securities.

If the cash available for investment goes above an individual's authorised limit, he or she must notify the appropriate person (e.g. a supervisor) and ask for instructions.

4.2 INVESTMENT GUIDELINES

Organisations might have guidelines for their cash managers about how any surplus cash should be invested. For example, a company might have a rule that all surplus cash should be held in bank deposit accounts and available for immediate withdrawal without notice. Alternatively, a company might have a stated policy of investing surplus cash in short-dated gilts.

In public sector organisations, investment guidelines are likely to be very strict. This is because any surplus cash is 'public money', and a public organisation should not be exposed to the risk of large investment losses. Such organisations are therefore likely to specify how any surplus cash should be used.

The following investment guidelines applied in a UK local borough council have been published on the Internet. They provide a useful example of what the nature of investment guidelines can be.

1 **Maturity and liquidity parameters**

   Minimum of 50% of the investment portfolio should have a maturity of one year or less.

   The maximum average maturity of the total portfolio should be three years.

   All investments with over three months to maturity must be in negotiable instruments (i.e. investments that can be sold if required).

   The maturity of any one investment in the portfolio must not exceed 10 years.

2 All investments must be in sterling-denominated instruments.

3 All investments must be made through banks or building societies that are on an approved list.

4 The amount invested through/with any individual bank or building society must not exceed 25% of the total value of the investment portfolio.

5 Investments must have a credit rating of no less than a certain grade. (The minimum credit rating is specified, and the authority requires all investments to have a high 'investment grade' credit rating.

6 The total value of gilts and corporate bonds in the portfolio must not exceed 50% of the value of the portfolio.

7 The maximum that can be invested with any individual borrower, with the exception of the UK government, is 10% of the value of the portfolio.

8 The investment guidelines end with a list of the types of securities that can be purchased for the portfolio. They include government securities (Treasury bills and gilts), local authority bills and bonds, bank bills, sterling CDs, commercial paper and corporate bonds.

Local authorities regularly invest short-term because they raise a large part of their taxes early in the year, and hold the money until it is needed for spending.

4.3 LEGAL RESTRICTIONS ON LOCAL AUTHORITIES

Various rules affect the ways that public sector organisations can handle cash and invest any surplus funds they have.

- Section 43 of the Local Government and Housing Act 1989 empowers councils to borrow money.
- Under Section 111 of the Local Government Act 1972, local authorities also have the power to lend surplus funds to facilitate the discharge of their functions.
- The Local Government Act 2003, and subsequent regulations, introduced a new 'prudential' framework that governs the capital financing and treasury management arrangements of local authorities. This framework replaced the previous rules whereby local authorities could only borrow to finance capital expenditure if given approval by the Government through the credit approval system.

  The implicit policy objective of the current regime is to encourage authorities to place their funds in forms of deposit that are relatively safe and quickly accessible. The underlying idea is that authorities should normally keep only the funds needed in the reasonably near future for their expenditure programmes and that in the meantime they should not take undue risks with the public money they hold in trust.

  The regulations do not prohibit any forms of investment. However, non-approved investments must be charged in-year when made and, when realised, up to 75% of the proceeds have to be set aside as provision for credit liabilities (PCL). This is a powerful incentive to use only the listed options, which are:

  - UK clearing banks and wholly owned subsidiaries where the repayment is guaranteed by a parent bank with the appropriate ratings
  - building societies
  - non-UK deposit taking banks:

    (i) local authorities

    (ii) gilts

    (iii) Euro-Sterling bonds permitted by the Regulations

    (iv) Public Works Loans Board/Government.
  - In accordance with the Code of Practice for Treasury Management in the Public Services, the annual Treasury Management and Investment Strategy has to be approved by the full Council.

4.4 CASH HANDLING PROCEDURES

Management is responsible for ensuring that cash, cheques, credit and debit card receipts are safeguarded against loss or theft, promptly deposited into the enterprise's bank account, and accurately recorded in the accounts. To fulfil this responsibility each unit receiving cash and equivalent should develop appropriate procedures that reflect the unit's size, complexity and method of operation.

There are four critical areas:

1 Accountability

2 Segregation of duties

3 Physical security

4 Reconciliation.

Accountability – this requires the person to have the authority to carry out the task. Any person who has delegated a task to someone remains accountable for ensuring the task is properly performed. Tasks can be delegated to someone only if that individual:

- possesses the appropriate knowledge and technical skill
- is actively involved in the task being performed.

Segregation of duties – the essence of the segregation of duties is that no one is to be put in a position in which they are able to both commit and conceal an error or fraud. Staff duties should be developed so that cash receipt and initial recording is assigned to one individual and reconciling duties are assigned to another. Cash handling work must be subject to daily review. Functions that need to be separated include:

- record keeping – creating and maintaining department records
- authorisation – review and approval of transactions
- asset custody – access to and/or control of physical assets, i.e. cash, cheques
- reconciliation – assurance that transactions are properly recorded.

These functions are separated when a different employee performs each of these four major functions. Often these duties are performed by different levels of personnel.

Physical security is assurance that the safety of people and assets (specifically cash) is maintained and controlled. It is effective when:

- assets are properly stored
- shortages/excesses are reported
- keys are secured
- cash counting is not visible
- safe combinations are changed
- background checks on personnel are performed.

Equipment and forms used should be appropriate for the amount of cash handled by the department and the number of individuals handling the cash. This applies to equipment used for both recording cash transactions and safeguarding cash (safes and lock boxes).

Reconciliation requires assurance that transactions are properly documented and approved and competent and knowledgeable individuals are involved. A reconciliation is performed to verify the processing and recording of transactions.

Documentation

Another important area is documentation. Current documentation of procedures should be maintained, regularly reviewed and updated. This should include a description of the responsibilities of staff and supervisors; operating instructions for equipment used in the cash handling process; and clear rules about who should have the authority to perform certain actions. For example, there should be rules about:

(i) Opening new bank accounts. Who is authorised to open a new account, and who should be the authorised signatories for the account? Who is authorised to specify what payments should be made into the account?

(ii) Borrowing. Who is authorised to negotiate new borrowing arrangements with banks, and up to what borrowing limits?

(iii) Who is authorised to invest surplus cash, and up to what investment limits?

(iv) Holding cash in the office. Who has the keys for the safe? Who has the duplicate keys for the safe?

(v) Existing bank accounts. Who are the authorised signatories? Are two signatories needed for payments above a certain amount?

(vi) Authorising payments. Who authorises purchase invoices and who decides when payments should be made?

CONCLUSION

This chapter has considered the importance of cash management, looking at the use of overdrafts, cash budgeting and cash management models, and the importance of the treasury department.

SELF-TEST QUESTIONS

		Paragraph
1	Give at least two objectives of a cash budget.	1.1
2	Describe two types of float.	1.2
3	What are the three motives for holding cash?	1.3
4	Outline two advantages of overdrafts.	1.4
5	What is the most liquid of assets?	2.2
6	What are the costs that are taken into account in the Baumol model?	2.6
7	Give three advantages of the centralisation of treasury activities.	3.3
8	What is the essence of the segregation of duties?	4.4

PRACTICE QUESTION

CASH MANAGEMENT

(a) 'Cash is no different from any other asset – if it is not being utilised properly it is going to result in lower profits.'

Discuss this statement, in particular referring to the motives for holding cash.
(8 marks)

(b) The AB Credit Collection Company employs agents who collect hire purchase instalments and other outstanding accounts on a door-to-door basis from Monday to Friday. The agents bank the cash collected to be remitted to head office once per week at the end of the week. The budget for next year shows that the total collections will be $5,200,000 and that the estimated bank overdraft rate is 9%. The collection manager has suggested that a daily remitting system should be introduced for collectors.

Comment on the significance of this system, stating clearly any assumptions you are required to make. **(12 marks)**

(Total: 20 marks)

For the answer to this question, see the 'Answers' section at the end of the book.

Chapter 4

INVESTING SURPLUS FUNDS

We have already noted that a business has to ensure that it has sufficient cash for all its day-to-day activities but, if the firm has surplus cash for its day-to-day needs, it should perhaps think about investing it. This means understanding the nature of the money markets, and the various opportunities that exist for investing the cash for the short term. When deciding which instrument to choose, management must assess the trade-off between the risks to the balances invested against the returns that can be achieved when investing funds.

This chapter covers Syllabus parts C2 and C4.

CONTENTS

LEARNING OUTCOMES

At the end of this chapter you should be able to:

- Define what is meant by 'surplus funds'
- Explain how surplus funds may arise
- Discuss the objectives to be considered in the investment of surplus funds
- Invest surplus funds according to organisational policy and within defined financial authorisation limits
- Define the risk-return trade-off
- Outline what is meant by risk of default, systematic risk and unsystematic risk
- Explain the purpose and main features of bank deposits, certificates of deposit, government stocks, local authority bonds and bills of exchange
- Explain the purpose and main features of debentures, unsecured loan stock, convertible and redeemable debts, warrants, equity and preferred shares.

1 SURPLUS FUNDS

1.1 WHAT IS MEANT BY SURPLUS FUNDS?

So far, cash management has been described in the context of ensuring that a business has sufficient cash and funding for its needs. Another aspect of cash management/treasury management is making use of cash surpluses that might arise from time to time.

Surplus funds comprise liquid balances held by a business, which are neither needed to finance current business operations nor held permanently for short-term investment.

Surplus funds can fall into two categories:

1. Long-term surpluses. Permanent cash surpluses and long-term cash surpluses are rare. These are cash surpluses that a business has no foreseeable use for. When they arise, the business is likely to repay liabilities or pay out the money to its owners in the form of dividends or drawings.

2. Short-term surpluses that need to be invested temporarily (perhaps in short-term securities or deposit accounts) until they are required.

The availability of surplus cash is temporary, awaiting employment either in existing operations or in new investment opportunities (whether already identified or not). The 'temporary' period can be of any duration from one day to the indefinite future date at which the new investment opportunity may be identified and seized. The business will need its cash at some future time in the not-too-distant future, but for a short time, perhaps several months, the business has more cash than it needs.

Cash surpluses should be used, and should not be left in a current bank account earning no interest. The cash might be transferred to a deposit account that does pay interest, or it might be invested in 'financial securities' such as government bonds (in the UK, gilt-edged securities or gilts). When cash surpluses are large, the interest income from investing the money can be quite large, adding to cash flow and profit.

1.2 HOW SURPLUS FUNDS MAY ARISE

Short-term surplus funds arise due to timing differences between the receipt of revenue and payment of expenditures i.e., a temporary surplus of cash inflows over cash outflows. This can be due to:

- unexpectedly large amounts of cash that have been generated from operations; this could be higher income from sales due to an increase in sales revenue

- lower costs maybe because of improved productivity or a cost-cutting exercise

- improvements in working capital management

- sales of non-current assets

- seasonal factors – surpluses generated in good months are used to cover shortfalls later.

2 INVESTING CASH SURPLUSES

When a business forecasts that it will have surplus funds, it should consider how to make the most profitable use of the cash surplus, without risking the liquidity of the business.

If a cash surplus is expected to be permanent, this means that it has no use for the cash and so there is no reason to keep it. The most appropriate decision is probably to pay the money back to the business owners.

If a cash surplus is expected to be temporary, the business should use the surplus to obtain additional income, but without exposing itself to unacceptable risk of losses.

The amount of surplus cash to invest, and the length of time for investing it, should be guided by the cash budget or cash forecast. The main points to remember are that:

- cash in a current bank account earns no interest and so should be kept to a minimum
- but at the same time, a business must have adequate liquidity, and it might therefore be prudent to keep some cash in the current account to meet unforeseen demands for payment.

2.1 INVESTING OBJECTIVES

Four factors need to be taken into account when deciding how a company should invest its cash surpluses:

1. **Risk** – the degree of risk attached to the investment in terms of variability of return and potential loss of principal.
2. **Liquidity** – the cash must be available for use when needed. How quickly the investment can be converted back to cash is of major importance. Factors such as how good a market exists for the chosen investment and the settlement period on any transaction should be considered.
3. **Maturity** – means the length or duration of investments.
4. **Return** – the income and capital gain from the chosen security. The aim is to earn the highest possible after tax returns.

These factors must be considered in the light of the firm's individual circumstances, in particular, the amount of funds available for investment and the duration of the surplus.

The firm might have specific policies regarding the level of risk it is prepared to take in its investments, and the proportions of cash invested in long term v short term deposits. There may be specific authorisation limits which need to be adhered to when investments are made.

Many investment opportunities are only available to large sums of cash. On the other hand, too much money concentrated on one security would impair its liquidity (it would be difficult to sell even 10% of the equity of a company in one day without affecting market price). Funds available for long periods of time can be safely tied up in longer-term investment opportunities, whereas funds that may be needed at short notice should be placed in highly liquid investments.

In general, the lower the liquidity of an investment, and the higher its risk, the higher its expected return will be. This is known as the 'risk-return trade-off'.

Most treasurers will be concerned with preserving the value of their investment and having access to funds at short notice, and will usually not look to maximise returns.

2.2 TYPES OF RISK

Everyone has heard the saying 'don't put all your eggs in one basket'. This concept can be applied to investing. Although we will be mainly focusing on the more conservative investing options available, no investment is without risk.

Companies need to manage risk. It is present whenever there are two or more possible future outcomes. Risk can manifest itself as an unexpected change in interest rates – relevant for companies that have to pay interest on loans – or an unexpected change in exchange rates – relevant for companies with overseas operations. It can also show up in unexpected changes in the company's business environment e.g. the market for its products or services that can significantly impact the company's cash flows. Sound financial planning – both in the short and long term – is the key to survival.

There are two main categories of risk:

- The first is **systematic**; it affects a large number of assets and is practically impossible to protect yourself against. An example of a systematic risk is a political event.

- The second is **unsystematic**, or 'specific risk'; it affects a small number of assets – a workers' strike or bad press, for example. Other types of unsystematic risk include: credit or default risk (the company cannot pay the contractual interest and principal on debt obligations), country risk (a country cannot honour its financial obligations), foreign exchange risk (the fluctuation in currency exchange rates), interest rate risk (an increase of interest rates hurts the price of bonds and stocks), political risk (changes in government policies, which are more common in second- and third-world countries), and market risk (the volatility of the stock market or fluctuations in stock prices which are the effect of market forces). The amount of risk the enterprise takes directly corresponds with the rate of return. For instance, a higher risk yields a higher potential return and a lower risk yields a lower rate of return.

In measuring investment risk we sometimes have to distinguish systematic risk from unsystematic risk.

Systematic risk is the variability of returns caused by factors affecting the whole market. It can never be eradicated so, if an investor wants to avoid risk altogether, he or she must steer well clear of the stock exchange. You only have to look at the effects of the global COVID-19 pandemic in 2020 to see how sudden unexpected events can turn the stock market into chaos. Share prices plummeted, and recovery was slow.

Unsystematic risk is the variability of returns caused by factors just affecting a specific market sector or group of companies. This element of risk can be eradicated by holding a well-diversified portfolio of investments. For example, an investor buys shares in two companies, one of which manufactures umbrellas and the other of which makes ice creams. During a wet summer, the umbrella business booms and its share price rises, but the ice cream business does badly. During a hot summer the ice cream business booms and its share price rises, but the umbrella business does badly. By investing in different types of company, the risk of overall share prices being affected by good or bad weather is eradicated.

The distinction between systematic and unsystematic risk only matters from the investor's point of view. The company is still subject to the total risk.

ACTIVITY 1

Which of the following would you classify as systematic risk and which as unsystematic risk?

Risk	Definition
Inflation risk	The probability that prices will rise by more than expected during the holding period
Interest rate risk	The probability that interest rates will move adversely during the holding period
Price risk	The probability that the prices of financial instruments will move adversely during the holding period
Reinvestment risk	The probability that reinvestment rates will move adversely during the holding period
Default (credit) risk	The probability that the borrower will fail to make timely principal and interest payments
Tax rate risk	The probability that tax laws will change during the holding period
Call (prepayment) risk	The probability that the borrower will recall and pay off the debt before maturity
Liquidity (market) risk	The probability that the market for a particular financial instrument will dry up
Currency risk	The probability that the value of one country's currency will move adversely against the value of another's during the holding period
Political risk	The probability that changes in governments, or their laws or regulations, will reduce the rate of return for foreign holders

For a suggested answer, see the 'Answers' section at the end of the book.

2.3 EXPOSURE TO INVESTMENT RISK

A problem with investing money is that the value of an investment can go down as well as up. If a business puts money into an investment that then loses value, it would have been better to hold on to the cash and keep it in the current account at the bank.

Deciding how to invest surplus cash therefore involves making a judgement about how much risk to accept. 'Risk' in this sense means the risk that the investment will lose value. As a general rule, higher-risk investments offer a higher potential return and low-risk investments offer a lower return.

- The lowest-risk investments are deposit accounts with a reputable bank (or with National Savings). It is most unlikely that the bank will suffer a financial collapse, which means that any money placed in a deposit account will be safe and will not go down in value. However, interest rates on bank deposits are lower than the rates of interest on other investments.
- Higher-risk investments are money market investments and government securities. These are described later in this chapter.

When a business has surplus cash, it should therefore consider what level of exposure to risk is acceptable. In other words, what losses would be acceptable if the investments were to fall in value?

Example

Suppose a business has $100,000 to invest for three months, it might decide that it should be invested to earn an expected return of 6% if there is a risk that the investments could fall in value by up to $5,000. If this risk is unacceptable, the business might decide to put the cash into a bank deposit account for three months and earn interest of, say, 3%.

Alternatively, it might be decided to split the investment and put $50,000 into the higher-risk investment expected to earn 6% (but with a risk of loss in value of up to $2,500) and the other $50,000 into a bank deposit account to earn 3%.

It would be unusual for a business to invest short-term cash in shares of other companies. This is because share prices are often volatile, and there is a high risk of losing money from a fall in the share price. The potential returns from investing in shares are therefore generally not worth the risk.

2.4 LIQUIDITY AND MATURITY

Liquidity is the ease and speed with which a financial instrument can be turned into cash without loss. For example a bank deposit is easily and quickly turned into cash and so is seen as very liquid. However, a stock in a small company may not be easy to sell at short notice so is deemed to be illiquid.

Term to maturity refers to the remaining time to maturity for a financial instrument. At maturity the instrument is repaid by the borrower. Term to maturity ranges from zero in the case of bank deposits that are easily withdrawn on demand to instruments such as shares which have no maturity date.

If a company knows that it will need the funds in three days (or weeks or months), it simply invests them for just that period at the best rate available with safety. The solution is to match the maturity of the investment with the period for which the funds are surplus.

- The exact duration of the surplus period is not always known. It will be known if the cash is needed to meet a loan instalment, a large tax payment or a dividend. But it will not be known if the need is unidentified, or depends on the build-up of stock, the progress of construction work, or the hammering out of an acquisition deal.

- Expected future trends in interest rates affect the maturity of investments. For example, if interest rates are forecast to fall, the returns on longer term investments might well be lower than those on short term investments.

- Bridging finance may be available to bridge the gap between the time when the cash is needed and the subsequent date on which the investment matures.

- An investment may not need to be held to maturity if either an earlier withdrawal is permitted by the terms of the instrument without excessive penalty, or there is a secondary market and its disposal in that market causes no excessive loss. A good example of such an investment is a certificate of deposit (CD), where the investor 'lends' the bank a stated amount for a stated period, usually between one and six months. As evidence of the debt and its promise to pay interest the bank gives the investor a CD. There is an active market for CDs issued by the commercial banks and turning a CD into cash is easy and cheap.

2.5 RETURN

Rational investors are both greedy and risk-averse. This means that they would like to gain as much as possible from their investments for as little risk as possible. But this is impossible. If they want to increase their return, they have to be prepared to take on more risk.

Although the whole purpose of investing cash is to receive a return, the rate of return is really the last factor to consider when investing cash surpluses. This is because it is largely dictated by the risk, liquidity and maturity. Once management has decided on the appropriate level of risk, liquidity and maturity, it has substantially narrowed down the types of investment that are appropriate. The market then dictates the rates of return on these investments.

2.6 MANAGEMENT OF SHORT-TERM AND LONG-TERM INVESTMENTS

The management of short-term investments and long-term investments calls for different approaches.

A **short-term investment** is intended to earn a return over a short time period until a business needs the cash. The aim of investing short term should be to earn a higher return than could be obtained by keeping the surplus cash in a current bank account. The investment should avoid an excessive risk of loss in value, usually because of a rise in interest rates. The investment should also be sufficiently liquid that it can be sold off quickly without much cost to raise cash.

Investing short term is therefore concerned primarily with:

- getting a good return, in terms of interest and, where possible, capital gains due to favourable movements in market prices
- avoiding excessive exposure to the risk of capital losses
- making sure that liquidity remains adequate.

Long-term investments have a different purpose, and so should be managed differently. They are intended to provide a suitable return over the long term (several years) and could well have a strategic value as well as a monetary value. Although there should be the aim of obtaining a suitable long-term return, short-term fluctuations in value or profitability are comparatively unimportant.

With long-term investments there is an investment risk, and the level of risk that is considered acceptable should be consistent with the size of the expected returns. In other words, exposures to risk are higher with long-term investments, but expected returns should also be higher.

Liquidity management is not an issue with long-term investments. A long-term investment does not need to be readily convertible into cash at short notice.

3 TYPES OF INVESTMENT

A wide (and expanding) number of short-term investment opportunities are available offering various degrees of liquidity, risk and return. They include:

Deposits

These are available for various maturity dates and offer varying returns. Interest rates are normally variable. Examples:

- **Money market deposits** for periods of overnight upwards to six months or, occasionally, a year. Usually a minimum of $10,000 is required.

- **Bank deposits** are similar to personal deposit accounts, with seven days' notice required for withdrawal. Interest penalties are usually levied for faster withdrawal.

- **Local authority deposits** with various maturities available; often the stocks are negotiable.

- **Certificates of deposit** are certificates issued by a bank when funds are deposited. The certificates may be sold to a third party, being fully negotiable instruments, and this makes the deposits highly marketable.

Loan stocks and equities

- **Loan stocks** are issued by governments (UK and foreign) and companies. Maturities, risks and returns vary.

- **Equities** are probably the riskiest short-term investment opportunities and are, therefore, not popular with most corporate treasurers. If chosen, they are best used in the context of a well-diversified portfolio.

3.1 RETAIL BANK AND BUILDING SOCIETY ACCOUNTS

Traditionally, retail banks provide banking services to individuals and small businesses dealing in large volumes of low value transactions. This is in contrast to wholesale banking which deals with large value transactions, generally in small volumes.

All of the high street banks and building societies offer different types of interest-earning accounts. For example:

A **deposit account** is an account for holding cash for a longer term. Banks pay interest on the money held in a deposit account. These accounts can be divided into:

- **Instant access accounts** that obviously allow instant access to your cash.

- **Notice accounts**, where savings earn a better rate of interest if you agree to lock them away for some time. The trade-off is that you cannot get at your money immediately. With notice accounts, you can only get your cash by giving notice of your intention to withdraw it. For example, with a 90-day notice account you would have to wait three months to get your money. You pay a penalty to access it earlier.

- **High interest accounts** are preferable when larger sums are available to invest (minimum $500). These usually give instant access to funds as well as a higher rate of interest.

Other types of investment with banks include:

Money market deposits offer real flexibility for larger amounts of money. For example, with $50,000 or more, fixed-term, fixed-rate deposits can be arranged for periods from overnight to five years.

Option deposits are arrangements for predetermined periods of investment, ranging from two to seven years. Interest rates are generally linked to base rates, giving a guaranteed return in real terms but restricted access to funds is the price paid for higher guaranteed interest rates. Investors would have to be sure of their cash position for that period before considering investing in an option deposit account.

Specialist bonds – all with different objectives – for those with at least $5,000 to invest.

An important feature of the banking system in the UK is that it is financially stable. Investment in a bank or building society deposit account offers high security with relatively low returns. In the event of default, investors are protected by statutory compensation schemes that will refund any funds lost, but only up to specified limits. The income received depends on the type of account and in some circumstances payment of interest can be made without deduction of tax. The risk factor on deposit accounts is very low although the real return (i.e. the return in excess of inflation) is also likely to be low. Deposit accounts are useful for short-term investment or as a readily accessible emergency fund.

4 MARKETABLE SECURITIES

Marketable securities are those that can be traded between investors. They represent stocks and bonds that are easily sold. Some are traded on highly developed and regulated markets while others can be traded between individual investors with brokers acting as middlemen. A marketable security has a readily determined fair market value and can be converted into cash at any time.

They can be classified into:

Money market securities which are short-term debt instruments sold by governments, financial institutions and corporations. The important characteristic of these securities is that they have maturities when issued of one year or less. The minimum size of transactions is typically large, usually exceeding $50,000. Money market securities tend to be highly liquid and safe assets. These investments include certificates of deposit, gilts, bills of exchange and treasury bills.

Capital market securities which have long maturities. These securities include instruments having maturities greater than one year and those having no designated maturity at all e.g. equities and preferred shares. They include fixed income securities, e.g. bonds, that promise a payment schedule with specific dates for the payment of interest and the repayment of principal. Any failure to conform to the payment schedule puts the security into default with all remaining payments. The holders of the securities can put the defaulter into bankruptcy. However, if an investor sells a bond before maturity the price that will be received is uncertain.

Indirect investments which can be undertaken by purchasing the shares of an investment company, which sells shares in itself to raise funds to purchase a portfolio of securities. The motivation for doing this is that the pooling of funds allows advantage to be taken of diversification and of savings in transactions costs. Many investment companies operate in line with a stated policy objective, for example on the type of securities that will be purchased and the nature of the fund management.

4.1 CERTIFICATES OF DEPOSIT

When banks accept deposits from customers, they are usually prepared to pay a higher interest rate for fixed long-term deposits than for deposits where the customer might withdraw the money at short notice. For example, suppose that an investor has $1 million to invest for three months. A bank might offer to pay 4% on a deposit if the customer has the right to withdraw the money at any time. However, if the investor agrees to keep the money on deposit for the full three months, the bank might be willing to pay 4.25%.

The investor would presumably prefer to invest at 4.25%, but only if they knew that they would not want any of the money during the fixed three-month deposit period.

Certificates of Deposit offer a way round this problem – they are marketable securities.

Definition A **Certificate of Deposit (CD)** is a financial instrument issued by a bank, certifying that the holder has the right to a fixed-term deposit of funds earning a specified interest rate. A CD is negotiable, which means that it can be sold by its original holder to another investor at any time before the end of the deposit period.

Example

An investor agrees to deposit $1 million with a bank for a fixed three-month period to earn interest at 4.25%. This means that at the end of the deposit period, the deposit with interest will be about $1,010,625. The bank issues a CD to the investor, certifying the investor's entitlement to the deposit plus interest after three months.

- If the investor holds the CD to maturity, he or she will be able to withdraw the $1,010,625.

- However, if the investor wants cash earlier, he or she can sell the CD in the money market. There is a market for trading in 'second-hand' CDs. The sale value of a CD will depend on how much a buyer is willing to pay to obtain the right to the deposit plus interest at maturity.

In this example, if the investor decided to sell the CD after two months, the sale value would depend on what a buyer would be willing to pay to receive the right to $1,010,625 in one month's time, when the deposit period ends. A buyer will offer a price that gives a suitable return on the investment.

For example, a buyer might offer $1,006,600 for the CD. If the CD is sold for this amount after two months (and so with one month to maturity):

- The buyer of the return will receive $1,010,625 in one month's time, for an investment of $1,006,600. This gives a return of just over $4,000 in one month.

- The original investor has made a return of $6,600 on the deposit of $1,000,000 in two months.

Investing in CDs

Banks and building societies issue CDs. The amount of the deposit and the date of repayment will be stated on the certificate. The deposit amount will usually be at least $100,000 and the repayment date will be anything from one week to five years.

Repayment is obtained by presenting the CD to the issuer on the designated date. Since CDs are negotiable, the holder can sell them at any time. This makes them far more liquid than a money-market time deposit, with the same bank.

CDs usually offer an attractive rate of interest and a low credit risk. They are useful for investing funds in the short term since they can be sold at any time on the secondary market. If a high level of liquidity is not required, however, an investor may prefer to place money on a time deposit which, being less liquid, will probably pay a higher level of interest.

4.2 GILT-EDGED SECURITIES (GILTs)

These are marketable British Government securities. The government issues them to finance its spending, but also uses them to control the money supply. Most gilts have a face value of $100 at which the government promises to buy the gilt back on a specific date in the future.

Gilts usually have fixed interest rates, although there are also various index-linked gilts. Where they are the index-linked type, both the interest and the redemption value are linked to inflation, ensuring that a decent real return is gained.

For example, here are just a few gilts currently in issue:

Treasury Stock 8½% 2025
Treasury Stock 7¼% 2027
Treasury Stock 5¾% 2029
Treasury Stock 5% 2032
Treasury Stock 6% 2038
3½% War Loan

For investment purposes, gilts are categorised according to how long it will be before they reach their redemption date. The main categories are:

- short-dated: these have up to 5 years remaining to maturity
- medium-dated: these have between 5 and 15 years remaining to maturity
- long-dated: these have over 15 years remaining to maturity
- perpetuals: there are some issues of gilts, such as 3.5% War Loans, that will never be redeemed, unless the government chooses to redeem them.

Gilts are also traded on the stock market. Their price can go up or down, depending on what people think will happen to interest rates. When interest rates are expected to fall, the price of the gilt rises, and when interest rates are expected to rise, the gilt price falls. Using gilts in this way makes them a more risky investment, but still relatively safe when compared with other types of investments. Gilts are transferable on the secondary market in multiples of a penny, but if they are bought from new, the minimum investment is $1,000. There is no maximum investment limit. They are easy to transfer and nowadays the title can even be passed electronically. Gilts are a good choice of investment for risk-averse investors.

Gilt yields are measured and reported in three ways.

- **Coupon yield**. The coupon yield is the fixed rate of interest, expressed as a percentage of nominal value. So 7% Treasury Stock 2031 would have a coupon yield of 7%, regardless of its market price.
- **Interest yield**. The interest yield on gilts is the annual interest receivable, expressed as a percentage of the market price. For example, if 7% Treasury Stock 2031 has a market price of 103.80, the interest yield is 6.7% (100% × 7/103.80).

- **Redemption yield**. The interest yield measures the interest return on gilts, but ignores any capital gain or loss on investment when the gilts are eventually redeemed. Redemption yield is the interest yield plus or minus an amount to reflect the difference between the market price of the gilt and its eventual redemption value.

The current interest yield and redemption yield on each issue of gilts is reported continually to investors in the gilts market and daily in the financial press.

The redemption yield is more significant for investors.

Example

An issue of 9% Treasury Stock has a market value of $105.80, and it is redeemable at par in two years' time.

The interest yield on the stock is 8.5% (100% × 9/105.80). However, an investor buying a quantity of the stock now at 105.80 and holding it until maturity will only receive $100 for every $105.80 of investment. Although the investor will receive an interest yield of 8.5% per annum, there will be a capital loss of $5.80 for each $105.80 invested. Since the stock has two years remaining to maturity this represents an average loss of $2.90 each year, which is 2.7% of the investment value.

As a rough approximation, the redemption yield on the stock is 5.8% (8.5%–2.7%).

ACTIVITY 2

An issue of 4% Treasury Stock has a current market price of $94.00. The stock has exactly three years to redemption, when it will be redeemed at par.

Required:

(a) Calculate the current interest yield on the stock.

(b) Calculate an approximate redemption yield.

For a suggested answer, see the 'Answers' section at the end of the book.

4.3 LOCAL AUTHORITY STOCK

Definition **Local authority stock** is issued by local government authorities ('local councils') with the ultimate backing of the government.

Local authority debt instruments are issued with a period to maturity ranging from as little as two days to 10 or 15 years. Local authority bonds are longer-dated stock, and most new issues have a maturity of one to four years. The most popular local authority bonds are called 'yearlings' which have a maturity of one year and six days. Local authority bills are shorter-dated stock, which are issued to meet short-term liquidity problems.

Local authority bonds pay a fixed coupon rate of interest, and interest is paid every six months. The minimum investment is $1,000. Investors can subscribe to a new issue and purchase bills or bonds from the local authority, or they can buy and sell bonds on the stock exchange.

The yield to investors on local authority debt instruments is usually slightly higher than the yield currently available on gilt-edged stock or Treasury bills. The credit risk is low, but any issue of local authority bills or bonds is only as secure as the local authority issuing them. The market for local authority bills and bonds is much smaller than for central government stock, which is another reason why yields are a bit higher.

Conclusion Local authority securities offer slightly higher yields than government stock because the market is less liquid and the security of a local authority is not regarded quite so highly as that of central government.

4.4 BILLS OF EXCHANGE

A bill is a short-term debt instrument. There are different types of bill.

- There are bills issued by the government. Central government bills are called Treasury bills.
- There are also bills of exchange. Bills of exchange are either trade bills or bank bills. Trade bills can be either term bills or sight bills.

Definition A **bill of exchange** is an unconditional order in writing from one person to another, requiring the person to whom it is written to pay a specified sum of money. The money might be payable immediately, in which case the bill is a sight bill. Alternatively, and more usually, the money might be payable at a specified future date, in which case it is a term bill. A bill of exchange could therefore be described as a 'You Owe Me' demand for payment.

The money markets in bills are largely for Treasury bills and bank bills, but it is useful to begin by looking at trade bills.

Trade bills might be used in commerce, particularly international trade, as a mechanism for the payment of a debt.

A bill is drawn by one person on another. With a trade bill, the person drawing the bill (the drawer) is the supplier of goods and the person who is required to pay (the drawee) is the customer.

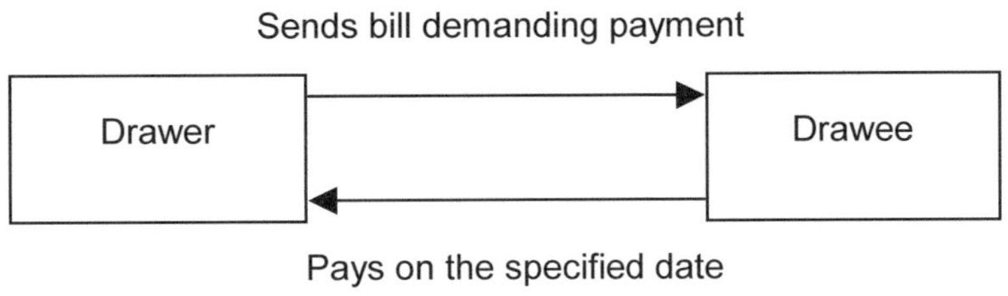

The drawer prepares a bill of exchange by obtaining a blank bill from its bank.

When the bill is a term bill, payable at a future date, the drawee is required to sign the bill as an indication that he or she acknowledges the debt and agrees to pay the money on the due date. Signing the bill in this way is called **accepting** the bill. An example of a trade bill is shown below.

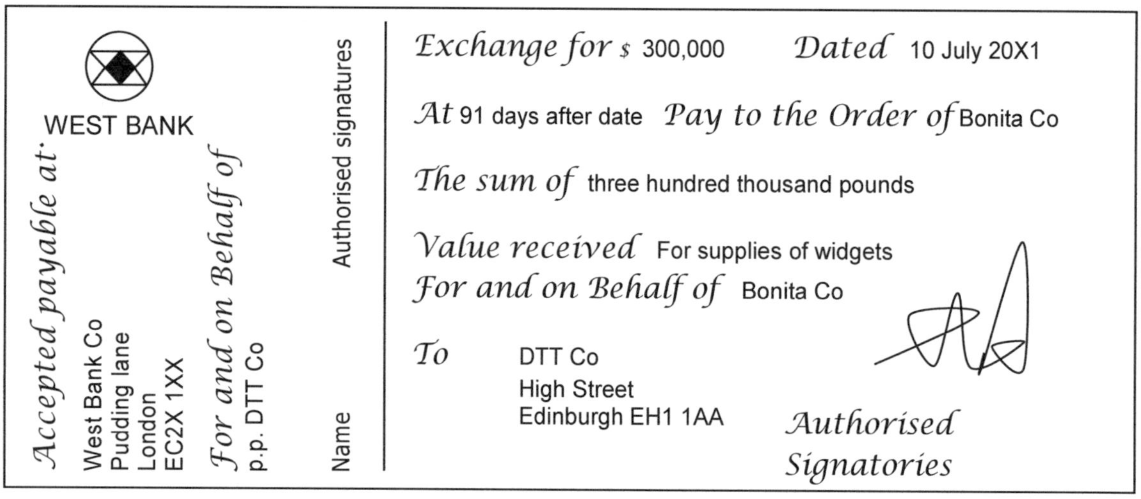
WEST BANK
Accepted payable at:
West Bank Co
Pudding lane
London
EC2X 1XX
For and on Behalf of
p.p. DTT Co
Authorised signatures
Name

Exchange for $ 300,000 Dated 10 July 20X1
At 91 days after date Pay to the Order of Bonita Co
The sum of three hundred thousand pounds
Value received For supplies of widgets
For and on Behalf of Bonita Co
To DTT Co
High Street
Edinburgh EH1 1AA
Authorised Signatories

The accepted bill is returned to the drawer. The drawer of a term bill can now do either of two things.

- She can wait until the date on which payment is due, and then present the bill to the bank for payment by the drawee.

- Alternatively, if the drawer needs the money sooner, he or she can sell it. The bank might be willing to buy the bill itself; otherwise it can arrange to sell the bill on behalf of the drawer in the bills market.

When a bill is sold, its sale value will be less than the amount payable on the bill. For example, if the bill is for $300,000 payable in 90 days' time, the sale value of the bill will be less than $300,000. The bill is therefore sold at a discount to its face value, and selling a bill in the market is therefore commonly known as 'discounting a bill'. The amount of the discount is to give the buyer a return on the investment in the bill. For example, if a bill for $300,000 payable in 90 days' time is discounted to $297,000, the difference of $3,000 between the market price and the eventual payment value represents interest for the buyer of the bill on an investment of $297,000 for 90 days.

A bill of exchange therefore provides a source of cash to the drawer of the bill, who can sell it in the bills market. It also provides a short-term investment to the buyer of the bill, who effectively earns interest on the investment by buying the debt at a discount to the amount he or she will eventually receive when the bill is paid.

Bank bills – a problem with trade bills is that the bill is a promise by the drawee to pay the money at a future date. The holder of a bill has to rely on the expectation that the drawee is creditworthy, and will pay the money on the due date.

Because there is an element of 'credit risk' in a trade bill, the buyer of the bill might want a higher return to compensate for the risk of non-payment. In other words, the trade bill might have to be sold at a fairly high discount to its face value in order to attract a buyer.

A bank bill is similar to a trade bill, except that the drawee is a bank, not a trading business. Banks are generally more creditworthy than non-bank businesses, therefore a term bill drawn on a bank is less risky than a trade bill and can be sold at a lower discount.

- The drawer of the bill will get more money from selling a bank bill than a similar trade bill.

- The buyer of the bill is prepared to take a lower return on the investment because the credit risk is much lower.

A company might therefore make an arrangement with its bank whereby the bank agrees to accept bills drawn on it. When the bill is accepted, it can be sold in the bills market (or 'discount market') and the money used to provide finance to the drawer. When the bill reaches its payment date, the bank pays the bill to the bill holder, and recovers the money from its customer, the company.

Bank bills are used in two ways.

- When a bill of exchange is used as a method of payment for a business transaction, the buyer of goods can arrange for its bank to accept a bill drawn by the supplier.

- If a company needs to borrow short-term funds, one way of arranging this is to get the bank to accept bills drawn on it by the company, which can then be discounted in the market. The money is then given to the company (as drawer of the bill, and so the seller of the bill). The bank pays the bill at maturity, but reclaims the money from the company. This type of short-term financing arrangement is called an acceptance credit facility.

The process of discounting bank bills is summarised in the diagram below.

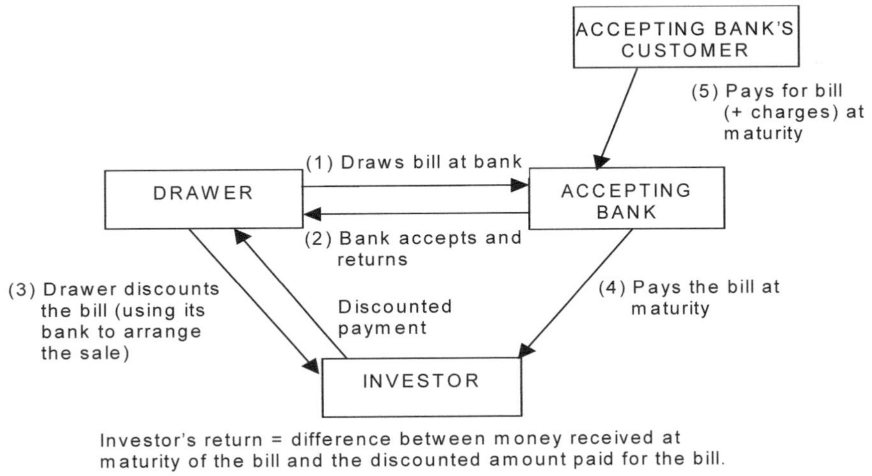

Treasury bills are short-term debt instruments issued and sold by the central government. They usually have a term of 91 days when issued.

A bill of exchange can be described as a 'You Owe Me' issued by the drawer and sent to the drawee for acceptance. A Treasury bill is not the same, because it is an IOU issued by the government. The government undertakes to pay the face value of the bill 91 days after the date of issue.

The government issues new Treasury bills regularly, and invites investors to subscribe by submitting a tender. Organisations wanting to buy Treasury bills can therefore put in a bid for a quantity of bills, and the government accepts the highest bids. The bills are then issued at a price equal to the lowest accepted bid.

Treasury bills are issued at a face value that the government will pay after 91 days, and they are sold at a discount to their face value. In the same way as for bills of exchange, the difference between the purchase price of a bill and its eventual redemption value (face value) represents interest for the investor in the bill.

Buyers of Treasury bills are mainly large financial institutions, including banks, but there is an active 'second-hand' market in bills. Investors buying bills from the government can sell them on at any time up to the eventual maturity date for the bill. The second-hand market value of a bill will always be at a discount to the bill's face value, and the amount of the discount always represents the interest or return on investment that the buyer of the bill will receive if he or she holds the bill to maturity.

4.5 THE DISCOUNT MARKET

A business with a short-term cash surplus can arrange through its bank to invest in the discount market, by purchasing either Treasury bills or bills of exchange (preferably bank bills, for which the credit risk is much lower). Since Treasury bills are an undertaking to pay by the central government, the risk to an investor is even lower than for bank bills. Treasury bills and government bonds (gilts) are commonly described as 'risk-free investments'.

An investor in bills needs to consider the risks and returns involved. There are two risks for an investor in bills.

- Credit risk. This is the risk that the bill will not be paid at maturity. As explained above, this risk is non-existent with Treasury bills and should be low for bank bills. It can be high for trade bills.
- The risk of a change in interest rates. This risk does not exist for any investor who buys a bill and then holds it to maturity. Interest rate risk only exists for investors who buy bills with the intention of re-selling them before maturity. The risk arises because if market rates of interest go up, the market value of bills will fall. (Equally, if market rates of interest fall, the market value of bills will rise.)

Example

An investor buys a 91-day bank bill with a face value of $1 million in the discount market for $987,500. Although the calculations are not shown, the bill will give the investor a return of 5% per annum if he or she holds the bill to maturity and takes the $1 million payment.

However, suppose that the investor sells the bill seven days later, when interest rates in the discount market have risen to 6%. The sale value of the bill would be about $986,000 (workings not shown) and the investor would have made a loss on the investment.

The market value of a bill goes down when interest rates rise, because when interest rates go up, investors want a bigger return. To get a bigger return, they will buy bills at a bigger discount to face value, in other words, bill prices will fall.

ACTIVITY 3

Your company has $5 million to invest for 50 days. You are interested in investing the money in bills, but you want to do so at a low risk.

Required:

Advise your manager what might be a suitable way of investing in bills to obtain a fairly low-risk return.

For a suggested answer, see the 'Answers' section at the end of the book.

4.6 RISK AND RETURN

As a general rule, money market investments should offer a higher yield to investors than ordinary bank deposits, as compensation for the higher risk (an example of the 'risk return trade-off'). Whenever a business is planning to invest surplus cash, it should look at the interest rates currently obtainable.

Example

The interest yields on a range of investments are currently as follows:

Investment	Current yield
Short-dated gilts	4.73%
Bank bills (1 month)	4.5625%
Bank bills (3 months)	4.5%
Treasury bills (3 months)	4.4375%
CDs	4.625%
Bank deposit	4.30%

Your company has $10 million to invest for three months. How should it invest the money?

Solution

It is essential to understand that unless there are clear guidelines and policies within the organisation about how surplus cash should or should not be invested, the choice between different investments is a matter of judgement and preference.

In this example:

- The lowest yield would be obtained by putting the money into a bank deposit account for three months, but it should be possible to secure a fixed interest rate for the three-month period, and there is no risk that the money held on deposit will lose value.

- Short-dated gilts offer the highest yield, but to cash in the investment, the gilts will have to be sold in the market, and there is a risk of a fall in market value due to an increase in interest rates over the next three months. If an increase in interest rates is not expected, gilts could be the favoured investment option.

- Of the money market investments, CDs offer a higher yield than three-month bank bills or three-month Treasury bills. All these investments can be held until maturity in three months' time, which means that there is no interest rate risk unless the business has to sell off its investments unexpectedly before the end of the three-month period.

- The yield on one-month bank bills is higher than the yield on three-month bills. However, it is not yet clear what interest rates will be available on investments at the end of one month, when the bills mature and are redeemed. The business will need to invest for a further two months, and there is a risk that interest rates could fall over the next month.

Whatever investment decision is taken, the choice of investments should be made for clear and logical reasons.

5 CAPITAL MARKET INSTRUMENTS

The term 'capital markets' means the markets for raising long-term finance, investing in long-term financial instruments, and trading in those instruments 'second hand' (i.e. in a secondary market).

The types of goods traded on the stock exchange are commonly referred to as securities. These can be classified as share capital and fixed income securities.

5.1 SHARE CAPITAL

A share is a security that represents a portion of the owner's capital in a business. Shareholders are the owners of the business. They share in the success or failure of the business. This can be measured by the amount of dividends that they receive and by the price of the share, quoted on the stock market.

The different types of share include:

Ordinary shares – also called equity shares, this is the risk capital of a company. Ordinary shares give holders the rights of ownership in the company, such as the right to share in the profits, to vote in general meetings and to elect and dismiss directors. Obligations of ownership are also conferred and this may result in the loss of an investor's money if the company is unsuccessful. Ordinary shares usually form the bulk of a company's capital and have no special rights over other shares. In the event of liquidation, ordinary shares rank after all other liabilities of the company.

Preferred shares are comparable to loan notes in that they yield fixed rate dividends. (Preferred shares are known as preference shares in the UK and loan notes are known as debentures in the UK.) The main difference, however, is that dividends on preferred shares are paid provided the company makes a profit, whereas dividends on loan notes need to be paid irrespective of whether the company makes a profit or a loss.

Preferred shares may be preferred also as regards distribution of assets upon dissolution of the company. There are various types of preferred shares:

- **Participating preferred shares** are entitled to participate in the profits beyond the fixed dividends, by way of an additional fluctuating dividend if the company is successful.

- **Cumulative preferred shares** are preferred shares which, apart from having a preferential right to receive a fixed dividend ahead of ordinary shares, also carry the right of any arrears of the preferred dividends which may have built up.

- **Non-cumulative preferred shares** are preferred shares which are not entitled to any arrears in dividends.

- **Redeemable preferred shares** may be redeemed by the company at a stated redemption price on advance notice of a period of time. It is usual to set a redemption price above the par value to compensate the owner for the involuntary loss of the investment.

- **Convertible preferred shares** are preferred shares, which carry the right to be made convertible, at the option of the holder, into another class of shares, normally into ordinary shares.

5.2 FIXED INCOME SECURITIES

The holders of fixed income securities are payables of the company rather than shareholders. Holders of fixed income securities have no rights in the company beyond the payment of a fixed interest on their loans and repayment of the loans in accordance with the terms on which they were issued. Fixed income securities may be secured or unsecured, with the secured fixed income securities ranking before the unsecured.

The two principal types of fixed income securities are loan notes and loan stocks:

Loan notes (debentures/debenture stocks) – a loan note or a debenture is similar to a mortgage. It is a long-term loan secured on certain fixed or floating assets of a company. A debenture stock is a debenture issued as a fixed-interest stock. Such securities are issued under trust deeds and, in the event of the borrower defaulting on the interest or capital repayment, the debenture holder has the right to appoint a receiver to sell the company's assets and secure repayment of the loan.

Loan stocks – this is a security issued by a company in respect of a loan made by investors. Loan stocks may be secured, unsecured, convertible or non-convertible, but are often unsecured, unlike debentures (loan notes).

- **Unsecured loan stocks** carry higher risk than debentures (loan notes) and, in the event of a winding-up, unsecured loan stockholders rank alongside all other unsecured payables.

- **Convertibles** carry the right to convert into ordinary shares of the company on pre-arranged terms and within a limited period. The income received from convertibles is normally higher than that offered on the underlying ordinary shares, but the capital behaviour is different because of the right to convert to ordinary shares. The conversion rights are either stated in terms of a conversion ratio (i.e. the number of ordinary shares into which $100 stock may be converted) or in terms of a conversion price (i.e. the right to convert into ordinary shares at a price of x pence) e.g. '$100 of stock may be converted into 25 ordinary shares' is a conversion ratio; 'stock may be converted into shares at a value of 400 cents per share' is the equivalent conversion price. Depending upon the proximity of the conversion date, interest rate factors can have a bearing on the capital value of convertibles. If the final conversion date passes, investors may find that the capital value of their investment has fallen and assumes the characteristics of a conventional fixed interest security. Alternatively, some convertibles may contain provisions for compulsory conversion or redemption, at the option of the issuing company, on terms that may not necessarily be advantageous to the holder.

  From the investor's point of view, convertible stocks offer a low-risk security with the added advantage of an opportunity to study share price movements before deciding whether to invest in the equity.

Permanent interest bearing shares in a building society (PIBS)

Easier access to capital markets was part of the justification for conversion given by the Halifax, Alliance and Leicester, Northern Rock, and Woolwich building societies. Conversion provides access to equity capital, whereas building societies' capital sources are limited to accumulated profits and subordinated debt.

However, societies seeking access to capital do, in practice, have other options open to them. The Nationwide, currently the largest building society, is among several to have issued debt in the form of 'PIBS' (permanent or preferred interest-bearing securities). This is a special type of security created to enable building societies to raise funds while improving their capital ratios. PIBS are quoted on the London Stock Exchange.

CONCLUSION

Companies have a variety of opportunities for using their surplus funds, but when deciding on how they should invest, their choice will be determined by four considerations – risk, liquidity, maturity and return.

This chapter has looked at the nature of the money markets and the gilts market and the use of these markets by businesses, largely as an opportunity for short-term investment of surplus cash.

A business must have enough liquidity to survive, and careful cash management should help to ensure that liquidity remains sufficient.

KEY TERMS

Deposit account – interest-earning bank account, used for holding surplus funds. There is no risk of capital loss with money in a deposit account.

Bill of exchange – a 'You Owe Me', drawn by a payable on another person (the drawee). In the case of a bill payable at a future date (a 'term bill'), the drawee accepts the bill by signing it, thereby acknowledging the obligation to pay the debt at the specified future date.

Bank bill – a bill of exchange drawn on a bank. A bill accepted by a bank is usually regarded as a lower credit risk than a bill accepted by a non-bank company.

Treasury bill – an IOU issued by the government, promising to pay a fixed sum of money after a given period of time (usually 91 days after issue).

Discount market – a market for selling and buying bills of exchange and Treasury bills. Bills are bought and sold in this market at a discount to face value, the discount reflecting the interest rate return that the buyer of the bill obtains if he or she holds the bill to maturity.

Certificate of deposit (CD) – a negotiable instrument issued by a bank, giving its holder the right to a sum of money (with interest) in a bank deposit account, at a specified future date.

Gilts – gilt-edged securities. Long-term debt securities (bonds) issued by the UK government. Gilts are used extensively as both long-term and short-term investments, and there is a large and liquid secondary market for buying and selling gilts.

SELF-TEST QUESTIONS

		Paragraph
1	How might cash surpluses arise?	1.2
2	Give two examples of unsystematic risk.	2.2
3	What is a notice account?	3.1
4	Explain what a short-dated gilt is.	4.2
5	What are the two risks for an investor in bills?	4.5
6	How are preferred shares comparable to loan notes?	5.1

Chapter 5

WORKING CAPITAL MANAGEMENT

Working capital is the capital available for conducting the day-to-day operations of an organisation, represented by its net current assets. The managers have the responsibility to manage the levels of working capital in the best interests of the stakeholders.

This chapter starts with an examination of the general issues of working capital management, including ratio analysis. We then move on to look at how organisations that have too much working capital suffer from overcapitalisation, whilst those with too little may be overtrading.

This chapter covers Syllabus part A1.

CONTENTS

LEARNING OUTCOMES

At the end of this chapter you should be able to:

- Define working capital
- Explain why working capital management is important
- Explain the relationship between cash flows and the working capital cycle
- Demonstrate the calculation of the working capital cycle (also known as the cash operating cycle)
- Outline the possible relationships between inventory levels and sales
- Define and explain over-trading and over-capitalisation
- Identify and calculate over-trading and over-capitalisation financial indicators.

1 WORKING CAPITAL MANAGEMENT

1.1 DEFINING WORKING CAPITAL

Organisations need cash to pay for all their day-to-day activities. They have to pay wages, pay for raw materials, pay bills and so on. The money available to them to do this is known as their working capital. The main sources of working capital are the current assets as these are the short-term assets that the firm can use to generate cash. However, the organisation also has current liabilities and so these have to be taken account of when working out how much working capital the organisation has at its disposal.

WORKING CAPITAL = CURRENT ASSETS – CURRENT LIABILITIES

Thus working capital is the same as net current assets, and is an important part of the top half of the firm's statement of financial position.

In an organisation's statement of financial position, these components of working capital are reported under the following headings:

Current assets	**Current liabilities**
• Liquid assets (cash and bank deposits) • Inventory of raw materials • Work in progress and finished goods • Marketable securities • Receivables (debtors)	• Bank overdraft • Payables (creditors) • Tax payable • Dividend payments due • Other short-term liabilities

Working capital measures how much in liquid assets a company has available to build its business. The number can be positive or negative depending on how much debt the company is carrying. In general, companies that have a lot of working capital will be more successful since they can expand and improve their operations. Companies with negative working capital may lack the funds necessary for growth.

Different industries have diverse working capital profiles, reflecting their methods of doing business and what they are selling.

- Businesses with a lot of cash sales and few credit sales should have minimal trade receivables. Supermarkets are good examples of such businesses.
- Businesses that exist to trade in completed products will only have finished goods in held in inventory. Compare this with manufacturers who will also have to maintain stocks of raw materials and work in progress.
- Some finished goods, notably foodstuffs, have to be sold within a limited period because of their perishable nature.
- Larger companies may be able to use their bargaining strength as customers to obtain more favourable, extended credit terms from suppliers. By contrast, smaller companies, particularly those that have recently started trading (and do not have a track record of creditworthiness) may be required to pay their suppliers immediately.

- Some businesses will receive their monies at certain times of the year, although they may incur expenses throughout the year at a fairly consistent level. This is often known as 'seasonality' of cash flow. For example, travel agents have peak sales in the weeks immediately following Christmas.

Working capital needs also fluctuate during the year:

- The amount of funds tied up in working capital would not typically be a constant figure throughout the year.

- Only in the most unusual of businesses would there be a constant need for working capital funding. For most businesses there would be weekly fluctuations.

- Many businesses operate in industries that have seasonal changes in demand. This means that sales, inventory, receivables, etc. would be at higher levels during some predictable times of the year than at others.

1.2 WORKING CAPITAL MANAGEMENT AND ITS IMPORTANCE

Working capital management is the management of all aspects of both current assets and current liabilities, to minimise the risk of insolvency while maximising the return on assets.

The objective of working capital management is to maintain the optimum balance of each of the working capital components. This includes making sure that funds are held as cash in bank deposits for as long as possible and in the largest amounts possible, thereby maximising the interest earned. However, such cash may more appropriately be 'invested' in other assets or in reducing other liabilities.

In Chapter 1 we briefly looked at the connection between investment in working capital and cash flow and showed the operating cycle sometimes called the working capital cycle, cash cycle or the trading cycle.

Definition The **working capital cycle**, which is also called the operating cycle and the cash cycle, is the average length of time between paying for purchases of materials (for use or re-sale) and eventually receiving payment from customers after a sale has been made.

There are three elements in the working capital cycle or operating cycle:

- **The average inventory (stock) turnover period.** This is the average time between buying inventory and using it to create a sale. The inventory turnover period in manufacturing businesses can be divided into turnover periods for raw materials, work in progress (the production cycle) and finished goods.

- **The receivables collection period** (also known as debtor days). This is the average period of time from making a sale to receiving payment from the customer.

- **The payables payment period is the average period of credit taken from suppliers** (also known as creditor days). This reduces the length of the working capital cycle, because purchases of inventory are not paid for until after the period of credit allowed by suppliers.

The working capital cycle is also called the cash cycle, because it can be described broadly as the time between paying cash to start a sale transaction and receiving cash from the customer.

The working capital cycle

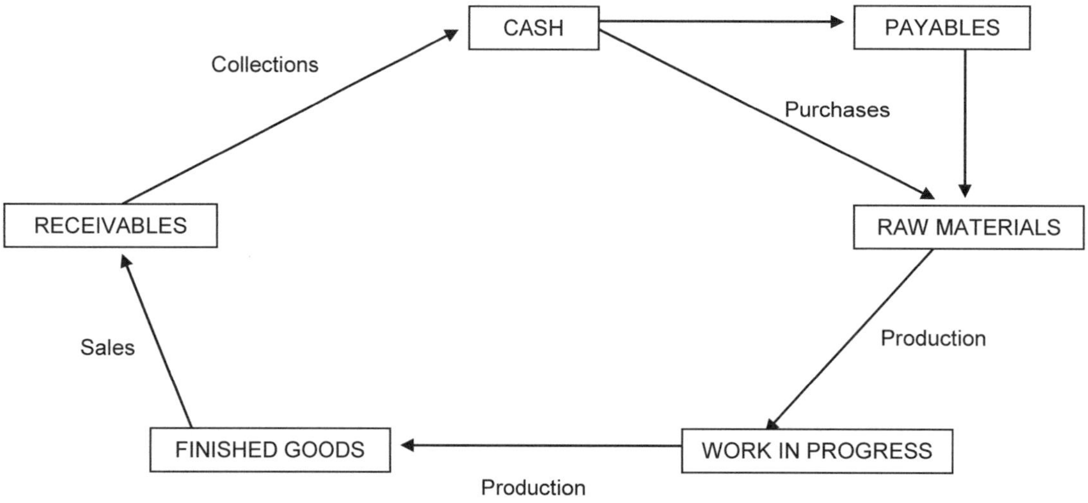

The cycle reflects a firm's investment in working capital as it moves through the production process towards sales. The investment in working capital gradually increases, firstly being only in raw materials, but then in labour and overheads as production progresses. This investment must be maintained throughout the production process, the holding period for finished goods and up to the final collection of cash from trade receivables. (**Note:** The net investment can be reduced by taking trade credit from suppliers.)

The faster a firm can 'push' items around the cycle, the lower its investment in working capital will be.

The cycle is measured in days (or months). It is an average measure only, and it is not exact. However, it is useful for monitoring liquidity, because changes in the length of the working capital cycle can indicate worsening or improving liquidity.

However, note that improving liquidity – identified by a shortening working capital cycle – is often achieved at the expense of profitability. For example, reducing inventory holdings and receivables collection period can make a business far less attractive to potential customers, so sales might well fall (damaging profitability) even though liquidity appears to be improving. It is very important that the managers of the business assess this **trade-off between profitability and liquidity** carefully. To be successful, the business needs to have a balance between good profitability and good liquidity.

1.3 CALCULATING THE WORKING CAPITAL CYCLE

With some fairly basic financial information it is possible to measure the length of the working capital cycle for a given firm.

For a **manufacturing business**, such as that illustrated in the diagram above, the working capital cycle will be measured by:

Working capital cycle = Raw materials holding period + WIP holding period + Finished goods holding period + Receivables collection period – Payables payment period.

For a **wholesale** or **retail** business, there will be no raw materials or WIP holding periods, and the cycle simplifies to:

Working capital cycle = Inventory holding period + Receivables collection period – Payables payment period.

Example

Suppose a company buys raw materials on one month's credit on 1 June. These are issued to the production department where they are transformed into finished goods. The production cycle lasts 1.5 months before the goods are sold. Receivables take 1.5 months' credit.

Purchase of raw materials	1 June
Payment made to suppliers	1 July
Sale of finished goods	15 July
Receipt of cash from receivables	1 September

+ Cash is locked up in work in progress = 1.5 months

+ Cash is locked up in receivables = 1.5 months

– Cash is free because goods bought on credit = 1 month

The working capital cycle is the period of 2 months from 1 July when payment is made to the suppliers until 1 September when cash is received from receivables.

A short cash conversion cycle is a sign of good working capital management. Conversely, a long cash conversion cycle indicates that capital is tied up while the business waits for customers to pay.

It is quite possible for a business to have a negative cash conversion cycle, i.e. receiving payment from customers before it has to pay suppliers. Examples are typically companies which employ 'just-in-time' (JIT) practices such as Dell, and companies which buy on extended credit terms and sell for cash, such as Tesco.

The longer the production process, the more cash the firm must keep tied up in inventory. Similarly, the longer it takes customers to pay their bills, the higher the value of accounts receivable. On the other hand, if a firm can delay paying for its own materials, it may reduce the amount of cash it needs. In other words, accounts payable reduce net working capital.

Summary

The working capital cycle is measurable in days as:

Inventory turnover period **plus** Receivables collection period **minus** Payables payment period

A longer inventory turnover period, or allowing receivables longer to pay lengthens the operating cycle. It also increases the investment in inventory or receivables, tying up more cash in working capital. A task for the financial manager is to maintain the length of the operating cycle at a level where the investment in working capital is not excessive, but at the same time liquidity is sufficient.

Good management of working capital is part of good financial management. Effective use of working capital will contribute to the operational efficiency of a department; optimum use will help to generate maximum returns. Ratio analysis can be used to identify working capital areas that require closer management.

ACTIVITY 1

A company generally pays its suppliers six weeks after receiving an invoice, while its credit customers usually pay within four weeks of invoicing. Raw materials inventory are held for a week before processing, which takes three weeks. Finished goods stay in inventory for an average of two weeks.

How long is the company's operating cycle?

For a suggested answer, see the 'Answers' section at the end of the book.

2 LIQUIDITY RATIOS

Liquidity means having cash or access to cash to meet payment liabilities. In the normal course of business, this usually means having enough cash coming in from sales to meet the payments to employees, suppliers, the tax authorities and so on.

A useful way of checking liquidity is to compare the amount of current assets in a business with the current liabilities. Current liabilities are amounts that have to be paid in the near future. Current assets – mainly inventory, receivables, short-term investments and cash – are items that are either cash, or readily sold for cash, or that will soon generate cash through sales and then payments by receivables.

Two ratios for measuring liquidity are:

- the current ratio
- the acid test ratio, also called the quick ratio.

The following statement of financial position figures will be used to illustrate how to calculate these ratios:

	Last year		This year	
	$000	$000	$000	$000
Non-current assets				
Freehold property		320		380
Equipment		120		130
Motor vehicles		60		50
		500		560
Current assets				
Inventory	70		160	
Receivables	65		120	
Cash at bank	125		–	
		260		280
Total assets		760		840
Equity and liabilities				
Share capital		200		250
Accumulated profits		330		356
Total shareholders' funds		530		606
Long-term loans		80		30
Current liabilities				
Bank overdraft	–		55	
Payables	130		125	
Tax payable	20		24	
		150		204
Total equity and liabilities		760		840

The credit sales for this year were $752,000, and the cost of sales for this year were $520,000.

2.1 THE CURRENT RATIO

Definition The **current ratio** is the ratio of current assets to current liabilities.

It can be used to assess the ability of a business to pay what it owes, and gives an indication of the margin of safety to meet the fluctuations which may arise from time to time in the flow of funds.

Using the figures in the example, we can calculate the current ratio in this year's and the previous year's statements of financial position.

Last year **This year**

$$\text{Current ratio} = \frac{\text{Current assets}}{\text{Current liabilities}} = \frac{260}{150} = 1.73 \quad \frac{280}{204} = 1.37$$

The current ratio for this year simply says that for every $1 owing as current liabilities there is $1.37 of cover provided by the current assets. According to a rough 'rule of thumb' the current ratio for a business ought to be around 2 to 1. The ratio this year does therefore appear to be on the low side. However, typical current ratios differ between industries. For example, supermarkets often sell goods before they pay for them, and so can usually survive and prosper with a current ratio below 1 to 1. However, it is also useful to look at trends, and here it is noticeable that the current ratio has come down to 1.37 this year from 1.73 last year. This could suggest that the liquidity position of the company is getting worse which may indicate cash flow problems.

2.2 THE ACID TEST RATIO (OR QUICK RATIO)

Definition The **acid test ratio** is the ratio of liquid assets (i.e. current assets excluding inventory) to the current liabilities.

In many businesses, inventory is not a very liquid asset. It could be held for a long time before it is used to generate sales and cash. If inventory is a slow-moving item and so not very liquid, it should be excluded from the measurement of liquidity. The acid test ratio is similar to the current ratio, with the exception that inventory is excluded from current assets.

The acid test ratio shows the extent to which liquid resources are available to meet current demands.

Using the figures in the example, we can calculate the acid test ratio in this year's and the previous year's statements of financial position.

Last year **This year**

$$\text{Acid test ratio} = \frac{\text{Current assets excluding inventory}}{\text{Current liabilities}} = \frac{190}{150} = 1.27 \quad \frac{120}{204} = 0.59$$

A rule of thumb for this ratio is that liquidity is good if the ratio is 1.0 or higher, although the 'norm' varies from one industry to another. The acid test ratio for this year is 0.59, which is low, indicating poor liquidity.

Again, it is useful to look at trends, and here it is noticeable that the current ratio has come down from 1.27 last year to 0.59 this year. This suggests that the liquidity position is getting worse which may indicate possible cash flow problems.

The poor liquidity position of the company, as indicated by the current ratio and acid test ratio, is confirmed simply by looking at the items in the statement of financial position. The business had a cash balance of $125,000 at the end of last year, and has an overdraft of $55,000 at the end of this year. The cash position had worsened by $180,000 over a 12-month period.

A credit manager looking at these ratios for a potential new customer is likely to limit the amount of any credit to the customer, or might even refuse to allow any credit at all. If the ratios are measured for an existing customer, the customer's account should be monitored constantly, and any deterioration in the customer's payment pattern should be a signal to take action (for example, to discuss the problem with the customer).

ACTIVITY 2

A company's annual sales are $8 million with a mark-up on cost of 60%. It normally pays payables two months after purchases are made, holding one month's worth of demand in inventory. The company allows receivables one and a half months' credit and its cash balance currently stands at $1,250,000. What are its current and quick ratios?

For a suggested answer, see the 'Answers' section at the end of the book.

3 WORKING CAPITAL CYCLE RATIOS

In addition to monitoring the current ratio and acid test ratio, a business can also monitor its working capital cycle.

The length of the cash cycle equals:

Raw material inventory	**less**	Payables payment period	**plus**	Production period	**plus**	Finished goods inventory period	**plus**	Receivables collection period

In addition to the liquidity ratios, cash flows and liquidity can be measured by the length of time the business takes on average to pay its payables, and the average length of credit it gives to its credit customers.

- If a business starts taking longer to pay its payables, this could be a sign of liquidity problems.
- If a business starts giving its customers a longer time to pay, this could be a sign of inefficient debt collection. If receivables take longer to pay, the cash flow position of the business will deteriorate.

Two ratios for measuring the length of the cash cycle are:

- receivables collection (debtor days)
- payables payment period (creditor days)

These ratios are not exact measurements, but are fairly reliable in measuring changes over time.

3.1 RECEIVABLES COLLECTION PERIOD (DEBTOR DAYS)

Definition **Receivables collection period (debtor days)** is the number of days on average that customers who have purchased goods and services take on credit to pay for them.

Receivables collection period can be calculated as $\frac{\text{Receivables}}{\text{Credit sales}} \times 365$

The figure for receivables can be either:

- the amount of receivables in the statement of financial position for this year, or
- the average amount of receivables during the year, which is assumed to be the average of the opening and closing statement of financial position figures.

Average receivables $= \frac{65+120}{2} = 92.5$

Receivables collection period for this year is therefore: $\frac{92.5}{752} \times 365 = 45$ days

Note: Where sales are a mix of cash sales and credit sales, the sales figure should exclude cash sales for greater accuracy in the ratio.

3.2 PAYABLES PAYMENT PERIOD (CREDITOR DAYS)

Definition **Payables payment period (creditor days)** is the average time taken to pay payables who have supplied goods and services on credit.

Payables payment period can be calculated as $\frac{\text{Average payables}}{\text{Credit purchases}} \times 365$

Note: If the purchases figure is not given in a question, we generally assume that cost of sales can be used as an appropriate approximation.

Using the figures in the example above, we can calculate the payables payment period for this year, given the cost of sales for the year (obtained from the statement of profit or loss and provided as data in the example). The payables payment period for last year cannot be calculated because we do not know the cost of sales for last year.

The amount of trade payables should be either:

- the amount of trade payables in the statement of financial position for this year, or
- the average value of trade payables during the year, which is assumed to be the average of the opening and closing statement of financial position figures.

In the calculation below, the figure for average creditors for the year is used to calculate the ratio.

Average payables over this year are $\frac{130+125}{2} = 127.5$

Payables payment period $= \frac{\text{Average trade payables}}{\text{Cost of sales}} = \frac{127.5}{520} \times 365 \text{ days} = 89 \text{ days}$

Thus if the average for the industry is, say, 45 days, which is not a typical, this company is taking twice as long to pay. This is of prime importance for credit management as it provides an indication of how long the company concerned (prospective customer) takes on average to pay for the purchases of goods and services it buys on credit.

It would be helpful to measure the payables payment period for the previous year, to see whether the average time to pay suppliers is getting longer.

3.3 INVENTORY TURNOVER RATIOS

A key indication of the efficiency of inventory management is shown in the following inventory measures:

- the inventory turnover ratio (how quickly inventory is sold)
- the inventory holding period (the average time inventory is held for)

Definition **Inventory turnover ratio** – how many times the average inventory held has been sold during the course of the trading year. It is measured as follows:

$$\textbf{Inventory turnover ratio} = \frac{\text{Cost of sales}}{\text{Average inventory held}}$$

For some businesses, such as wholesalers and some retailers, a high inventory turnover ratio is essential in order to make any profit. A low inventory turnover ratio could indicate the presence of slow moving inventory, which may be a problem that management will need to address.

An alternative calculation of the inventory turnover ratio is to show the result in days. When the result is shown in days, it is sometimes called the inventory holding period.

Definition **Inventory holding period** – this is a measure of the time (on average) that inventory is held before being sold. It is also known as the inventory turnover period. It is measured as follows:

$$\textbf{Inventory holding period} = \frac{\text{Average inventory held}}{\text{Cost of sales}} \times 365 \text{ days}$$

For a manufacturing company there will be three types of inventory – raw materials and components, work in progress and finished goods. The manufacturing staff convert raw materials and bought-in components into finished goods. At any given time there will be some inventory that has been processed but is not yet complete and that is referred to as 'work in progress'.

The inventory holding period therefore has three components for each of which a turnover ratio can be calculated. These are:

$$\text{Raw materials inventory holding period} = \left(\frac{\text{Average raw materials inventory}}{\text{Annual purchases}}\right) \times 365 \text{ days}$$

$$\text{Work-in-progress holding period} = \left(\frac{\text{Work - in - progress inventory}}{\text{Cost of goods sold} \times \text{degree of completion}}\right) \times 365 \text{ days}$$

$$\text{Finished inventory holding period} = \left(\frac{\text{Finished goods inventory}}{\text{Cost of goods sold}}\right) \times 365 \text{ days}$$

Note that the degree of completion of work in progress needs to be taken into account when calculating the work in progress holding period.

Using the example shown earlier, the inventory holding (or turnover) period would be calculated as follows:

Average inventory = (70 + 160)/2 = 115

The average inventory holding (turnover) period is:

$$\frac{115}{520} \times 365 \text{ days} = 81 \text{ days}$$

A fruit shop, for example, would expect an average holding period of no more than a couple of days otherwise the fruit will deteriorate and sales will be lost. A bookshop, on the other hand, might have an inventory turnover ratio of just 3 to 4 days and a holding period of around 90 to 120 days. This is because it needs to carry a very high level of inventory in order to give sufficient choice to its customers. Holding inventory for too long has serious implications for the amount of money that the business has tied up in inventory.

By adding the inventory days and the receivables collection period (in days) we can get an indication of the organisation's liquidity in terms of how soon inventory is converted into cash.

3.4 AVERAGE INVENTORY

Average inventory is sometimes calculated as the average of the opening inventory at the beginning of the year and the closing inventory at the end of the year. Strictly, it would be better to measure inventory at more frequent intervals throughout the year. In the absence of, say, monthly inventory figures it is acceptable to use either the mid-point of the opening and closing inventory or the closing inventory figure. (Sometimes, the inventory turnover period is calculated using closing inventory instead of average inventory, on the assumption that the closing inventory value is reasonably representative of average inventory levels.)

Example

The following information shows a firm's investment in working capital and its budgeted level for the coming year, which we can analyse from the viewpoint of its implications for working capital policy:

	Position as from now	**Budget position 1 year from now**
	$	$
Sales	250,000	288,000
Cost of goods sold	210,000	248,000
Purchases	140,000	170,000
Receivables	31,250	36,000
Payables	21,000	30,000
Raw materials inventory	35,000	60,000
Work-in-progress (80% complete)	17,500	30,000
Finished goods inventory	40,000	43,000

Assume all sales and purchases are on credit terms.

Solution

Workings:

	Current	Budget
(W1) **Payables**		
Payables payment period		
$= \left(\frac{\text{Payables}}{\text{Purchases}}\right) \times 365$	$\frac{21}{140} \times 365 = (55 \text{ days})$	$\frac{30}{170} \times 365 = (64 \text{ days})$
(W2) **Receivables**		
Receivables collection period		
$= \left(\frac{\text{Receivables}}{\text{Sales}}\right) \times 365$	$\frac{31.25}{250} \times 365 = 46 \text{ days}$	$\frac{36}{288} \times 365 = 46 \text{ days}$
(W3) **Finished inventory holding period**		
$= \left(\frac{\text{Finished goods inventory}}{\text{Cost of goods sold}}\right) \times 365$	$\frac{40}{210} \times 365 = 70 \text{ days}$	$\frac{43}{248} \times 365 = 63 \text{ days}$
(W4) **Raw materials inventory holding period**		
$= \left(\frac{\text{Raw materials stock}}{\text{Purchases}}\right) \times 365$	$\frac{35}{140} \times 365 = 91 \text{ days}$	$\frac{60}{170} \times 365 = 129 \text{ days}$
(W5) **Work-in-progress holding period**		
$= \left(\frac{\text{Work-in-progress inventory}}{\text{Cost of goods sold} \times \text{cost of completion}}\right) \times 365$		
Current $= \frac{17.5}{210 \times 80\%} \times 365 =$	38 days	
Budget $= \frac{30}{248 \times 80\%} \times 365 =$		55 days
Length of cash operating cycle	190 days	229 days

Analysis of the figures shows that working capital investment is being increased. Receivables balances are moving pro-rata with sales, the current and budgeted collection period both being 46 days. However, some additional finance will be taken from payables as a result of the payment period being increased from 55 days to 64 days. This increase represents about 16% and is not particularly significant unless suppliers demand payment within 60 days, or offer discounts for payment within that time (which will be lost).

A significant change in the turnover of inventory levels is anticipated. Raw materials inventory turnover will be decreased by 41% and work-in-progress by 45%, while finished goods stock turnover will increase by 10%. The implication is that production will increase while sales will fall; in the period following the budget, inventory levels will be very high. The overall impression is that unnecessarily high investment in raw materials and work-in-progress is being undertaken. A reappraisal of the situation should be made to see if these inventory levels could be reduced, thereby releasing funds for other uses. It may also be possible to reduce debtors to their current levels.

ACTIVITY 3

Extracts from the statement of profit or loss for the year and the statement of financial position as at the end of the year for a company show the following:

	$
Sales	250,000
Cost of goods sold	210,000
Purchases	140,000
Receivables	31,250
Payables	21,000
Inventory	92,500

Note: Assume all sales and purchases are on credit terms.

Calculate the length of the working capital or cash operating cycle.

For a suggested answer, see the 'Answers' section at the end of the book.

3.5 MONITORING THE WORKING CAPITAL CYCLE

In the example used to illustrate the working capital turnover periods, the working capital cycle would be calculated as follows:

	Days
Average inventory turnover	81
Average credit to customers	45
	126
Average credit from suppliers	(89)
Average working capital cycle	37

The length of the working capital cycle, or the length of the individual elements of the cycle, might provide useful information to management, by suggesting that the average period is too long or too short. For example, if average receivables collection period is found to be 100 days, this would normally be regarded as excessively high.

More usually, however, the length of the working capital does not provide useful information to management unless there is something to use for comparison. A useful comparison is to look at the length of the cycle in the past, and to assess whether the cycle is getting longer or shorter.

- A longer working capital cycle will indicate a larger investment in inventory plus trade receivables less trade payables, which could result in worse cash flows.

- A shorter working capital cycle will indicate a smaller investment in inventory plus trade receivables less trade payables, which could result in improved cash flows.

The reasons for a significant change in the length of the working capital cycle should be investigated, to establish whether control measures are needed to improve liquidity.

Liquidity ratios and cash budgets and forecasts

Managers use both cash budgets and liquidity ratios to manage cash flows and liquidity.

Cash budgets and forecasts are used to manage cash flows. They indicate whether there is likely to be a shortage or surplus of cash overall, so that appropriate measures can be taken. They include all receipts and payments, from whatever source. Cash budgets can also be used for comparing actual cash flows with the budget, and adjusting expectations to prepare revised forecasts.

Liquidity ratios and working capital cycle ratios are average measures, and lack the detail of cash budgets. They also concentrate on one aspect of liquidity, namely the liquidity generated by the operating cycle and cash flows from day-to-day operations. They can be calculated easily and quickly, and are more useful than cash budgets in identifying improving or worsening trends.

4 THE RELATIONSHIP OF WORKING CAPITAL MANAGEMENT TO BUSINESS SOLVENCY

A firm needs a flow of cash to carry out the day-to-day transactions which form its business activity. Some cash payments (e.g. to small payables) can be delayed without endangering the company's prospects, but others must be paid on time.

If loan note (debenture) interest is not paid, the trust deed may allow the loan note holders to appoint a receiver to sell sufficient assets for the loan note to be repaid.

Employees must be paid their wages and salaries on time, otherwise they will leave and the business will cease to function.

A major responsibility of the financial manager is to ensure that an **adequate flow of cash** is available to enable the business to operate efficiently.

Cash must be in place to meet obligations as they fall due. If insufficient cash is available, the company will suffer from lack of liquidity. At the extreme, the company may fail due to it.

Profit earned will, to a certain extent, alleviate the effect of lack of liquidity, but the strain on operating cash flow will be accentuated by the need to provide for investment in non-current assets for the firm's future, dividends and interest for the providers of long-term capital, and taxation.

Management of cash flows therefore involves the interrelationship of the following items:

- profits
- working capital levels
- capital expenditure
- dividend policy
- taxation.

The emphasis in this section of the text is on the control of levels of working capital.

4.1 SHORT-TERM CASH CONTROL

Control of cash over short periods is best achieved by preparing short-term cash forecasts for comparison with actual results. If the cash forecast shows an unacceptable cash balance or a cash deficit, then it will be necessary to review a number of items as follows:

- profit levels, including changes in selling price or improvements in operating efficiency
- working capital requirements, i.e. inventory holdings, credit periods given and taken, invoice processing procedures, etc.
- non-current asset requirements, having regard to the timing and amounts of capital projects
- dividend policy.

4.2 OVERCAPITALISATION

A firm is **overcapitalised** if its working capital is excessive for its needs.

Excessive inventory, receivables and cash and very few payables will lead to a low return on investment, with long-term funds tied up in non-earning short-term assets.

Overcapitalisation can normally be identified by poor accounting ratios. For example:

- a current ratio higher than 2:1 or a quick ratio more than 1:1 may be an indication of an over investment in working capital
- inventory and receivables collection periods being too long could indicate that the volume of inventories or receivables is very high
- shorter periods of credit taken from suppliers might indicate the volume of payables is too low
- by comparing the volume of sales as a multiple of the working capital investment with previous years or with similar companies, it should indicate whether the total volume of working capital is too high.

4.3 OVERTRADING

Definition **Overtrading** occurs when a business is conducting its business operations with inadequate capital. It is also called under-capitalisation.

Overtrading takes place when a business accepts work, and tries to fulfil it at a level that cannot be supported by its working capital or net current assets. This means that it does not have enough cash and cannot obtain enough cash quickly.

Typically, a business can start to overtrade when it is growing, and finds it difficult to obtain long-term finance to pay for its growth. As a result, it pays for its growth in inventory and receivables with short-term credit, particularly trade credit and a larger bank overdraft. A business might even try to purchase long-term assets with short-term credit.

Essentially a business that is overtrading is chasing sales and growth in order to make it profitable, but as discussed earlier, there is a trade-off between profitability and liquidity and unfortunately an overtrading business is not managing this trade-off effectively. If a business is profitable, but at the same time is suffering from poor and worsening liquidity, it could be in serious danger of insolvency.

Symptoms of overtrading are:

- greatly increased turnover
- sometimes, a large increase in receivables, with receivables also taking longer to pay (a rapidly growing businesses might sell on easy credit terms to win new customers)
- taking longer credit from suppliers, because the business does not have the cash flows to pay sooner
- unusual inventory movements – inventory levels could fall sharply in response to growing sales demand, creating a threat of inventory shortages. Alternatively, inventory levels could increase significantly as the business buys more to meet growing sales demand
- a falling current ratio and quick ratio, because increases in inventory and receivables are financed mainly by increases in trade payables and overdraft
- a rising bank overdraft.

Overtrading is a common problem, and it often happens to recently started businesses and to rapidly expanding businesses.

Cash often has to leave the business before more cash comes into it. For example, wages and salaries are usually payable weekly or monthly, and there may also be other expenses that need to be met promptly, such as telephone bills and rent.

Although suppliers may be paid on credit, customers may also pay on credit and it does not take much to upset the balance.

It is also possible to run out of cash, even if the enterprise's customers pay cash and do not have credit accounts, for example if the enterprise has to pay suppliers quickly and holds inventory for a long time. What matters is the amount of working capital and the timing of cash coming in and going out.

Businesses that overtrade run a serious risk by over-relying on short-term finance, because they could find that:

- trade payables insist on earlier payment, or threaten legal action for non-payment
- a bank calls in an uncommitted overdraft, forcing the business into liquidation.

An example of overtrading

Jack's business is three years old. His annual turnover is $200,000 and his annual profit is $18,000. He operates with a bank overdraft of up to $25,000. His working capital is sufficient to steadily expand the business.

Jack succeeds in winning a contract to supply Business X. The order is for $40,000 a month for two years. He will be paid 75 days after delivery. He phones his suppliers and orders everything that he will need to fulfil the contract in the first few months. He tells them all to deliver everything as soon as possible.

In the first month things go very well. All the suppliers start delivering as promised. The only problem is that he is short of space. During the second month things still look good. He has made the first delivery to Business X. He increases his overdraft.

Unfortunately, during the third month Jack has problems. He has made more deliveries to Business X but his overdraft is at the limit and he is getting calls from unpaid suppliers.

Jack has a crisis in the fourth month. He cannot pay all his suppliers. Some have stopped delivering and are threatening legal action. However, he thinks that he will be fine because he is still supplying Business X.

By the fifth month his overdraft is $4,000 over the limit. Three suppliers start legal action. The bank refuses to pay any more cheques. But his first payment from Business X arrives on time. This does not happen the following month and he cannot fulfil any more orders. The bank demands that the overdraft be repaid within seven days and Jack closes the business and blames the bank. But, if timings and payments of deliveries from suppliers and to customers had been negotiated and regulated more successfully beforehand and at the start, the closure may have been avoided.

Avoiding overtrading

With hindsight what could Jack have done differently?

- He could have asked Business X to pay him in 45 days in return for a small reduction in the contract price.
- He could have ordered carefully and scheduled the delivery dates so that his payments were delayed for as long as possible.
- He could have asked his biggest suppliers to wait an extra 15 days for payment in view of the bigger orders they are getting.
- He could have drawn up an impressive written plan and presented it to the bank so that the bank might have agreed to increase the overdraft limit to $50,000.

An example of key performance and liquidity ratios

Main is a small owner-managed company producing a range of high quality hi-fi products, which it sells to specialist hi-fi shops. The products are a unique mix of state-of-the-art electronics combined with rare, traditional components renowned for producing high quality sound. Recently, sales have begun to rise rapidly following excellent reviews in consumer magazines and a general increase in consumer confidence The Chairman is delighted at the firm's improved performance but the other directors are concerned that Main may be overtrading as it is getting close to agreed overdraft limit of $50,000. Main's accounts for the past two years are summarised below.

Statement of profit or loss for the year ended 31 December

	20X4	20X5
	$000	$000
Revenue	2,400	3,200
Cost of sales	850	1,200
Gross profit	1,550	2,000
Other operating costs	640	813
Operating profit	910	1,187
Interest	–	3
Profit before tax	910	1,184
Taxation	200	234
Profit after tax	710	950
Dividends	210	250
Retained profit	500	700

Statement of financial position as at 31 December

	20X4		20X5	
	$000	$000	$000	$000
Non-current assets (net)		1,800		2,400
Current assets				
Inventory of finished goods	300		475	
Inventory of components	100		150	
Receivables	350		600	
Cash	300		10	
		1,050		1,235
Total assets		2,850		3,635
Ordinary shares ($0.50)		1,000		1,000
Accumulated profits		1,450		2,150
Shareholders' fund		2,450		3,150
Current liabilities				
Overdraft	–		45	
Trade payables	300		400	
Other payables	100		40	
		400		485
Total equity and liabilities		2,850		3,635

Solution

We can analyse Main's current working capital position and assess whether or not the firm can be said to be overtrading.

Working:

		20X4		**20X5**
Gross margin	1,550/2,400	64.6%	2,000/3,200	62.5%
Net margin	910/2,400	37.9%	1,187/3,200	37.1%
Asset turnover	2,400/2,450	0.98	3,200/3,150	1.02
Current ratio	1,050/400	2.6	1,235/485	2.5
Quick ratio	650/400	1.6	610/485	1.3
Receivables collection period	350/2,400 × 365	53	600/3,200 × 365	68
Payables payment period	300/850 × 365	129	400/1,200 × 365	122
Inventory days (finished goods)	300/850 × 365	129	475/1,200 × 365	144
Inventory days (components)	100/850 × 365	43	150/1,200 × 365	46
Operating cycle		96		136

*Due to the purchases figures not being given, cost of sales has been used to calculate the components holding period and the payables payment period figure.

Analysis of Main's working capital position

The Chairman is right to be pleased with Main's profitability:

- Main has achieved an operating profit of $1,187,000 in 20X5.
- Sales have risen by 33%.
- Gross profit has increased by 29%.
- Profit after tax has increased by 34%.

However, some aspects of profitability have worsened:

- The gross margin has fallen from 64.6% to 62.5%.
- The net margin has fallen from 37.9% to 37.1%.

More significantly, the improvements in profitability appear to be at the expense of liquidity:

- Cash has fallen by $335,000, with the firm now close to its overdraft limit.
- The operating cycle has increased dramatically from 96 to 136 days.
- Receivables collection period has increased from 53 to 68 days.
- The holding period of finished goods has increased from 129 to 144 days.
- The holding period of components has increased from 43 to 46 days.
- An extra $475,000 is tied up in inventory and receivables.
- The current ratio has fallen from 2.6 to 2.5.
- The quick ratio has fallen from 1.6 to 1.3.

Together with the declining margins, these are typical symptoms of 'overtrading' companies.

- Overtrading companies are often unable or unwilling to raise long-term capital and thus tend to rely more heavily on short-term sources such as payables and bank overdrafts.
- Receivables usually increase sharply as the company follows a more generous trade credit policy in order to win sales, while inventory tends to increase as the company attempts to produce at a faster rate ahead of increases in demand.
- Overtrading is thus characterised by rising borrowings and a declining liquidity position in terms of the quick ratio, if not always according to the current ratio.

However, Main is not showing all of the signs of overtrading:

- Overtrading firms usually see the payables payment period increasing as the firm exploits the generosity of suppliers in order to enhance sales. With Main the payables payment period has fallen slightly from 129 to 122 days.
- Overtrading firms usually see an increase in gearing. Main continues to have no long-term debt finance.
- Overtrading firms usually see a sharp increase in the asset turnover ratio as output increases are often obtained by more intensive utilisation of existing non-current assets, and growth tends to be financed by more intensive use of working capital. For Main, this has increased slightly from 0.98 to 1.02 because the increase in sales has been supported by an increase in non-current assets, suggesting that the output increase was well planned.

In summary, there is evidence that Main is overtrading but not disastrously so. The main areas of concern are receivables and inventory management and these must be addressed to convince the bank to continue to support the firm. This is of particular concern for Main as it is a private owner-managed firm that is likely to find raising finance more difficult than a quoted company and will thus be more reliant on the bank.

ACTIVITY 4

What does the term 'overtrading' mean? Describe some of the symptoms.

For a suggested answer, see the 'Answers' section at the end of the book.

4.4 CONTROL OF ORDERS RECEIVED

Overtrading can cause grave financial problems, so it may be vital to limit the amount of business that is accepted. In a manufacturing firm, for instance, each order must be analysed to discover the following:

- its effect on factory capacity
- the amount of working capital tied up in the order
- the length of time for which the company must provide finance
- the estimated profit or contribution of the order.

Management will wish to select the most profitable orders and could perhaps formulate a selection factor relating the contribution to the total order value and the total financing period, e.g.:

$$\text{Selection factor} = \frac{\text{Contribution}}{\text{Order value} \times \text{Financing period}}$$

It might also be possible to limit the orders taken by a salesperson to a certain order value, with an overall ceiling any month. Beyond this, the salesperson must obtain approval from the sales manager. In that way, a profitable mix of orders could be selected which can be handled comfortably by the firm. Another aspect of orders is the relationship between quotations sent and orders received: if, say, 90% of quotations are accepted and firm orders received, the company may be under-pricing its products.

4.5 CONTROL OF PURCHASE COMMITMENTS

A firm's payables can put the firm into liquidation if their demands for settlement are not satisfied. It is clearly important therefore to apply controls to the routines which create the liabilities, i.e. purchasing of material and plant, etc. The purchasing manager should verify that materials to be purchased would be resold or used in production within a reasonable time – say two months. In many cases this factor should carry greater weight than the savings that can be made by bulk buying. The purchasing manager should, however, seek to negotiate with suppliers in an attempt to obtain bulk discounts by placing larger orders, but taking delivery over a long period – thereby reducing the total initial liability.

CONCLUSION

This chapter has discussed the basic principles involved in working capital management, including financing issues and ratio analysis. The importance of liquidity to business survival and growth was emphasised.

KEY TERMS

Working capital cycle – also called the operating cycle and the cash cycle, is the average length of time between paying for purchases of materials (for use or re-sale) and eventually receiving payment from customers after a sale has been made.

Inventory turnover period – the average time between buying inventory and using it to create a sale. The stock turnover period in manufacturing businesses can be divided into turnover periods for raw materials, work in progress (the production cycle) and finished goods.

Receivables collection period (also known as debtor days) – the number of days on average that customers take to pay for the goods and services that they buy.

Payables payment period (also known as creditor days) – the average time taken to pay suppliers for goods and services that have been bought on credit.

Current ratio – the ratio of current assets to current liabilities.

Acid test ratio – the ratio of liquid assets (i.e. current assets excluding inventory) to the current liabilities.

Inventory turnover ratio – how many times the average inventory held has been sold during the course of the trading year. It is measured as follows:

$$\textbf{Inventory turnover ratio} = \frac{\text{Cost of sales}}{\text{Average inventory held}}$$

Inventory holding period – this is a measure of the time (on average) that inventory is held before being sold. It is also known as the inventory turnover period. It is measured as follows:

$$\textbf{Inventory holding period} = \frac{\text{Average inventory held}}{\text{Cost of sales}} \times 365 \text{ days}$$

Overtrading – occurs when a business is conducting its business operations with inadequate capital. It is also called under-capitalisation.

SELF-TEST QUESTIONS

		Paragraph
1	What is the working capital cycle?	1.2
2	What is the current ratio, and what is commonly regarded as an optimal current ratio?	2.1
3	What is the acid test ratio or quick ratio, and what is commonly regarded as an optimal value for this ratio?	2.2
4	What is the formula for calculating the average debt collection period (receivables collection period)?	3.1
5	What is the formula for calculating the average credit period taken from trade payables (payables payment period)?	3.2
6	What is the formula for calculating average inventory turnover?	3.3

PRACTICE QUESTION

EWDEN

Ewden is a medium-sized company producing a range of engineering products which it sells to wholesale distributors. Recently, its sales have begun to rise rapidly following a general recovery in the economy as a whole. However, it is concerned about its liquidity position and is contemplating ways of improving its cash flow.

Ewden's accounts for the past two years are summarised below:

Statement of profit or loss for the year ended 31 December

	20X2	**20X3**
	$000	$000
Revenue	12,000	16,000
Cost of sales	7,000	9,000
Operating profit	5,000	7,000
Interest payable	200	400
Profit before tax	4,800	6,600
Taxation*	1,000	1,600
Profit after tax	3,800	5,000
Dividends	1,500	2,000
Retained profit	2,300	3,000

(* after capital allowances)

Statement of financial position as at 31 December

		20X2		20X3
		$000		$000
Non-current assets (net)		9,000		12,000
Current assets:				
Inventory	1,400		2,200	
Receivables	1,600		2,600	
Cash	1,500		100	
		4,500		4,900
Total assets		13,500		16,900
Ordinary shares ($0.50)		3,000		3,000
Accumulated profits		6,500		9,500
Shareholders' funds		9,500		12,500
10% Loan stock		2,000		2,000
Current liabilities:				
Overdraft	–		200	
Trade payables	1,500		2,000	
Other payables	500		200	
		2,000		2,400
Total assets		13,500		16,900

Required:

Write a report which identifies the reasons for the sharp decline in Ewden's liquidity, assesses the extent to which the company can be said to be exhibiting the problem of 'overtrading', and offer suitable advice to Ewden's management.

Illustrate your answer by reference to key performance and liquidity ratios computed from Ewden's accounts.

Note: It is not necessary to compile a cash flow statement. **(20 marks)**

For a suggested answer, see the 'Answers' section at the end of the book.

Chapter 6

MANAGING INVENTORY AND PAYABLES

This chapter deals with the general principles of short-term asset management before taking a more detailed look at inventory control. The chapter then goes on to the monitoring, management and control of payables.

This chapter covers Syllabus parts A2, A3 and C3.

CONTENTS

LEARNING OUTCOMES

At the end of this chapter you should be able to:

- Explain the nature of trade credit and its use as a short-term source of finance
- Discuss the key considerations when developing an inventory ordering and storage policy
- Define and explain work in progress
- Define economic order quantity (EOQ)
- Apply the EOQ model
- Discuss the effects of just-in-time on inventory control
- Explain the role of accounts payables in the working capital cycle
- Explain the need to monitor accounts payables

- Explain accounts payables control operations and the importance of accounts payables management
- Describe the various types and form of accounts payables
- Describe the various accounts payables payment methods and procedures (for example, direct debit, cheque)
- Evaluate and demonstrate the issues involved with early payment and settlement discounts
- Identify the risks of taking increased credit and buying under extended credit terms.

1 MANAGEMENT OF INVENTORY

1.1 DEFINITIONS

The following terms will recur throughout this chapter:

Lead time – the time interval between the start of an activity or process and its completion e.g. the time between ordering goods and their receipt, or between starting production of a product and its completion. Thus, a supply lead time of three months means that it will take three months from the time an order is placed until the time the goods are delivered into stores.

Stock-out – a situation where there is a requirement for an item of inventory, but the stores or warehouse is temporarily out of inventory.

Buffer (or safety) inventory – a stock of materials, or of work in progress, maintained in order to protect user departments from the effect of possible interruptions to supply. Buffer inventory should only be required intermittently during the lead time between re-ordering an item and its re-supply. If there is excessive demand, or a delay in re-supply, the buffer inventory might be used. At all other times, buffer inventory represents 'excess' inventory being held which in turn gives rise to 'extra' inventory holding costs.

Re-order quantity – this is the number of units of an item in one order.

Re-order level – a level of inventory at which a replenishment order should be placed.

Economic order quantity – the most economic inventory replenishment order size, which minimises the sum of inventory ordering costs and holding costs.

1.2 MANAGING INVENTORY

Managing inventory is a juggling act. Excessive inventory can place a heavy burden on the cash resources of the business. Insufficient inventory can result in lost sales, delays for customers, etc. The objective of inventory management is to ensure sufficient levels of inventory to maintain an acceptable level of availability on demand whilst minimising the associated holding, administrative and stock-out costs.

For manufacturing companies, inventory may include raw materials, work in progress and finished goods waiting to be consumed in production or to be sold.

- Raw materials are substances in a natural state before they go through manufacturing or other processing, or components that require assembly purchased from outside suppliers.

- Work in progress may be described as products and services in the intermediate stages of completion. It includes items which, at a given time, are going through the production process. Some products have a long production process – so the value of work in progress is often substantial – e.g. construction projects.

- Finished goods are goods that are complete. They may be held in stores awaiting delivery to a customer or they may have been produced some time in advance ahead of seasonal increases in demand.

The total balance of inventory is the sum of the value of each individual inventory line. Inventory records are needed:

- to provide an account of activity within each inventory line

- as evidence to support the balances used in financial reports.

A department also needs a system of internal controls to efficiently manage inventory and to ensure that inventory records provide reliable information.

1.3 COSTS OF INVENTORY

Inventory management is an important aspect of working capital management because inventories themselves do not earn any revenue. Holding inventory is an expensive business – it has been estimated that the cost of holding inventory each year is one third of its production or purchase cost.

Apart from the actual cost of buying inventory, there are three other inventory costs to consider. These are the costs of holding, obtaining and running out of inventory. The two major quantitative problems of determining re-order levels and order quantities are essentially problems of striking the optimum balance between holding costs, stock-out costs and order set-up costs.

Holding costs (sometimes called carrying costs) include the opportunity cost of forgone interest, storage space and equipment, administration and staff costs, warehouse rental and lease costs, deterioration, obsolescence, insurance and pilferage.

Order set-up costs are incurred each time a batch of inventory is ordered. Costs include freight, order administration and loss of quantity discounts. Administrative costs and, where production is internal, costs of setting up machinery will be affected in total by the frequency of orders.

Stock-out costs, or the cost of running out of inventory, also incur a cost. If, for example, a shop is persistently out of inventory on some lines, customers will start going elsewhere. Stock-out costs are difficult to estimate, but they are an essential factor to consider in inventory control.

Carrying costs can be minimised by making frequent small orders but this increases ordering costs and the risk of stock-outs. Risk of stock-outs can be reduced by carrying 'safety inventory' (at a cost) and re-ordering ahead of time.

The best ordering strategy requires balancing the various cost factors to ensure the department incurs minimum inventory costs. The optimum inventory position is known as the Economic Order Quantity (EOQ). Analytical review of inventory can help to identify areas where inventory management can be improved. Slow moving items, continual stock-outs, obsolescence, inventory reconciliation problems and excess spoilage are signals that inventory lines need closer analysis and control.

However, it is important to keep an overall perspective. It is not cost effective to closely manage a large number of low value inventory lines, nor is it necessary. A usual feature of inventory is that a small number of high value lines account for a large proportion of inventory value. The '80/20' rule (PARETO) predicts that 80% of the total value of inventory is represented by only 20% of the number of inventory items. Those high value lines need reasonably close management. The remaining 80% of inventory lines can be managed using 'broad-brush' strategies.

2 THE ECONOMIC ORDER QUANTITY AND ITS APPLICATION

2.1 ECONOMIC ORDER QUANTITY (EOQ) MODEL

We now turn to the theoretical side of inventory control. Essentially, two inventory problems need to be answered under either of two assumptions:

- How much to order? When an order is placed with a supplier, what quantity should be ordered?
- When to order? How frequently should inventory be ordered? Should it be ordered at regular intervals, or when the inventory level has fallen to a re-order level?

The trade-off is:

Ordering more frequently	**Ordering less frequently**
Higher ordering costs	Lower ordering costs
Smaller average inventory	Larger average inventory

The different departments within a firm (finance, production, marketing, etc.) often have differing views about what is an 'appropriate' level of inventory.

- Financial managers would like to keep inventory levels low to ensure that funds are wisely invested.
- Marketing managers would like to keep inventory levels high to ensure orders could be quickly filled.
- Manufacturing managers would like to keep raw materials levels high to avoid production delays and to make larger, more economical production runs.

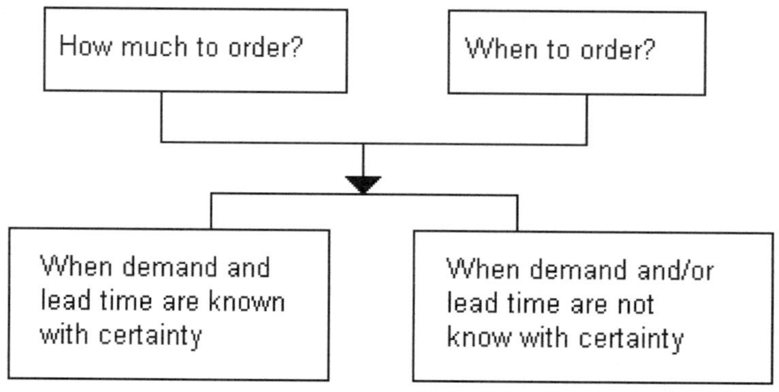

When should inventory be re-ordered?

A gap (the lead time) inevitably occurs between placing an order and its delivery. Where both that gap and the rate of demand are known with certainty, an exact decision on when to re-order can be made.

In the real world both will fluctuate randomly and so the order must be placed so as to leave some buffer stock (inventory) if demand and lead time follow the average pattern. The problem is again the balancing of increased holding costs if the buffer inventory is high, against increased stock-out costs if the buffer inventory is low.

How much inventory should be re-ordered?

Large order quantities reduce order set-up and stock-out costs each year. On the other hand, inventory volumes will on average be higher and so holding costs increase. The problem is balancing one against the other.

Economic order quantity (EOQ) is the quantity of inventory ordered each time which minimises annual costs (order set-up + holding costs). Note that the EOQ is not affected by uncertainty of demand and lead times, as long as demand is independent of inventory levels.

The EOQ model is based on several assumptions:

- There are no price discounts available for larger-sized orders.
- Demand for the item of inventory is a constant amount each day/week/month.
- Re-supply is immediate, so that the supply lead time is 0 days. (Alternatively, the supply lead time is constant, so that the re-order level can be fixed in order to ensure re-supply immediately the inventory level falls to 0 units.)

If none of these assumptions is valid (or largely accurate), the EOQ model is of doubtful accuracy and reliability.

Example

Watallington is a retailer of barrels. The company has an annual demand of 30,000 barrels. The barrels are purchased for inventory in lots of 5,000 and cost $12 each. Fresh supplies can be obtained immediately, with ordering and transport costs amounting to $200 per order. The annual cost of holding one barrel in inventory is estimated to be 10% of the purchase cost, or $1.20.

Thus Watallington orders 5,000 barrels at a time and these are used from inventory at a uniform rate.

Every two months inventory levels are zero and a new order is made. The average inventory level is: $\frac{5{,}000}{2}$ barrels, i.e. half the replenishment level.

Watallington's total annual inventory costs are made up as follows.

Ordering costs	$\frac{30{,}000}{5{,}000} \times \$200$	$1,200
Cost of holding inventory	$\frac{5{,}000}{2} \times \$1.20$	$3,000
Total inventory costs		$4,200

2.2 THE EOQ FORMULA

The EOQ formula allows us to calculate the optimal amount of inventory to be re-ordered every time an order is placed. Total inventory costs are minimised when the combined cost of ordering inventory and holding inventory each period (each year) is minimised. To decide what to do, we must look at the demand and costs using the standard ACCA notation in which:

C_H = cost of holding a unit of inventory for a year

C_O = cost of placing an order

D = annual demand

also:

TOC = total annual re-ordering cost

THC = total annual holding cost

x = order quantity

The equation below is the **economic order quantity** or **EOQ** formula. Note that you won't be asked to derive the formula in the exam, but you may well be asked to use it, so make sure that you learn the formula.

$$\text{EOQ} = \sqrt{\frac{2C_OD}{C_H}}$$

$$\text{For Watallington, EOQ} = \sqrt{\frac{2 \times 200 \times 30{,}000}{1.20}} = 3{,}162 \text{ barrels}$$

Total annual costs for the company will comprise holding costs plus re-ordering costs.

= (Average inventory × C_H) + (Number of re-orders p.a. × C_O)

$$= \left(\frac{3{,}162}{2} \times £1.20\right) + \left(\frac{30{,}000}{3{,}162} \times £200\right) = \$1{,}897.20 + \$1{,}897.53$$

= $3,794.73

In practice, this would mean taking 9.488 orders a year (annual demand/EOQ = 30,000/3,162 = 9.488), which is nonsense. It is more sensible to order in lots of 3,000 barrels at a total inventory cost of $3,800 per annum which is only $5 more than the theoretical minimum cost. This example does illustrate a problem with the EOQ model – it sometimes gives awkward answers. This is called the problem of discontinuities i.e. it may only be feasible to order in steps of large whole numbers e.g. multiples of 500.

ACTIVITY 1

Calculate the economic order quantity given the following data:

Annual demand	5,000 units
Ordering cost	$150 per order
Annual holding cost	$2 per unit

For a suggested answer, see the 'Answers' section at the end of the book.

3 DISCOUNTS AND ECONOMIC ORDER QUANTITIES

A common twist to exam questions is to ask students to evaluate whether bulk discounts are worth taking. While prices fall, total annual holding costs will increase if more inventory is ordered each time an order is placed, so the matter needs a little thought. The common approach is one of trial and error. This involves finding the total annual cost (holding cost, re-ordering cost and purchasing cost) at the level indicated by the EOQ and at the level(s) where a discount first becomes available.

3.1 BULK DISCOUNTS

We do not always buy the lowest total cost quantity when we buy a quantity-discounted item. We often spend more than we should. Often, bulk purchase discounts are offered for placing large orders so, when we buy more of an item, we pay a lower unit cost. However, we should be interested in the total purchase cost (quantity × unit cost). The problem is: if the order quantity required to obtain a discount exceeds the EOQ, is the discount worth taking? The problem may be solved by the following procedure:

Step 1 Calculate the EOQ ignoring discounts.

Step 2 If this is below the level for discounts, calculate total annual inventory costs.

Step 3 Recalculate total annual inventory costs using the order size required to just obtain the discount.

Step 4 Compare the cost of steps 2 and 3 with the saving from the discount, and select the minimum cost alternative.

Step 5 Repeat for all discount levels.

Annual inventory costs consist of:

- the annual purchase costs of the item
- annual inventory ordering costs
- annual inventory holding costs.

3.2 EXAMPLE

In the Watallington example above, suppose additionally that a 2% discount is available on orders of at least 5,000 barrels and that a 2.5% discount is available if the order quantity is 7,500 barrels or above. With this information, would the economic order quantity still be 3,000?

Steps 1 and 2	We know the EOQ is about 3,000 barrels	$
	Purchase costs (30,000 barrels × $12)	360,000
	Inventory holding costs (3,000/2 × $1.20)	1,800
	Order costs (30,000/3,000 × $200)	2,000
		363,800

Step 3	At an order quantity 5,000, the total cost is	$
	Purchase costs (30,000 × 98% × $12)	352,800
	Inventory holding costs (5,000/2 × 10% × 98% × $12)	2,940
	Order costs (30,000/5,000 × $200)	1,200
		356,940
Step 4	Net cost saving = $(363,800 – 356,940)	$6,860
	Buying in batches of 5,000 is worthwhile, compared with buying in the EOQ quantities of 3,000	
	Similarly, purchasing in batches of 7,500 results in:	$
	Purchase costs (30,000 × 97.5% × $12)	351,000
	Inventory holding costs (7,500/2 × 10% × 97.5% × $12)	4,388
	Order costs (30,000/7,500 × $200)	800
		356,188

A further small saving can be made by ordering in batches of 7,500.

3.3 WHEN TO RE-ORDER INVENTORY

Having decided how much inventory to re-order, the next problem is **when** to re-order. The firm needs to identify a level of inventory which can be reached before an order needs to be placed. The **re-order level (ROL)** is the quantity of inventory on hand when an order is placed. When demand and lead time are known with certainty the re-order level may be calculated exactly:

Demand for the item each day/week × Supply lead time in days/weeks.

(The supply lead time is the length of time between initiating a new order for an inventory item and receiving the delivery of the item from the supplier.)

For example, if the daily demand for an inventory item is 10 units and the supply lead time is two weeks, the re-order level should be 20 units, so that there will be enough units of the item in inventory to meet the demand during the supply lead time. Similarly, if re-supply is 'instantaneous' and the supply lead time is 0, the re-order level can be 0 units. (This is the principle applied with just-in-time purchasing.)

ACTIVITY 2

Return to the original Watallington example. Assume that the company adopts the EOQ as its order quantity and that it now takes two weeks for an order to be delivered. How frequently will the company place an order? How much inventory will it have on hand when the order is placed?

For a suggested answer, see the 'Answers' section at the end of the book.

3.4 THE RE-ORDER LEVEL: UNCERTAIN DEMAND AND LEAD TIMES

In practice, the demand for an inventory item is rarely predictable or constant, and the supply lead time might also be variable. When there is uncertain demand or an uncertain supply lead time, there could be some risk that demand during the lead time will exceed the re-order level quantity, and there will be a 'stock-out'. When a stock-out occurs, there will be some delay in operations until the new delivery of the item is made. There could possibly be a major disruption in operations, resulting in loss of output and sales or bottlenecks in production.

Because demand will vary from period to period re-order levels must allow some buffer (or safety) inventory, the size of which is a function of three factors:

- variability of demand
- cost of holding inventory
- cost of stock-outs.

You will not be required to perform this calculation.

3.5 MAXIMUM AND MINIMUM WARNING LEVELS

When a safety (or buffer) inventory is held, there should be a control mechanism to warn management:

- if the size of the buffer inventory might be too high, or
- if there is still some risk of a stock-out during the supply lead time.

A control mechanism can be provided by having, for each inventory item:

- a maximum inventory level, and
- a minimum inventory level.

If the actual inventory level exceeds the maximum warning level, this could be an indication that the buffer inventory is too large, and the re-order level should perhaps be reduced. If the actual inventory level falls below the minimum warning level, this would give a notification of a possible stock-out during the supply lead time. If the actual inventory level falls below the minimum level during most supply lead times, this could indicate that the buffer inventory is too small, and the re-order level should therefore be increased.

Formulae for establishing a maximum warning level and a minimum warning level for an item of inventory are as follows:

- Maximum inventory level =

  Re-order level + Re-order quantity – (Minimum demand per day/week × minimum supply lead time in days/weeks)

- Minimum inventory level =

  Re-order level – (Average demand per day/week × Average supply lead time in days/weeks)

3.6 FEEDBACK CONTROL

It is important that an inventory control system should have some mechanism whereby re-order levels and re-order quantities are adjusted according to changes in demand or lead time supply. Consequently, an inventory control system should incorporate a feedback system to make new rules for obtaining more effective control in the future.

More sophisticated inventory control methods are possible through computerisation. As pointed out earlier, if inventory records are inaccurate, the inventory control method will also be inaccurate.

ACTIVITY 3

The following data relates to an item of raw material:

Cost of the raw material	$10 per unit
Usage per day	100 units
Minimum lead time	20 days
Maximum lead time	30 days
Cost of ordering material	$400 per order
Carrying costs	10% per annum

Note: Assume that each year consists of 48 working weeks of five days per week.

Re-order level is set at maximum expected requirement in lead time plus 20%.

You are required:

(a) to calculate the re-order level

(b) to calculate the re-order quantity

(c) to calculate the maximum level

(d) to calculate the minimum level.

For a suggested answer, see the 'Answers' section at the end of the book.

4 JUST-IN-TIME (JIT) AND LEAN MANUFACTURING

JIT is a series of manufacturing and supply chain techniques that aim to minimise inventory levels and improve customer service by manufacturing not only at the exact time customers require, but also in the exact quantities they need and at competitive prices.

Definition **Just-in-time** – a system whose objective is to produce or to procure products or components as they are required by a customer or for use, rather than for holding in inventory. A just-in-time system is a 'pull' system, which responds to demand, in contrast to a 'push' system, in which inventory acts as a buffer between the different elements of the system, such as purchasing, production and sales.

Just-in-time production – a production system which is driven by demand for finished products whereby each component on a production line is produced only when needed for the next stage.

Just-in-time purchasing – a purchasing system in which material purchases are contracted so that the receipt and usage of material, to the maximum extent possible, coincide.

Lean manufacturing – an approach to manufacturing

This system has gained considerable popularity in both the United States and Europe. It has a wide ranging impact upon many of the traditional organisational functions.

The production of components only when they are needed and in the quantity that is needed shortens lead times and virtually eliminates work in progress and finished goods inventories. The resulting differences in production are:

- **Conventional production**

  Provides monthly production schedules to every process including the final assembly line. The preceding process supplies the parts to the subsequent process (push-through system) which is unable to respond quickly. Each process must adjust their schedule simultaneously requiring back-up inventory between processes.

- **JIT**

  Does not provide simultaneous schedules to every process, only for the final assembly line. Goods are built for the customer, not for holding as inventory. The system works on a pull-through basis, drawing components through the system. It can respond quickly drawing parts as required. As soon as items are completed in one process, so the next process produces to replace.

A production system which maximises the rate of movement of inventory and minimises the costs of holding inventory is called a 'lean' production system. It is designed to pare down ancillary costs to the bare minimum thought to be consistent with efficiency and flexibility. Lean production systems are the product of intensive scrutiny of the whole production process and usually require very close co-operation and communication with suppliers and very intensive training of operatives.

4.1 IMPACT ON PURCHASING AND PRODUCTION

(a) Under JIT, companies aim to reduce the number of their suppliers. Long-term contracts and single sourcing are advocated to strengthen buyer-supplier relationships. Inventory problems are shifted back onto suppliers, with deliveries being made as required.

(b) **JIT delivery and transportation**

The spread of JIT in the production process inevitably impinges upon those in delivery and transportation. For example, the company Ryder has established centres close to its manufacturing plants. These are not warehouses, but rather extensions of the production process. As soon as an order to move material or to call off material is received, the truck moves and delivers. This means smaller more productive loads, more frequently. The use of freight cars and railways fits less well into the JIT pattern, although Union Pacific, in the USA, has developed a system whereby freight can be moved on a JIT basis.

The use of JIT puts new demands on the schedules of the hauliers. Tighter schedules are required, with penalties for non-delivery. The haulier is regarded as almost a partner to the manufacturer.

(c) **Inventory valuation**

The inevitable reduction in inventory levels will reduce the time taken to count inventory and the clerical cost. As for valuing inventory, Hewlett-Packard no longer adds conversion costs to inventory, but treats them as period costs.

JIT renders the EOQ model virtually useless!

JIT causes the ordering cost to decline towards zero and since the model is optimal when holding costs equal ordering costs, the optimum becomes a virtually zero inventory level.

JIT is part of a broader management philosophy aimed at eliminating waste and inefficiency, and improving production quality. It seeks to minimise inventory levels, but this depends on having reliable processing systems (e.g. avoiding breakdown) and high quality standards (e.g. avoiding rejects).

JIT extends much further than a concentration on inventory levels. It centres on the elimination of waste at every stage of the manufacturing process, notably by the elimination of:

- WIP, by reducing batch sizes (often to one)
- raw materials inventory, by the suppliers delivering direct to the shop floor just in time for use
- scrap and rework, by an emphasis on total quality control of the design, of the process, and of the materials
- finished goods inventory, by reducing lead times so that all products are made to order
- material handling costs, by re-design of the shop floor so that goods move directly between adjacent work centres.

The combination of these concepts in JIT results in:

- a smooth flow of work through the manufacturing plant
- a flexible production process which is responsive to the customer's requirements
- reduction in capital tied up in inventory.

ACTIVITY 4

What potential benefits would an organisation hope for by the introduction of JIT/lean manufacturing?

For a suggested answer, see the 'Answers' section at the end of the book.

5 MANAGEMENT OF TRADE PAYABLES

Definition **Trade credit** is the term used to describe the situation whereby a company is able to obtain goods (or services) from a supplier without immediate payment, the supplier accepting that the company will pay for the goods at a later date.

Trade credit periods vary from industry to industry and each industry will have what is a generally accepted norm which would be from seven days upwards. The usual terms of credit range from four weeks to the period between the date of purchase and the end of the month following the month of purchase. However, considerable scope for flexibility exists and longer credit periods are sometimes offered, particularly where the type of business activity requires a long period to convert materials into saleable products e.g. farming.

However, some businesses do not confine the period of credit taken to that allowed by suppliers, and may take longer. Suppliers may attempt to stop their customers taking extended credit by refusing future supply, quoting COD (cash on delivery) terms, or by incorporating an incentive to pay on time in their standard sales terms e.g. a discount.

Managing trade payables involves getting satisfactory credit from suppliers, attempting to extend this credit in periods of cash shortage whilst maintaining good relations with regular and important suppliers.

5.1 ROLE OF PAYABLES IN THE WORKING CAPITAL CYCLE

Trade payables, representing amounts owed by the business for supplies and services, are a plus in the working capital equation. The higher the figure, the more credit has been extended by others (usually at no cost) towards working capital needs. The practice of businesses extending trade credit to one another is probably the most important source of short-term funding available to most organisations, especially when we consider the alternatives e.g. overdraft, loan, factoring or invoice discounting.

At first glance trade credit appears to represent a short-term interest-free loan which enables a higher level of trade than if everything were paid for immediately in cash. However, if we take a closer look at trade credit we can see that there are costs associated with it. The costs of making the maximum use of trade credit include the loss of the supplier's goodwill and the loss of any available discounts for early payment of debts.

Another cost of trade credit, which is often ignored, is its impact upon the creditworthiness of a business. If a business consistently exceeds the credit period imposed by suppliers, in the long term its credit rating will be damaged. In the worst-case scenario, suppliers will be forced to take legal action and may even withdraw their credit facility, requiring cash on delivery.

A proportion of the firm's suppliers will normally offer **settlement discounts** which should be taken up where possible by ensuring that special clearing treatment is given where settlement discount is allowed. However, if the firm is short of funds, it might wish to make maximum use of the credit period allowed by suppliers regardless of the settlement discounts offered.

It is a mistake to reduce working capital by holding on to a supplier's money for a longer period than is allowed as, in the long term, this will affect the supplier's willingness to supply goods and raw materials, and cause further embarrassment to the firm.

Favourable credit terms are one of several factors which influence the choice of a supplier. Furthermore, the act of accepting settlement discounts has an opportunity cost, i.e. the cost of finance obtained from another source to replace that not obtained from trade payables.

Whilst trade credit is undoubtedly a useful facility, it is important that businesses do not become too dependent upon it.

5.2 TYPE AND FORM OF PAYABLES

There are types of payables other than trade payables. Whilst these may not offer the same flexibility in terms of payment they can be planned for in the budget and the finance made available in plenty of time. For example:

- Rent is generally paid on the quarter days (25 March, 24 June, 29 September and 25 December).
- Tax (corporation, income and sales tax (VAT in the UK)) are paid on specific dates prescribed by regulation or statute.
- Payment to employees are usually at the end of each month.
- Utilities' bills tend to be paid quarterly on certain specific dates.

However, payables such as the utility companies and local authorities, that would normally issue bills quarterly or half-yearly, recognise the importance of offering some customers the option of paying weekly, fortnightly or monthly and also of paying in cash either at a post office or PayPoint outlets. Where there is a clear dispute about an account they will suspend the arrears management and debt recovery procedures while they try to resolve the matter.

5.3 MONITORING PAYABLES

Trade payables are shown in a company's statement of financial position as **amounts falling due within one year** and represent a source of short-term finance. The period of the short-term finance is from the date on which the goods or services are received to the date of payment i.e. the credit period, which is explained in more depth below.

Trade payables have to be monitored and managed in much the same way as other liabilities:

(a) They have to be **verified** to ensure that they are authentic and show a true and fair view of the amount for statement of financial position purposes.

Verification will involve checking various documents such as invoices, credit notes and statements with the order and goods received notes. Such checks are in place to help avoid errors and fraud.

(b) This involves having sound/effective/efficient **recording systems**. For example, an account will need to be kept for each individual supplier to whom money is owed.

(c) A **purchases day book (journal)** could also form a useful important part of the recording system. This lists all the invoices for goods/services which have been purchased on credit or could be an actual file of purchase invoices.

(d) The monitoring should ensure that appropriate early settlement discounts are taken and that payments are made within the agreed credit periods.

(e) **Control accounts** will also help keep an arithmetic check on the balances in the purchases ledger.

If payables are paid:

- too quickly without receiving an early settlement discount, this is considered to be poor financial management. You are in effect not obtaining the maximum use of this particular source of short-term finance
- too slowly – this could cause problems such as not being able to order more until the debt or part of the debt is settled, or having to face legal proceedings.

Each organisation will need to establish a policy for paying its suppliers and other payables, covering matters such as payment periods/methods etc.

Example

Honest Ed was a Canadian supermarket owner. He arranged with his suppliers for goods on 90 days' credit. As soon as he had sold the goods, he had the use of the cash for quite a considerable number of days before he had to pay it over to his suppliers. He used a treasury function to invest this surplus cash short-term, and became very rich on the strength of the income from his investments (**a true story**).

Supplier reliability

It might sometimes be prudent to monitor the financial position of a key supplier, when it is suspected that the supplier could be in financial difficulties. When a firm relies on a key supplier, its operations could be seriously disrupted if the supplier went out of business. A supplier who is in financial difficulties might:

- press for earlier payment
- offer discounts for early payment.

To monitor the financial position of a supplier, a firm can:

- check the published financial statements of the supplier, giving particular attention to the supplier's profitability, liquidity and working capital cycle
- alternatively, obtain regular credit status reports on the supplier from an agency.

When a key supplier is thought to be in financial difficulties, it might be appropriate to search for alternative sources of supply.

6 PAYABLES CONTROL OPERATIONS

If payments are made by an organisation then it is obviously extremely important that they are only made for genuine goods, services and expenses incurred by the organisation. Therefore if a cheque is required for payment of an item there must be sufficient evidence of that item existing for the payment to appear reasonable e.g. check the invoice with the order and goods received note.

Most payments that a business makes will be for transactions of one sort or another that have some sort of documentary evidence. The main types of **documentary evidence** will be considered later in this chapter.

Once the documentary evidence of an expense has been established it will then be necessary for the payment of the expense to be **authorised**. This is a routine part of business life and each organisation will set up its own procedures for authorisation e.g. who signs cheques and who countersigns cheques. A key element of control concerns the use of suppliers' invoices and statements.

6.1 CHECKING INVOICES TO SUPPORTING DOCUMENTATION

When an invoice is received by a business then it should be checked against the available supporting documentation to ensure that it is both valid and correct. Businesses should not pay for anything they haven't bought!

The accuracy of a purchase invoice will depend upon factors such as the price used, trade and settlement discounts offered, additions and other calculations on the invoice.

An invoice should be checked for **validity**. Has it been raised for goods that were actually received or for services that were actually provided? Only a thorough check of the supporting documentation for an invoice will determine its validity.

Many of the invoices that a business receives will be for goods. These may be raw materials that are to be made into a product, items being purchased for resale or other items necessary for the running of the business such as stationery or canteen supplies.

If goods of any type have been purchased then there should normally have been a **purchase order** sent out for these goods. In order to ensure that the invoice received is for goods that are genuinely required by the business and that have been correctly purchased and authorised then the invoice should be matched to the related purchase order.

Copies of purchase orders are likely to be filed and kept in the accounting department or possibly in the stores department. Often the supplier invoice received will refer to the purchase order number although in other instances a search of purchase orders in order to find the relevant one may be necessary.

Even when it has been determined that the goods were properly ordered the purchase order only agrees goods that are due to be delivered. The purchase invoice must not be passed for payment until it is also certain that the goods being invoiced have actually been received in good condition by the organisation. The evidence of receipt of the goods is the **goods received note** which will normally either be filed with the purchase order or separately in the stores department.

When the goods received note is checked to the purchase invoice it is important to note two things in particular:

- the goods received note should adequately describe the goods that were actually received and these should be exactly the same as the goods described on the supplier's invoice
- the goods received note should also make clear the quantity of goods that were actually delivered and again this should agree with the quantity being charged for on the supplier's invoice.

In a number of instances a bill will be received for services that have been used rather than an invoice being issued. This is the case for payments for gas, electricity, telephone etc. The bill will be used as evidence for payment in exactly the same way as an invoice would.

6.2 SUPPLIERS' STATEMENTS

Many organisations will tend to make their payments at a particular time each month, for example on the last Friday of each month. During the month it is quite possible that a number of invoices might have been received from the same supplier.

In order to summarise the invoices that have been sent out and the monies due, the supplier may send the organisation a statement summarising the balance brought forward from the last statement, invoices for the month in question, monies received and the balance outstanding.

Example

An example of a supplier's statement addressed to John Forrester Wholesale Supplies from Disks and Labels is given below.

DISKS AND LABELS

76 Wood End Road
Newcastke Upon Tyne
NE4 9AJ
Tel: 0141 839 4444

John Forrester Wholesale Supplies
Unit 79b
Oakhampton Industrial Estate
Bristol BS27 4JW

VAT Reg No. 341 5079 584

Date: 5 June 20X3

STATEMENT OF ACCOUNT

Date	Description	$	$	Balance owing ($)
14 May	Balance B/f			1,729.46
26 May	Invoice 314/X3	397.42		2,126.88
29 May	Invoice 386/X3	927.04		3,053.92
3 June	Cheque rec'd		1,729.46	1,324.46
4 June	Invoice 419/X3	1,062.96		2,387.42
5 June	Credit note CR174		123.26	2,264.16
			Amount now due	**2,264.16**

Note that the statement shows the following amounts:

(a) the balance brought forward as owing at the beginning of the period

(b) the invoices issued during the period

(c) the credit note issued in the period (deducted from the total due to be paid)

(d) the balance due at the end of the period.

Checking supplier's statements

Although the supplier's statement is evidence that payment is due to that supplier, the amounts on the statement should always be checked to the original invoices to ensure that the statement itself is correct, before payment is made.

Example

Suppose that the invoices shown on the statement above were checked and invoice 386/X3 from 29 May appears as follows. Can you spot the error that has occurred?

DISKS AND LABELS

76 Wood End Road
Newcastke Upon Tyne
NE4 9AJ
Tel: 0141 839 4444

John Forrester Wholesale Supplies
Unit 79b
Oakhampton Industrial Estate
Bristol BS27 4JW

No. 386/X3
VAT Reg No. 341 5079 584
Order No. 227P
DN No. 1489

Date: 29 May 20X3

INVOICE

Ref.	Description	Quantity	Item value	Discount	Balance
P 180	Boxed disks	30	2.63		78.90

	Amount now due	**78.90**
Terms	**VAT @ 17.5%**	**13.81**
E&OE	**Total**	**92.71**

Solution

An error has been made on the statement from Disks and Labels as the invoice on 29 May has been included in the balance as $927.04 rather than the correct amount of $92.71.

The actual amount due from John Forrester to Disks and Labels is therefore substantially less than that which appears on the statement.

The amount due should be:

	$
Balance b/f	1,729.46
26 May Invoice 314/X3	397.42
29 May Invoice 386/X3	92.71
4 June Invoice 419/X3	1,062.96
	3,282.55
Less: Cheque received	1,729.46
Credit note CR 174	123.26
	1,429.83

Once this discrepancy has been discovered, then Disks and Labels should be informed of the error that they have made on the statement by letter. This letter would probably be written by the purchasing manager or payables ledger manager or accounts department supervisor.

7 SUPPLIER PAYMENT METHODS AND PROCEDURES

Some methods chosen to pay for goods and services, rent and salaries will probably not vary much. Businesses tend to use cheques more often than other methods for paying suppliers but employees are generally paid using electronic banking methods. The payroll is prepared using a standard package run on a PC and the pay details are remitted directly to the entity's bankers. The pay is then credited to the employee's account using the BACS (Bankers Automated Clearing Services) system.

Cash payments

Cash is sometimes used for small payments; however, for security reasons, it is not recommended for organisations to carry large quantities of cash. Apart from small items paid for through the petty cash system or the special provisions such as those made by cash and carry warehouses, most purchases for goods and services by a business will be arranged on credit terms, i.e. payment will follow at a later stage after receipt. Wherever possible it is suggested that all transactions should be paid for in non-cash form, i.e. cheques, direct debits, etc. This will aid security, both from the point of view of reducing the risk of theft and, with the availability of the supporting primary records, from the control aspect.

Where payment is by cash e.g. payroll, the following procedure is typical.

- **Cash drawn from the bank** – An amount equivalent to the net wages is drawn from the bank. The amount will be made up of the correct analysis of each coin and type of note required.

- **Wages 'made up'** – Preferably made up by teams of two people who are not wages office staff. One counts out the money and the other checks it before inserting it with a pay slip into the wage packet.

- **Wages 'paid out'** – Employees will be correctly identified before wage packets are handed over. Any unclaimed packets will be retained in the wages office until claimed by the employee or someone holding written authorisation.

- Various security precautions will be incorporated into the procedures, e.g. varying time and route to the bank, and security organisations can be engaged to take over some parts of the procedures.

Petty cash procedure

Inevitably there will be a need for a petty cash procedure. Payments should only be against properly authorised petty cash vouchers, with supporting documents if available. These will then be recorded and probably analysed in a petty cash book, which is ruled off periodically. The person in charge of petty cash will have a float of cash out of which small disbursements are made and periodically he or she in turn is reimbursed by the cashier to bring the float back to its 'imprest' amount. Any discrepancy that cannot be resolved, and losses that are uncovered, should be reported via a formal reporting system.

Payments by cheque

Cheques drawn on a current account at a bank are the most popular payment method for goods and services purchased on credit. They are convenient to use for payments of any amount (provided sufficient funds are in the bank or the organisation has negotiated an overdraft for the amount). Using the counterfoil to fill in with details of the cheques you have written will help you to monitor how much is in your account and provide details for tracing past payments whenever any queries arise.

The disadvantages of cheque payments include security problems, e.g. theft and misuse, and the time it takes for a cheque to be processed.

Lost cheques

If a supplier fails to receive a cheque that is sent by post the procedures include:

- check to make sure that it has been sent
- check the name, address and department of the supplier to which the cheque was sent. Payment might have been sent to the wrong person or wrong department
- if it has gone through the bank and the supplier has been paid, the error is in the supplier's records. Give the details of the cheque to the supplier
- confirm that it has not been processed by checking the latest bank statement or telephoning the bank. If it hasn't you should stop the lost cheque and prepare a new one. To 'stop' a cheque being paid, phone your branch and then confirm the telephone call in writing. Your branch will need to know the cheque number, the amount and the date it was issued. A bank cannot accept instructions to stop a cheque guaranteed by a current account debit card or cheque guarantee card because it has already promised to pay cheques up to the card guarantee limit.

Bank giro payments

Bank giro is a system that enables customers of the bank to use only one cheque to pay several bills simultaneously. This is useful where there are periodic payments to regular suppliers of goods and services. Details of the supplier, its bank account and the amount due are supplied to the business's normal branch of the bank, together with a cheque for the total amount. These details are then circulated through the bank clearing system in exactly the same way as individual cheques. A particular application of the use of this service is the payment of salaries direct to the bank accounts of employees.

In addition you may well be familiar with the use many large undertakings make of the service. The gas, water and telephone authorities, together with mail order companies, are examples of businesses that supply ready-printed credit slips with their bills so that customers can pay their account due at a bank. The slip is then cleared very speedily through the system and the account of the undertaking is credited with the due amount more quickly than when bills are paid through showrooms or the post.

Payments by Bankers' Draft

Bankers' drafts are cheques drawn directly on the account of a bank rather than the account of a customer. The comfort they provide is that it is highly unlikely they would be returned unpaid due to lack of funds. However it is important to note that there is no guarantee against fraudulent use – for example, they may be lost or stolen and then used fraudulently.

Plastic cards

Plastic cards are another popular form of payment in the UK. They allow users to pay for goods and services virtually anywhere in the world, easily and conveniently, and provide a secure alternative to cash and cheques.

Plastic cards are issued to users by a variety of organisations or card issuers such as banks, building societies, financial services companies and retailers. The types of card issued and their levels of functionality vary from card issuer to card issuer and between the different card schemes under which the cards are issued.

The major plastic card schemes include American Express, Diners Club, JCB International, Maestro, MasterCard and Visa. These schemes are the operators of the payment card systems that govern transaction processes and transmission of money through the card network.

Payments by Direct Debits

A Direct Debit is when you give an organisation permission to withdraw money from your account and pay it into your account. The payment is likely to be repeated – often monthly or quarterly – but the amount and the exact date it is taken can vary. This is why Direct Debit is an easy and useful way to pay bills.

Also for recurring transactions, if you have a current account debit card, you can set up payments with companies allowing them to charge amounts to your debit card regularly. You set up a recurring transaction by providing the company with your card details.

Payments by Standing Order

Standing orders are regular payments that you set up with the bank (unlike Direct Debits, which are set up with the company that collects the payments). Any person or company with a current account at a bank or building society in the UK can give a standing order instruction.

The bank or building society will, on the day specified in the order, debit your account and transfer the money through the BACS system to the bank or building society account of the recipient. Note that the key difference between a direct debit and a standing order is that under a standing order your bank organises the payment whereas under a direct debit the recipient requests the amount from your bank.

Currently the money arrives with the recipient within three working days, e.g. for a standing order initiated on a Monday, the earliest it could arrive would be the Wednesday.

Clearing House Automated Payments (CHAPS)

CHAPS is an electronic bank-to-bank same-day value payment made within the UK in either sterling or euro. The main benefit of CHAPS is that it is fast, secure and efficient and the money is transferred the same day. Unlike other forms of payment such as cheques, CHAPS payments are irrevocable.

CHAPS is one of the largest real-time gross settlement (RTGS) systems in the world. Banks themselves use CHAPS to move money around the financial system, but it is also used regularly:

- for business-to-business payments
- by solicitors/licensed conveyancers to transfer the purchase price of a house between the bank accounts of those involved
- by individuals buying or selling a high-value item, such as a car, who need a secure, urgent, same-day guaranteed payment.

BACS Payment Schemes

BACS Payment Schemes (BACS) operates an electronic funds transfer service whereby customers may inject certain debit and/or credit entries directly into the UK clearing system. Use of the BACS service enables same day debiting/crediting settlements to be achieved, and the day on which the entries are applied to the destination accounts can be controlled with a greater degree of certainty than can be necessarily achieved with paper-based systems. As a general rule input in whatever form must be received by BACS by the evening two English bank working days before the day on which the debit and/or credit entries are to be applied to the destination accounts. It is used for making payments direct to the accounts of individuals or other organisations in respect of payroll, pensions, payments to suppliers, annuities, commission and many other applications. For example the great majority of staff salaries in the UK are paid via BACS.

It is essential to control those who can make changes or additions to the details, and all data should be independently checked and authorised. Dual control may be advisable.

Telegraphic transfer

If you need to pay someone very quickly you can use a telegraphic transfer. This allows you to send money directly to someone's bank account as long as you have the correct account information for the person you want to pay and the details of their bank. Telegraphic transfers can be sent in most currencies.

The money should normally arrive in the account of the person you want to pay within two to five working days, if you are transferring to a country in the European Union.

7.1 EARLY PAYMENT AND SETTLEMENT DISCOUNTS

As we have already noted, most suppliers offer customers a discount for early payment. For example, a supplier might allow 30 days' credit on all sales; but to encourage early settlement of debts, customers paying within seven days are offered a cash discount equating to 2.5% of the invoice total. On an invoice of $10,000 (excluding sales tax) this would equate to a saving of $250 ($10,000 × 2.5%).

Even if an organisation has an overdraft it may still be beneficial to take advantage of a cash discount. For example:

Faisal purchases $5,000 of goods from Anna who offers all customers the option of either 30 days' credit or a 1.5% discount if cash is received within five days. If Faisal takes the cash discount he will incur an overdraft on which interest is charged at 20% per annum. Is the cash discount beneficial to Faisal?

If Faisal takes the cash discount he will save: $5,000 × 1.5% = $75

However, he will incur an overdraft for 25 days (30 – 5 days) which will cost:
$5,000 × [20% × 25/365] = $68.49

In this example Faisal will benefit by $6.51 if he pays the invoice within five days.

In order to compare the cost of different sources of finance, all costs are usually converted to a rate **per annum** basis. The cost of extended trade credit is usually measured by loss of discount, but the calculation of its cost is bedevilled by such variables as the number of alternative sources of supply, and the conditions which exist in the general economic environment.

Certain assumptions have to be made concerning (a) the maximum delay in payment which can be achieved before the supply of goods is withdrawn by the supplier, and (b) the availability of alternative sources of supply.

Example

A business is buying $1,000 worth of goods per month and can take 2.5% discount if it settles accounts within one month. It will lose that source of supply if it delays payment for more than three months.

It has a supplying industry that is organised in such a way that an alternative supply of goods will be difficult to obtain in the event of the business obtaining a bad name.

To work out the cost to the business of taking the extra two months' credit and losing the discount, carry out the following steps.

Step 1 Work out the discount available and the amount due if the discount were taken.

Discount available = 2.5% × $1,000 = $25

Amount due after discount = $1,000 – $25 = $975.

The idea here is that the business is effectively borrowing $975 from the supplier for two months, and paying $1,000 back at the end – an interest charge of $25 on the 'loan'.

Step 2 The effective interest cost of not taking the discount is approximately:

$$\frac{\text{Discount available}}{\text{Discounted amount due}} \times \frac{\text{365 days or 12 months}}{\text{Reduction in payment time}} \times 100\%$$

This applies to the maximum credit period available after losing the discount (i.e. three months – one month).

The **simple** interest cost of taking two months' credit $= \frac{\$25}{\$975} \times \frac{12}{2} \times 100\%$

$= 15.4\%$

Step 3 To calculate the **compound interest**:

For compound interest, the rate will be: $(1 + \text{interest cost for period})^n - 1$, where 'n' is the number of periods in a year.

As there are approximately six 60-day periods in a year the compound annual cost is:

$$\left(1 + \frac{25}{975}\right)^6 - 1 = 0.164 \text{ or } 16.4\%$$

Note that this calculation contains only the explicit costs of trade credit. The implicit costs of delaying payment to the three-month point should also be considered. For example, although suppliers may not cut off future supplies, they may put a low priority on the quality of service given to late paying customers.

ACTIVITY 5

Beast Co buys $10,000 of goods per month from its supplier. Normal credit terms are that payment is due after 60 days, but a 2% discount can be taken if payment is made after 15 days.

Calculate the annual percentage cost of forgoing the discount and paying after 60 days.

For a suggested answer, see the 'Answers' section at the end of the book.

7.2 RISKS OF EXCESS CREDIT

Businesses should establish a policy for taking credit from suppliers.

- They should avoid paying for purchases earlier than they have to, unless an attractive early payment discount is offered.
- However, they should also ensure that they will have the cash available to make the payments on time, when they eventually fall due.

The risk of taking too much credit is that when payments fall due, a business will be able to pay only some and not all of its debts on time. The consequences could be that:

- key suppliers will refuse to make further deliveries until existing debts are paid
- suppliers will reduce their credit terms on future purchases
- in some cases, suppliers might take legal action for the recovery of an unpaid debt. (Any court judgement against a customer, ordering a debt to be paid, will become a matter of public record.)

CONCLUSION

This chapter has looked at various policies and techniques for managing inventory levels and managing credit from suppliers. In the next chapters, we shall go on to consider the management of credit given to customers.

KEY TERMS

Lead time – the time interval between the start of an activity or process and its completion e.g. the time between ordering goods and their receipt, or between starting production of a product and its completion.

Stock-out – a situation where there is a requirement for an item of inventory, but the stores or warehouse is temporarily out of stock.

Buffer (safety) inventory – a stock of materials, or of work in progress, maintained in order to protect user departments from the effect of possible interruptions to supply.

Re-order quantity – this is the number of units of an item in one order.

Re-order level – a level of inventory at which a replenishment order should be placed.

Economic order quantity – the most economic inventory replenishment order size, which minimises the sum of inventory ordering costs and holding costs.

Maximum level – an inventory level, set for control purposes, which actual inventory held should never exceed.

Minimum level – an inventory level, set for control purposes, below which actual inventory held should not fall without being highlighted.

Just-in-time – a system whose objective is to produce or to procure products or components as they are required by a customer or for use, rather than for inventory. A just-in-time system is a 'pull' system, which responds to demand, in contrast to a 'push' system, in which inventory acts as a buffer between the different elements of the system, such as purchasing, production and sales.

Just-in-time production – a production system which is driven by demand for finished products whereby each component on a production line is produced only when needed for the next stage.

Just-in-time purchasing – a purchasing system in which material purchases are contracted so that the receipt and usage of material, to the maximum extent possible, coincide.

Trade credit – the term used to describe the situation whereby a company is able to obtain goods (or services) from a supplier without immediate payment, the supplier accepting that the company will pay for the goods at a later date.

SELF-TEST QUESTIONS

		Paragraph
1	What is the 'lead time'?	1.1
2	What is the definition of buffer inventory?	1.1
3	Give three examples of 'holding costs'.	1.3
4	Explain the objective of using the EOQ model.	2.1
5	What are the assumptions upon which the EOQ model is based?	2.1
6	Set out the five steps whereby bulk discounts can be incorporated into the analysis of inventory costs.	3.1
7	What is the contribution of JIT to efficient inventory control?	4.1
8	What is the danger of paying suppliers too slowly or the disadvantage of paying too quickly?	5.3
9	Why is authorisation a key element of the control process?	6

PRACTICE QUESTION 1

COMPUTER BUREAU ORDER QUANTITY

It has been estimated that a computer bureau will need 1,000 boxes of line printer paper next year. The purchasing officer of the bureau plans to arrange regular deliveries from a supplier, who charges $15 per delivery.

The bureau's accountant advises the purchasing officer that the cost of storing a box of line printer paper for a year is $2.70. Over a year, the average number of boxes in storage is half the order quantity (that is the number of boxes per delivery).

The ordering cost is defined as the delivery cost plus the storage cost, where the annual costs for an order quantity of x boxes will be:

Delivery cost:

Number of deliveries × Cost per delivery = $\frac{100}{x} \times \$15$

Storage cost:

Average inventory level × Storage cost per box = $\frac{x}{2} \times \$2.70$

Required:

(a) Calculate the delivery cost, storage cost and ordering cost for order quantities of 50, 100, 150, 200 and 250 boxes. **(8 marks)**

(b) Using your answer to part (a) above, estimate the order quantity which will minimise cost. **(2 marks)**

(Total: 10 marks)

For a suggested answer, see the 'Answers' section at the end of the book.

PRACTICE QUESTION 2

K & L GAMES

K&L Games is re-evaluating its inventory control policy. Its daily demand for wooden boxes is steady at 40 a day for each of the 250 working days (50 weeks) of the year. The boxes are currently bought weekly in batches of 200 from a local supplier for $2 each. The cost of ordering the boxes from the local supplier is $64, regardless of the size of the order. The inventory holding costs, expressed as a percentage of inventory value, are 25% pa.

Required:

(a) Determine the economic order quantity and frequency of replenishment, and the annual saving to be made by implementing these. **(12 marks)**

(b) Recommend whether or not it is worthwhile to make use of the local supplier's new quantity discount scheme, shown below.

Local Supplier's New Discount Scheme

Quantity	**Discount**
0 – 999	0%
1,000 – 4,999	5%
5,000 +	10%

(8 marks)

(Total: 20 marks)

For a suggested answer, see the 'Answers' section at the end of the book.

PRACTICE QUESTION 3

DOCUMENTARY CHECKS

Describe the various documentary checks which have to be made before an invoice is passed and authorised for payment. **(10 marks)**

For a suggested answer, see the 'Answers' section at the end of the book.

Chapter 7

MANAGING RECEIVABLES

The previous chapters have looked at cash management and liquidity management within a business. This chapter looks at yet another aspect of working capital management: the management of receivables, or 'credit management'. This involves decisions about credit policy and credit terms for individual customers.

This chapter covers Syllabus parts A3, F1, F2 and F3.

CONTENTS

LEARNING OUTCOMES

At the end of this chapter you should be able to:

- Explain the role of accounts receivables in the working capital cycle
- Explain the importance of credit management, including the level of trade credit, the role of the credit control function and the activities of the credit control function
- Explain the need to establish a credit policy and outline the steps involved, including setting maximum credit amounts and periods and total credit levels
- Explain the key categories that should be considered when assessing the credit-worthiness of a customer
- Outline the various internal sources of information that may be used in assessing the credit-worthiness of a customer
- Outline the various external sources of information that may be used in assessing the credit-worthiness of a customer
- Define and explain credit scoring
- Identify possible reasons for rejecting an application for credit or extending credit
- Outline how the financial statements of a customer can be used to assess the credit-worthiness of a customer
- Identify and apply the common ratios that may be used to analyse the financial statements of a customer in order to assess their credit-worthiness
- Evaluate the usefulness and limitations of ratio analysis in assessing credit-worthiness
- Identify the main data protection issues that should be considered when dealing with accounts receivables records
- Describe the main external sources that may be used to monitor receivables (including credit agencies, industry sources, financial reports, press coverage, official publications, bank or supplier reference)
- Explain the key elements of a basic contract (offer, acceptance, remedies for breach of contract etc.)
- Briefly outline specific terms and conditions that may be included in contracts with credit customers (e.g. length of credit period, amount of interest on late payments, retention of title).

1 ROLE OF RECEIVABLES IN THE WORKING CAPITAL CYCLE

1.1 KEEPING THE WORKING CAPITAL CYCLE TURNING

Cash flow is vital to the livelihood of a business. It should be every manager's primary task to help keep it flowing and to use the cash flow to generate profits.

If a business is operating profitably, then it should, in theory, generate cash surpluses. If it does not generate surpluses, the business will eventually run out of cash and collapse. The faster a business expands, the more cash it will need for working capital and investment. Good management of working capital will generate cash, will help improve profits and reduce risks.

Cash from sales is usually the most important source of liquidity for an organisation but the cost of providing credit to customers can represent a substantial proportion of an organisation's total profits.

Each component of working capital (namely inventory, receivables and payables) has two dimensions – time and money. When it comes to managing working capital – time **is** money. If companies can get money to move faster around the cycle (e.g. collect monies due from receivables more quickly) or reduce the amount of money tied up (e.g. reduce inventory levels relative to sales), the business will generate more cash or it will need to borrow less money to fund working capital.

1.2 RECEIVABLES COLLECTION PERIOD

In its pursuit of its objectives for profit, cash flow, asset use and lower interest costs, the organisation has to balance the total level of credit that it can offer between encouraging customers, with the considerable costs of offering credit, and refusing opportunities for profitable sales. In some cases receivables can account for nearly a third of the total assets of the organisation.

Businesses that sell goods on credit terms specify a credit period. Failure to send out invoices on time or to follow up late payers will have an adverse effect on the cash flow of the business. As we saw in an earlier chapter, the receivables collection period measures the average period of credit allowed to customers.

	20X7	**20X6**
Average daily sales	$\frac{\$209,000}{365} = \$573$	$\frac{\$196,000}{365} = \$537$
Closing trade receivables	\$29,000	\$23,000
Receivables collection period	$\frac{\$29,000}{\$573} = 50.6$ days	$\frac{\$23,000}{\$537} = 42.8$ days

Compared with 20X6 the receivables collection period has worsened in 20X7. If the average credit allowed to customers was, say, 30 days, then something is clearly wrong. Further investigation might reveal delays in sending out invoices or failure to 'screen' new customers.

In general, the shorter the receivables collection period the better because customers are effectively 'borrowing' from the company. Remember, however, that the level of receivables reflects not only the ability of the credit controllers but also the sales and marketing strategy adopted, and the nature of the business. Any change in the level of receivables must therefore be assessed in the light of the level of sales.

Note: The quickest way to compute the receivables collection period is to use the following formula (we are assuming that all sales are on credit):

$$\frac{\text{Closing trade receivables}}{\text{Credit sales for year}} \times 365$$

20X7	**20X6**
$\frac{29{,}000}{209{,}000} \times 365 = 50.6 \text{ days}$	$\frac{23{,}000}{196{,}000} \times 365 = 42.8 \text{ days}$

Note: Instead of using the current value of trade receivables to calculate the receivables collection period, the average value of receivables could also be used.

2 CREDIT AND THE COST OF GIVING CREDIT

2.1 THE NEED TO GIVE CREDIT

Trade credit is credit given to customers in the normal course of business operations. Most businesses are forced to give some credit in order to make sales, although the amount of credit will vary from one industry to another depending on what the average for the industry is. For example, supermarkets don't normally offer any credit (this seems perfectly normal in their industry) whereas in many industries 30 days credit is more normal. However, even a supermarket will often have to accept credit card payments, which means that the credit card company is effectively a 'receivable' until the balance is finally settled.

2.2 THE COST OF GIVING CREDIT

Although credit usually has to be given to win sales, there is also a cost to giving credit. There are two main aspects to this cost:

- the costs of irrecoverable debts
- the cost of the capital tied up in receivables.

Irrecoverable debts

When buying goods or services on credit, there is always a risk that the customer will be unable or unwilling to pay for them when payment falls due. If a debt cannot be collected, it has to be written off as 'irrecoverable'. Such debts are a cost.

Example

A business sells goods to a customer on credit for $3,000. The cost of sales was $2,200.

- When the goods are sold, the business will make a profit of $800 on the sale.
- However, if the customer fails to pay and the debt is written off as irrecoverable, the business will actually lose $2,200, which is the cost of making the sale.

In the financial accounts of the business, this would be reported as:

	$
Sales	3,000
Cost of sales	(2,200)
Gross profit	800
Irrecoverable debt written off	(3,000)
Net profit	(2,200)

The cost of capital tied up in receivables

There is also a cost of tying up capital in receivables. This can be measured as an interest cost, which is the amount of interest a business has to pay (or the interest income that it loses) by allowing sales on credit instead of making all sales for cash.

Suppose for example that a business makes $100,000 of sales on credit. It will have $100,000 of receivables. However, if the sales had been made for cash instead of on credit, it would have no receivables but $100,000 in cash. By having receivables, the business is delaying the receipt of cash. We can measure the cost of this by applying an interest rate to the total amount of receivables.

A simple way of calculating the annual cost of investing in receivables is:

Average receivables during the year × Annual interest cost (as a percentage rate of interest)

Example

The management of a business has estimated that, by allowing credit to customers, its annual sales are $2 million higher than they would be if all sales were for cash. The business makes a contribution (gross profit) of 60% on its sales. Irrecoverable debts are 2% of total sales of $3 million. Average receivables are $1 million and the annual cost of interest is 7%.

The benefits and costs of giving credit can be measured as follows:

	$	$
Extra contribution from higher sales (60% of $2m)		1,200,000
Costs		
Irrecoverable debts (2% of $3 million)	60,000	
Interest cost of receivables (7% of $1 million)	70,000	
Total costs of credit		130,000
Net benefit of giving credit		1,070,000

Most businesses believe that it is more profitable to give credit than to insist on sales for cash. However, credit has to be controlled. If too much credit is given, it is likely that both the cost of irrecoverable debts and the interest cost of the investment in receivables would become unacceptably high.

2.3 CREDIT AND CASH FLOWS

It is also important to remember that giving credit affects cash flows. Cash from sales is usually the most important source of liquidity for a business, and unless it is able to collect cash from its sales, it could run out of cash and so go out of business. Another reason for having to control credit is therefore the need for cash. A business must not give more credit than it can safely allow without endangering liquidity, and when credit is allowed to customers it is important to get customers to pay up on time, and not take longer credit than they have been allowed.

2.4 CREDIT TERMS

There are two inter-related aspects to giving credit to a customer:

- setting a credit limit, which is the total amount of credit allowed to the customer
- setting a latest date for payment, which might be 30 days, 60 days, 90 days, etc. after the invoice date.

A customer might therefore be allowed credit of up to $20,000, and required to pay invoices within 60 days of the invoice date. Credit management involves controlling both the amount of credit given and the length of credit.

ACTIVITY 1

The receivables of LCBN Co have been categorised into four groups according to the average time they take to pay and the probability that they will become irrecoverable debts, as follows:

Receivable category	**Average collection period**	**Irrecoverable debts**
	days	**% of sales**
V	15	0.75
W	20	2.00
X	25	3.00
Y	30	5.00
Z	60	8.00

Variable costs are 60% of sales. Next year, the company has an opportunity to increase its credit sales by $2,500,000, by offering better credit terms to certain potential customers. Of these sales, it is expected that the receivable categories would be as follows:

Receivable category	**Additional sales**
	$
W	500,000
Y	500,000
Z	1,500,000

The company's short-term borrowing rate is 7.5% per annum.

Required:

Calculate the effect on profit of the proposal to increase sales.

Note: You can calculate the increase in receivables as:

$$\text{Additional sales (in \$)} \times \frac{\text{Average collection period (days)}}{\text{365 days}}$$

Use the following table to prepare your answer:

	Category W	Category Y	Category Z	Total
	$	$	$	$
Additional sales				
Additional contribution (40%)				
Additional irrecoverable debts:				
2% of $500,000				
5% of $500,000				
8% of $1,500,000				
Interest cost				
Total additional cost				
Net benefit				

For a suggested answer, see the 'Answers' section at the end of the book.

3 ELEMENTS OF CREDIT CONTROL

Credit control (or credit management) is necessary:

- to achieve a balance in giving credit between the benefits from extra sales and the resulting costs of higher irrecoverable debts and higher finance costs (investing in additional receivables)
- to limit the total amount of trade credit in order to avoid a liquidity shortage from over investment in receivables.

These objectives are achieved largely by:

- setting limits and restrictions on granting credit, as a matter of credit policy
- credit risk assessment: assessing the creditworthiness of individual customers
- agreeing credit terms with individual customers (deciding how much credit each customer should be allowed, and on what payment terms)
- collecting payments in accordance with the agreed credit terms.

Essentially, these aspects of credit control divide into two broad areas: granting credit and collecting payments.

Some of the detailed aspects of credit control are:

- setting credit policy
- credit analysis (analysing the credit status of individual customers)
- credit terms and credit limits
- credit insurance

- collecting debts
- deciding when to write off debts as irrecoverable
- factoring debts and invoice discounting
- monitoring credit risks and collections (e.g. through aged receivables analysis)
- involvement with the accounting system (sales ledger, cash book)
- legal issues relating to credit control, such as contracts with the customer, data protection law, etc.
- co-ordination of credit control and sales.

These are explained in more detail in the following chapters.

4 POLICY AND PROCEDURES FRAMEWORK

When a business sells goods on credit, it does not offer the same credit terms to every customer.

- Some customers are allowed a higher credit limit, partly because they buy more goods or services, and partly because they are a lower credit risk than other customers.
- Some customers might be given a longer time to pay than others.
- Some customers might be refused credit altogether, and asked to pay in advance for everything they buy.
- Individual customers should be assessed for creditworthiness, and on the basis of this assessment, credit terms should be offered.
- Different organisations use different methods of assessing credit. For example, some might use a credit scoring system, others might ask for a reference from a credit reference agency, and others might simply ask for a bank reference and references from other suppliers to the customer. Whatever method is used, the required procedures should be specified and credit controllers should be required to follow them.

4.1 CREDIT POLICY

The granting of credit to individual customers should be within the framework of the organisation's policy on credit terms and established procedures for assessing creditworthiness. Most businesses must be prepared to offer reasonable credit terms to remain competitive and stay in business. The aim of credit policy should therefore be to control the credit terms offered and to monitor for all credit customers their ability and willingness to pay on time.

A credit policy should set out the standard payment terms the business is prepared to offer. These terms can be written into the terms and conditions of business and brought to the attention of new customers. The new customer might be asked to sign a form agreeing to comply with the terms offered.

The business could also formulate policies for settlement discounts and penalties for late payment.

- Settlement discounts are discounts from the amount payable for payment within a given number of days after the invoice date. For example, a business could have a policy of offering a cash discount of 1% for payment within 30 days, otherwise payment is required within 60 days of the invoice date.
- A business could specify in its terms and conditions a penalty for late payment, so that interest is charged on overdue payments. The threat of charging interest can be useful in persuading customers to pay, but it is difficult in practice to make a customer pay any such interest charged. A late payer might eventually agree to pay the overdue invoice, but refuse to pay the interest. A business might allow its customers to do this because they want to retain the customer's goodwill, and do not think it is worth the effort to dispute a small interest charge.

ACTIVITY 2

Sawdust Co is considering a change in its credit policy. Currently it offers terms of 60 days net (two months) to all its customers, but it is considering a change to 90 days net (three months).

The company estimates that the easier credit terms will lead to an increase of 7% in total sales revenue, which are currently $80 million each year. The contribution margin on sales is 30%, and there should be no increase in fixed costs if the sales volume increases as expected.

It is estimated that as a result of the increase in sales volume, inventory levels will rise by $4 million and trade payables by $1 million. Currently all customers take the full 60 days credit offered, and it is assumed that all customers will take 90 days if this is offered.

The company has a target rate of return of 15%.

Required:

Calculate whether the change in credit policy is financially justified.

For a suggested answer, see the 'Answers' section at the end of the book.

5 THE CREDIT APPLICATION

The process of granting credit to an individual customer should begin with an application from the customer. This could be a new customer asking for credit for the first time, or an existing customer who is asking for more credit.

A business might ask its customers to apply for credit on a standard application form. If the business uses a sales force, a sales representative will usually help the customer to prepare the application.

Not all businesses use credit application forms. However, the benefits of such forms are that:

- the customer (or prospective customer) formally authorises the business to carry out credit checks
- using standard forms makes it easier to apply standard credit checking procedures.

6 ASSESSING CREDITWORTHINESS

Some businesses assess the credit status of their customers by giving them a formal rating or credit score. Credit status will be based on an assessment of:

- the customer's financial health
- the customer's history of late payments.

A business could establish a number of different credit status categories, and assign each customer to one of these categories. For example, customers might be assessed as financially strong, financially stable or financially weak, and as late payers or prompt payers, to give six credit status ratings, as follows:

	Financially strong	Financially stable	Financially weak
Prompt payer	A rating	B rating	E rating
Late payer	C rating	D rating	F rating

The amount of credit and the direct terms offered to a customer can then be based on the credit rating. In addition, the procedures for monitoring the creditworthiness of customers could be varied according to credit status, with customers with weaker credit ratings being monitored more closely than stronger credits.

The systems of credit ratings used by businesses vary widely, and there are no standard systems in use.

It is also important to remember that not all organisations measure the credit status of customers. Instead, they use a less formal system to decide whether to give credit to a customer, and if so how much and on what terms.

6.1 SOURCES OF CREDIT STATUS INFORMATION

There are different sources of information for assessing the credit status of a new customer. Generally, a firm will start the assessment of a new customer by generating internal information about that customer, for example records of previous sales to the customer and a review of the customer's financial statements. Then, extra information is generated from external sources, for example asking the customer's bank and/or other suppliers to provide references.

The sources of information differ to some extent between business customers and private (individual) customers. These sources are:

For businesses

Internal sources

- visit to customer/sales representative report
- financial statements of the business

External sources

- bank reference/bank status report
- trade references
- the Individual Insolvency Register
- the Register of County Court Judgements
- credit reference agency report (see Section 7).

For individuals

Internal sources

- information provided by the customer, on a credit application form

External sources

- bank reference
- credit reference agency report (see Section 7).

Banks and credit card companies are the main types of organisation that ask for credit status information about individuals. If you have ever applied yourself for a credit card, you should know how much detail the card issuer asks for. An application form for a credit card commonly asks for details of the individual's monthly income and main outgoings, so that the card issuer can reach a decision about whether to issue a card to the individual and if so, what the credit limit should be.

Most businesses other than banks and credit card companies are more likely to seek credit status information about businesses, because trade credit is generally given to businesses but not private individuals.

6.2 BANK REFERENCE/BANK STATUS REPORT

A customer can be asked to provide the name and address of his bank, and to give consent to the bank providing a reference or status report. This is a report in which the bank provides an opinion about the customer.

When a potential new customer consents to a bank reference being provided, the credit controller submits the request for a report to its own bank, for passing on to the potential customer's bank. The request for a reference should indicate the amount of credit that is under consideration.

A problem with bank references, however, is that banks are generally reluctant to provide a bad reference for any of its customers. A bank will certainly not want to make a credit decision as part of its reference.

Because banks are reluctant to give bad reports or firm credit judgements, some businesses might take the view that they are not worth the trouble and cost of obtaining.

6.3 TRADE REFERENCES

A customer can also be asked to provide the names and addresses of two or three other businesses from which it buys on credit, and to consent to these suppliers being asked for a reference.

A trade reference can be asked for in writing or by telephone. When a trade reference is requested in writing, it is helpful to submit a standard form, together with a covering letter.

- The covering letter should ask for the supplier's co-operation in providing a trade reference about the customer, stating that the customer has given its consent to the reference being given and indicating the amount of credit that has been asked for.

- The standard form helps the supplier by specifying the information required. Unless the required information is specified, the supplier might fail to provide it. The form should emphasise the fact that any information provided will be in the strictest confidence. The words 'STRICTLY CONFIDENTIAL' (or something similar) should be printed at the top of the form.

The information required in a trade reference will be:

- the name of the supplier providing the reference
- the name of the customer
- the length of time that the customer has been trading with the supplier
- whether or not the customer supplied trade references before becoming a customer of the supplier
- the customer's credit limit with the supplier
- payment terms, for example 30 days' net
- the payment history of the customer: is the customer a good payer, a fairly slow payer or a very slow payer
- whether the supplier has ever had to suspend credit to the customer (and, if yes, when did this happen and what were the reasons?)
- a few lines for adding any other information the supplier considers relevant. (For example, the supplier might want to add a comment such as 'X Co is an important and very good customer of this business'.)

The standard form should end by thanking the supplier for taking the time to complete the form, and stating the name and address of the person to whom the form should be returned.

A supplier who is asked to supply a trade reference is not obliged to give a reference at all, and (like a bank) might be unwilling to give a bad reference about an existing customer. However, it might be possible to find out whether the customer:

- buys extensively on credit, and
- pays promptly for its purchases, or has a habit of paying late.

The quality of a trade reference depends on the nature of the information the other supplier is willing to give.

It should be remembered, however, that when a potential new customer gives the names of existing suppliers who can be asked for a trade reference, the customer is likely to select suppliers that are paid on time or suppliers with which it has a particularly good relationship.

Trade references, like bank references, can provide some reassurance to a credit controller, but are by no means wholly reliable.

6.4 VISIT TO CUSTOMER/SALES REPRESENTATIVE REPORT

When a business has a field sales force, its sales representatives can go out to meet with potential new customers on their premises. They also meet existing customers regularly. They are 'in the front line' and in a unique position to provide information on customer creditworthiness. They can provide valuable feedback on developments taking place amongst customers in terms of product sales, expansion plans, laying off staff, and so on. They can judge whether the customer's business seems to be doing well or badly. They can also discuss the problems of customers who are slow payers.

If a business does not have a sales force, it may still be possible to visit a prospective applicant for credit or an existing customer on their 'home ground' i.e. at their own premises. The main purpose of such a visit should be to establish a good relationship with the (potential) customer concerned. In addition, the visit could also provide a valuable insight into the way in which the customer's business operates and is being managed. The 'three Cs' used by some banking organisations could be a useful starting point. An assessment could be made of capacity, capability and character of the company/organisation being visited, as follows:

- Capacity – does the company have the necessary capacity to achieve their objectives, formulate necessary policies in terms of non-current assets, products, personnel, etc?
- Capability – how capable is the company at producing its products or delivering a service e.g. in terms of expertise and managerial skills?
- Character – can we trust and work hand in hand with the personnel involved?
- In addition it can provide a mutual understanding for the company concerned and its products (or services), and the problems it has to face.

6.5 SOME OTHER SOURCES

Occasionally, some other sources of information about a customer might be available. These could include:

- references to the customer's business in a trade journal
- the customer's web site, which should provide background information about the customer's business.

The Individual Insolvency Register and individual bankruptcies

The Individual Insolvency Register is a register of judgements by the country courts against individuals who have not paid a debt. The register gives details of bankruptcy orders against individuals in England and Wales.

The register database includes the name of the bankrupt, his or her last known address, details of the bankruptcy order and, if known, the bankrupt's date of birth, occupation and trading details. Bankruptcy records are usually held on the register for five years after the date of the bankruptcy order. (If the bankruptcy order is cancelled because the individual subsequently pays the debts, the record is removed from the register after two years.)

The register can be searched without charge, either by:

- emailing, posting or faxing a request to the office where the register is held, giving details of the individual to be searched (name, address, occupation or business and age if known), or
- visiting a local office of the official receiver.

The Register of County Court Judgements

Payables (for example, unpaid suppliers) can apply to the County Court for a judgement. A County Court Judgement (CCJ) is an order by the court for a debt to be paid. Unless the debt is paid within one month, a CCJ is entered in the Register of County Court Judgements. This register is held at the Registry Trust and is available for public inspection.

It can be checked to find out whether there has been a County Court Judgement against the potential customer. CCJs are kept on the register for six years.

Companies House and company insolvencies

The Individual Insolvency Register contains details about individual bankruptcies, but not about company insolvencies. For information about company insolvencies, details can be obtained from the Register of Companies which is held at Companies House.

There is also a register of disqualified company directors, which is available on the Internet at www.companieshouse.gov.uk.

Internet

The Internet is a potential source of credit information, but finding information can be a hit-and-miss affair. A useful procedure is to use a search engine on the Internet to find out whether there is any information about named individuals, such as the owner or director of a business, or information about the business itself.

Two popular Internet search engines are Yahoo! and Google.

These search engines allow you to enter any words or phrases and search the Internet for any references to those words or phrases.

Suppose that you are a credit controller checking the credit status of William Batty, a business owner. You can use a search engine to key in a search for 'William Batty'. If there are any references to this name on the Internet, you can then check out any of them that could relate to the individual you are checking. While this could yield some useful information, it could take a great deal of time to sift through the large number of references that can be found. Even people with unusual names can have dozens of namesakes who are to be found on the Internet.

7 CREDIT REFERENCE AGENCY REPORTS

Credit reference agencies, also known as credit bureaux, can provide credit information about businesses and individuals in the form of a credit status report, in return for a fee. The fee for a standard short report is usually quite small, perhaps about $20.

Reference agencies offer a range of services to clients, ranging from supplying copies of the recent annual financial statements of the business (if it is a company) to a detailed credit status report. A status report can include the agency's own assessment of the credit status of the business or individual concerned. Agencies provide an on-line service, so that clients can ask for reports through the agency's web site.

The largest credit reference agencies in the UK include Dun & Bradstreet, Equifax and Experian.

You might have heard of credit rating agencies, such as Moody's and Standard & Poor's. These agencies provide a credit rating system for very large companies that borrow in the corporate bond markets. Credit reference agencies, in contrast, provide credit information about small and medium-sized businesses and about individuals.

7.1 WHY USE A CREDIT REFERENCE AGENCY?

Agencies can provide information about potential new customers and also new information about an existing customer that could affect its credit status.

The purpose of using a credit reference agency is to obtain information about the credit status of a potential or existing customer from a single source, without having to do much work to get it. Agency reports are convenient and fairly inexpensive. However, a credit controller must know how to use agency reports and judge how much they can be relied on for an accurate and meaningful credit assessment.

7.2 WHERE DOES AN AGENCY GET ITS INFORMATION FROM?

A credit reference agency gets its information from a variety of sources, many of them published sources. These sources include:

- in the case of companies, copies of its annual accounts. UK companies are required by law to file a copy of their annual accounts at Companies House. Copies of the accounts for the most recent years can be obtained and analysed. Credit reference agencies carry out a simple analysis of these accounts, by measuring some key accounting ratios

- the Individual Insolvency Register and the Register of County Court Judgements. These show whether there has ever been a court order against the customer for non-payment of a debt. Although this information is publicly available, credit reference agencies are accustomed to obtaining data from these sources, and holding it on file

- its accumulated history of credit information about businesses, supplied by other clients of the agency.

In the case of an individual, a credit reference agency will even check the electoral roll, to confirm that the customer's address in the credit application is the same as his or her address on the electoral roll.

A credit controller can check the **published sources of information** himself/herself, but when a business wants to check these sources, it is often much more convenient to use an agency and pay the fee.

7.3 WHAT DOES A CREDIT REFERENCE AGENCY'S REPORT CONTAIN?

Credit status reports vary in format and content, and a business can ask for a detailed status report provided it is willing to pay the required fee. A standard credit status report from an agency for a small or medium-sized business will give a basic credit assessment of and a limited amount of information about the customer.

Although different agencies have different styles of report, it might be helpful for the purpose of illustration to look at the contents of a 'customer report' that can be obtained from Dun & Bradstreet. A D&B customer report includes:

- a risk rating of the customer, based on a four-star rating system (with one star = high credit risk, 2 stars = slightly greater-than-average risk, 3 stars = slightly less-than-average risk and 4 stars = low credit risk

- a recommended credit limit. This is an amount in $

- payment performance. This is a five-star rating measurement, with one star indicating a poor payment record and five stars indicating a prompt payer. Three stars, for example, indicate payment on average 6 to 15 days late

- trading opinion. This is an opinion about how to handle the customer's account. For example, the opinion could be: 'Give credit but monitor the account closely'
- how the risk rating for the customer compares with the risk rating for other businesses in the same industry. This is a five-star rating system, with one star indicating much worse than average and five starts indicating much better than average.

A customer report also includes some factual information, such as:

- the year the business was first started
- details of any significant legal proceedings against it (e.g. County Court judgements, whether the business is wound up or whether its owner has gone through personal bankruptcy proceedings)
- the names of the owners or directors
- the size of the business, in terms of annual sales turnover and the number of employees
- a few key financial figures for the previous three years (sales turnover, profit, the 'net worth' of the business assets and the ratio of the current assets to current liabilities)
- bank details (name of bank and sort code of the branch).

8 FINANCIAL STATEMENT ANALYSIS

Some businesses carry out checks themselves on the creditworthiness of potential new customers. This might be appropriate when the customer has applied for a large amount of credit, which means that the credit risk (the risk of losses from irrecoverable debts) could be high if the credit is granted. Thorough credit checking should help to reduce irrecoverable debts.

The financial statements for analysis can come from either of two sources:

- in the case of a corporate customer, historical financial accounts filed at Companies House. A copy of these can be obtained directly from Companies House, or through a credit reference agency
- directly from the customer/applicant for credit.

8.1 KEY QUESTIONS IN FINANCIAL ANALYSIS

A credit analyst can analyse the financial statements of a corporate customer's business to extract information about how the business is doing and its apparent financial performance and position. There are several aspects of performance and financial position to look at.

- **Liquidity** – Is the company able to meet its short-term obligations as they fall due from the resources immediately available to it? How long on average does it take to pay its debts?
- **Profitability** – Is the company making a profit, and if so is it enough? What is its return on capital employed?

- **Efficiency** – Is the company making best use of its resources, generating adequate sales from its investment in equipment and people and is it managing its working capital levels adequately?
- **Stability** – How much debt does the company have already? Is it heavily in debt and 'highly geared', or is it in a good financial position and able to take on more debt?

8.2 COMMON RATIOS USED IN CREDIT CONTROL

The answer to questions in the areas above will come from a careful, analytical review of the financial statements and in particular:

- calculating key financial ratios from the figures in the financial statements
- making comparisons and identifying trends. Ratios and other financial numbers are not always useful when looked at in isolation. We need to compare ratios calculated from recent financial statements with ratios for earlier years (to look for any improving or worsening trends) or similar ratios for other businesses in the same industry (to assess how well the customer's business is performing in comparison with the 'industry norm').

Some of the ratios commonly used to assess a customer's business are explained below.

Liquidity ratios and working capital cycle ratios were described in an earlier chapter.

8.3 PROFITABILITY RATIOS

Profitability ratios can be used to judge the profitability of a customer's business. If a business is losing money, or if it is making only small profits, its credit status will be lower than for a more profitable business. This is because in the long run, a business needs profits to survive, and it needs adequate profits to prosper.

We could simply look at the amount of profit the business has earned. However, a profit figure taken in isolation does not mean anything. For example, if you are told that a company has made a profit of $100,000 for the year, would you take this as a sign of financial strength or not? The answer should be that it depends on how big the business is and the volume of its business. A profit of $100,000 is probably extremely good for a window cleaning company but very poor for a large public company whose shares are traded on the stock exchange.

Useful ratios for measuring profitability are:

- net profit margin
- gross profit margin
- earnings per share (EPS)
- return on capital employed (ROCE).

Example

The following example will be used to illustrate the calculation of these ratios.

A company has reported the following results for the year just ended:

	$000	$000
Sales revenue		2,450
Cost of sales		950
Gross profit		1,500
Administration costs	370	
Selling and distribution costs	610	
		980
Profit before interest and taxation		520
Interest costs		70
Profit before taxation		450
Taxation		120
Profit for the year		330
Dividends		170
Retained profit for the year		160

	End of this year	**Start of this year**
	$000	$000
Share capital ($1 shares)	1,000	1,000
Reserves	3,760	3,600
Long-term debt	1,000	1,000
Total capital employed	5,760	5,600

Net profit margin/operating profit margin

The net profit margin is usually measured for a company as:

$$\frac{\text{Net profit before interest (sometimes called operating profit)}}{\text{Sales revenue}} \times 100\%$$

Gross profit margin

The gross profit margin is measured as:

$$\frac{\text{Gross profit}}{\text{Sales revenue}} \times 100\%$$

In the example above, the net margin is (520/2,450) × 100% = 21.2%. The gross margin is (1,500/2,450) × 100% = 61.2%.

The profitability of a business is usually assessed by comparing net and gross margins with other businesses in the same industry, and by monitoring trends in profitability over time. However, in this example it is probably safe to assume that the company has strong operating profits, since it has made $0.21 in profit before interest for every $1 of sales.

Earnings per share (EPS)

$$\text{EPS is } \frac{\text{Profit after tax}}{\text{Number of shares}}$$

It measures the amount of profit generated per share. A growing EPS figure would reassure shareholders that the company is moving in the right direction and will probably be able to pay out an increasing level of dividends.

Here, the EPS is $330,000/1,000,000 = $0.33

Return on capital employed (ROCE)

The net profit ratio and gross profit ratio provide a measure of profitability in relation to sales revenue, but they do not compare the size of the profit with the size of the business.

The return on capital employed (ROCE) is a measure of profitability in relation to the size of the business. The most usual method of calculating ROCE for a company is:

$$\text{ROCE} = \frac{\text{Profit before interest and taxation}}{\text{Total capital employed}} \times 100\%$$

Total capital employed = shareholders' funds (equity) + long-term debt

In most cases this is the same as total assets less current liabilities.

In the example above, ROCE is calculated as follows:

Average capital employed = (5,600 + 5,760)/2 = 5,680.

$$\text{ROCE} = \frac{520}{5{,}680} \times 100\% = 9.2\%$$

The ROCE of a business can be assessed by comparing it with the ROCE of other businesses, and also by looking at historical trends to see whether ROCE is improving or getting worse over time, or remaining fairly stable.

8.4 EFFICIENCY RATIOS AND ACTIVITY RATIOS

Efficiency and activity ratios are not directly relevant to creditworthiness, although a business that uses its assets efficiently is likely to have a stronger financial position than businesses that use their assets inefficiently.

Two financial ratios for monitoring the efficiency of asset use are:

- the asset turnover ratio
- inventory turnover.

Asset turnover ratio

This is the ratio of sales revenue each year to the value of the assets employed in the business. It measures the amount of sales revenue for each $1 invested in assets.

$$\text{Asset turnover ratio} = \frac{\text{Sales}}{\text{Capital employed}}$$

For example, if a business has annual sales revenue of $10 million and its total capital employed is $5 million, the asset turnover is 2 times. This means that every $1 of assets has generated $2 of sales revenue.

Inventory turnover

Inventory turnover is relevant to an assessment of liquidity and so creditworthiness, because if a business ties up money in stocks (inventories), its cash flow will be affected. Slow inventory turnover could be an indication of poor cash management.

Have they got too much money tied up in inventory? An increasing figure or one much greater than the 'yardstick' industry norm may indicate poor inventory management. We use the cost of sales rather than sales revenue in its ratio because inventory is stated in the balance sheet at cost rather than at sales value.

$$\text{Inventory turnover} = \frac{\text{Cost of sales}}{\text{Inventory}}$$

Measured this way, inventory turnover is measured in times per year.

Average inventory turnover can also be measured in days:

$$\text{Inventory turnover} = \frac{\text{Inventory}}{\text{Cost of sales}} \times 365$$

In both cases, the figure for inventory can be either the value of inventory in the end-of-year balance sheet or the average of the opening and closing balance sheet figures.

8.5 LONG-TERM SOLVENCY RATIOS (STABILITY RATIOS)

When a business is heavily in debt, it could be at risk from a fall in sales revenue and profits, because a fall in revenue could leave it without enough profits and cash to meet the interest payments on the debt. Clearly, this would affect the cash flows of the business and its ability to pay its trade payables.

Unlike short-term liquidity ratios, the risk from high levels of borrowing is more long-term.

Two ratios for measuring long-term solvency are:

- gearing ratio
- interest cover ratio.

Gearing

Gearing (or 'leverage' as it is known in the US) is the proportion of the net assets of a business financed by long-term borrowing. Basically, the higher the borrowing, the higher the risk to the business from a fall in sales.

$$\text{Gearing} = \frac{\text{Borrowing}}{\text{Total capital employed}} \times 100\%$$

There is no official or standard definition of gearing. Borrowing is usually just long-term borrowing, but can include short-term loans (with less than 12 months to maturity) and any bank overdraft.

A business is said to be 'high-geared' if its total borrowings exceed 50% of its total capital employed.

Example (continued)

In the example above, this year's statement of financial position showed share capital and reserves of $4,600,000 and long term debt of $1,000,000, giving total capital employed of $5,600,000. Therefore, the gearing ratio is ($1m/$5.6m =) 17.9%. This company is therefore a 'low-geared' company.

Interest cover

Interest cover is a measure of the extent to which profits are sufficient to cover the interest costs payable by the business.

$$\text{Interest cover} = \frac{\text{Profit before interest}}{\text{Interest}}$$

An interest cover of less than 3 would be regarded as fairly risky, leaving the business vulnerable to a fall in sales and profits.

8.6 OTHER FINANCIAL RATIOS

The most common financial ratios have been described and explained, but credit controllers might use other ratios for credit analysis. If you are asked to calculate financial ratios from a customer's financial statements, the nature of any unfamiliar ratio should be specified exactly to you. It is essential to calculate ratios correctly, and office procedures should therefore state how ratios should be calculated, to avoid the risk of error.

8.7 LIMITATIONS OF RATIO ANALYSIS

Some financial ratios, such as liquidity ratios, only show the position as the date of the balance sheet.

- Ratios are derived from 'one-off' annual accounts at one point in time. The figures in the accounts may be susceptible to 'window dressing' or seasonal abnormalities, and therefore might not show a representative position.
- Ratios are historic i.e. they help to show what has happened, but not what is going to happen in future.
- Ratios are in any case approximate measures and not exact.

- Comparisons of ratios between similar/same industry companies may be obscured because of the application of different accounting policies.

- There is a danger that ratios will be used in isolation or as the only evidence in analysis, rather than as one part of a jigsaw to be used in conjunction with other credit status data.

- Financial ratio analysis is carried out by an 'outsider looking in' and the information for analysis is inevitably limited. A credit analyst can use ratio analysis only to obtain a broad overall picture.

9 CREDIT SCORING

Financial ratio analysis can provide some information about a customer's business. Other sources of credit status information can also be valuable, such as trade references (for potential new customers) and the customer's payment history (for existing customers).

Some businesses that carry out their own in-house credit assessment of customers need a way of analysing the credit status data and reaching a decision about offering credit. One technique that can be used is to use key information to build up a credit score for the customer. Depending on the customer's credit score, a suitable amount of credit is then allowed (or credit is refused).

Definition **Credit scoring** is a technique that enables companies to apply a systematic approach to the granting of credit, by building up a score to assess the customer's credit rating.

Credit scoring can be applied in all circumstances where credit is under consideration, to businesses and to private individuals. However, it is more applicable where sales are to the public, and the use of other credit assessment methods are either not possible or are too expensive.

Banks use credit scoring to assess a customer's application for a loan. In the areas of hire purchase and personal loans, the companies/institutions involved have been able to streamline their processing of applications via credit scoring systems based on the information extracted from the application forms.

Each organisation that uses credit scoring has to develop its own system, and there are wide variations in credit scoring methods. In general terms, however:

- A number of key items are measured. For a business, these can be a mixture of financial ratios and other items (such as the length of time that the customer's business has been established. For an individual, key factors can include age, job, whether married or not, whether owning a property or not, annual salary and so on.

- For each of these items a maximum score is allocated.

- A customer is then scored, up to the maximum allowed, for each item, according to specified criteria/guidelines.

- The total credit score for all items is then calculated, and the customer's credit score determines its credit status.

Businesses can also purchase a credit scoring system from specialist suppliers, provided they are willing to use a system devised by another organisation.

Example

A sample of past customers would identify the factors associated with irrecoverable debts. Age, sex, marital status, family size, occupation, etc. may be significant factors.

The company may allocate a points score to potential customers as follows:

Factor	Points score
Aged over 40	15
Married with fewer than three children	20
Home owner	20
At same address for over three years	15
At existing job for over two years	20
Car owner	10
Total	100

Past records may show that there had been no records of payment difficulties with customers with a score of 80 or over, irrecoverable debts of 10% for scores between 35 and 80, and irrecoverable debts of 25% where customers had a score of less than 35. A 'cut-off' point of 35 would probably be established, and credit refused to any potential customer with a score of less than 35.

It may be considered worthwhile to carry out some further form of credit evaluation for potential customers with scores between 35 and 80, in order to reduce the irrecoverable debts below 10%. The costs of the further analysis would have to be compared with the financial benefits from the reduction in irrecoverable debts.

The factors which are considered most likely to influence creditworthiness are of course a matter of judgement, as are the respective weights which should be attached to each factor.

Conclusion There are a number of internal and external sources of information which can be used to assist the credit control function/department in the performance of their duties, and which are as follows.

10 OPENING A NEW CUSTOMER ACCOUNT

When a decision is taken to grant credit to a customer for the first time, an account has to be opened for the customer. This is an account for the individual customer in the receivables ledger (sales ledger).

There should be established procedures within the organisation for authorising the opening of a new account. Without strict controls, there is a risk of fraud, whereby unauthorised accounts are opened and goods are sold on credit to 'non-existent' customers.

The procedures for opening a new account should include:

- notifying the customer that credit has been granted, the size of the credit limit and the credit terms

- creating a new account in the receivables ledger for the customer, and giving the customer a unique identity code

- recording in the account details of the credit limit and credit terms, for monitoring and control purposes
- recording in the account the address to which invoices should be sent and a contact name and number (for chasing up payment).

10.1 CREDIT TERMS IN A CONTRACT WITH THE CUSTOMER

Many contracts between a supplier and a customer are in writing. The terms and conditions are drawn up by the supplier, and the customer agrees to them by signing the contract. In many cases, there is a general contract between the supplier and the customer that covers all the individual business transactions between them.

For example, a pharmaceuticals distribution company might enter a contract with a private hospital for the supply of medicines and drugs. A single contract would probably be drawn up, to cover all purchase orders and deliveries.

A written contract should include some reference to credit terms. Here is an example of a term that could be included:

'The time and payment of invoices shall be of the essence of the contract. Credit terms shall only be accepted after completion and acceptance of a credit account. The Company reserves the right to make credit checks and request payment in advance in certain circumstances.'

Here, the contract states that one of its conditions is that the customer should comply with the credit terms that are agreed, even though the contract itself does not stipulate what the credit terms should be. These are left for negotiation and separate consideration.

A contract could include other terms.

- There could be a term that tries to limit the delay in payment due to a customer raising a query about an invoice. For example, the contract might state:

  'Any queries relating to an invoice must be raised as soon as reasonably possible and not exceeding 30 days after receipt of the invoice, otherwise it will be deemed to be approved and any client's query waived.'

- There could be a term that allows the supplier to charge interest on overdue payments. For example:

  'The Company reserves the right to charge interest on overdue accounts. Interest, where applicable, will be charged at 3% per annum over the base rate of Royal Bank of Scotland plc at the time the debt becomes due, such interest to accrue from day to day.'

- There could also be a term in the contract stating the supplier's right to take legal action for the recovery of an unpaid debt. For example:

  'The Company reserves the right to pass accounts not settled within the specified terms to solicitors or a bailiff for collection.'

> **Key point**
>
> When there is a written contract between a supplier and a customer, covering a series of future transactions, it is appropriate to include terms and conditions relating to credit, although in general terms.
>
> Where a written contract covers just one business transaction, the specific credit terms should be included, stating when the customer should pay the amounts due.

A potential problem arises when there is no written contract between supplier and customer, and the customer has not been notified in writing of the credit terms. In such a situation, a business might supply goods on credit to a customer, without specifying when payment is due until the invoice is sent out. Although the invoice will state when payment is due, the customer could argue that it had not accepted these credit terms, and so is entitled to a longer period to pay.

11 OFFERING SETTLEMENT DISCOUNTS

When credit terms are offered to a customer, a settlement discount might also be offered as an incentive to pay early. The offer of a settlement discount allows a credit customer to pay less than the full debt by paying sooner than the end of the normal credit period.

Definition A **settlement discount** is a discount allowed off the invoiced payment due, if the invoice is paid within a specified number of days of the invoice date. A settlement discount is also called a **cash discount**.

For example, suppose that a business has a standard policy of granting 60 days' credit to customers. In order to speed up payments and so reduce the total amount of receivables, the business might decide to offer a settlement discount of, say, 2% for payment within 14 days.

The customer should be notified of any settlement discount, either by a sales representative or a credit controller. The details of the discount should also be included on the invoice, usually toward s the bottom of the invoice where the payment terms are specified.

Typical wording might be: 'Discount of 2% for payment within 14 days of invoice date, net 60 days'.

This means that a settlement discount of 2% is available for payment within 14 days, otherwise the full invoice amount is payable within 60 days of the invoice date.

Example

A company offers its credit customers 60 days' credit, with a settlement discount of 2% for payment within 14 days. It wishes to invoice a customer for $1,000 plus sales tax at 17.5%.

When the invoice is sent out, the company does not know if the customer will take the discount, so the invoice will be for $1,000 plus sales tax. However, the amount of sales tax payable is calculated on the assumption that the customer will take the settlement discount. In this example, the settlement discount would be $20 (2% of $1,000), so sales tax should be charged at 17.5% of $980 (= $171.50). This is the sales tax charge regardless of whether or not the customer decides to take the discount.

	$
Amount payable	980.00
Sales tax	171.50
Total amount payable	1,151.50

The customer has the choice between paying $1,151.50 after 14 days and taking the discount, or paying $1,171.50 after day 14 but within 60 days of the invoice date.

11.1 THE COST OF OFFERING SETTLEMENT DISCOUNTS

A business must ensure that offering settlement discounts is financially sensible. Settlement discounts are a way of easing liquidity problems by improving cash flows. However, discounts have a cost, because the business gives up income and cash receipts.

The cost of offering settlement discounts can be calculated as one of the following interest costs:

- effective interest rate
- simple annual interest rate
- compound annual interest rate.

Example

Suppose that a business allows customers to pay after 90 days, but offers a settlement discount of 2.5% for payment within 7 days. The cost of the discount, as an interest cost, can be calculated by considering an invoice for $100.

- If there is no settlement discount, the business will receive $100 after 90 days.
- If there is a settlement discount and the customer takes it, the business will receive $97.50 after 7 days.

The business therefore receives $2.50 less (the amount of the discount) but it receives its cash – $97.50 – 83 days earlier than it otherwise would.

The discount is therefore financially worthwhile if the business could invest $97.50 for 83 days and earn interest on its investment of at least $2.50.

Effective interest rate

$$\text{Effective interest rate} = \frac{\$2.50}{\$97.50} \times 100\% = 11.3\% \text{ in 83 days}$$

Simple annual interest rate

$$\text{Simple annual interest rate} = 2.56\% \times \frac{365\,\text{days}}{83\,\text{days}} = 11.3\%$$

Compound annual interest rate

$$\text{Compound annual interest rate} = [1.0256^{365/83} - 1] \times 100\% = 11.8\%$$

Alternatively, you might find it easier to use the following formula for calculating the simple annual interest of a settlement discount.

$$\frac{D}{(100-D)} \times \frac{365\text{days}}{(X-Y)\text{days}} \times 100\%$$

where

D is the size of discount offered (e.g. 3% = 3, 1.5% = 1.5, etc.)

X is the normal credit period in days

Y is the maximum number of days for payment to take advantage of the discount.

Simple annual interest rate = $\frac{\$2.50}{\$97.50} \times \frac{365\text{days}}{83\text{days}} \times 100\% = 11.3\%$ (as calculated above).

Once you have calculated the simple annual interest rate in this way, you can calculate the annual compound interest rate in the same way as shown above.

ACTIVITY 3

A company is concerned about the size of its receivables and its cash flows. It therefore decides to offer a 'prompt payment discount' of 1.5% for payment within 14 days. Without the discount, customers take 60 days' credit.

Required:

Calculate the cost of offering the discount in terms of:

(a) effective rate of interest

(b) simple annual rate of interest

(c) compound annual rate of interest.

For a suggested answer, see the 'Answers' section at the end of the book.

Another way of assessing the cost of a settlement discount is to measure the effect on annual profit.

- The cost of offering settlement discounts is the amount of the discounts taken by customers.
- The benefit from offering settlement discounts comes from improved cash flow and the reduction in receivables. This can be measured as:

  Reduction in receivables × Annual cost of interest (%).

Example

A company currently has annual sales of $1.5 million each month. All its sales are on credit, and customers take 60 days to pay. The company believes that if it offers a settlement discount of 2% for payment within 10 days, 25% of customers will take the discount. The annual cost of interest is 8%.

Required:

Calculate the effect of offering the discount on annual profits. Assume that there are 360 days in the year.

Solution

Annual sales are \$1.5 million per month × 12 months = \$18 million.

The cost of the discounts allowed each year will be 2% × 25% × \$18 million = \$90,000.

Receivables without the discount will be (average 60 days):

$$\$18\text{million} \times \frac{60}{360} = \$3.0\text{million}$$

Receivables with the discount will be (average 60 days for 75% of receivables and average 10 days for 25% of receivables):

$$75\%\text{of}\,\$18\text{million} \times \frac{60}{360} + 25\%\text{of}\,\$18\text{million} \times \frac{10}{360}$$

= \$2.25 million + \$0.125 million

= \$2.375 million

Receivables will be reduced by \$625,000 (\$3 million – \$2.375 million) if the discounts are offered.

The reduction in receivables will mean a reduction in annual interest costs of 8% of \$625,000 = \$50,000.

Summary	\$
Cost of discounts allowed	90,000
Saving in interest cost	50,000
Net cost of offering discounts	40,000

11.2 WHY GIVE SETTLEMENT DISCOUNTS?

Settlement discounts usually have a fairly high cost for the business that offers them. This is because the discount needs to be reasonably attractive to persuade a customer to take it. If the discount is small, a customer has no incentive to take it.

The purpose of a settlement discount is to:

- improve cash flow, by
- getting some customers to pay early, and so reducing the total amount of receivables.

It is fairly common for credit terms to be offered on the basis that payment is expected at the end of the month following the month of delivery of goods. This will give rise to an average credit period of 45 days (½ of the month of delivery + the following month = 45 days). In practice, however, many customers take longer credit than they should, and trade credit can be outstanding for two to three months, or even longer. Offering settlement discounts is a way of controlling credit better, provided a significant number of customers can be persuaded to take the discount and pay early.

11.3 INTEREST ON OVERDUE AMOUNTS

If an organisation grants a discount for prompt payment then it follows on that it is possible it will charge interest on overdue amounts. It is possible to include a provision for doing so in the terms of trade. In the UK there are even statutory provisions that permit customers to charge interest on overdue amounts, without any prior contractual agreement to do so. While this could be effective, particularly in discouraging a large customer from taking advantage of a weaker supplier's inability to press for payment, taking interest could cost customer goodwill and cost the company future sales.

12 REJECTING AN APPLICATION FOR CREDIT

12.1 DEALING WITH REJECTIONS

Businesses cannot and should not provide credit to all applicants. If they did, they would give credit to high-risk customers and the level of irrecoverable debts could be extremely high.

When an application for credit is rejected, the rejection must be notified to the would-be customer, who might want to ask about the reasons for the rejection. Any discussions with the customer must be carried out in a tactful manner, and in accordance with the organisation's guidelines.

The goodwill of the potential customer should be maintained, as far as this is possible. A business cannot gain anything by treating a potential customer badly, but there can be a lot to gain from acting courteously and tactfully.

- Having been rejected for credit, the customer might nevertheless decide to buy and pay in advance or on delivery.
- The customer might apply again at a future date, when his financial position is stronger.

Procedures for dealing with rejections should be established. For example, would-be customers could be informed in person, by phone, fax or letter. Whichever method is adopted the tone should be clear, concise, tactful and polite. The notification could also include some indication if and when and under what circumstances it would be possible to provide credit in the future. Alternatives could also be suggested so as not to close the door completely e.g. offering to supply on COD (cash on delivery terms) or by getting the customer to agree to pay by direct debit. In such situations, the way in which the customer performed could be monitored, and after a time credit granted and credit limits/terms etc., agreed with the customer.

The customer might also be told of the reason for the rejection, for example because his credit score was not high enough or because of an adverse credit reference agency report. With credit scoring systems it would not be possible to disclose all of the reasons, and in certain cases a concise and polite rejection may be the best course of action.

12.2 REASONS FOR REJECTING AN APPLICATION FOR CREDIT

These may include one or more of the following:

- a poor credit score, calculated with a credit scoring system
- a poor track record of financial performance, identified through financial ratio analysis of the applicant's accounts, for example downward trends in profits and liquidity

- no track record because the applicant is a new business
- the customer might already be heavily in debt, and yet asking for a large amount of trade credit
- information from third parties e.g. banks, credit rating agencies, existing customers, suppliers, etc.

In conclusion, remember that all dealings should be conducted in a business like, courteous and polite manner. This could well result in being able to do business at some future date, for example when the new company has become established and can successfully pay its way.

It might be company policy to keep a record of any dealings with the customer to discuss his credit application, for example by taking a note or record of telephone conversations and filing emails for future reference.

13 LEGAL ISSUES: CONTRACT LAW

When a business sells goods or services to a customer, there is a contract between them. A contract is an agreement between two or more parties that is enforceable in law. If a customer is late with a payment, it could be in breach of contract. If so, legal action can be taken if necessary to try to obtain payment of the debt.

The basic elements of a contract are:

Offer: a firm proposal to give or do something. It can be made expressly or impliedly, and it does not need to be in writing. It can be withdrawn by the offeror at any time before acceptance. It can be express or implied, and made orally or in writing.

Acceptance: the unconditional agreement to all the terms of the offer. It can be oral, written or implied from a person's conduct. So, for example, if you start supplying goods to a customer, but they fail to sign the contract you sent them, they cannot turn round at a later date and say that they did not agree to your terms. They have implied agreement by continuing to trade with you. Similarly, if they send you back the contract, signed, but with some amendments that they put in, if you then commence/ continue to trade with them you will be deemed to have accepted those terms.

Consideration: one party does something in exchange for another party doing something. Often, there is simply an exchange of promises. For example, Alpha Ltd promises to supply cakes to Beta Ltd and Beta Ltd promises to pay. If Alpha Ltd then fails to make the supply, and Beta Ltd is forced to buy the cakes at a higher price elsewhere in order to meet its commitments, Beta Ltd can sue Alpha Ltd for the difference in price, provided that all the other essential elements of a contract are there. Note, however, that consideration does not need to be adequate, that is, the law does not require a fair deal to have been struck in the first place.

Legal intention: both parties must have intended the agreement to be a legally binding one. This is assumed in commercial arrangements but, if you entered into an agreement in a social situation, for example, agreeing to supply cakes to your friend when you were out for dinner with him, then such legal intention must be proved.

Form: most contracts do not need to be in any strict legal form but, if your company is entering into an agreement for the sale or purchase of land, this must be in writing under UK law. Consumer credit agreements must also be in writing.

Specific terms and conditions that could be included in contracts

In order to manage receivables better and minimise losses, certain terms should be included from the outset, where relevant. These are as follows:

- State clearly the **length of free credit** provided to customers in your initial agreement with each customer. Each invoice should also clearly state this credit period. If the customer then breaks this agreement, they are in breach of contract and the relevant remedies can be pursued if and when necessary.

- Since the fact is that all customers will not pay on time, **interest should be charged on late payment** and this should also be set out in the original contract with the customer. As with the credit period, the amount of interest to be charged should also be printed on each invoice, as a reminder to the customer that you mean business. Once payments are overdue, interest should be charged as warned, otherwise customers will automatically assume that your charges are not genuine, and they may start paying late as a matter of routine.

- A **retention of title clause** can be put into your contracts with customers. This clause states that the buyer does not obtain ownership of the goods unless and until payment is made. Therefore, in theory, if the buyer goes out of business before paying for the goods, the supplier can retrieve the goods. It is often not as simple as that but such clauses certainly can work and are used on a regular basis against liquidators with great effect.

13.1 GROUNDS FOR REFUSAL TO PAY A DEBT

If a customer does not pay a debt on time, is the customer in breach of contract? For a credit controller, there are two legal issues to consider.

- Does the customer have grounds for refusing to pay the debt at all?

- Does the customer have grounds for delaying payment?

A customer could refuse to pay a debt on the grounds either that there is no contract, or that there is a contract but the supplier is in breach of the contract's terms and conditions.

It can be very useful to have some understanding of contract law, in order to respond to a customer in the event of any dispute. Some of the key issues are set out below.

- For a contract to exist, there must be an **offer and** an **acceptance** of the offer. The offer could come from the customer, who asks to purchase goods or services, and the acceptance comes from the supplier, who agrees to provide them. Alternatively, the offer could come from the supplier, for example in the form of a tender or bid, and the acceptance then comes from the customer. A customer could possibly claim that he or she did not offer to buy anything from the supplier, nor did he or she accept any offer from the supplier.

An offer and acceptance can be either in writing or given orally.

- **Consideration** must be given by both parties. In a normal trade transaction, consideration is given by the supplier in the form of delivery of goods or services, and consideration is given by the buyer in the form of payment for the goods or services. For a contract to exist and be binding on both parties, the consideration does not have to be adequate. This means that if there is a claim by the customer that the price is too high, this does not matter, unless it can be shown that the price charged is in breach of the terms and conditions of the agreement.

- A contract between a supplier and a business customer is usually subject to certain **terms and conditions**. These are often set out in writing. A breach of a condition by the supplier could give the customer grounds for claiming that there has been a breach of contract.

- The **sale of goods by a business to consumers** (the general public) could be subject to special laws. In the UK, the sale of goods to consumers is regulated by the Sale of Goods Act 1979 and the Unfair Contract Terms Act 1977.

The Sale of Goods Act 1979

The Sale of Goods Act states that in any sale of goods by a business to a consumer, there are three implied terms in the contract:

- **Implied term as to title**. The seller has title to the goods and therefore has the right to sell them.

- **Implied term as to description**. Where the goods are sold by description (for example in a catalogue or advertisement, or on the wrapping or packaging for the goods) they correspond with the description.

- **Implied term as to quality and fitness of purpose**. The goods must be of suitable quality and fit for their intended purpose.

The implied term as to satisfactory quality is intended to protect consumers from shoddy goods and faulty workmanship. For example, if a purchaser buys a pair of shoes, there is an implied term that they will not fall apart after a reasonable period of wear.

The implied term as to fitness for purpose is designed to protect against goods that do not do what they are supposed to do. For example, if a purchaser buys a football that does not bounce, it is not fit for its purpose. Often, a seller is in breach of the implied terms about both quality and fitness of purpose, because goods are not fit for their purpose, they might not be of satisfactory quality.

The Sale of Goods Act regulates business-to-consumer sales but not business-to-business sales. Most business-to-consumer sales are for cash, so when a customer claims that a sale has been in breach of the implied terms of the Sale of Goods Act, the customer will normally be asking for his money back rather than refusing to pay a debt.

Unfair Contract Terms Act 1977

Sometimes, businesses try to exclude liability for breaches of contracts, so that they will not be liable to pay damages should there be a breach. You might have seen notices along the lines of: 'The company accepts no responsibility for any loss or damage suffered'.

The Unfair Contract Terms Act 1977 restricts the extent to which this can legally happen in a contract for the sale of goods. In a consumer sale (i.e. where a business sells to a consumer) it is not possible to exclude liability for any of the implied terms discussed above. In a business-to-business sale, such exclusions are permissible but only if they are reasonable.

ACTIVITY 4

(a) Jane buys a video camera from Stan, who has advertised it for sale in the 'small ads' column of the local newspaper. The camera never works properly, and after a few weeks ceases working altogether. Jane wants her money back from Stan.

Advise Jane.

(b) Sarah buys a coat from a department store. A notice at the counter says that goods will not be exchanged for any reason. When she gets home, Sarah finds that some of the buttons are missing. Sarah wants to return the coat and get her money back.

Advise Sarah.

(c) Mark buys some all-weather boots from Outdoor Outfitters, and wears them to go fishing. He discovers that they leak. When he takes them back to the shop, the sales assistant says that no refund can be given as Mark has obviously used them for something other than their proper purpose, and in any event Outdoor Outfitters does not accept responsibility for any faults in its products.

Advise Mark as to whether he is entitled to a refund.

For a suggested answer, see the 'Answers' section at the end of the book.

13.2 REMEDIES FOR BREACH OF CONTRACT

When a customer refuses to pay for goods or services on the grounds that there has been a breach of contract, the argument needs to be resolved. In many cases, disputes between supplier and customer are resolved by negotiation rather than referring the matter to lawyers and the courts.

The likely outcomes are that:

- the customer agrees to pay in full, or
- the supplier allows the customer to return the goods and cancels the debt (by issuing a credit note) or cancels the debt for a service provided, or
- the customer agrees to keep the goods but pay a smaller price (in which case a credit note is issued for the reduction in the price).

14 LEGAL ISSUES: DATA PROTECTION ACT

The Data Protection Act 1998 regulates the holding of personal data by businesses (and other organisations and individuals) and provides some protection to individuals. When data protection legislation was first introduced in the UK, it only covered personal data held on computer files. The 1998 Act, however, has extended the legislation to manual records as well as computer records.

Personal data is data:

- about a living person who can be identified from the data itself, and
- which is in the possession (or likely to come into the possession) of a 'data controller', such as a business or other organisation.

A person who is the subject of personal data held by a data controller is known as a **data subject**.

The Act gives rights to individuals:

- to access personal data held about them by a data controller, and
- to seek compensation for any loss or damage suffered from the misuse of such personal data.

A Data Protection Register is maintained by the Data Protection Commissioner. This is a register of data users or controllers, listing their names and addresses together with general details of the nature of the personal data held and the purposes for which it is held. An address is provided for each data controller, to which data subjects may write to request access to the personal data that relates to them.

14.1 PROVISIONS OF THE ACT

The 1998 Act gives a data subject, with some exceptions, the right to examine the personal data that a data controller is holding about him or her. Individuals may write to a data controller to ask whether they are the subject of personal data, and are entitled to a reply.

The data controller may charge a nominal fee for providing the information, but is required to reply within a certain time.

Where personal data is being held, the data subject has the right to receive details of:

- the personal data that is being held
- the purposes for which the information is being processed
- the recipients to whom the information might be disclosed.

If any of the personal data is incorrect, the data subject can ask for it to be removed from the file or corrected.

Any individual who suffers damage as a result of improper use of the data by the data controller is entitled to compensation for any loss suffered.

14.2 RULES FOR DATA PROTECTION COMPLIANCE

The 1998 legislation spells out the conditions under which processing is lawful. Filing systems that are structured so as to 'facilitate access to information about a particular person' are now included in the Act. This includes systems that are paper-based or on microfiche or film.

The ten rules for data protection compliance are:

1 **Consent**

Wherever possible obtain consent before acquiring, holding or using personal data. Any forms, whether paper or web-based, which are designed to gather personal data should contain a statement explaining what the information is to be used for and to whom it may be disclosed.

2 Sensitive data

Be particularly careful with sensitive personal data (i.e. information relating to race, political opinion, physical or mental health, religious belief, trade union membership, sexuality, criminal offences, etc.). Such information should only be held and used where strictly necessary. Always obtain the consent of the individual concerned and notify them of the likely use(s) of such data.

3 Individual rights

Wherever possible be open with individuals concerning the information being held about them. When preparing reports or appending notes to official documents, bear in mind that individuals have the right to see all personal data and could therefore read any 'informal' comments made about them. Also be aware that this includes emails containing personal data and so the same caution should be used when sending emails.

4 Review files

Only create and retain personal data where absolutely necessary. Securely dispose of or delete any personal data which is out of date, irrelevant or no longer required. Hold regular reviews of files and discard unnecessary or obsolete data systematically.

5 Disposal of records

When discarding paper records that contain personal data treat them confidentially (i.e. shred such files rather than disposing of them as waste paper). Similarly any unnecessary or out-of-date electronic records should be deleted. The organisation's computers should not be given away or sold unless all information stored on them has been removed or deleted.

6 Accuracy

Keep all personal data up to date and accurate. Note any changes of address and other amendments. If there is any doubt about the accuracy of personal data then it should not be used.

7 Security

Keep all personal data as securely as possible (e.g. in lockable filing cabinets or in rooms that can be locked when unoccupied). Do not leave records containing personal data unattended in offices or areas accessible to the members of the public. Ensure that personal data is not displayed on computer screens that are visible to passers-by. Be aware that these security considerations also apply to records taken away from the organisation e.g. for work at home or for an external meeting. Also bear in mind that email is not necessarily confidential or secure so should not be used for potentially sensitive communications.

8 Disclosing data

Never reveal personal data to third parties without the consent of the individual concerned or other reasonable justification. This includes parents, guardians, relatives and friends of the data subject who have no right to access information without the data subject's consent. Requests for personal information are received from time to time from organisations such as the police and other government bodies (for example, HM Revenue & Customs). The organisation should endeavour to co-operate with these organisations but steps should first be taken to ensure that requests are genuine and legitimate.

9 Worldwide transfer

Always obtain consent from the individual concerned before placing information about them on the Internet (apart from basic office contact details) and before sending any personal data outside the European Union, Iceland, Lichtenstein or Norway.

10 Third party processors

Be aware that, if you are using a third party data processor e.g. for bulk mailings or database management and are giving them access to personal data, then you must have a written contract in place with them to ensure that they treat such information confidentially, securely and in compliance with the Data Protection Act 1998.

14.3 THE DATA PROTECTION ACT AND CREDIT CONTROL

The Data Protection Act is relevant for credit control whenever personal data is used to carry out credit checks. It therefore applies in cases where consumers or sole traders are vetted, because they are living persons.

If a business turns down a customer for credit or a loan, it does not have to tell the individual why the credit has been refused, except to say that he or she has failed to reach a pass mark in its credit scoring system or that a credit reference agency has provided information suggesting that the individual might be a bad credit risk. If the individual has applied for credit of up to $25,000 and has been refused because of a report from a credit reference agency, the individual is entitled to know the name of the credit reference agency. He or she can then make an application to the agency for a copy of his or her personal file, on payment of a small fee. The individual is then entitled to a copy of the personal data held, clearly explained.

The personal data held ought to be based on the information available to the credit reference agency from:

- the electoral roll (so that a check can be made that the individual is living at the stated address)
- a register of County Court judgements and bankruptcies (which shows whether there has been a court judgement against the individual for non-payment of a debt)
- any other previous or current credit accounts of the individual with other organisations (showing whether the individual has a history of keeping up-to-date with payments).

If there are any errors in the personal data, the individual can ask for the data to be corrected or removed, and he or she could also be entitled to compensation.

Remember, however, that the Data Protection Act applies only to data about individuals. It does not apply to information about companies and other organisations.

CONCLUSION

Decisions about granting credit call for careful judgement. Refusing credit will means fewer sales, but granting credit to a high-risk customer could result in irrecoverable debt losses. Credit policy and credit procedures should therefore be formulated clearly, to help the credit controller make his or her decisions.

Granting credit is one aspect of credit management. Once credit has been granted, it is critically important to make sure that the customer pays what he or she owes, and on time. Collections policy and procedures are explained in the next chapter.

KEY TERMS

Receivables collection period – the number of days on average that receivables take to pay for the goods and services they buy.

Trade credit – credit given to customers in the normal course of business operations.

Irrecoverable debt – a debt that cannot be collected and it has to be written off as 'bad'. Bad debts are a cost.

Credit limit – the total amount of credit allowed to the customer.

Credit policy – the aim of credit policy should be to control the credit terms offered and to monitor for all credit customers their ability and willingness to pay on time.

Settlement discount – discount from the amount payable for payment within a given number of days after the invoice date.

Credit status – some businesses assess the credit status of their customers by giving them a formal rating or credit score. Credit status will be based on an assessment of the customer's financial health and the customer's history of late payments.

Bank status report – report in which the bank provides an opinion about the customer.

Trade reference – a customer can be asked to provide the names and addresses of two or three other businesses from which it buys on credit, and to consent to these suppliers being asked for a reference.

Individual Insolvency Register – a register of judgements by the country courts against individuals who have not paid a debt. The register gives details of bankruptcy orders against individuals in England and Wales.

County Court Judgement (CCJ) – an order by the court for a debt to be paid.

Profitability ratios – ratios that can be used to judge the profitability of a customer's business.

Asset turnover ratio – this is the ratio of sales revenue each year to the value of the assets employed in the business. It measures the amount of sales revenue for each $1 invested in assets.

Credit scoring – a technique that enables companies to apply a systematic approach to the granting of credit, by building up a score to assess the customer's credit rating.

Data Protection Act 1998 – regulates the holding of personal data by businesses (and other organisations and individuals) and provides some protection to individuals.

SELF-TEST QUESTIONS

		Paragraph
1	What is a credit application form?	5
2	List five sources of credit status information for a business.	6.1
3	What is the official source of information about court decisions against non-payers of debts?	7.2
4	What is credit scoring?	9
5	What terms and conditions about credit might be included in a written contract with a customer?	10.1
6	What is a settlement discount?	11
7	How do you calculate the cost of a settlement discount in terms of both simple annual interest and compound annual interest?	11.1
8	Name two reasons for offering settlement discounts.	11.2
9	What are the rights of an individual under the Data Protection Act if he/she is refused credit?	14.3

PRACTICE QUESTION

CRUST CO

A new customer, Crust, has asked your company for credit terms. Your company has a policy of carrying out an analysis of a customer's financial statements as a part of an internal credit checking exercise, before deciding whether to agree to granting credit.

Required:

You have been given the financial statements of Crust (extracts shown below) and you are required to calculate the following financial ratios for the past two years:

(a) the ratio of working capital to total assets

(b) the no credit interval. This is the ratio of liquid assets (receivables plus short-term investments plus cash) to daily cash operating expenses. Assume a 365-day year

(c) the ratio of retained earnings to total assets

(d) the ratio of earnings before interest and taxation to interest charges plus annual loan repayments

(e) the gearing ratio.

Note: Earnings is a term that can be taken to mean 'profit'.

Extracts of accounts of Crust

	Current year	Previous year
	$	$
Sales revenue	3,100,000	3,350,000
Cash operating expenses	2,400,000	2,700,000
Profit before interest and taxation	105,000	53,000
Interest charges	4,000	3,000
Non-current assets	310,000	367,000
Current assets		
Inventory	62,000	66,000
Receivables	75,000	86,000
Cash and short-term investments	30,000	8,000
	167,000	160,000
Total assets	477,000	527,000
Called up share capital	100,000	100,000
Accumulated profits		
Brought forward	225,000	260,000
Retained for the year	35,000	22,000
Shareholders' funds	360,000	382,000
Bank loans	40,000	30,000
Current liabilities		
Bank overdraft	5,000	28,000
Trade payables	70,000	75,000
Other payables	2,000	12,000
	77,000	115,000
Total equity and liabilities	477,000	527,000

Note: Last year, bank loan repayments totalled $10,000. **(10 marks)**

For a suggested answer, see the 'Answers' section at the end of the book.

Chapter 8

DEBT COLLECTION

This chapter looks at how debts are collected and what companies do about bad debts and doubtful debts.

This chapter covers Syllabus parts D4, F1, F3 and F4.

CONTENTS

LEARNING OUTCOMES

At the end of this chapter you should be able to:

- Identify the main contents of accounts receivables records
- Describe the main internal sources that may be used to monitor accounts receivables (including aged trade receivables analysis, average periods of credit, incidence of bad debts)
- Describe ways in which credit customers could be encouraged to pay promptly, including effects of offering discounts
- Identify the main methods used to identify potential problems with credit customers meeting their payment obligations
- Describe the main techniques and methods that may be used to assist in the collection of overdue debts
- Describe how factoring works and the main types of service provided by factors
- Define invoice discounting and outline how this form of factoring works
- Calculate the cost of factoring arrangements, invoice discounting and changes in credit policy
- Outline the basic legal procedures for the collection of debts
- Explain bankruptcy and insolvency
- Identify debt recovery methods appropriate to individual customers
- Explain procedures for writing off debts (double entry recording is excluded).

1 THE NEED FOR EFFICIENCY IN COLLECTING DEBTS

It is tempting to think that a business makes its profits when it makes a sale, but this is not true. If a customer buys on credit but then fails to pay the debt, there will be a loss, and not a profit, on the sale. If a customer pays late, the cash flows of the business will be worse than they should be, and this means either extra cost in the form of a higher overdraft interest charge or the loss of investment income.

Collecting debts is therefore an extremely important function in any business that sells on credit. Effective debt collection helps to avoid losses and also improves liquidity and cash flow.

It is important to manage debt collection as efficiently as possible, to avoid unnecessary delays in collecting payment. The need for efficiency starts with sending out the invoices.

- Invoices should be sent out promptly, as soon as the sale is made. It is essential to minimise the time lag between delivery of the goods or service and invoicing, for example by streamlining authorisation and administrative procedures. The customer's period of credit starts from the date of the invoice, so the sooner the invoice goes out, the sooner the payment should come in. Some businesses might have an 'invoice run' every week, but longer delays in sending out invoices should not be acceptable. For example, if a business makes a sale and then waits three weeks before sending out the invoice, there will be a long delay in getting paid that could have been avoided. Small and medium-sized businesses can be badly-organised when it comes to sending out invoices with the minimum of delay!

- The customer's account should contain the invoicing address. Invoices should be sent to the person in the customer's organisation responsible for processing them. This is often the accounts department. However, delays can arise simply because the authorised person in the customer organisation has not received the invoice.

- Another delay can arise when the customer queries the invoice or makes a complaint about the goods or services delivered. The customer is unlikely to pay the invoice until the query or complaint has been dealt with. It is therefore important to respond to customers promptly, and try to resolve the problem quickly. The collections staff should be notified of any unresolved difficulties so that they can monitor the situation.

- Some customers do not decide which invoices to pay until they have received and checked a statement. Sending out statements regularly should therefore be an element of the standard debt collection procedures.

1.1 INTERNAL CONTROLS AND AUTHORISATION

There should be internal controls over debt collection, to prevent error and fraud, and areas of authority should be specified, to indicate what individuals can and cannot do. For example specific individuals should have the responsibility for opening bank accounts, banking payments received, signing cheques, counter-signing cheques, granting credit to customers, recording payments received and discounts allowed in the receivables ledger, invoicing, and so on.

Responsibility and delegated authority relating to the management and control of receivables could include:

Dealing with cash from receivables

- Receiving cash from customers (opening the post).
- Paying the cash into the bank.
- Writing up the cash book and receivables ledger.
- Having the keys or duplicate keys to the office safe.

Granting credit

- Vetting applicants for credit.
- Checking orders/credit limits and giving the go-ahead for granting credit and giving terms of payment.

Documentation

- Authorising invoices and credit notes.
- Issuing invoices and credit notes.

Others

- Writing off irrecoverable debts.
- Offering cash discounts.

1.2 PREVENTING CREDIT LIMITS FROM BEING EXCEEDED

Credit limits should be controlled properly, and additional sales to a customer refused if the credit limit would be exceeded. When a new order is received, checks should be made with the customers' account in the receivables ledger before delivery/fulfilment of the order is authorised. In cases where the amount outstanding would exceed the credit limit if the order went ahead, the credit control department could request full or part-payment in advance, as the circumstances dictate.

1.3 RELATIONSHIPS

It can be very useful to have a good working relationship with your customer's accounts department. This will ensure that any payment problems are normally quickly resolved.

If a payment is late, it is much easier to call the customer if you know him or her well, than if the relationship is more distant and formal. However, a good working relationship calls for mutual trust and respect, and this can take quite a long time to build up.

1.4 KNOWING CUSTOMERS' 'PASS FOR PAYMENT' SYSTEMS

Most firms and other organisations in both the private or public sectors operate a 'pass for payment' system.

Definition A **pass for payment system** is a system in which several checks are made before an invoice is authorised for payment.

The checks involved could include:

- comparing invoice details with the original order
- checking with the delivery note/goods received notes to ensure the goods have in fact been received
- checking the calculations of sales tax (VAT), discounts, denomination of quantity, etc.
- where appropriate, compare with estimates/tenders received, etc.
- ensuring that the goods have been received by the stores or that the service to be paid for has been performed to the satisfaction of internally appointed inspectors.

These procedures take time to carry out, and invoices may be processed in batches at certain times of the month. It could well happen that if an invoice arrives as little as one day later, it could miss out on being included in the next batch of invoices to be processed. It could be very useful to find out about a customer's payment systems and then make sure that invoices arrive before the appropriate deadlines, so that they can be processed quickly. This should help to reduce the lead times that customers take to process invoices and pass them for payment.

Information about customer pass for payment systems may not always be easy to obtain. However, where the firm has established a good working relationship with a customer's accounts department, it may be possible to obtain enough information to arrange the timing of invoices.

1.5 PAYMENT METHODS

Many business customers pay by cheque or by credit card. A problem for the supplier with these methods of payment is that the customer can choose when to make the payment. It might be possible to agree other methods of payment, whereby the supplier has more control over the timing of payments.

- For regular payments, such as rent and insurance premiums, or electricity, gas and water bills to domestic customers, it might be possible to encourage the customer to pay by direct debit or standing order. The supplier should then be fairly certain of receiving payments on the due dates.
- For business customers buying regularly, it might be possible to persuade the customer to make payments by bank transfer using BACS (Bankers Automated Clearing System). Businesses that use BACS to pay employees and regular suppliers often have a monthly 'payment run', at the time they pay the monthly salaries to employees. This arrangement could improve the likelihood that invoices will be paid on time, as part of the customer's established payments procedures. If a customer then fails to pay on the date for the monthly BACS run, debt collection staff can chase the customer to find out the reason for non-payment.

2 DEBT COLLECTION AND THE RECEIVABLES LEDGER

It is perhaps an obvious point to make, but the receivables ledger is fundamental to efficient debt collection. The receivables ledger includes an individual account for each credit customer, showing details of sales to the customers, payments, sales returns and discounts taken. The details in a customer account can be used to provide information such as which invoices have been paid and which are still unpaid, the dates of the invoices, the credit terms to the customer, the contact name and address for the customer's business.

Collections staff need this information to do their job properly.

The receivables ledger can also be used to produce an aged receivables list (described later), which is a useful report for monitoring debt collection and deciding how to chase unpaid debts.

3 PROCEDURES FOR COLLECTING OVERDUE DEBTS

When a business uses its in-house staff to collect debts, there should be clear policy guidelines and procedures instructing staff what should be done – and when – to make sure that debts are collected. The longer a debt is allowed to go unpaid, the higher the probability of eventual default. A systematic progression of follow-up procedures is therefore required, bearing in mind the risk of offending a valued customer to the point where their business is lost.

Collection procedures for overdue debts vary between different organisations, but will involve the following measures.

3.1 STATEMENTS

Definition A **statement** to a customer shows details of transactions between the business and the customer since the last statement was produced. It shows the unpaid balance brought forward from the last statement, plus details of invoices for goods supplied on credit, credit notes, discounts taken and payments received, and the balance outstanding at the end of the period. Many companies send them out to credit customers at the end of each month.

The use of statements has been found to be valuable aid to credit control.

Customers often wait until they receive a statement before they pay and use them, in part, as a double check on the amount owing. The statement may also have a remittance advice attached. This gives details of the balance outstanding and should be detached by the customer and sent back to the company concerned together with the payment.

Customers might also use a statement to decide which invoices to pay, or as a prompt to raise any query with the supplier about the details of an invoice. (It might seem improbable, but it is actually quite common for a customer to admit to not knowing what she has paid and what she hasn't paid, and so would like to receive a statement to sort the matter out!)

3.2 REMINDER LETTERS

When a debt becomes overdue, a reminder letter can be sent out. This is simply a letter reminding the customer that the payment is overdue, and asking for immediate payment. Reminder letters are often regarded as being a relatively poor way of obtaining payment, as many customers simply ignore them. However, they might be a necessary option for businesses with large numbers of credit customers for small amounts of debt, such as electricity supply companies and telephone companies.

A collection system might provide for a series of reminder letters. The first letter should be polite, courteous and to the point. The might be a second reminder letter, which is more forceful in its language. The final letter should use much stronger language and possibly threaten further action if the debt is not paid.

Final reminder letters are sometimes called 'red letters' because at one time, they were often printed in red ink. A telephone company can threaten disconnection if a debt is not paid. Other businesses could threaten legal action, but it is probably unwise to warn about such action unless there is a real intention to carry out the threat.

A typical first reminder letter could be drafted, as follows:

Leswick Co
4 Westcroft Court
Huntingdon

Accounts Dept
RY Co
Hardup House
2 Debt Alley
London SE2 4RR

April 20X4

Dear Sir or Madam

We would like to point out that our invoice number X01712 dated 19 January 20X4 for $12,100 has now been outstanding for over two months and we would be pleased if you would settle it within the next fourteen days.

If there are any problems concerning this invoice, will you please contact Brian Nile in our accounts department?

Yours faithfully,

T Watts
Credit Controller

3.3 TELEPHONE CALLS

Making telephone calls to the customer are more expensive than reminder letters but where large sums are involved they can be an efficient way of speeding up payment. You will also find out why the customers have not paid, and it could even be your fault. For example a customer could be waiting for a credit note before he pays the balance on the account. The impact of making telephone calls can be noticeable, making it an effective method of chasing debts.

Some computerised systems, in addition to producing aged lists of receivables (described later), also print out the telephone number of debts over a certain age. This is rather like saying to the credit control department/accounts department, 'ring them up as soon as you can, and find out the reasons why they have not paid'. In such cases it may be possible to at least get a payment on account and sort out how and when the balance will be forthcoming.

Customers might make excuses, such as 'The payment is in the post' or 'I shall send you a cheque today', but if he is chased often enough, he will run out of excuses. Making phone calls is therefore only effective if the caller is prepared to be persistent. An effective debt collector is therefore often a person with the character to keep up the pressure on a customer, and not take 'no' for an answer.

3.4 STOP ORDERS

At some stage, if a debt is still unpaid, a business must decide that no further goods or services can be sold to the customer until a payment is made. When such a decision is taken, a STOP order is issued.

- The customer's account should be noted to show that no further orders should be accepted until the stop order is lifted.
- The customer should be notified.
- Even more important, sales staff within the organisation should be notified, so that they do not agree to any further sales. In some businesses, the sales department has a 'stop list', showing customers who cannot at the moment make any purchases. When a new stop order is made, the list should be updated.
- As well as notifying sales staff, it might also be necessary to inform other individuals within the organisation. For example, the business might offer a maintenance support service to the customer. If so, the maintenance department should be informed, so that they can refuse any request from the customer for assistance.

3.5 CHARGING INTEREST ON OVERDUE ACCOUNTS

Some businesses charge interest on overdue payments, if the customer has been notified in advance that this is a term of the contract. The threat of charging interest can have an effect, and persuade a customer to pay. However, collecting the interest charge is not so easy. When the customer eventually pays, she is likely to refuse to pay the interest charge, and the supplier then has the problem of deciding whether to chase the customer for the interest. It is not usually worth the effort needed to chase the payment or the bad feeling it will create.

3.6 DEBT COLLECTION AGENCIES

An unpaid debt might be put into the hands of a debt collection agency, if it is unpaid after a certain length of time. Debt collection agencies offer a debt collection service on either a fixed fee basis or on 'no collection, no charge' terms. The quality of service can vary considerably between agencies, and care should be taken in selecting an agent. Using a poor-quality agent could seriously damage the relationship between the business and its customer.

3.7 LEGAL ACTION

Legal action is a last resort. A **solicitor's letter** often prompts payment and many cases do not go to court. The threat of court action in a solicitor's letter can often persuade a customer to pay up. However court action is usually not worth the time and expense, particularly if the customer doesn't have the money to pay.

Even so, some businesses might decide that they have a 'moral responsibility' to pursue a dishonest customer, even if they do not expect to benefit financially from their action.

Legal measures to obtain payment are explained in more detail later.

ACTIVITY 1

A company offers standard credit terms to customers of 30 days net.

Required:

Suggest the procedures the company might adopt for collecting unpaid debts, using the table below for your answer.

Number of weeks after the due payment date	Action

Note: There isn't a 'right' and 'wrong' answer to this activity, and your solution might differ from the one we provide.

For a suggested answer, see the 'Answers' section at the end of the book.

3.8 KEEPING INDIVIDUALS INFORMED

It is important for the credit controller to keep other individuals within the organisation informed about any developments that can affect their work. In particular, if there is a sales force, it is important to keep the sales department notified of any developments. If there is a problem with the non-payment of a debt, a sales representative could be asked to contact the customer and discuss the problem. If a stop order is issued prohibiting any further sales to the customer, the sales force should be informed immediately.

If the unpaid debt is large, senior management should also be notified, because of the potential risk of losses from an irrecoverable debt.

We can conclude, therefore, that the collection procedures used should be appropriate to the circumstances of the business, and in many cases the circumstances of the individual customer. Legal action should only ever be a last resort, because it can be slow and expensive, and not always effective in collecting money.

Selecting the most appropriate collection procedures, and knowing when to use them, is by no means an easy task. A person responsible for collections should apply the company procedures, and should always deal courteously with customers (no matter how annoying they might seem). However, doing the job effectively often comes gradually with experience and by getting to know your customers.

4 CREDIT INSURANCE

Credit insurance can be purchased to obtain protection against the non-payment of debts by customers. An insurance company will be prepared to provide insurance, but only for approved debts.

When an insured debt is unpaid and, under the terms of the insurance policy becomes an irrecoverable debt, the insurance company will pay for the loss. For the cost of the insurance premium, a business can therefore eliminate irrecoverable debt risk (credit risk).

Example

A business might be about to sell goods to a customer for $20,000, and is interested in buying credit insurance for the debt. An insurance company has indicated that it will insure 90% of the debt for a premium of $600.

By paying $600 for insurance, the business will have net receipts of $19,400 if the customer pays. If the customer fails to pay, the insurance company will pay for $18,000 of the loss, giving the business net receipts of $17,400.

A company can choose to obtain credit insurance:

- for all its credit sales, on a regular basis. The insurance company will not wish to approve every invoice but will want to impose limits on the total amount of credit that can be insured
- for selected parts of its business operations
- for occasional, large-value invoices. These are approved by the insurance company as part of the process of arranging the insurance policy.

5 FACTORING DEBTS

Many businesses use their own staff to collect debts. However, other arrangements can be made and other debt collection methods used. These include using the services of a factor.

Definition A **factor** is a financial institution that accelerates the cash conversion cycle for client companies, allowing them to gain access to receivables more quickly than if they waited for the normal trade credit period to elapse.

There are three elements to a factor's services:

- **Providing finance.** A factor provides short-term finance to a business, based on the value of its unpaid invoices. A factor will pay an agreed proportion of the value of new invoices as soon as they are sent out to customers. It is repaid when the debt is eventually collected.

- **Administration of the sales ledger.** A factor also takes over the responsibility for administering the client's receivables ledger and debt collection procedures.

- **Credit protection.** A factor might also agree to insure the debts of a client against irrecoverable debt risk. If a customer becomes an irrecoverable debt, the factor takes the loss.

Some companies realise that, although it is necessary to extend trade credit to customers for competitive reasons, they need payment earlier than agreed in order to assist their own cash flow. Factors exist to help such companies.

Factoring is most suitable for:

- small and medium-sized firms which often cannot afford sophisticated credit and sales accounting systems, and

- firms that are expanding rapidly. These often have a substantial and growing investment in inventory and receivables, which can be turned into cash by factoring the debts. Factoring debts can be a more flexible source of financing working capital than an overdraft or bank loan.

Conclusion Factoring is primarily designed to allow companies to accelerate cash flow, providing finance against outstanding trade receivables. This improves cash flow and liquidity.

5.1 A FACTOR'S SERVICES

As stated above, a factor's services consist of providing short-term finance, receivables ledger administration and debt collection, and credit protection. The provision of finance and the debt collection services are closely linked, although there are separate charges for each of these services. A factor only provides finance on condition that it can collect the debts.

Occasionally, a factor will provide a sales ledger administration service without providing short-term finance, but this type of arrangement (called 'service factoring') is less common than a finance-plus-receivables ledger administration service.

Factoring can be arranged on either a 'without recourse' basis or a 'with recourse' basis.

- When factoring is without recourse or 'non-recourse', the factor provides protection for the client against irrecoverable debts. The factor has no 'come-back' or recourse to the client if a customer defaults. When a customer of the client fails to pay a debt, the factor bears the loss and the client receives the money from the debt.
- When the service is with recourse ('recourse factoring'), the client must bear the loss from any irrecoverable debt, and so has to reimburse the factor for any money it has already received for the debt.

Credit protection is provided only when the service is non-recourse.

5.2 RECEIVABLES LEDGER ADMINISTRATION

A factor assumes the various functions of receivables ledger administration, including:

- recording sales details in the receivables ledger (i.e. in the accounts of the individual customers)
- sending out statements
- sending out reminders
- collecting payment.

The factor might refer to this service as 'credit management and administration'. In some cases, the factor also sends out the invoices. However, it is more usual for the business (the factor's client) to send out the invoices, and to send a copy to the factor. The factor then enters the details in the receivables ledger. Invoices must specify clearly that payments must be made to the factor.

The benefits for the client are the cost savings from reducing in-house administration and access to a more efficient, specialist credit management team. This is particularly valuable to a young fast-growing company, which may outgrow its administration system and otherwise be exposed to the liquidity risks of over-trading.

The fee for such an administration service would lie in the range of 0.75% to 2.5% of the value of sales revenue handled.

A company with about 50 customers, sending out 1,000 invoices a year and with annual sales revenue of $1 million might pay 1% or $10,000 a year.

5.3 CREDIT PROTECTION FROM A FACTOR

The factor can also provide a credit protection and evaluation service for clients, analysing customer characteristics before deciding on their creditworthiness.

When factoring is without recourse, the factor is providing credit protection. Under this arrangement, the factor requires total control of credit approval and decides the credit limits for each customer of the client.

(When factoring is with recourse, most factors do not insist on setting the credit limits for the client's customers because the client must bear the loss from any irrecoverable debt.)

The typical charge for credit protection ranges from 0.5% to 2% of annual sales revenue.

Example

Edden is a medium-sized company producing a range of engineering products which it sells to wholesale distributors. Recently, its sales have begun to rise rapidly due to economic recovery. However, it is concerned about its liquidity position and is looking ways of improving cash flow.

Its annual sales are $16 million, and average receivables are $3.3 million (representing about 75 days of sales).

One way of speeding up collection from receivables is to use a factor. The factor will operate on a service-only basis, administering and collecting payment from Edden's customers. This is expected to generate administrative savings of $100,000 each year. The factor has undertaken to pay outstanding debts after 45 days, regardless of whether the customers have actually paid or not. The factor will make a service charge of 1.75% of Edden's turnover. Edden can borrow at an interest rate of 8% per annum.

Required:

Determine the relative costs and benefits of using the factor.

Solution

Reduction in receivables collection period = (75 – 45) = 30 days

Reduction in receivables = $\frac{30}{365} \times \$16\text{m} = \$1{,}315{,}068$

Interest saving = (8% × $1,315,068) = $105,205, say $105,000

Administrative savings = $100,000

Service charge = (1.75% × $16m) = $280,000

Summary	$
Service charge	(280,000)
Interest saved by reducing receivables	105,000
Administration costs saved	100,000
Net annual cost of the service	(75,000)

Edden will have to balance this cost against the security offered by improved cash flows and greater liquidity.

5.4 PROVISION OF FINANCE – FACTORING

Definition **Finance factoring** is where the factor makes a cash advance to the client, as well as conducting receivables ledger administration and debt collection services.

A factor will advance money to a client, based on a proportion (usually 80% to 85%) of approved invoices. Approved invoices are invoices to customers within credit limits. For example, a company with sales on 30-day credit terms from reliable customers of $500,000 per month might receive an advance of $400,000 (80%) each month. Interest is charged on the money advanced. If the factor is a subsidiary of a bank, the interest rate is typically 1.5% to 3% above the bank's base rate, and charged on a daily basis.

When the customer eventually pays the debt to the factor, the client receives the balance of the payment less interest and other charges from the factor.

The following diagram shows how this operates.

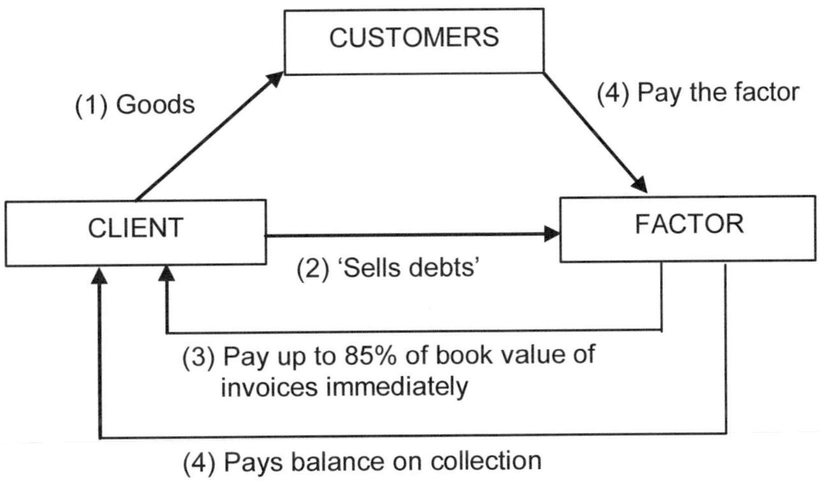

5.5 NON-RECOURSE FACTORING: HOW THE FULL SERVICE WORKS

It might help now to go through the stages in a non-recourse factoring service, to see how all three services of the factor can link together.

- Most factoring agreements cover all sales by the client's business. The factor decides the credit limits for each customer of the client.
- The client business makes a sale and produces the invoice. (In some cases, the factor might produce the invoice itself from data supplied by the client.) The invoice must make it clear that payment must be made to the factor.
- The invoice goes to the customer and a copy goes to the factor.
- The factor is responsible for receivables ledger administration, and recording the sale and debt in the customer's account in the receivables ledger.
- The factor pays the client an agreed percentage amount of the invoice, typically 80% to 85% of the invoice value. (**Note:** Typically, the client will produce a number of invoices at the same time, so the factor provides finance for a number of invoices.) Payment of this advance is usually made within 24 hours.

- The factor issues statements to customers and collects payments. The debt collection service includes contacting late payers and chasing payment of overdue debts. (This happens with recourse factoring as well as non-recourse factoring.)

- When the factor receives payment, the factor pays the client the balance of the invoice amount, less charges.

- The factor provides regular reports on the status of the client's receivables ledger, and the client can usually access customer account information on-line.

5.6 GETTING STARTED WITH A FACTOR

When a business decides that it wants to use the services of a factor, it has to find a factor willing to adopt it as a client that will provide the type of service that the business wants. There is a Factors and Discounters Association which provides a list of factors, with contact numbers.

Alternatively, a business can obtain advice from a factoring broker, who might also be able to arrange a better deal. Most brokers do not charge clients for their service, because they get paid commission by the factoring company.

What the factor looks for in a client business

When a business asks a factor to provide a factoring service, the factor will check the accounts of the business to find out whether it meets the factor's criteria for taking on a client.

- Most companies that use factoring have an annual sales revenue of at least $200,000.

- Some factors are willing to take on start-up businesses as clients or businesses with an annual sales revenue of as little as $50,000.

- The business should not have just a small number of customers. In general, no single customer should account for more than 25% to 40% of the annual sales revenue.

- On the other hand, if there are large numbers of small-value invoices, factoring could be uneconomical.

- Factors prefer businesses that offer the standard credit terms for the industry.

Before signing up with a factor

A business should confirm before signing any agreement with a factor that the factor can provide all the services it requires at an acceptable price. It is worth going into the detail of how the system will work.

- If the factor is providing a non-recourse factoring service, it will want to set the credit terms for each of the client's customers, using its own credit assessment system. A business should want to find out details of how credit limits will be set and how quickly applications for credit from new customers will be processed. If the business wants to increase the credit limit for a particular customer, will the factor be willing to agree?

- How will the factor chase overdue debts? In the case of seriously overdue debts, will the factor want to issue STOP instructions to the client, to prevent further credit sales to the customer? Will the factor take customers to court?

- How will disputed invoices be handled?

- How will the factor and the business communicate with each other? Will there be an on-line connection for information transmission?

The factor's fees and charges are negotiable, and it might be possible to obtain better terms through negotiation, especially if the business is profitable and expanding, offering the factor the prospect of a larger volume of business in the future.

It is also sensible to check the terms and conditions for terminating the agreement with the factor. There may be a notice period, which is typically three months and a cancellation fee.

5.7 ADVANTAGES OF FACTORING AND PROBLEMS WITH FACTORING

Advantages of factoring

The benefits of factoring are as follows:

- A business improves its cash flow, because the factor provides finance for up to 80% or more of debts within 24 hours of the invoices being issued. A bank providing an overdraft facility secured against a company's unpaid invoices will normally lend up to 50% only of the invoice value. (Factors will provide 80% or so because they set credit limits and are responsible for collecting the debts.)

- A factor saves the administration costs of keeping the receivables ledger up-to-date and the costs of debt collection.

- A business can use the factor's credit control system to assess the creditworthiness of both new and existing customers.

- Non-recourse factoring is a convenient way of obtaining insurance against bad debts.

Problems with factoring

Although factors provide valuable services, companies are sometimes wary about using them. A possible problem with factoring is that the intervention of the factor between the factor's client and the client's customers (receivables) could endanger trading relationships and damage goodwill. Customers might prefer to deal with the business, not a factor.

When a non-recourse factoring service is used, the client loses control over decisions about granting credit to its customers.

For this reason, some clients prefer to retain the risk of irrecoverable debts, and opt for a 'with recourse' factoring service. With this type of service, the client and not the factor decides whether extreme action (legal action) should be taken against a non-payer.

On top of this, when suppliers and customers of the client find out that the client is using a factor to collect debts, it may arouse fears that the company is beset by cash flow problems, raising fears about its viability. If so, its suppliers may impose more stringent payment terms, thus negating the benefits provided by the factor.

Using a factor can therefore create problems with customers who may resent being chased for payment by a third party, and may question the supplier's financial stability.

Finally, ending a factoring arrangement can be difficult, because a business must either switch to another factor or buy back its receivables ledger from the factor. This will cost money and in the short run it will result in more receivables and the risk of a shortfall in cash flow and liquidity.

ACTIVITY 2

The outstanding balances on a company's receivables ledger total $125,000, representing three months' sales. A factor will operate the ledger on a non-recourse basis, for an annual charge of 2% of sales revenue. There is a danger of loss of business if it is generally known that the firm is using a factor: annual sales revenue could fall by $30,000 and annual cash profits are 50% of sales. Using the factor would generate annual administration savings of $20,000. Irrecoverable debts currently run at 3% of sales revenue.

Required:

Assess whether it is financially worth using the factor. For the purpose of this activity, you should ignore interest costs.

For a suggested answer, see the 'Answers' section at the end of the book.

ACTIVITY 3

A company has monthly credit sales of $200,000, and it gives customers 60 days credit. All customers take the full credit allowed. It has irrecoverable debts each year amounting to about 2.5% of sales revenue. It operates with a bank overdraft and pays interest at 8% on its overdraft balance.

The company's management is considering whether to use a factor to collect is debts, under a non-recourse factoring arrangement. A factor has indicated that it will take over the administration of the receivables ledger and debt collection for a fee of 2% of annual credit sales revenue. This would save the company internal operating costs of $30,000 each year.

The factor would also charge 1.5% of sales revenue for credit insurance.

The factor will advance 80% of the value of invoices as soon as they are sent out, and charge interest at 7.75%.

If the services of the factor are used, it is anticipated that there will be no change in annual sales revenue and no change in the collection period of 60 days.

Required:

Assess the financial consequences of using the factor for non-recourse factoring and factor finance.

For a suggested answer, see the 'Answers' section at the end of the book.

5.8 EXPORT FACTORING

Export factoring is a factoring service where the debts are for customers in other countries. The service can be a great benefit to firms selling abroad, because the factor takes on the task of collecting the payments. Obtaining payment from customers in other countries is often far more difficult than getting payment from 'domestic' customers.

The cost of export factoring is a bit higher than the cost of domestic factoring, and the factor's services include credit protection. Credit protection from a factor can be cheaper than normal export credit insurance from an insurance company.

6 INVOICE DISCOUNTING

Definition **Invoice discounting** is a method of raising finance against the security of receivables without using the receivables ledger administration services of a factor.

Firms of factors will also provide invoice discounting to clients.

With invoice discounting, the business retains control over its receivables ledger, and confidentiality in its dealings with customers.

- The business sends out invoices, statements and reminders in the normal way, and collects the debts. With 'confidential invoice discounting', its customers are unaware that the business is using invoice discounting.
- The invoice discounter provides cash to the business for a proportion of the value of the invoice, as soon as it receives a copy of the invoice and agrees to discount it. The discounter will advance cash up to 80% of face value.
- When the business eventually collects the payment from its customer, the money must be paid into a bank account controlled by the invoice discounter. The invoice discounter then pays the business the remainder of the invoice, less interest and administration charges.

Invoice discounting can help a business that is trying to improve its cash flows, but does not want a factor to administer its receivables ledger and collect its debts. It is therefore equivalent to the financing service provided by a factor.

Administration charges for this service are around 0.5–1% of a client's sales revenue. It is more risky than factoring since the client retains control over its credit policy. Consequently, such facilities are usually confined to established companies with an annual sales revenue above $500,000, and the business must be profitable. Interest costs are usually in the range 3–4% above base rate, although larger companies and those which arrange credit insurance may receive better terms.

The invoice discounter will check the receivables ledger of the client regularly, perhaps every three months, to check that its debt collection procedures are adequate.

6.1 HOW INVOICE DISCOUNTING WORKS – EXAMPLE

At the beginning of August, Basildon Co sells goods for a total value of $300,000 to regular customers but decides that it requires payment earlier than the agreed 30-day credit period for these invoices. A discounter agrees to finance 80% of their face value, i.e. $240,000. Interest is 9% p.a. The invoices were due for payment in early September, but were subsequently settled in mid-September, exactly 45 days after the initial transactions. The invoice discounter's service charge is 1%. A special account is set up with a bank, into which all payments are made. The sequence of cash flows is:

August	Basildon receives cash advance of $240,000	
Mid-September	Customers pay $300,000	
	Invoice discounter receives the full $300,000, paid into the special bank account	
	Basildon receives the balance payable receivable less charges, i.e.	
	Service fee = 1% × $300,000 =	$3,000
	Interest = 9% × $240,000 × 45/365 =	$2,663
	Total charges	$5,663
	Basildon receives:	
	Balance of payment from customer	$60,000
	Less charges	$5,663
		$54,337
Summary	Total receipts by Basildon: $240,000 + $54,337	$294,337
	Invoice discounter's fee and interest charges	$5,633

ACTIVITY 4

Distinguish between factoring and invoice discounting, explaining the benefits that companies obtain from each.

For a suggested answer, see the 'Answers' section at the end of the book.

7 MONITORING DEBT COLLECTION: ANALYSING INFORMATION ABOUT RECEIVABLES

In addition to having established procedures for chasing late payers, credit controllers should also monitor the credit situation continually. There are several reasons for needing to monitor receivables.

- The overall situation on receivables should be kept under review, to make sure that debt collection procedures appear to be working. Any signs of slower payments from customers should be identified as soon as possible, so that swift corrective measures can be taken.

- The position with regard to individual customers should also be kept under review. If some customers are regular late payers, the credit controller should consider whether any suitable measures can be used to improve the payments pattern without antagonising the customer. If a customer has an excellent payment record, it might be worthwhile informing the sales team, so that more credit can be offered to encourage the customer to buy more. The measures that ought to be taken for each customer are likely to vary with circumstances, and with the judgement of the credit controllers.

- At some stage, decisions have to be taken about making allowances for receivables or writing off irrecoverable debts.

Methods of monitoring receivables include:

- measuring days sales outstanding (DSO), and trends in DSO

- producing aged receivables lists regularly, for detailed information about overdue debts.

These methods (internal sources of information) can be supplemented by other information from external sources, such as credit references, bank references and monitoring press reports on the customer to evaluate its ongoing creditworthiness (all covered in more detail in Chapter 7 of this Text).

All these methods of monitoring allow the credit control team to identify problems and consider appropriate measures to resolve them.

8 DAYS SALES OUTSTANDING (DSO)

In earlier chapters, two of the financial ratios described were receivables collection period and payables payment period. These are measurements of the average credit period given to customers and received from trade payables.

Receivables collection period and payables payment period are usually measured by taking average receivables and average trade payables.

$$\text{Receivables collection period} = \frac{\text{Average receivables}}{\text{Sales for the year}} \times 365 \text{ days}$$

$$\text{Payables payment period} = \frac{\text{Average trade payables}}{\text{Cost of sales for the year}} \times 365 \text{ days}$$

Days sales outstanding (DSO) is similar to receivables collection period, except that the figure used for receivables is the current level of receivables.

DSO is used by credit controllers to check on the current level of receivables, and to assess whether the average collection period is getting shorter, longer or staying about the same.

$$\text{DSO} = \frac{\text{Current receivables}}{\text{Sales for the year}} \times 365 \text{ days}$$

Another way of measuring DSO, when monthly sales fluctuate with seasonal variations, is to work out how many recent months of sales volume is represented by the current receivables level.

Example

The monthly sales of GHB Co vary from month to month with seasonal demand. Credit sales for the past few months have been as follows:

	$
January	350,000
February	40,000
March	120,000
April	240,000
May	220,000

Receivables at the end of May are $520,000.

Required:

Calculate the days sales outstanding as at the end of May.

Solution

When sales vary from month to month, DSO is calculated by assuming that the current receivables represent the most recent credit sales.

The receivables of $520,000 at the end of May therefore represent the following sales:

	Sales in month	**Cumulative**	
	$	$	
May	220,000	220,000	
April	240,000	460,000	
March	60,000	520,000	(balance)

The receivables therefore represent all sales in May and April, and $60,000 of sales in March, which are one half of March sales. DSO are therefore 2.5 months. If we assume a 30-day month, we can say that days sales outstanding are 75 days (30 × 2.5).

Management can monitor the trend in DSO, and if the trend is worsening, or if the collection period seems unacceptably long, measures for improving the speed of payments can be considered.

ACTIVITY 5

A company currently has outstanding debts of $425,000 owed by its customers. Its sales for the past four months have been:

Month	**Sales**
	$
September	420,000
October	503,000
November	210,000
December	103,000

Required:

Calculate the current days sales outstanding. Assume a 30-day month.

For a suggested answer, see the 'Answers' section at the end of the book.

9 AGED DEBTS (RECEIVABLES) ANALYSIS

Definition An **aged debts analysis** (or an aged receivables list) is a report showing the total amount of debts owed to the business, analysed between debts that are not yet due for payment and payments that are overdue. Overdue payments are also categorised according to the length of time for which payment has been due.

An aged debts report can be produced for receivables in total, for management information purposes.

A report can also be produced providing an aged debts analysis for each individual customer. This type of report is used by credit controllers to:

- identify problems customers, and
- consider measures for dealing with them.

An aged debts analysis for individual customers give the organisation an indication of the time being taken by each customer to pay debts, and also of any problem debts that there might be, i.e. any potential irrecoverable debts.

9.1 LAYOUT

An aged debts analysis might be set out in the following manner:

Credit customer	**Total owing**	**Outstanding for:**			
		Less than (<) 30 days	**30–60 days**	**61–90 days**	**More than (>) 90 days**
	$	$	$	$	$
C N Lawson Co	551.86	279.30	272.56	–	–
Grainger Co	713.59	–	–	279.03	434.56
Burdon Co	518.47	219.50	248.30	50.67	–
P Roper	700.00	450.00	–	–	250.00
Total	2,483.92	948.80	520.86	329.70	684.56

This indicates the amount of each total debt that relates to each period of time.

When standard credit terms are 30 days, most organisations would normally hope for the majority of their debts to be clustered in the 'less than 30 days' category and only a few debts outstanding for more than that period.

For a large receivables ledger it is common practice to calculate totals and percentages for each of the overdue columns and monitor the 'ageing' of the ledger in total. This analysis can then be compared to stated credit terms. A high percentage in the 30–60 day column would be of no concern to an organisation offering terms of 30 days following month of invoice but would be of concern if standard terms were 'net 14 days'.

9.2 INTERPRETING AND USING AN AGED DEBT ANALYSIS

Aged debt analyses are produced for the management of an organisation in order to provide them with information about the payment patterns of customers.

Example

The aged debts report shown is reproduced below, with percentages added. This can be used to make recommendations to a supervisor or senior manager in the organisation. Normal credit terms are 30 days.

Credit customer	**Total owing**	**Outstanding for:**			
		Less than (<) 30 days	**30–60 days**	**61–90 days**	**More than (>) 90 days**
	$	$	$	$	$
C N Lawson	551.86	279.30	272.56	–	–
Grainger Co	713.59	–	–	279.03	434.56
Burdon	518.47	219.50	248.30	50.67	–
P Roper	700.00	450.00	–	–	250.00
Total	2,483.92	948.80	520.86	329.70	684.56
Percentage	100%	38%	21%	13%	28%

This could possibly be interpreted as follows:

- C N Lawson would appear to pay its debts reasonably promptly as nothing has been owing for more than 60 days.
- Grainger's debts show a potentially rather worrying position. Most of the total debt has been owing for more than 90 days and the remainder for 60–90 days. As there are no more recent amounts owing, this suggests either that sales to this customer have been stopped or that the customer has chosen to stop buying.
- Burdon's debts show perhaps the most common position for a credit customer who tends to pay after about 60 days. Only a small amount of the debt has been outstanding for longer than this period.
- P Roper's debt is mainly less than 30 days old and so not yet due for payment. However, there is an unpaid amount of $250 over 90 days old. This could be a disputed invoice. It might be an invoice the customer has overlooked and we have failed to chase for payment.

Recommendations

1. **C N Lawson** and **Burdon**. We should continue to pursue normal debt collection procedures with these customers, and try to persuade them to pay earlier.
2. **Grainger.** It might be appropriate to ask a sales representative to visit this customer and find out more about the situation from the customer's point of view.
3. **P Roper.** Check whether there is a problem with the unpaid debt of $250 and see if it is something that can be resolved.

4 The company's normal credit terms are 30 days, but **only 38% of outstanding receivables are for 30 days or less**. This means that 62% of debts are overdue for payment. This suggests that we should be reviewing our debt collection procedures. Either they are not effective enough, or they are not being applied properly by debt collection staff.

5 The offer of **settlement discounts** may also affect the aged debt analysis in that a greater proportion of customers would pay within the period qualifying them for a discount.

10 PREPARING AN AGED DEBTS (RECEIVABLES) ANALYSIS

If the accounting system is computerised, preparing an aged debts analysis is simply a matter of entering an instruction into the system with keyboard and mouse. However, you need to understand how it would be done in a manual accounting system. The process is much slower and more laborious!

The key records for preparing an aged receivables analysis are the individual customer accounts in the receivables ledger. Each account shows, for that customer, the date of invoices and credit notes issued and the dates of payments received and cash discounts allowed. From this, an aged debt analysis for the customer can be produced.

Example

Given below is the receivables ledger account for T K Glade as at 30 June 20X7.

T K Glade

		$			$
14 March	Inv 20391	48.39	30 April	Cash	64.90
29 March	Inv 20405	64.90	22 May	Cash	51.51
7 April	Inv 20436	13.28	31 May	Cash	17.38
15 April	Inv 20487	51.51	15 June	Cash	19.30
25 April	Inv 20511	17.38	28 June	Cash	80.00
3 May	Inv 20552	72.45			
27 May	Inv 20599	80.00			
6 June	Inv 20683	19.30			
15 June	Inv 20697	12.57			
20 June	Inv 20724	62.39	30 June	Balance c/d	209.08
		442.17			442.17

Note: 'Inv' means invoice number'.

Required:

Prepare an aged receivables analysis for T K Glade.

Solution

Step 1 The first step is to work out which invoices have been settled, by matching the invoices to the cash payments received, credit notes issued and discounts allowed. In this example, there are no credit notes or discounts, so the task is simply to match the payments received to the invoices.

T K Glade

		$				$	
14 March	Inv 20391	48.39		30 April	Cash	64.90	✓
29 March	Inv 20405	64.90	✓	22 May	Cash	51.51	✓
7 April	Inv 20436	13.28		31 May	Cash	17.38	✓
15 April	Inv 20487	51.51	✓	15 June	Cash	19.30	✓
25 April	Inv 20511	17.38	✓	28 June	Cash	80.00	✓
3 May	Inv 20552	72.45					
27 May	Inv 20599	80.00	✓				
6 June	Inv 20683	19.30	✓				
15 June	Inv 20697	12.57					
20 June	Inv 20724	62.39		30 June	Balance c/d	209.08	
		442.17				442.17	

Step 2 Next, analyse the remaining unpaid invoices according to their date. Today's date is 30 June. If we assume a 30-day month for convenience (which is normal):

- < 30 days = invoices with a June date
- 30–60 days = invoices with a May date
- 60–90 days = invoices with an April date
- > 90 days = invoices with a March date (or earlier).

	Date	**Amount**
		$
> 90 days	14 March	48.39
60–90 days	7 April	13.28
30–60 days	3 May	72.45
< 30 days	15 June	12.57
	20 June	62.39
		209.08

Step 3 We can now prepare an aged analysis report for this customer.

Customer	**Total owing**	**Outstanding for**			
		< 30 days	**30–60 days**	**60–90 days**	**> 90 days**
	$	$	$	$	$
T K Glade	209.08	74.96	72.45	13.28	48.39

In practice most of the customers with outstanding balances will have settled their accounts up to a particular date e.g. up to the date of the last but one statement or last but two statements. In these cases, only the invoices from these dates will be outstanding.

ACTIVITY 6

Given below are two receivables ledger accounts as at 31 March 20X4.

Gilde & Co

		$			$
20 Dec	Inv 2946	118.38	30 Jan	Credit note	172.48
28 Dec	Inv 2983	72.03	15 Feb	Cash	228.36
17 Jan	Inv 3029	228.36	28 Feb	Cash	72.03
25 Jan	Inv 3046	172.48	12 March	Cash	48.30
2 Feb	Inv 3103	48.30	14 March	Credit note	49.20
11 Feb	Inv 3135	69.02			
26 Feb	Inv 3157	159.27			
12 March	Inv 3204	49.20			
15 March	Inv 3221	49.20			
28 March	Inv 3252	169.39	31 March	Balance c/d	565.26
		1,135.63			1,135.63

Brandreth Co

		$			$
3 Jan	Inv 2999	378.29	12 Jan	Cash	363.16
12 Jan	Inv 3012	115.29	12 Jan	Discount	15.13
26 Jan	Inv 3047	39.20	25 Feb	Cash	398.59
13 Feb	Inv 3140	415.20	25 Feb	Discount	16.61
18 Feb	Inv 3145	415.20	28 Feb	Credit note	162.41
25 Feb	Inv 3156	162.41	28 Feb	Cash	115.29
4 March	Inv 3178	441.79	4 March	Credit note	39.20
18 March	Inv 3229	150.39	16 March	Cash	424.12
20 March	Inv 3237	66.20	16 March	Discount	17.67
27 March	Inv 3250	551.29	30 March	Cash	415.20
			31 March	Balance c/d	767.88
		2,735.26			2,735.26

Required:

Prepare an aged debt analysis for each customer and in total, using the following layout.

Customer	**Total owing**	**Outstanding for**			
		< 30 days	**30–60 days**	**60–90 days**	**> 90 days**
	$	$	$	$	$

For a suggested answer, see the 'Answers' section at the end of the book.

The preparation of an aged debts analysis should be done at frequent intervals e.g. monthly. It highlights problem customers, and in effect directs the energy and effort of the credit control function to the accounts that really need their attention. It provides a focus and forces them into action. Making good use of the aged analysis can provide an early warning of problems ahead, improve cash flow and reduce irrecoverable debts e.g. by talking to a customer before a minor problem becomes a major problem via granting a temporary increase in the credit period.

11 IRRECOVERABLE DEBTS AND ALLOWANCES FOR RECEIVABLES

An aged receivables analysis is a useful aid to management in making decisions about irrecoverable debts and allowances for receivables because it draws attention to problem customers and shows how much debt is seriously overdue.

Writing off irrecoverable debts and making allowances for receivables are essentially accounting measures rather than debt collection measures. When a debt is written off as irrecoverable, it does not mean necessarily that all efforts to collect it are brought to an end, although it could be a signal for taking an extreme measure. For example, when a debt is written off, it might be decided to apply to the court for a bankruptcy order against an individual customer or a winding up order against a company, or to put the debt into the hands of a debt collection agency.

Allowances for receivables are unnecessary until the organisation is preparing financial statements for the period, because making provisions is a step in the process of preparing a statement of profit or loss and statement of financial position.

- When a customer's debt is written off, it is decided that the debt is unlikely to be collected, and that it should therefore be removed from the customer's account in the receivables ledger. The customer might have gone into liquidation, or even disappeared without trace. In all probability, the customer's account will be closed. In the accounts, the debt is written off to an irrecoverable debts expenses account, and charged against profits for the period.

- When an allowance is made for a receivable, the business does not give up hope of collecting payment from the customer, and the debt remains in the customer's account in the receivables ledger. (In this respect, an irrecoverable debt and a receivables allowance are different.) However, it is recognised that the prospects for collecting payment are not good and in due course of time, the debt might have to be written off as irrecoverable.

11.1 DECIDING WHEN TO WRITE OFF AN IRRECOVERABLE DEBT

As indicated above, a decision to make an allowance for receivables is not necessary until the end of an accounting period. Writing off an irrecoverable debt, on the other hand, can happen at any time.

When a debt is written off, it has probably been outstanding for a very long time. The debt collection procedures might have a guidelines, for example, that debts should be written off when they are, say, 120 days overdue, unless there are good reasons for not writing it off.

Usually, the decision is taken by a senior manager, and the decision is notified to the accounts department (including debt collection staff) and the sales force, who should be told that the customer's account has been closed.

Each organisation has its own procedures about writing off irrecoverable debts. However, debts should not be written off until every effort has been made to collect the debt, especially when the amount involved is large.

Management might ask for a recommendation from the debt collection staff, saying that every effort has been made to collect the money, and indicating why the customer as not paid, before a decision is taken to write it off.

12 LEGAL ACTION: INTRODUCTION

You need to have some understanding of what happens when legal action is taken to collect an unpaid debt, and the effects of a customer's bankruptcy or insolvency.

Bankruptcy and insolvency are last-resort measures against a customer, and before a business takes action of this sort, it will have tried other legal measures to get the money. If a solicitor's letter threatening legal action has no effect on a non-paying customer, the next step could be to apply to the court for an order to the customer to pay the debt.

If the court makes such an order but the customer still does not pay, it is necessary to go back to the court for an enforcing order. Only if payment is still not forthcoming should bankruptcy or insolvency proceedings be taken.

- Bankruptcy occurs when an individual is unable to pay his or her debts, and the court makes a bankruptcy order against the individual. When such an order is made, measures are taken to raise as much money as possible by selling off the individual's assets, and distributing the amounts collected between all the unpaid payables.
- Insolvency occurs when a company is unable to pay its debts. Various legal measures can be taken by an unpaid payable. These include action to wind up the company and then dissolve it.

The rules governing bankruptcy and insolvency are governed by the Insolvency Act 1986.

Credit controllers need to know these rules for two reasons.

- The business might consider taking legal action to recover an unpaid debt. If so, it needs to know what measures can be taken, and what the consequences might be.
- Another individual or organisation might take legal action against a credit customer of your business. In such cases, you need to know your rights as an unpaid payable of the customer, and what needs to be done to make sure that your entitlement to payment is recognised in bankruptcy or insolvency proceedings.

13 TAKING LEGAL ACTION TO RECOVER AN UNPAID DEBT

As a last resort, legal action can be taken to obtain payment of a debt. However, making a claim through the courts can be time-consuming and there is no certainty that the action will be successful and result in payment. For example, the receivable might not have enough money or other assets to pay the debt. The services of a solicitor will be needed, and for debts of less than $5,000, the costs of the solicitor cannot be recovered from the 'opponent'.

A business might therefore consider legal action only in certain circumstances:

- when the amount of the debt is quite large
- as an example to other customers, and a warning of what could happen if they do not pay their debts.

To avoid such considerations, businesses sometimes insert 'retention of title' clauses into their sales contracts with customers. These ensure that the goods legally remain the property of the seller until the debt is paid, so mean that the seller will be able to take back the goods sold if the payment is not forthcoming.

Alternatively, a business might use a lien agreement, where again the seller is allowed to take back the goods if the payment is not made by the customer.

13.1 ADMINISTRATION ORDER

If legal action is taken against a customer, and the court agrees that the supplier is entitled to payment, the customer might be able to apply for an administration order if he is unable to pay the debt. The customer must have total debts of less than $5,000.

By applying for an administration order, the customer who owes money seeks the protection of the courts against further action by his payables. The court decides whether the arrangement will be fair to all the payables, and if it is satisfied it issues an administration order. Under this arrangement, the customer makes regular payments to the court, which are then used to settle the debts in a manner that is fair to all the payables.

If the customer subsequently fails to maintain the payments to the court, a payable can apply to the court again for a judgement order or a bankruptcy order.

13.2 COUNTY COURT JUDGEMENTS

When a claim is made through the courts, the County Court might issue a County Court Judgement, ordering the customer who owes money to pay either in full immediately or in instalments. The customer is then required to comply with the order.

13.3 WHAT HAPPENS IF THE SUPPLIER HAS A JUDGEMENT BUT THE CUSTOMER DOESN'T PAY?

If the court issues a County Court Judgement, it will not enforce the judgement if the customer fails to pay unless the supplier asks it to. The supplier who is owed money can try to enforce the judgement by applying to the court for any of the following:

- a warrant of execution
- an attachment of earnings order
- a third party debt order, also called a garnishee order
- a charging order.

The selection of which type of order to apply for will depend on the circumstances of each case.

A warrant of execution

A warrant of execution gives the court bailiff the authority to take goods from the customer's home or business. However, if the debt is for more than $5,000, the County Court cannot issue a warrant and instead the payable has to apply to the High Court to ask for the sheriff's officer to collect the money owed or remove goods belonging to the customer owing money.

Goods seized by the bailiff are sold at public auction and the money obtained is used to pay off the debt.

An attachment of earnings order

An attachment of earnings order might be appropriate where the customer is an employee (and not self-employed or unemployed). The order is sent to the customer's employer, instructing the employer to take an amount from the customer's wage or salary on each pay day. The money deducted is sent to a collection office, which then passes it on to the payable.

Third party debt order or garnishee order

A third party debt order is usually issued to prevent a customer who owed money from taking money out of a bank or building society account. On receiving the order, the bank or building society freezes the account, and the money in the account on that date is used to pay as much of the debt as possible.

Charging order

A charging order is an order made by the court that 'charges' a customer's property, such as her house or any stocks and shares she might own. When the charge is made on land (e.g. the customer's home), it must be registered with the Land Registry. This means that the customer cannot subsequently sell the land until the charge is removed. The effect of a charging order is that if the customer later sells the property, the unpaid supplier should receive payment out of the proceeds of the sale.

14 PERSONAL BANKRUPTCY

Another method of trying to obtain payment from an individual is to apply to the court for a bankruptcy order. The debt needs to be at least $750 before bankruptcy proceedings can be started.

- The unpaid payable must first serve a 'statutory demand' on the customer who owes money, explaining why the debt is due and that a court judgement has been obtained.
- If the debt is not paid within three weeks of serving the statutory demand, the payable can petition the court for a bankruptcy order against the customer.
- The court considers the petition at a hearing, and if it is satisfied, it issue the bankruptcy order.

A court will not issue a bankruptcy order if the debt is in dispute. For example, a supplier might apply for a bankruptcy order because of an unpaid debt of $1,500. If the customer successfully claims that there is a dispute about the payment (for example, because the supplier had failed to supply goods of a suitable quality) the court will not issue an order.

Once an individual has been made bankrupt, no other proceedings can be started against him. A 'trustee' is appointed to collect together the assets of the bankrupt person, and a list of unpaid payables. (The trustee must be a licensed insolvency practitioner.) Payables must apply to the trustee, and notify him of the debt they are owed. In addition, the bankrupt individual is expected to be honest in notifying the trustee of his unpaid debts. The trustee then shares out the proceeds between the payables. The payable who has applied for the bankruptcy order does not get any special treatment (e.g. priority for payment) from the trustee.

A bankruptcy normally lasts three years after the bankruptcy order is issued. During that time, the individual cannot become a company director or run a business, nor apply for credit of over $250 without notifying the payable that issued the bankruptcy proceedings.

14.1 DISADVANTAGES OF BANKRUPTCY PROCEEDINGS

When an individual owes money to more than one supplier, bankruptcy proceedings could be unsuitable, because there may be not enough money to provide a reasonable settlement for all the payables. Experience has shown that in most bankruptcies, unsecured payables do not get much money.

14.2 INDIVIDUAL VOLUNTARY AGREEMENTS (IVAs)

An individual who is threatened with legal proceedings by unpaid payable could take the initiative in trying to resolve the problem, and try to arrange an Individual Voluntary Agreement (IVA). The initiative for an IVA comes from the customer who owes money, not the payable.

The individual must obtain the assistance of a licensed insolvency practitioner, who accepts him or her on to an IVA programme. The insolvency practitioner then contacts all the payables of the individual, notifying them that he represents the individual and that an IVA is proposed. A court order, called an interim order, is then obtained. This protects the customer who owes money against further action by his payables while the IVA arrangement is being drawn up.

When the IVA proposal is drawn up, the payables (or unpaid suppliers) are contacted to discuss arrangements relating to the settlement of the debts. The basis of an IVA is that the customer will make payments out of his disposable income – i.e. out of what he can easily afford – and the proposal is to make monthly payments to settle the debts. The payables might even agree to payment of only a proportion of the debts, on the grounds that some payment is better than nothing. The insolvency practitioner then prepares a nominees report' about the proposed IVA and shortly afterwards calls a meeting of payables to approve the arrangement. At least 75% of payables must agree to it.

Once approved, the customer who has unpaid debts is legally obliged to keep up the payments he has promised to settle the debts. Details of IVAs are recorded on the Individual Insolvency Register.

15 COMPANY INSOLVENCY

Procedures against a company for unpaid debts are different from procedures against an individual. There are several possible courses of action, all regulated in the UK by the Insolvency Act 1986.

The options available for recovering unpaid debts from a company depend on whether the payable has a fixed charge or a floating charge over assets of the company. When security has been provided in the form of a fixed or floating charge, the secured payable has priority over unsecured payable and can seek repayment from the secured assets. Secured payable are usually banks or, in the case of large companies, holders of bonds or debentures (loan notes).

When a company is insolvent and unable to pay its debts, the courses of action available are:

- administration order
- company voluntary arrangement
- receivership (including administrative receivership)
- liquidation (or 'winding up').

15.1 ADMINISTRATION ORDERS

The court might agree to issue an administration order, on application by the company owing money or by a payable. The purpose of such an order is to give the company time to seek a settlement with its payables and survive, without going into liquidation.

A payable applying for an administration order is likely to be an unsecured payable. (A secured payable is more likely to seek the appointment of a receiver.) An unsecured payable might prefer a settlement with the company owing money than to apply for the company to be wound up.

An administration order by the court results in the appointment of an administrator, commonly called a 'company doctor', who must be a licensed insolvency practitioner. The administrator is given wide powers to manage the company, with a view to ensuring its survival and reaching a settlement with all its creditors. An administration order gives the company owing money a breathing space, because while it is in force:

- none of the debts are payable until agreement is reached with all the payables, and
- secured payables cannot try to enforce their security by appointing a receiver (see below).

15.2 COMPANY VOLUNTARY ARRANGEMENT (CVA)

A company that is in debt and unable to pay might be able to come to an agreement with its payables, whereby the payables agree to an arrangement as settlement of their debts. A proposal for a CVA should come from:

- the company's directors, provided the company is not subject to an administration order or in the process of being wound up
- the administrator, if the company is subject to an administrator
- the liquidator, if the company is in the process of being wound up.

The purpose of a CVA is to reach an agreement with the company's payables offering them something better than if the company were to be wound up. The terms of an agreement can vary, but could involve any of the following arrangements:

- An agreement by the payables to give the company more time to pay its debts.
- An agreement by the payables to swap their debt for ordinary shares in the company that owes them money, or long-term loan stock in the company.
- An agreement by the payables to accept a smaller payment in final settlement of their debts, for example a payment of 75 pence for every $1 owed.

In order to negotiate a CVA with payables, a 'nominee' must be appointed, who must be a licensed insolvency practitioner. (The nominee could be the administrator if the company is subject to an administration order, or the receiver if the company is being wound up.)

If an arrangement is agreed with the payables, it is implemented by a 'supervisor', who is usually the person who acted as nominee in negotiating it.

15.3 RECEIVERSHIP

A receiver is a person appointed by a payable, or by the court on behalf of a payable, to realise a security (under a fixed or floating charge or a loan note) and obtain payment for the payable.

There are two types of receiver:

- a receiver, and
- an administrative receiver.

A **receiver** might be appointed under a **fixed charge** to take control of the specific asset or assets that are subject to the charge. For example, if a debt is secured by a fixed charge on a company's building, the receiver takes control of the building and can dispose of it to raise cash to pay the payable.

The appointment of a receiver is unusual in practice, because companies normally give a fixed and floating charge as security for a debt, and when a floating charge is involved, an administrative receiver is appointed.

An **administrative receiver** might be appointed under a **floating charge**, or under a fixed and floating charge, to take control of and manage the entire company. An administrative receiver is often called a 'receiver and manager'.

Receivers and administrative receivers are appointed in one of two ways:

- Under the powers of a legal agreement, such as a loan note (debenture) trust deed, giving the payable a fixed or a floating charge. When an administrative receiver is appointed, the payable holding the charge makes the appointment.
- A receiver can be appointed by the court, but this is not common.

When an administrative receiver is appointed, she takes control of the company and its business operations, with a view to keeping the company in business until she has been able to raise the money to pay the secured payable. Until she has completed her task, the administrative receiver effectively runs the company. When her task is completed, the company could go back under the control of its management.

Order of payment in a receivership

The receiver must use the money raised from selling the company's assets to pay off the secured payables. However, there is a strict order of priority for payment, as follows:

- the costs of the receivership (legal fees, the receiver's fees and so on)
- money due to the holder of a fixed charge, payable from the proceeds from disposal of the charged asset
- certain preferential creditors, such as the government for unpaid tax and employees for unpaid wages or salary
- money due to the holder of a floating charge.

Any surplus proceeds are then either returned to the company or, if the company is being wound up, passed on to the receiver for distribution to other payables.

15.4 LIQUIDATION (WINDING UP)

A company is **dissolved** when it is struck off the Register of Companies. Dissolution usually occurs after liquidation, when the company is 'wound up' and its affairs brought to an end. A liquidation begins with a formal decision to liquidate. This decision is taken either:

- by the court, in the case of a **compulsory liquidation**, or
- by the shareholders of the company, in the case of a **voluntary winding up**, which can be either a **members' voluntary winding up** or a payables' **voluntary winding up**.

When a decision is taken to wind up the company, a liquidator is appointed. The liquidator takes over the control of the company from its directors.

The difference between members' voluntary winding up and a payables' voluntary winding up is that:

- a members' voluntary winding up is allowed if the company is able to pay all its debts in full
- a payables' voluntary winding up is required when the company cannot pay all its debts in full, so that the payables have a major part to play in the voluntary liquidation arrangements.

Compulsory liquidation

A compulsory liquidation starts with a petition to the court. A petition can be presented by a payable. This does not have to be the original payable, which means that a non-recourse factor or a debt collection agency can submit a petition. The payable must be able to demonstrate that the company is unable to pay its debts, and there are several ways of doing this.

One way of proving inability to pay debts is that the payable has obtained a court judgement for payment of the debt and has attempted to enforce the judgement, but the debt is still unpaid.

In practice, a payable must normally be owed at least $750 to be successful with a petition.

When the court is petitioned for a compulsory winding up order, a **provisional liquidator** is appointed. This is usually someone called the official receiver, and when the court eventually makes the liquidation order, the official receiver then becomes the **liquidator**.

The liquidator then winds up the company's affairs, raising what money it can from the company's assets, and using the money to pay as much to creditors as possible.

Voluntary winding up

A company's shareholders can take a voluntary decision to wind up the company. If they are able to declare that the company can pay all its debts in full, the liquidation can be a members' voluntary winding up. The shareholders appoint a liquidator, who winds up the company's affairs and uses the cash from disposing of the company's assets to:

- pay off the payables in full, and
- distribute any surplus to the shareholders.

If the shareholders want to wind up the company but are unable to make a declaration that the company will be able to pay its debts in full, they must seek a payables' voluntary winding up. A creditors' meeting must be held to approve the liquidation. If both shareholders and payables agree to the liquidation, a liquidation committee (with representatives of both shareholders and payables) is set up to monitor the winding up. However, the actual winding up is conducted by the receiver, not the liquidation committee.

Priorities for payment in a winding up

In a winding up, the money obtained from disposing of the company's assets must be paid out to payables in the following order:

- The costs of the winding up are paid first.
- Secured payables holding a fixed charge are paid out of the proceeds from disposing of the asset that is subject to the charge.
- Preferential payables (see above) must be paid next.
- Debts that are secured by a floating charge are paid next.
- If there is any money left after all the secured payables have been paid, the money remaining is then used to pay unsecured payables. However, if there is only, say, $100,000 left to pay unsecured debts of $200,000, unsecured payables receive a proportion of the debt. In this example, unsecured payables would receive $0.50 in the $1.
- If all unsecured payables are paid in full, the surplus is available for distribution to the shareholders.

Collecting debts in a liquidation

A business that is owed money by a company must think carefully before petitioning for a compulsory liquidation. This is because the process can be time-consuming and costly, and unless the company's assets can be sold off to raise a large amount of money, it is doubtful whether much of the debt will actually be paid.

CONCLUSION

Debt collection procedures vary widely between different organisations, but for all businesses that sell on credit, debt collection is an important activity.

This chapter has explained a range of procedures, reporting systems and legal measures. However, you also need to recognise that collecting debts successfully calls for good judgement and persistence on the part of the credit controller, who has to press customers for payment without antagonising them and losing their goodwill.

KEY TERMS

Pass for payment system – a system in which several checks are made before an invoice is authorised for payment.

Statement – a report to a customer listing the transactions on the customer's account since the previous statement. It details purchases by the customer, credit notes issued, payments received and discounts allowed. The statement also shows the balance owed by the customer as at the statement date. Statements are sent out regularly by some businesses, to prompt customers into making a payment.

Stop order – an internal instruction that no further sales should be made to a specific customer until payment is received for an outstanding debt.

Solicitor's letter – a letter sent to a credit customer by a solicitor on behalf of a client, threatening legal action unless payment is received.

Credit insurance – insurance against the risk of non-payment by credit customers.

Factoring – services provided by a factor. These consist of receivables ledger administration and debt collection, credit insurance (non-recourse factoring only) and the provision of short-term finance based on the value of receivables.

Invoice discounting – the provision of short-term finance against the security of approved debts.

Aged receivables list – a report analysing unpaid debts and the length of time for which unpaid debts have been outstanding.

County court judgement – an order issued by a county court in the UK, ordering a customer who owes money to pay debt.

Insolvency – inability to pay, giving rise to legal action.

Bankruptcy – a bankruptcy order issued by a court makes an individual bankrupt. The assets of a bankrupt individual may be seized and sold off to raise money to pay unpaid payables.

Liquidation – winding up of a company's affairs, which is followed by dissolution of the company. A compulsory liquidation order might be issued by a court against an insolvent company.

Receivership/administrative receivership – putting a company's secured assets under the control of a receiver (fixed charge) or an administrative receiver (floating charge). An unpaid payable with a fixed or floating charge can apply to the court for a receivership/administrative receivership order when the customer owing money is in default.

SELF-TEST QUESTIONS

		Paragraph
1	What payment methods other than payment by cheque or credit card might be used to speed up collections from credit customers?	1.5
2	What is a statement?	3.1
3	What is a reminder letter?	3.2
4	What is a stop order?	3.4
5	How do debt collection agencies charge for their services?	3.6
6	What is credit insurance?	4
7	What are the three main elements of a factoring service?	5
8	What is non-recourse factoring?	5.1
9	What proportion of the face value of invoices will a factor normally provide to a client?	5.4
10	What is invoice discounting?	6
11	What is an aged receivables report?	9
12	What is the difference between an irrecoverable debt and an allowance for receivables?	11
13	What is the difference between bankruptcy and insolvency?	12
14	What action can be taken against an individual to recover an unpaid debt when a county court judgement order has been made but the debt is still uncollected?	13.3
15	What is a warrant of execution?	13.3
16	What happens when a bankruptcy order is issued against an individual?	14
17	What is an individual voluntary agreement (IVA)?	14.2
18	What legal actions are available when a company cannot pay its debts?	15
19	What is administrative receivership?	15.3
20	What are the two main forms of company liquidation?	15.4
21	What are the priorities for payment in a company winding up?	15.4

PRACTICE QUESTION

NITTON CO

Here is an aged receivables report for Nitton Co as at 30 June 20X5. The normal credit terms for this company are 30 days net.

Customer	**Total owing**		**Outstanding for**		
		< 30 days	**30–60 days**	**60–90 days**	**> 90 days**
	$	$	$	$	$
Smith	41,000	27,000	14,000	–	–
Brown	78,000	36,000	25,000	17,000	–
Jones	159,000	42,000	39,000	41,000	37,000
Shah	40,000	32,000	–	–	8,000
West	35,000	35,000	–	–	–
	353,000	172,000	78,000	58,000	45,000
	100%	49%	22%	16%	13%

Required:

Prepare a report for your supervisor analysing the aged receivables list and recommending a suitable course of action for each customer. **(10 marks)**

For a suggested answer, see the 'Answers' section at the end of the book.

Chapter 9

FINANCIAL MANAGEMENT ENVIRONMENT

This chapter is the first in Part C of this text, which is concerned with raising finance. It looks at the role of the financial sector, concentrating on the major suppliers of finance – banks and other financial institutions known as financial intermediaries.

This chapter covers Syllabus part C2.

CONTENTS

LEARNING OUTCOMES

At the end of this chapter you should be able to:

- Explain the role and functions of various types of banks (including the structure of the banking system)
- Identify the major financial intermediaries
- Outline the general roles of financial intermediaries
- Outline the key benefits of financial intermediation
- Outline the relationships between financial institutions
- Explain the basic nature of a money market.

---

1 THE STRUCTURE OF A BANKING SYSTEM

The financial institutions of a country may be represented as an organisational hierarchy with its central bank at its apex and the two main groups below.

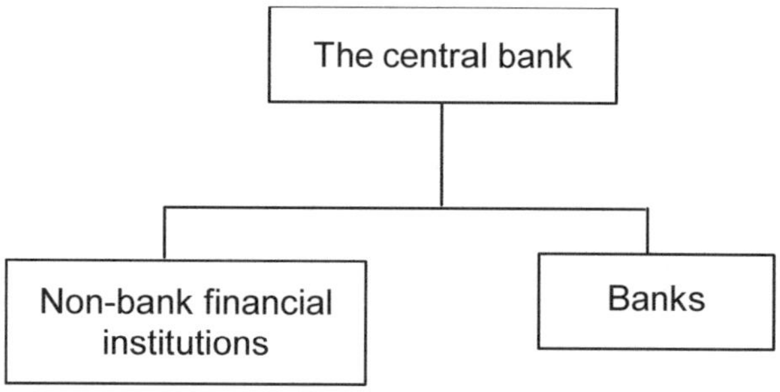

The most visible units in the banking system are the privately owned banks that deal with the ordinary public. These banks are profit-seeking firms. They accept deposits and transfer sight deposits among their customers and banks when ordered to do so by cheque. They make loans, called advances, to customers and charge them interest in return and they invest in interest-earning financial assets.

The second main element of the UK banking system is the wholesale banks (also known as investment banks or merchant banks).

The third main element of the banking system is the central bank, whose functions are to be banker to the government and the commercial banking system, to manage the public debt, to control the money supply and to regulate the country's monetary and credit system.

Most banking systems have a variety of other specialised institutions – some accepting time deposits from the public and lending money out on a longer term basis. UK examples are finance houses and building societies. The institutions are often called financial intermediaries, since they stand between those who save money and those who ultimately borrow it.

1.1 THE MAJOR FINANCIAL INTERMEDIARIES

Intermediation refers to the process whereby potential borrowers are brought together with potential lenders by a third party, the intermediary.

The savings/investment process in capitalist economies is organised around financial intermediation, making them a central institution of economic growth.

Banks and other financial institutions such as building societies and insurance companies are known as **financial intermediaries**. They all have the common function of providing a link between those who wish to lend and those who wish to borrow. In other words, they act as the mechanism whereby the supply of funds is matched to the demand for funds.

The major financial intermediaries in the UK include the following:

Clearing banks – the familiar high street banks provide a payment and cheque clearing mechanism. They offer various accounts to investors and provide large amounts of short to medium-term loans to the business sector and the personal sector. They also offer a wide range of financial services to their customers.

Investment banks, sometimes called merchant banks, concentrate on the following:

- **Financial advice to business firms** – few manufacturing or commercial companies of any size can now afford to be without the advice of a merchant bank. Such advice is necessary in order to obtain investment capital, to invest surplus funds, to guard against takeover, or to take over others. Increasingly, the merchant banks have themselves become actively involved in the financial management of their business clients and have had an influence over the direction these affairs have taken.

- **Providing finance to business** – merchant banks also compete in the services of leasing, factoring, hire purchase and general lending. They are also the gateway to the capital market for long-term funds because they are likely to have specialised departments handling capital issues as 'issuing houses'.

- **Foreign trade** – a number of merchant banks are active in the promotion of foreign trade by providing marine insurance, credits, and assistance in appointing foreign agents and arranging foreign payments.

Not all merchant banks are large and not all offer a wide range of services: the term is now rather misused. However, it is expected that a merchant bank will operate without the large branch network necessary for a clearing bank, it will work closely with its business clients, and will be more ready to take business risks and promote business enterprise than a clearing bank. It is probably fair to say that a merchant bank is essentially in the general business of creating wealth and of helping those who show that they are capable of successful business enterprise.

Savings banks – public sector savings banks (e.g. the National Savings Bank in the UK) are used to collect funds from the small personal saver, which are mainly invested in government securities.

Building societies – these take deposits from the household sector and lend to individuals buying their own homes. They have recently grown rapidly in the UK and now provide many of the services offered by the clearing banks. They are not involved, however, in providing funds for the business sector. Over recent years many have converted to banks.

Finance companies – these come in three main varieties:

(i) **Finance houses**, providing medium-term instalment credit to the business and personal sectors. These are usually owned by business sector firms or by other financial intermediaries. They offer services similar to the clearing banks.

(ii) **Leasing companies**, leasing capital equipment to the business sector. They are usually subsidiaries of other financial institutions.

(iii) **Factoring companies**, providing loans to companies secured on trade receivables, are usually bank subsidiaries. Other debt collection and credit control services are usually on offer.

Pension funds – these collect funds from employers and employees to provide pensions on retirement or death. As their outgoings are relatively predictable they can afford to invest funds for long periods of time.

Insurance companies – these use premium income from policyholders to invest mainly in long-term assets such as bonds, equities and property. Their outgoings from their long-term business (life assurance and pensions) and their short-term activities (fire, accident, motor insurance, etc.) are once again relatively predictable and therefore they can afford to tie up a large proportion of their funds for a long period of time.

Investment trusts and unit trusts – are limited liability companies collecting funds by selling shares and bonds and investing the proceeds, mainly in the ordinary shares of other companies. Funds at their disposal are limited to the amount of securities in issue plus retained profits, and hence they are often referred to as 'closed end funds'. Unit trusts on the other hand, although investing in a similar way, find that their funds vary according to whether investors are buying new units or cashing in old ones. Both offer substantial diversification opportunities to the personal investor.

1.2 THE GENERAL ROLES OF FINANCIAL INTERMEDIARIES

There will always have to be some mechanism for channelling the savings of households into the investments of firms. From the perspective of financial markets, businesses need capital and will supply assets to the market to get this capital. Households are the ultimate holders of these assets – either directly or through various types of investment pool – and so provide the ultimate demand. The financial intermediary moves resources between these two groups – businesses and households. This is the fundamental role of a financial intermediary. In this process, they provide four important services.

1 **Expert advice** – financial intermediaries can advise their customers on financial matters: on the best way of investing their funds and on alternative ways of obtaining finance. This should help to encourage the flow of savings and the efficient use of them.

2 **Expertise in channelling funds** – financial intermediaries have the specialist knowledge to be able to channel funds to those areas that yield the highest return. This too encourages the flow of savings as it gives savers the confidence that their savings will earn a good rate of interest. Financial intermediaries also help to ensure that projects that are potentially profitable will be able to obtain finance.

In addition to channelling funds from depositors to borrowers, certain financial institutions have another important function. This is to provide a means of transmitting payments. Thus by the use of cheques, debit cards, credit cards, standing orders, etc., money can be transferred from one person or institution to another without having to rely on cash.

3 **Maturity transformation** – many people and firms want to borrow money for long periods of time, and yet many depositors want to be able to withdraw their deposits on demand or at short notice. If people had to rely on borrowing directly from other people, there would be a problem here: the lenders would not be prepared to lend for a long enough period. Imagine lending a friend $150,000 of savings to buy a house if the friend was going to take 25 years to pay it back. Even if there was no risk whatsoever of your friend defaulting, most people would be totally unwilling to tie up their savings for so long. This is where a bank or building society comes in. It borrows money from a vast number of small savers, who are able to withdraw their money on demand or at short notice. It then lends the money to house purchasers for a long period of time by granting mortgages (typically these are paid back over 20 to 30 years). This process whereby financial intermediaries lend for longer periods of time than they borrow is known as maturity transformation. They are able to do this because with a large number of depositors it is highly unlikely that they would all want to withdraw their deposits at the same time. On any particular day, although some people will be withdrawing money, others will be making new deposits.

4 **Risk transformation** – you may be unwilling to lend money directly to another person in case they do not pay up. You are unwilling to take the risk. Financial intermediaries, however, by lending to large numbers of people, are willing to risk the odd case of default. They can absorb the loss because of the interest they earn on all the other loans. This spreading of risks is known as risk transformation. What is more, financial intermediaries may have the expertise to be able to assess just how risky a loan is.

1.3 THE KEY BENEFITS OF FINANCIAL INTERMEDIATION

- **Financial intermediaries bring together providers and users of finance**. They act between individuals and businesses and other institutions who need to borrow or those with surplus funds to invest. A financial intermediary may act as a broker (an agent handling transactions on behalf of others for a fee) or as principal (taking deposits or lending money for its own account).

- **The economic benefits of financial intermediation arise from the problem of scarcity**. Capital is one of the scarcest resources. A financial intermediary, such as a commercial bank, leasing company, or investment fund, gathers financial resources from sources of cash such as savers and investors and distributes them to productive units in need of debt or equity financing. When financial intermediaries operate well, they enable their ultimate beneficiaries to tap sources of funding that would otherwise be unavailable.

- **Firms and individuals borrowing funds to finance investment will tend to want to repay the borrowing over the expected life of the investment.** In addition the claims issued by firms will have a relatively high default risk reflecting the nature of business investment. In contrast, lenders will generally be looking to hold assets which are relatively liquid and low-risk. To reconcile the conflicting requirements of lenders and borrowers a financial intermediary will hold the long-term, high-risk claims of borrowers and finance this by issuing liabilities, called deposits, which are highly liquid and have low default risk.

- **By linking lenders and borrowers the intermediary is able to aggregate the amount lent by savers into the amounts which borrowers require.** For example, numerous building society accounts containing deposits of relatively small sums may be used to finance the smaller number of relatively large sums which mortgage borrowers require.

- **Intermediaries are able to reduce the transaction costs entailed during the process of matching borrowers with lenders.** Intermediaries are also able to reduce the transactions costs associated with the writing and communicating of contract terms for borrowers and lenders, particularly in cases where the contract terms are highly specialised to the situation at hand. In addition, information costs incurred as a result of monitoring and enforcement of contract terms are reduced by centralising these functions with one agent that has extensive experience. This is particularly important in cases in which would-be lenders are relatively unsophisticated compared to would-be borrowers. As long as the intermediary's own return is tied to the success of these monitoring and enforcement functions, it has an incentive to perform these functions in a reliable manner.

- **Intermediaries expend considerable resources investigating the anticipated profitability of the projects they finance.** Individual lenders in general have neither the resources nor the incentive to carry out such extensive investigations. Moreover, the information gathered by the intermediary about an investment project is generally not made public; it is used to construct investment opportunities (mutual funds, etc.) for those who supply the intermediary with loanable funds. This is to the advantage of both the borrowers (who wish to keep trade secrets secret) and the lenders (who wish to take advantage of 'inside information' about investment opportunities). In this way, the production of information is tied in with the management of customer accounts. The principal insurance which a supplier of funds has that an intermediary will perform reliably is the stake which the owners and/or managers of the intermediary themselves have in the investments they choose for their customers.

ACTIVITY 1

What are 'financial intermediaries'? How can you tell whether they are acting as a broker or principal?

For a suggested answer, see the 'Answers' section at the end of the book.

2 BANKS IN THE UK

By far the largest element of money supply is bank deposits. Banks can be divided into two main groups: **retail banks** and wholesale banks.

2.1 RETAIL BANKS

Retail banks in the UK are the familiar high street banks such as Barclays and Lloyds TSB and HSBC. They specialise in providing branch banking facilities to members of the general public, but they also lend to businesses, albeit often on a short-term basis.

Their business is in **retail deposits and loans**. These are deposits and loans made through their branch network at published rates of interest. The branches are like 'retail outlets' for banking services.

2.2 WHOLESALE BANKS

The other major category of banks is the wholesale banks, also known as investment banks. These include merchant banks such as Kleinwort Hambros and Rothschild & Co. They often act as 'brokers', arranging loans for companies from a number of different sources. They also offer financial advice to industry and provide assistance to firms in raising new capital through the issue of new shares.

Wholesale banks include many overseas banks, especially Japanese and American, specialising in the finance of international trade and capital movements, and dealing extensively in the foreign exchange market. Most of their deposits are in foreign currencies. They also include finance houses, which specialise in lending to businesses and in providing hire purchase finance for the purchase of consumer durables, such as cars, furniture and electrical goods.

They are called wholesale banks because they specialise in receiving large deposits from and making large loans to industry and other financial institutions (normally of a minimum of $250,000): these are known as **wholesale deposits** and **loans**. Banks also lend and borrow wholesale funds to and from each other. This inter-bank lending has grown enormously in recent years. Banks that are short of funds borrow large sums from others with surplus funds, thus ensuring that the banking sector as a whole does not have funds surplus to its requirements. The rate at which they lend to each other is known as the IBOR (inter-bank offer rate). The IBOR used to be the main reference rate to help determine interest rates for all borrowers and investors, but due to the manipulation scandal following the 2008 credit crunch, it has now been replaced by other reference rates such as SOFR (secured overnight financing rate).

2.3 BUILDING SOCIETIES

These UK institutions specialise in granting loans (mortgages) for house purchase. They compete for the savings of the general public through a network of high street branches. Unlike retail banks, they are not public limited companies, their 'shares' being the deposits made by their investors. In recent years, many of the building societies have converted to banks (including all the large building societies except the Nationwide Anglia).

In the past, there was a clear distinction between banks and building societies. Today, however, they have become much more similar, with building societies now offering current account facilities and cash machines, and retail banks granting mortgages. This is all part of a trend away from the narrow specialisation of the past and towards the offering of a wider and wider range of services. This has been helped by a process of **financial deregulation**. Inevitably, as this trend continues, the services offered by the various institutions will increasingly overlap.

2.4 DEPOSIT TAKING AND LENDING

Banks are in the business of deposit taking and lending. To understand this, we must distinguish between banks' liabilities and assets.

Liabilities – customers' deposits in banks (and other deposit-taking institutions such as building societies) are **liabilities** to these institutions. This means simply that the customers have the claim on these deposits and thus the institutions are liable to meet the claims.

There are four major types of deposit: sight deposits, time deposits, certificates of deposit and 'repos'.

1 **Sight deposits** are any deposits that can be withdrawn on demand by the depositor without penalty. In the past, sight accounts did not pay interest. Today, however, there are some sight accounts that do.

   The most familiar form of sight deposits are current accounts at banks. Depositors are issued with cheque books and/or debit cards (e.g. Switch or Connect) that enable them to spend the money directly without first having to go to the bank and draw the money out in cash. In the case of debit cards, the person's account is electronically debited when the purchase is made and the card is 'swiped' across the machine. This process is known as EPTPOS (electronic funds transfer at point of sale).

   An important feature of current accounts is that banks often allow customers to be overdrawn. That is, they can draw on their account and make payments to other people in excess of the amount of money they have deposited.

2 **Time deposits** require notice of withdrawal. They are not cheque book or debit card accounts. The most familiar form of time deposits are the deposit and savings accounts in banks and the various savings accounts in building societies. No overdraft facilities exist with time deposits.

3 **Certificates of deposit** are certificates issued by banks to customers (usually firms) for large deposits of a fixed term (e.g. $100,000 for 18 months).

4 **Sale and repurchase agreements** (REPOS) – If banks have a temporary shortage of funds, they can sell some of their financial assets to other banks or to the central bank – the Bank of England in the UK and the European Central Bank in the eurozone – and later repurchase them on some agreed date, often about a fortnight later. These **sale and repurchase agreements** (REPOS) are

in effect a form of loan, the bank borrowing for a period of time using some of its financial assets as the security for the loan. The most usual assets to use in this way are government bonds (gilts). Sale and repurchase agreements involving gilts are known as gilt REPOS. As we shall see, gilt repos play a vital role in the operation of monetary policy.

Other liabilities include 'Items in suspense and transmission' – these are funds in the process of being transferred from one customer's account to another. 'Capital and other funds' include shareholders' funds and internal funds of the banks themselves.

Assets – a bank's financial assets are its claims on others. There are three main categories of asset:

1 Cash and operational balances in the central bank (Bank of England in the UK, ECB in the eurozone). Banks need to hold a certain amount of their assets as cash. They also keep 'operational balances' in the central bank. These are like the banks' own current accounts and are used for clearing purposes i.e. for settling day-to-day claims between banks. They can be withdrawn in cash on demand and are thus also totally liquid.

2 Loans to individuals and firms, to other financial institutions and to the government – make up the vast majority of banks' assets. These are 'assets' because they represent claims that the banks have on other people. Loans can be grouped into two types: short- and long-term.

3 Investments – partly in government bonds (gilts), which are effectively loans to the government. The government sells bonds, which then pay a fixed sum each year as interest. Once issued, they can then be bought and sold on the stock exchange.

The example below shows the approximate statement of financial position of UK banks.

Sterling liabilities	$bn	%	**Sterling assets**	$bn	%
Sight deposits	628.7	(36.2)	Notes and coins	7.2	(0.4)
UK banks, etc.	105.1				
UK public sector	4.6		Balances with B. of E.	1.7	(0.1)
UK private sector	459.7		Market loans	401.7	(22.9)
Non-resident	59.3		UK banks	236.1	
			CDs, etc.	77.5	
Time deposits	604.1	(34.8)	Non-residents	88.1	
UK banks, etc.	142.4				
UK public sector	9.1		Bills of exchange	30.1	(1.7)
UK private sector	299.6		Treasury	12.3	
Non-residents	153.0		UK Bank bills	6.8	
			Other	11.0	
Certificate of deposit	157.7	(9.1)	Reverse repos	92.0	(5.2)
Sale and repurchase agreements (repos)	104.2	(6.0)	Investments	128.6	(7.3)
			Advances	1034.8	(59.0)
Other	242.9	(13.9)	Miscellaneous	58.8	(3.4)
Total sterling liabilities	1737.6	(100.0)	Total sterling assets	1754.9	(100.0)
Liab's in other currencies	2133.4		Assets in other currencies	2116.1	
Total liabilities	**3871.0**		**Total assets**	**3871.0**	

ACTIVITY 2

What are 'REPOS'?

For a suggested answer, see the 'Answers' section at the end of the book.

3 THE CENTRAL BANK

The Bank of England is the UK's central bank. The European Central Bank (ECB) is the central bank for the countries using the euro, and the Federal Reserve Bank (Fed) is the USA's central bank. All countries have a central bank and they fulfil two vital roles in the economy.

The first is to oversee the whole monetary system and ensure that banks and other financial institutions operate as stably and as efficiently as possible.

The second is to act as the government's agent, both as its banker and in carrying out monetary policy. The Bank of England traditionally worked in very close liaison with the Treasury, and there used to be regular meetings between the Governor of the Bank of England and the Chancellor of the Exchequer. Although the Bank may have disagreed with Treasury policy, it always carried it out. With the election of the Labour government in 1997, however, the Bank of England was given independence to decide the course of monetary policy. In particular, this meant that the Bank of England, and not the government, would now decide interest rates.

If the UK adopts the euro, there will be a much reduced role for the Bank of England. At present, however, within its two broad roles, it has a number of different functions.

- **It issues notes** – the amount of banknotes issued by the Bank of England depends largely on the demand for notes from the general public. If people draw more cash from their bank accounts, the banks will have to draw more cash from their balances in the Bank of England. These balances are held in the Banking Department. The Banking Department will thus have to acquire more notes from the Issue Department, which will simply print more in exchange for extra government or other securities supplied by the Banking Department. Thus the amount of notes in circulation is always more at Christmas time.

- **It acts as a banker to the government** – it keeps two major accounts: The 'Exchequer' – for taxation and government spending and the 'National Loans Fund' for government borrowing and lending.

- **It manages the government's borrowing programme** – whenever the government runs a budget deficit (i.e. spends more than it receives in tax and other revenues), it will have to finance that deficit by borrowing. It can borrow by issuing bonds (gilts), National Savings certificates or Treasury bills. Even when the government runs a budget surplus, the Bank of England will still have to manage the national debt (the accumulated borrowing from the past).

- **It advises banks on good banking practice**. It discusses government policy with them and reports back to the government. It requires all recognised banks to maintain adequate liquidity: this is called prudential control.

- **It provides liquidity, as necessary, to banks** – ensuring that there is always an adequate supply of liquidity to meet the legitimate demands of depositors.

- **It is a lender of the last resort** – commercial banks often have sudden needs for cash and one way of getting it is to borrow from the central bank to avoid the negative consequences of a credit crunch on the real sector of the economy.

- **It operates the government's monetary and exchange rate policy** managing the issue and repurchasing of gilts and Treasury bills.

4 FINANCIAL MARKETS

4.1 THE RELATIONSHIP BETWEEN FINANCIAL INSTITUTIONS

The financial markets, both capital and money markets, are places where those requiring finance (deficit units) can meet with those able to supply it (surplus units). They offer both primary and secondary markets.

The financial markets can be divided into different subtypes:

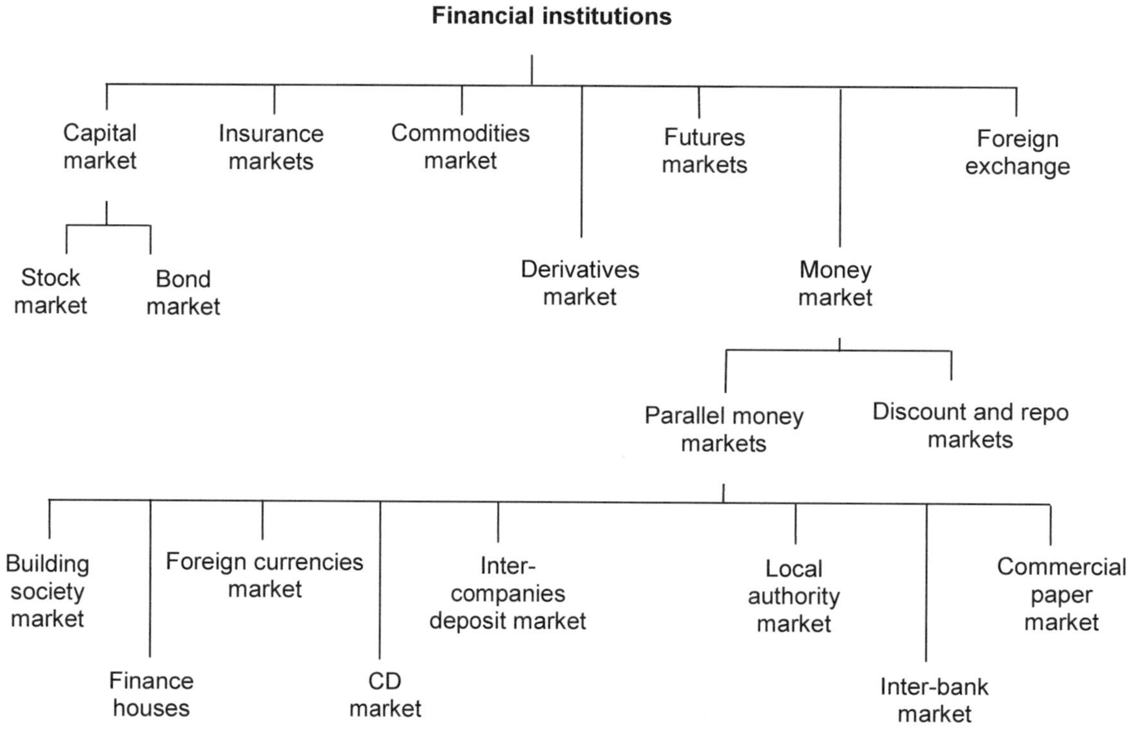

Capital markets which consist of:

- Stock markets, which provide financing through the issue of shares or common stock, and enable the subsequent trading of them.

- Bond markets, refer to people and entities involved in buying and selling of bonds and the quantity and prices of those transactions over time. Participants in the market trade bonds issued by corporations and various government bodies.

Commodity markets are markets where raw or primary products are exchanged. These raw commodities are traded on regulated exchanges, in which they are bought and sold in standardised contracts.

Money markets, which provide short-term debt financing and investment.

Derivatives markets, which provide instruments for the management of financial risk.

Futures markets, which provide standardised forward contracts to buy or sell a particular commodity or financial instrument at a predetermined price in the future. Futures contracts detail the quality and quantity of the underlying asset; they are standardised to facilitate trading on a futures exchange. Some futures contracts may call for physical delivery of the asset, while others are settled in cash.

Insurance markets, which facilitate the redistribution of various risks.

Foreign exchange markets, which exist wherever one currency is traded for another. It is by far the largest market in the world, in terms of cash value traded, and includes trading between large banks, central banks, currency speculators, multinational corporations, governments, and other financial markets and institutions. Retail traders (small speculators) are a small part of this market. They may only participate indirectly through brokers or banks.

The **capital markets** consist of primary markets and secondary markets. Newly formed (issued) securities are bought or sold in primary markets. Secondary markets allow investors to sell securities that they hold or buy existing securities.

4.2 THE ROLE OF FINANCIAL MARKETS

Primary markets provide a focal point for borrowers and lenders to meet. The forces of supply and demand should ensure that funds find their way to their most productive usage. Primary markets deal in new issues of loanable funds. They raise new finance for the deficit units.

Secondary markets allow holders of financial claims (surplus units) to realise their investments before the maturity date by selling them to other investors. They therefore increase the willingness of surplus units to invest their funds. A well-developed secondary market should also reduce the price volatility of securities, as regular trading in 'second-hand' securities should ensure smoother price changes. This should further encourage investors to supply funds.

Secondary markets help investors achieve the following:

- **Diversification** – by giving investors the opportunity to invest in a wide range of enterprises it allows them to spread their risk. This is the familiar 'Don't put all your eggs in one basket' strategy.

- **Risk shifting** – deficit units, particularly companies, issue various types of security on the financial markets to give investors a choice of the degree of risk they take. For example, company loan stocks secured on the assets of the business offer low risk with relatively low returns, whereas equities carry much higher risk with correspondingly higher returns.

- **Hedging** – financial markets offer participants the opportunity to reduce risk through hedging which involves taking out counterbalancing contracts to offset existing risks. For example, if a UK exporter is awaiting payment in francs from a Swiss customer the exporter is subject to the risk that the Swiss franc may decline in value over the credit period. To hedge this risk he or she could enter a counterbalancing contract and arrange to sell the Swiss francs forward (agree to exchange them for pounds at a fixed future date at a fixed exchange rate). In this way he or she has used the foreign exchange market to insure the future sterling receipt. Similar hedging possibilities are available on interest rates and on equity prices.

- **Arbitrage** – this is the process of buying a security at a low price in one market and simultaneously selling in another market at a higher price to make a profit.

Although it is only the primary markets that raise new funds for deficit units, well-developed secondary markets are required to fulfil the above roles for lenders and borrowers. Without these opportunities more surplus units would be tempted to keep their funds 'under the bed' rather than putting them at the disposal of deficit units. However, the emergence of disintermediation (reduction in the use of intermediaries) and securitisation (conversion into marketable securities), where companies lend and borrow funds directly between themselves, has provided a further means of dealing with cash flow surpluses and deficits.

4.3 THE MONEY MARKETS

It is through the London money market that the Bank of England exercises its control of the economy. The market deals in short-term lending and borrowing. It is normally divided into the 'discount' and 'repo' markets and the 'parallel' or 'complementary' market.

The discount and repo markets

The markets for bills of exchange (the discount market) and for repos play a crucial role in ensuring that banks have sufficient liquidity to meet all their needs.

Assume that bank customers start drawing out more cash. As a result, banks find themselves short of liquid assets. What can they do? The answer is that they borrow from the Bank of England. There are two ways in which this can be done.

- Method 1 – enter a repo agreement, whereby the Bank of England buys gilts from the banks (thereby supplying them with money) on the condition that the banks buy the gilts back at a fixed price and on a fixed date, typically two weeks later. The repurchase price will be above the asked price. The difference is the equivalent of the interest that the banks are being charged for having what amounts to a loan from the Bank of England. The repurchase price (and hence the 'repo rate') will be set by the Bank of England to reflect its chosen rate of interest, i.e. the rate chosen by the Bank of England's Monetary Policy Committee.

- Method 2 – sell Treasury bills back to the Bank of England before they have reached maturity (i.e. before the three months are up). This process is known as rediscounting. The Bank of England will pay a price below the face value, thus effectively charging interest to the banks. The price is set so that the 'rediscount rate' reflects the interest rate set by the Monetary Policy Committee.

In being prepared to rediscount bills or provide money through gilt repos, the Bank of England is thus the ultimate guarantor of sufficient liquidity in the monetary system and is known as lender of last resort.

The need for banks to acquire liquidity in this way is not uncommon. It is generally a deliberate policy of the Bank of England to create a shortage of liquidity in the economy to force banks to obtain liquidity from it. But why should the Bank of England do this? It does it as a means of controlling interest rates. If the banks are forced to obtain liquidity from the Bank of England, they will be borrowing at the Bank of England's chosen rate (i.e. the repo rate). The banks will then have to gear their other rates to it, and other institutions will gear their rates to those of the banks.

The parallel money markets

The parallel money markets include the following:

- The inter-bank market (wholesale loans from one bank to another from one day to up to several months).
- The market for certificates of deposit.
- The inter-companies deposit market (short-term loans from one company to another arranged through the market).
- The foreign currencies market (dealings in foreign currencies deposited short term in London).
- Finance house market (short-term borrowing to finance hire purchase).
- Building society market (wholesale borrowing by the building societies).
- Local authority market – local authorities have a special market where they can borrow short-term funds. Local authority bonds have a maturity of around one year and Local authority bills are short-term debt similar to Treasury bills.
- Commercial paper market – borrowing in sterling by companies, banks and other financial institutions by the issue of short-term (less than one year) 'promissory notes'. These, like Bills of exchange, are sold at a discount and redeemed at their face value, but in the interim can be traded on the market at any time.

CONCLUSION

In this chapter we have looked at financial intermediaries and their important functions. As part of the banking system they deal in deposits and loans. The money market consists of the discount and repo markets and the parallel money markets (consisting of various markets in short-term finance between various financial institutions).

SELF-TEST QUESTIONS

		Paragraph
1	What are the wholesale banks also known as?	1
2	List the major financial intermediaries in the UK.	1.1
3	Banks are in the business of deposit taking and lending. What are four major types of deposit?	2.4
4	What acts as a lender of the last resort?	3
5	Briefly describe how hedging works.	4.2

Chapter 10

THE ECONOMIC ENVIRONMENT

We have already discussed the main providers of finance and in this chapter we will be looking at the major economic influences that affect the finance available to an enterprise as well as other aspects of business. The main economic influences are inflation and interest rates. As a determinant of the cost of capital that an organisation faces, interest rates are also the target of government and central bank monetary policy.

This chapter covers Syllabus part D1.

CONTENTS

LEARNING OUTCOMES

At the end of this chapter you should be able to:

- Define what is meant by 'money supply' in an economic context
- Outline how money supply may be controlled in an economy
- Outline the basic relationship between the demand for money and interest rates
- Describe how the application of different monetary policies can affect the economy
- Explain briefly and illustrate the interaction between inflation and interest rates
- Discuss the possible consequences of inflation in an economy and its effects on organisations in general.

---

1 MONEY AND MONETARY POLICY

1.1 MONETARY POLICY IN THE UK

In the UK, the central bank has been given responsibility by the government for controlling short-term interest rates. These are controlled with a view to influencing the rate of inflation in the economy over the long term. In broad terms, an increase in interest rates is likely to reduce demand in the economy and so lower inflationary pressures, whereas a reduction in interest rates should give a boost to spending in the economy, but could result in more inflation. The aim of economic policy is to find a suitable balance between economic growth and the risks from inflation.

Central governments can control short-term interest rates through their activities in the money markets. This is because the commercial banks need to borrow regularly from the central bank. The central bank lends to the commercial banks at a rate of its own choosing (a rate known in the UK as the repo rate). This borrowing rate for banks affects the interest rates that the banks set for their own customers. Action by a central bank to raise or lower interest rates normally results in an immediate increase or reduction in bank base rates.

Monetary policy aims to influence the overall level of monetary demand in the economy so that it grows broadly in line with the economy's ability to produce goods and services. This stops output rising too quickly or slowly. Interest rates are increased to moderate demand and inflation and they are reduced to stimulate demand. If rates are set too low, this may encourage the build-up of inflationary pressure; if they are set too high, demand will be lower than necessary to control inflation. In particular, monetary policy may be concerned with:

(a) The **quantity** of money in circulation. The stock of money in the economy (the 'money supply') is believed to have important effects on the volume of expenditure in the economy. This in turn may influence the level of output in the economy or the level of prices.

(b) The **price** of money. The price of money is the rate of interest. If governments wish to influence the amount of money held in the economy or the demand for credit, they may attempt to influence the level of interest rates.

(c) The **availability of credit** in the economy.

The monetary authorities may be able to control either the supply of money in the economy or the level of interest rates but it cannot do both simultaneously. In practice, attempts by governments (such as the Thatcher government in the UK) to control the economy by controlling the money supply have failed and have been abandoned. However, growth in the money supply is monitored, because excessive growth could be destabilising.

1.2 THE MONEY SUPPLY

Money supply can be defined in a number of different ways, depending on what items are included. A useful distinction is between the monetary base and broad money.

Broad money also includes deposits in banks and possibly various other short-term deposits in the money market.

The monetary base (or 'high-powered money') consists of cash (notes and coins) in circulation outside the central bank.

In the UK, it is sometimes referred to as the 'narrow monetary base' or 'narrow money' to distinguish it from the wide monetary base, which also includes banks' balances with the Bank of England.

But the monetary base gives us a very poor indication of the effective money supply, since it excludes the most important source of liquidity for spending: namely, bank deposits. The problem is which deposits to include. We need to answer three questions:

- Should we include just sight deposits, or time deposits as well?
- Should we include just retail deposits, or wholesale deposits as well?
- Should we include just bank deposits, or building society (savings institution) deposits as well?

In the past there has been a whole range of measures, each including different combinations of these accounts. However, financial deregulation, the abolition of foreign exchange controls and the development of computer technology have led to huge changes in the financial sector throughout the world. This has led to a blurring of the distinctions between different types of account. It has also made it very easy to switch deposits from one type of account to another. For these reasons, the most usual measure that countries use for money supply is **broad money**, which in most cases includes both time and sight deposits, retail and wholesale deposits, and bank and building society (savings institution) deposits.

1.3 WHAT CAUSES INCREASES IN MONEY SUPPLY?

An increase in the money supply can occur as a result of banks and building societies choosing to hold a lower liquidity ratio, an inflow of funds from abroad or a public sector deficit.

Banks and building societies lend more money – if banks collectively choose to hold a lower liquidity ratio, they will have surplus liquidity. The banks have tended to choose a lower liquidity ratio over time because of the increasing use of direct debits, cheques and debit-card and credit-card transactions.

Surplus liquidity can be used to expand advances, which will lead to a multiplied rise in money supply. The impetus to expand advances may come from the banks themselves. The aggressive promotion of credit cards and the advertising of personal loans are familiar examples. The impetus may also come from the customer. As an economy pulls out of recession, the demand for loans is likely to rise.

An inflow of funds from abroad – if the government intervenes in the foreign exchange market to maintain a rate of exchange **below** the equilibrium, there will be an excess demand for sterling. To maintain the exchange rate at this level, the Bank of England has to buy up the excess foreign currencies on offer with **extra** pounds, thereby building up the foreign currency reserves. When this sterling is used to pay for UK exports and is then deposited back in the banks by the exporters, credit will be created on the basis of it, leading to a multiplied increase in money supply.

The money supply will also expand if depositors of sterling in banks overseas then switch these deposits to banks in the UK. This is a **direct** increase in the money supply. In an open economy like the UK, movements of sterling and other currencies into and out of the country can be very large, leading to large fluctuations in the money supply.

A public-sector deficit – the public-sector net cash requirement (PSNCR) is the difference between public-sector expenditure and public-sector receipts. To meet this deficit, the government has to borrow money. In general, the bigger the PSNCR, the greater will be the growth in the money supply. Just how the money supply will be affected, however, depends on who buys the securities.

Such securities could be sold to the central bank. In this case, the central bank credits the government's account to the value of the securities it has purchased. When the government spends the money, it pays with cheques drawn on its account with the central bank. When the recipients of these cheques pay them into their bank accounts, the banks will present the cheques to the central bank and their balances there will be duly credited. These additional balances will then become the basis for credit creation. There will be a multiplied expansion of the money supply.

Similarly, if the government borrows through additional Treasury bills, and if these are purchased by the banking sector, there will be a multiplied expansion of the money supply. The reason is that, although banks' balances at the central bank will go down when the banks purchase the bills, they will go up again when the government spends the money. In addition, the banks will now have additional liquid assets (bills), which can be used as the basis for credit creation.

If, however, the government securities are purchased by the 'non-bank private sector' (the name given to the general public and non-bank firms), the money supply will remain unchanged. When people buy the bonds or bills, they will draw money from their banks. When the government spends the money, it will be re-deposited in banks. There is no increase in money supply. It is just a case of existing money changing hands.

The government could attempt to minimise the boost to money supply by financing the PSNCR through the sale of gilts, since, even if these were partly purchased by the banks, they could not be used as the basis for credit creation.

1.4 THE MAIN MONETARY POLICY TECHNIQUES TO CONTROL MONEY SUPPLY

There are three ways in which the central bank may influence money supply.

- **Reserve requirements** – central bank sets a minimum ratio of cash reserves to deposits that commercial banks must meet.

- **Discount rate** – the interest rate that the central bank charges when the commercial banks want to borrow. Setting this at a penalty rate may encourage commercial banks to hold more excess reserves.

- **Open market operations** – actions to alter the monetary base by buying or selling financial securities (gilts and bills) in the open market. The weekly tender in Treasury bills is used to help manage the money market as well as raising cash for the government. The Public Sector Net Cash Requirement (PSNCR) is, however, funded mainly through the sale of gilt-edged securities which are long-term investments used to finance the shortfall between government revenues and expenditure.

The main instrument of monetary policy is the short-term interest rate. Central banks have a variety of techniques for influencing interest rates but they are all designed, in one way or another, to affect the cost of money to the banking system. In general this is done by keeping the banking system short of money and then lending the banks the money they need at an interest rate which the central bank decides. In this country such influence is exercised through the Bank of England's daily operations in the money markets.

A change in interest rates will affect the economy through a number of routes:

- First, a change in the cost of borrowing will affect spending decisions. Interest rates affect the relative attraction of spending today as against spending later, as a rise in rates will make savings more attractive and borrowing less so, and this will tend to reduce present spending, both on consumption and on investment. The opposite happens when an economy is slowing, or when imminent recession is feared. Lowering interest rates makes borrowing cheaper. Consumers have more spare cash to spend, companies can raise cheaper capital, and the economy starts to accelerate again.

- Second, a change in rates affects the cash flow of borrowers and payables. A rise or fall in interest rates affects the cash flow of those with floating interest rate assets or liabilities. For example, many households have floating interest rate deposits in banks and building societies. Floating interest rate receivables include households with mortgages, and companies. Fluctuations in cash flow may affect spending.

- Third, a change in interest rates affects the value of certain assets, notably housing and stocks and shares. Such a change in wealth may influence people's willingness to spend.

- Fourth, a particular pressure on prices comes through the exchange rate. For example, a rise in domestic interest rates relative to those overseas will tend to result in a net inflow of capital and an appreciation of the exchange rate. A rising pound will reduce prices for imports, thus increasing competitive pressures and supplementing the downward pressure on inflation arising from weakened demand.

All of these influences on demand are likely to affect prices and inflation. A rise in short-term interest rates can be expected to restrain demand for UK output in the way described. That in turn is likely to put downward pressure on UK prices and the rate of inflation.

1.5 FISCAL POLICY TECHNIQUES

An alternative to monetary policy that governments can use to influence the economy is fiscal policy. Fiscal policy is the use of government revenue collection (taxation) and expenditure (spending) to influence the economy.

The two main instruments of fiscal policy are changes in the level and composition of taxation and government spending in various sectors. These changes can affect the following macroeconomic variables in an economy:

- Aggregate demand and the level of economic activity

- The distribution of income

- The pattern of resource allocation within the government sector and relative to the private sector.

2 INTEREST RATES

The interest rate can be considered as the price of money. If you want to borrow money it is the percentage over and above the original loan that has to be paid back. This makes the interest rate a vital tool of economic management. A large amount of economic activity (both consumption and investment) is done on borrowed money, and so if the interest rate is changed it will either encourage or discourage borrowing and therefore tend to increase or decrease economic growth.

There are many different interest rates in the UK, as interest rates will vary according to the amount of time money is tied up for (the longer term the investment the higher the rate on offer and vice-versa) and the riskiness of the investment (the riskier the investment the higher the rate is likely to be). Financial institutions will therefore usually set their rates from a base rate. All other rates for saving and borrowing will often then be expressed as an amount above or below the base rate.

2.1 DEMAND FOR MONEY AND INTEREST RATES

There are four influences on the demand for money:

- **The price level** – as price levels rise, you need more money to take care of day-to-day transactions.
- **Income** – the higher your income, the more money you spend, hence the more money you need on hand.
- **The interest rate** – the interest rate is the price of money; therefore, the higher the interest rate the lower the quantity of money demanded and vice versa.
- **Credit availability** – the easier the credit, the less money you have to have on hand.

Although we have already discussed Keynes' three reasons to hold money, we need to mention it again because of its relationship with the demand for money and interest rates.

- **Transaction motive** – need a certain quantity of money just to carry out the day to-day-transactions of life.
- **Precautionary motive** – need to have a certain quantity of money to guard against the unexpected.
- **Speculative (or assets) motive** – idea that you want to keep a certain quantity of money available to take advantage of financial opportunities that might come along.

Keynes argued that people will need money to satisfy the transaction motive and the precautionary motive regardless of the level of interest. It is only the speculative motive that affects the demand for money as a result of interest rates.

Liquidity preference refers to people's preference to holding on to their savings as money rather than investing it. Unfortunately, when carried to its logical conclusion, the speculative motive for holding money would suggest that at very low rates of interest, people will choose to hold money:

- they won't spend it
- they won't loan it (interest rates are too low)
- they just hoard it.

This is called the 'the Liquidity Trap'. Japan has been caught in a liquidity trap since the late 1990s because of the following:

- very low interest rates for savers
- a large portfolio of non-performing loans banks will not foreclose on
- banks will not make new loans because of poor prospects for performance.

The conclusion is that demand for money will be high when interest is low because the speculative demand for money will be high when interest rates are low.

ACTIVITY 1

If interest rates fall significantly and unexpectedly, what effect would this have on a kitchen retailing company which has a large overdraft?

For a suggested answer, see the 'Answers' section at the end of the book.

2.2 GENERAL DEFINITIONS OF INTEREST

In finance, **interest** has three general definitions.

- Interest is a surcharge on the repayment of debt (borrowed money).
- Interest is the return derived from an investment.
- Interest is the right to one's claim in an organisation, such as that of an owner or creditor (payable).

In economics, interest is the return to capital achieved over time or as the result of an event.

In common use the term 'interest' is seen as rent paid for the use of money. As with any rental, the market price (or rate) is subject to change to reflect market conditions. The fraction by which the balances grow is called the interest rate. The original balance is called the principal. Interest rates are very closely watched indicators of a financial market, and have a dramatic effect on finance and economics.

The fact that lenders demand interest for loans can be attributed to the following reasons:

- Time value of money (TVM) or time preference (TP) – TVM: having money now is more valuable than having it at some future time because interest is earned: TP: interest is the value borrowers place on having money now.
- Opportunity cost – OC: The cost in terms of options no longer available once one particular option is chosen.

2.3 TYPES AND STRUCTURE OF INTEREST RATE

There are scores of interest rates – credit card rates, consumer loan rates, savings account rates, mortgage rates, etc. – but they are all either fixed or variable.

(i) **Fixed**. The interest rate stays fixed throughout the life of the debt. Most bonds are fixed rate bonds.

(ii) **Variable**. The interest rate is usually determined by a reference rate, such as SOFR or a consumer price index.

The structure of interest rates refers to many different interest rates, but these can be grouped into three broad classes – short-term, medium-term and long-term – according to the time which they reach maturity.

Longer-term financial assets generally offer a higher yield than shorter-term lending due to:

- investors needing compensation for tying up money in the asset for a longer period of time and going against their liquidity preference, and
- investors needing compensation for the greater risk associated with lending longer-term than shorter-term.

2.4 ANALYSIS OF INTEREST-RATE RISKS

Interest involves the future, which is uncertain. Some interest bearing investments are riskier than others. The greater the risk of the security, the more interest the investors will expect to receive.

The fundamental determinants of interest rate are the risks, which include:

Credit risk – the risk of default on the loan or of bankruptcy. This is the most commonly associated risk. It determines the different amount individuals or firms pay based on their creditworthiness. Different parties will be offered different rates on debt obligations (such as loans). The measure of creditworthiness of an individual is called a credit rating or credit score. Other entities (such as governments and companies) will acquire a bond rating if they are active in bond markets. The credit spread between an instrument and its risk-free equivalent is called the risk premium.

Maturity/term risk – the risk involved in a long-term investment. This is risk due to changes in the fixed income term structure. It arises if interest rates are fixed on liabilities for periods that differ from those on offsetting assets. One reason may be maturity mismatches. Suppose an insurance company is earning 6% on an asset supporting a liability on which it is paying 4%. The asset matures in two years while the liability matures in ten. In two years, the firm will have to reinvest the proceeds from the asset. If interest rates fall, it could end up reinvesting at 3%. For the remaining eight years, it would earn 3% on the new asset while continuing to pay 4% on the original liability. Term structure risk also occurs with floating rate assets or liabilities. If fixed rate assets are financed with floating rate liabilities, the rate payable on the liabilities may rise while the rate earned on the assets remains constant.

Liquidity risk – the need of compensating the illiquidity of the debt. This is the risk that the lender might not be able to liquidate the debt on short notice. The difference in interest rate due to liquidity risk is called liquidity spread. Instruments such as bonds have an active secondary market. Other instruments such as savings deposits are easily transferable to cash. On the other hand a 30-year Government savings bond is non-transferable. It can only be redeemed at half price before maturity. The savings bond will obviously offer a higher return.

Inflation risk – macroeconomic price changes.

Exchange rate risk – currency fluctuation.

Most of the inflation and exchange rate risk come from loans to developing countries. Therefore, loans offered by banks in developed countries usually denominate the loan contract in stable currencies such as the US Dollar, Pound Sterling or Euro. This has led to unfavourable consequences for the borrowers of developing countries because the economies of developing countries often have high inflation and an unstable exchange rate.

2.5 REAL RATES, NOMINAL RATES AND INFLATION

Nominal rates – compounding and discounting are normally at nominal rates of interest. These are interest rates reflecting market yields. For example, if interest paid per annum on a loan of $1,000 is $80, the rate of interest would be 8%. This rate might also be referred to as the money rate of interest.

Real rates – are a measure of the increase in real wealth, expressed in terms of the increase in purchasing power over goods as a result of postponing spending. A real rate of interest is the yield after allowing for inflation. For example, if the nominal or market yield on an investment is 8% and the rate of inflation is 3% the real return is only about 5%.

The exact relationship between nominal yield (money yield), the real yield and the annual rate of inflation is:

$$(1 + N) = (1 + R)(1 + I)$$

Where:

N is the nominal rate of interest

R is the real rate of interest and

I is the annual rate of inflation.

Example

A bank pays 5% on a deposit account. Annual inflation is 3.6%.

$$(1.05) = (1 + R)(1.036)$$

$$1 + R = 1.05/1.036$$

$$= 1.0135$$

The real rate on the deposit account is therefore 0.0135 or 1.35%.

3 INFLATION

3.1 THE RATE OF INFLATION

The rate of inflation measures the annual percentage increase in prices. The most usual measure is that of **retail** prices. The UK government publishes an index of retail prices (RPI) each month, and the rate of inflation is the percentage increase in that index over the previous 12 months.

The RPI, (or consumer price index (CPI) as it is known in some countries), tends to be constructed differently from one country to another, and this makes international comparisons difficult. An alternative measure is that used by the European Union. This is the harmonised consumer price index (HCPI). HCPIs are published monthly for each of the EU countries individually, plus composite ones for the whole of the EU and for the member states using the euro. The HCPI is the measure used by the European Central Bank when deciding what interest rates to set in the eurozone.

Before we proceed, a word of caution: be careful not to confuse a rise or fall in **inflation** with a rise or fall in prices. A rise in inflation means a **faster** increase in prices. A fall in inflation means a **slower** increase in prices (but still an increase as long as inflation is positive).

3.2 THE COSTS OF INFLATION

Why is inflation a problem? If prices go up by 10%, does it really matter? Provided your wages keep up with prices, you won't have to reduce your standard of living.

If people could anticipate the rate of inflation correctly and fully adjust prices and incomes to take account of it, then the costs of inflation would indeed be relatively small. For consumers, they would simply be the relatively minor inconvenience of having to adjust our notions of what a 'fair' price is for each item when we go shopping. For firms, they would again be the relatively minor costs of having to change price labels, or prices in catalogues or on menus, or adjust slot machines.

In reality, people frequently make mistakes when predicting the rate of inflation and are not able to adapt fully to it. This leads to the following problems, which are likely to be more serious the higher the rate of inflation becomes and the more the rate fluctuates.

Redistribution – inflation redistributes income away from those on fixed incomes and those in a weak bargaining position, to those who can use their economic power to gain large pay, rent or profit increases. It redistributes wealth to those with assets (e.g. property) that rise in value rapidly during periods of inflation, and away from those with types of savings that pay rates of interest below the rate of inflation and hence whose value is eroded by inflation.

Uncertainty and lack of investment – inflation tends to cause uncertainty among the business community, especially when the rate of inflation fluctuates. (Generally, the higher the rate of inflation, the more it fluctuates.) If it is difficult for firms to predict their costs and revenues, they may be discouraged from investing. This will reduce the rate of economic growth. On the other hand, policies to reduce the rate of inflation may themselves reduce the rate of economic growth, especially in the short run. This may then provide the government with a policy dilemma.

Balance of payment – inflation is likely to have a negative effect on the balance of payments. If a country suffers from relatively high inflation, its exports will become less competitive in world markets. At the same time, imports will become relatively cheaper than home-produced goods. Thus exports will fall and imports will rise. As a result, the balance of payments will deteriorate and/or the exchange rate will fall. Both of these effects can cause problems.

Resources – extra resources are likely to be used to cope with the effects of inflation. Accountants and other financial experts may have to be employed by companies to help them cope with the uncertainties caused by inflation.

The costs of inflation may be relatively mild if inflation is kept to single figures. They can be very serious, however, if inflation gets out of hand. If inflation develops into hyperinflation, with prices rising hundreds or even thousands of per cent per year, the whole basis of the market economy will be undermined.

3.3 REQUIRED RATE OF RETURN

Inflation affects the returns that a provider of funds will require. As inflation increases so will the minimum return required by an investor. For example, for an investment of \$100 now, a return of 5% will provide \$105 in one year's time. However, if inflation is expected to be 15%, then \$105 in one year's time will buy only 105/1.15 = \$91.30 worth of goods at today's prices. To be able to buy \$105 worth of goods at today's prices i.e. to give a real rate of return of 5%, the investor will need a nominal return of $105 \times 1.15 = 1.2075$ i.e. a return of 20.75%.

3.4 IMPACT OF INFLATION ON BUSINESS CASH FLOWS AND PROFITS

The real effects on the level of profits and the cash flow position of a business of a sustained rate of inflation depends on the form that inflation is taking and the nature of the markets in which the company is operating. One way of analysing inflation is to distinguish between demand-pull inflation and cost-push inflation.

Demand-pull inflation might occur when excess aggregate monetary demand in the economy and hence demand for particular goods and services enables companies to raise prices and expand profit margins.

Cost-push inflation will occur when there are increases in production costs independent of the state of demand, e.g. rising raw material costs or rising labour costs. The initial effect is to reduce profit margins and the extent to which these can be restored depends on the ability of companies to pass on cost increases as price increases for customers.

One would expect that the effect of cost-push inflation on company profits and cash flow would always be negative, but that with demand-pull inflation profits and cash flow might be increased, at least in nominal terms and in the short run. In practice, however, even demand-pull inflation may have negative effects on profits and cash flow.

Demand-pull inflation may in any case work through cost. This is especially true if companies use pricing strategies in which prices are determined by cost plus some mark-up.

- Excess demand for goods leads companies to expand output.
- This leads to excess demand for factors of production, especially labour, so costs (e.g. wages) rise.
- Companies pass on the increased cost as higher prices.

In most cases inflation will reduce profits and cash flow, especially in the long run.

ACTIVITY 2

How will inflation affect the pricing of goods and services?

For a suggested answer, see the 'Answers' section at the end of the book.

CONCLUSION

This chapter has given a brief overview of the ways in which monetary policies can impact on the financial management decisions of a business.

SELF-TEST QUESTIONS

		Paragraph
1	What is the monetary base sometimes called?	1.2
2	How does a change in interest affect the economy?	1.4
3	Describe the speculative motive for holding money.	2.1
4	Why do lenders demand interest for loans?	2.2
5	How do real rates of interest differ from nominal rates?	2.5
6	What is demand-pull inflation?	3.4

Chapter 11

SHORT- AND MEDIUM-TERM FINANCE

The assets of a business are financed from a variety of sources, which can be categorised into short-term and medium-term credit, long-term debt and equity and in this chapter we consider which sources of finance are likely to be appropriate in different circumstances. As the bank is a key provider of short and medium term finance, we concentrate on the features of overdraft and loan financing. We also look at the legal relationship between the bank and the customer. The other forms of finance that are covered in this chapter are hire purchase and leasing.

This chapter covers Syllabus parts C3, D2 and D3.

CONTENTS

LEARNING OUTCOMES

At the end of this chapter you should be able to:

- Discuss the relative merits and limitations of short-/medium-/long-term finance
- Describe the key factors that should be considered in deciding the mix of short-/medium-/long-term finance in an organisation
- Discuss situations where it may be appropriate to raise short-term finance
- Describe the different forms of bank loans and overdrafts, their terms and conditions
- Explain the legal relationship between bank and customer
- Evaluate the risks associated with increasing the amount of short-term finance in an organisation

- Discuss situations where it may be appropriate to raise medium-term finance
- Describe the main features of hire purchase, and leases
- Compare and contrast the main features of hire purchase, and leases (**Note:** Lease or buy decisions are not examinable).

1 THE CHOICE BETWEEN SHORT-, MEDIUM- AND LONG-TERM FINANCE

Companies need funds to bridge the gap between paying for production of finished goods and receiving money from their customers (working capital). They also need them for buying the non-current assets with which they operate, such as machinery, land and buildings (fixed capital).

The major source of finance for companies is cash from accumulated earnings, which can be used both for working capital and fixed assets, as they are funds which permanently belong to the business. However, these are insufficient for financing a business, particularly a new one, which has not yet had the opportunity to build up reserves of accumulated profits.

Short- or medium-term finance is obtained from the money markets as we will go on to discuss. The way in which a company can obtain long-term finance is by using the capital markets and issuing shares or loan notes (known as debentures in the UK).

1.1 MERITS AND LIMITATIONS OF SHORT-/MEDIUM-/LONG-TERM FINANCE

The largest source of finance for investment in the UK is firms' own internal funds. Given, however, that business profitability depends in large part on the general state of the economy, internal funds as a source of business finance are likely to show considerable cyclical variation. When profits are squeezed in a recession, this source of investment will decline.

Other sources of finance, which include borrowing and the issue of shares and loan notes (debentures), are known as 'external funds'. These are then categorised as short-term, medium-term or long-term sources of finance.

Short-term finance is usually in the form of a short-term bank loan or overdraft facility, and is used by business as a form of working capital to aid it in its day-to-day business operations.

Medium-term finance, again provided largely by banks, is usually in the form of a loan with set repayment targets. It is common for such loans to be made at a fixed rate of interest, with repayments being designed to fit in with the business's expected cash flow. Bank lending has been the most volatile source of business finance, and has been particularly sensitive to the state of the economy. While part of the reason is the lower demand for loans during a recession, part of the reason is the caution of banks in granting loans if prospects for the economy are poor.

Long-term finance, especially in the UK, tends to be acquired through the stock market. It will usually be in the form of **shares (or equities)**. This is where members of the public or institutions (such as pension funds) buy a part ownership in the company and, as a result, receive dividends on those shares. The dividends depend on the amount of profit the company makes and distributes to shareholders. The proportion of business financing from this source clearly depends on the state of the stock market. In the late 1990s, with a buoyant stock market, the proportion of funds obtained through share issue increased.

Alternatively, firms can issue loan notes **(or debentures)**. These securities are fixed-interest loans to firms. Loan note holders have a prior claim on company shares. Their interest must be paid in full before shareholders can receive any dividends.

Some investors are more flexible than others because they are not locked into a few available sources of funds. Investors would like many financing alternatives in order to minimise their cost of funds at any point in time. Unfortunately, not many firms are in this enviable position through the duration of a business cycle.

At the time the financing decision is made, the investor is never sure if it is the right one. Should the financing be long-term or short-term, debt or equity, and so on? At each point a decision is made until a final financing method is reached. In most cases the investor will balance short-term versus long-term considerations against a composition of the firm's assets and the firm's willingness to accept risk. The ratio of long-term financing to short-term financing at any point will be greatly influenced by the term structure of interest rates. (The term structure of interest rates refers to the way in which the yield on a security varies according to the term of the borrowing, that is the length of the time until the debt will be repaid as shown by the yield curve. Normally, the longer the term of an asset to maturity the higher the rate of interest paid on the asset.)

In conclusion, a company will generally use short-term finance to invest in short-term assets (such as working capital and short life non-current assets), but medium-term and long-term finance to invest in longer life non-current assets.

The advantage of short-term finance is that it is usually cheaper and the company doesn't have to lock itself into fixed interest rates for a long period, but can take advantage of any interest changes as it regularly renegotiates its financing terms. This will be particularly attractive if the interest rates are volatile and likely to fall. However, this regular renegotiating of interest rates for short-term finance can be time-consuming. Consequently, companies sometimes choose to use more expensive long-term finance because it is more secure and stable, and is therefore easier to manage. Medium-term finance can be used to balance the benefits of each of the other types of finance. For example, medium-term finance is more expensive than short-term finance but cheaper than long-term. However, it is more secure and stable than short-term finance but not as much so as long-term.

1.2 OVERVIEW OF SOURCES OF FINANCE

In order to provide a framework for study of finance, the sources of finance must be classified in an appropriate way. There are a number of possible classifications, but for the purposes of this text three distinctions are of particular importance:

- the distinction between equity and other finance
- the sub-division of equity into internally generated and new issues
- the division of non-equity finance into long-term, medium-term, short-term and special categories.

The following classification is therefore applied.

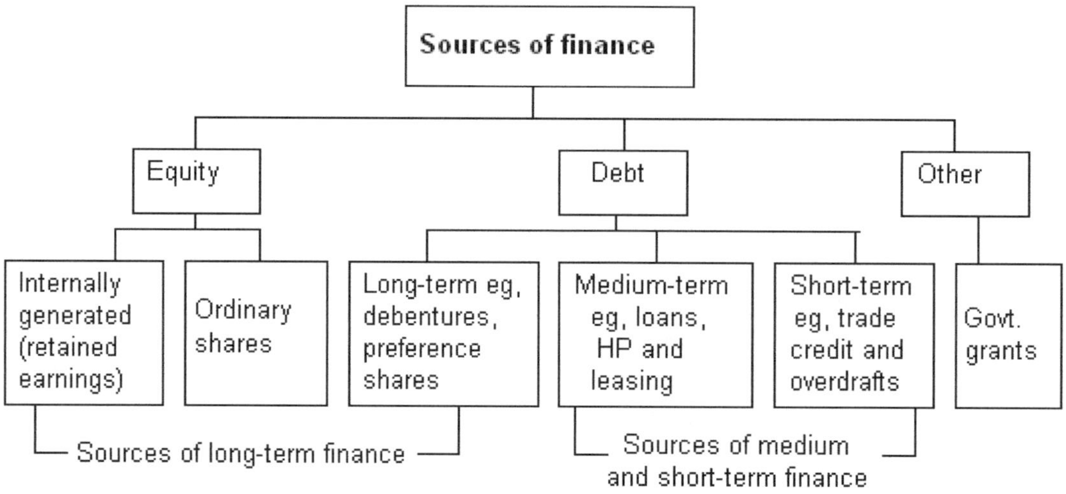

Each of these categories of finance will need to be considered in more detail as the text progresses.

Definitions of long-term, medium-term and short-term are somewhat elastic but as a rough guide the following durations can be taken:

- short-term = up to one year
- medium-term = 1 year to 7 years
- long-term = 7 years or more.

1.3 DECIDING THE MIX OF SHORT-, MEDIUM- AND LONG-TERM FINANCE

A vast range of funding alternatives is open to companies and new developments occur every day. Before examining the various sources of finance available, we are going to consider some of the criteria which a business owner may use when selecting sources of finance for a new project. The business faces at least two major decisions. Should it:

(i) use finance from internal resources?

(ii) raise finance externally from debt or equity and if so where should it be raised from and in which form?

For a new company just starting up, the choice might be very limited and they may be looking for sources of finance aimed specially at them. We will look at their predicament in a later chapter.

The internal resources – when looking at its internal resources, the company needs to consider certain issues:

- How much cash will be available. The company needs to consider the amount held in current and projected cash balances and short-term investments, and how much of this will be needed to support existing operations.
- If the company's projected cash flow is not sufficient to fund the new project then it could consider tightening its control of working capital to improve its cash position. For example, pressurising customers for early settlement, running down inventory levels and lengthening the payment period to suppliers could increase cash resources.

The external resources – if the necessary finance cannot be provided internally, then the company has to consider raising finance externally. Issues to be considered include:

- **Cost** – the higher the cost of funding, the lower the firm's profit. Debt finance tends to be cheaper than equity. This is because providers of debt take less risks than providers of equity and therefore earn less return. This is because:
  - interest has to be paid before dividends
  - in the event of liquidation, debt finance is paid off before equity
  - debt interest is tax deductible (unlike equity dividends) making it even cheaper to a taxpaying company
  - arrangement costs are usually lower on debt finance than equity finance and once again, unlike equity arrangement costs, they are also tax deductible.

- **Duration** – as noted above finance can be arranged for various time periods. Normally, but not invariably, long-term finance is more expensive than short-term finance. This is because lenders normally perceive the risks as being higher on long-term advances. Long-term finance does however, carry the advantage of security, whereas sources of short-term finance can often be withdrawn at short notice. Short-term loans have to be regularly renewed and the company carries the risk that lenders may refuse to extend further credit. This risk is at its highest on overdraft borrowing where the bank can call in the overdraft 'on demand'. With long-term borrowing, as long as the borrower does not breach the debt covenants involved, the finance is assured for the duration of the loan.

  In choosing between short-term, medium-term and long-term borrowing, the firm should consider the textbook rule of thumb for prudent financing: 'finance short-term investments with short-term funds and long-term investments with long-term funds'. Simply, this means use cheap short-term borrowing where it is safe to do so (investments that are short-term in nature and hence renewal risk is not a problem) but use medium- or long-term finance for longer lived investments.

- **Gearing** – this refers to the ratio of debt to equity finance. Although high gearing involves the use of cheap debt finance it does bring with it the risk of having to meet regular repayments of interest and principal on the loans. If these are not met the company could end up in liquidation. On the other hand too little debt could result in earnings dilution. For example the issue of a large amount of equity to fund a new project could result in a decrease in earnings per share despite an increase in total earnings.

- **Size of the company** – not all companies have access to all sources of finance. Small companies traditionally have problems in raising equity and long-term debt finance. These problems are investigated later but remember that many firms do not have an unlimited choice of funding arrangements.

  A quoted company is one whose shares are dealt in on a recognised stock exchange or on the Alternative Investment Market (AIM). The effect is that shares in such a company represent a highly liquid asset. This, in turn, makes it much easier to attract new investors to buy new shares issued by the company because these investors know that they can always sell their shares if they wish to realise their investment.

Dealings in second-hand shares may appear to be irrelevant so far as the company is concerned as they do not represent an extra inflow of funds. They are, however, relevant in that they provide an indication of the market valuation of the shares in that company, and hence the terms on which new shares could be issued.

Investment in shares of unquoted companies represents the acquisition of a highly illiquid investment. For this reason it is much more difficult for such a company to raise finance by new share issues.

- **Security available** – many lenders will require assets to be pledged as security against loans. Good quality assets such as land and buildings provide security for borrowing – intangible assets such as capitalised research and development expenditure usually do not. In the absence of good asset security, borrowing may not be an option.

- **Covenants** – if an entity has already borrowed money from one lender, that lender might have insisted on covenants in the original loan agreement which may now restrict the entity's behaviour. Covenants are agreements in the loan agreement which aim to protect the lender's position. For example, a covenant may prevent an entity from borrowing any more money from other lenders.

- **The current state of equity markets.** In a period of falling share prices many companies will be reluctant to sell new shares. They feel the price received will be too low. This will dilute the wealth of the existing owners. Note this does not apply to rights issues where shares are sold to the existing owners of the company. New issues of shares on the UK stock exchanges have been rare over the last few years due to the bear market.

After consideration of the above points the company will be in a position to decide between the use of debt or equity finance. The last major decision is what type of finance should be used and where should it be raised?

2 RAISING SHORT-TERM FINANCE

Credit is the capacity to borrow. It is the right to incur debt for goods and/or services and repay the debt over some specified future time period. Credit provision to a company means that the business is allowed the use of a productive good while it is being paid for.

The process of using borrowed, leased or 'joint venture' resources from someone else is sometimes called leverage. Using the leverage provided by someone else's capital helps the user business go farther than it otherwise would. For instance, a company that puts up $1,000 and borrows an additional $4,000 is using 80% leverage. The objective is to increase total net income and the return on a company's own equity capital.

2.1 BANK LOANS

Bank loans are a very flexible form of finance. Banks will consider applications for loans for virtually any term, from a few months to several years. Bank loans to businesses are rarely for more than seven years, unlike loans to individuals which can be for anything up to 25 years in the case of a mortgage for the purchase of a home.

Interest on a bank loan can be fixed for the duration of the loan, particularly if the loan is short-term. However, for longer-term loans, the interest is usually at a variable rate or 'floating rate'. Variable rate interest means that the interest payable is linked to a reference interest rate, which is either the bank's base rate or a money market interest rate such as the Secured Overnight Financing Rate (SOFR). For example, a business might pay 2% above base rate on a loan, or 1.5% above SOFR, and so on. At regular intervals throughout the term of the loan, the interest rate is adjusted if the reference interest rate has changed since the previous review date.

Example

BVC borrows $30,000 from its bank for three years. Interest is charged at 1.5% above the bank's base rate. The starting date for the loan is 1 April Year 1, and interest is charged every six months. The interest rate will be reviewed every six months, on 1 October Year 1, 1 April Year 2 and so on. On 1 April Year 1, the bank's base rate is 5%.

When the loan is provided, the bank will open a loan account for BVC, showing that BVC owes $30,000. (The borrowed money might be paid into BVC's current account, but the loan account shows how much BVC owes the bank.)

For the first six months of the loan period, BVC will pay interest at 6.5% on the $30,000. The interest will be charged to BVC's loan account, and under the terms of the loan agreement, BVC will be required to:

- pay the interest, probably from its current account, and
- possibly also repay some of the loan principal, depending on the repayment terms in the loan agreement.

After six months, the interest rate will be reviewed. If the bank's base rate has gone up since 1 April from 5% to, say, 5.5%, the interest on the loan for the next six months will be at the rate of 7%.

(**Note:** Interest rates are always quoted at an annual rate. So interest at 7% for six months will actually be $3.50 for each $100 borrowed.)

With a variable rate loan, the interest rate therefore goes up and down over the term of the loan depending on changes in the bank's base rate or the SOFR rate.

2.2 TYPES OF BANK LOAN

There are various ways of classifying loans:

- **payment terms**, e.g. instalment versus single payment
- **period-of-payment terms**, e.g. short-term versus intermediate-term or long-term
- **in the manner of its security terms**, e.g. secured versus unsecured
- **in interest payment terms**, e.g. simple interest versus add-on, versus discount, versus balloon.

On the basis of the above classification, there are twelve common types of loans, namely: short-term loans, intermediate-term loans, long-term loans, unsecured loans, secured loans, instalment loans, single payment ('bullet') loans, simple-interest loans, add-on interest loans, discount or front-end loans, balloon loans and amortised loans.

- Short-term loans are credit that is usually paid back in one year or less. They are usually used in financing the purchase of operating inputs, wages for hired labour, machinery and equipment, and/or family living expenses. Usually lenders expect short-term loans to be repaid after their purposes have been served, e.g. after the expected production output has been sold.

  Included under short-term loans are loans for operating production inputs, which are assumed to be self-liquidating. In other words, although the inputs are used up in the production, the added returns from their use will repay the money borrowed to purchase the inputs, plus interest.

- Intermediate-term (IT) loans are credit extended for several years, usually one to five years. This type of credit is normally used for purchases of buildings, equipment and other production inputs that require longer than one year to generate sufficient returns to repay the loan.

- Long-term loans are those loans for which repayment exceeds five to seven years and may extend to 40 years. This type of credit is usually extended on assets (such as land) which have a long productive life in the business. Some land improvement programmes like land levelling, reforestation, land clearing and drainage-way construction are usually financed with long-term credit.

- Unsecured loans are credit given out by lenders on no other basis than a promise by the borrower to repay. The borrower does not have to put up collateral and the lender relies on credit reputation. Unsecured loans usually carry a higher interest rate than secured loans and may be difficult or impossible to arrange for businesses with a poor credit record.

- Secured loans are those loans that involve a pledge of some or all of a business's assets. The lender requires security as protection for its depositors against the risks involved in the use planned for the borrowed funds. The borrower may be able to bargain for better terms by putting up collateral, which is a way of backing one's promise to repay.

- Instalment loans are those loans in which the borrower or credit customer repays a set amount each period (week, month, year) until the borrowed amount is cleared. Instalment credit is similar to charge account credit, but usually involves a formal legal contract for a predetermined period with specific payments. With this plan, the borrower usually knows precisely how much will be paid and when.

- Simple interest loans are those loans in which interest is paid on the unpaid loan balance. Thus, the borrower is required to pay interest only on the actual amount of money outstanding and only for the actual time the money is used (e.g. 30 days, 90 days, 4 months and 2 days, 12 years and 1 month).

- Add-on interest loans are credit in which the borrower pays interest on the full amount of the loan for the entire loan period. Interest is charged on the face amount of the loan at the time it is made and then 'added on'. The resulting sum of the principal and interest is then divided equally by the number of payments to be made. The company is thus paying interest on the face value of the note although it has use of only a part of the initial balance once principal payments begin. This type of loan is sometimes called the 'flat rate' loan and usually results in an interest rate higher than the one specified.

- Discount or front-end loans are loans in which the interest is calculated and then subtracted from the principal first. For example, a $5,000 discount loan at 10% for one year would result in the borrower only receiving $4,500 to start with, and the $5,000 debt would be paid back, as specified, by the end of a year.

  On a discount loan, the lender discounts or deducts the interest in advance. Thus, the effective interest rates on discount loans are usually much higher than (in fact, more than double) the specified interest rates.

- Bullet loans are those loans in which the borrower pays no principal until the amount is due. Because the company must eventually pay the debt in full, it is important to have the self-discipline and professional integrity to set aside money to be able to do so. This type of loan is sometimes called the 'lump sum' or 'single payment' loan, and is generally repaid in less than a year.

- Balloon loans are loans that normally require only interest payments each period, until the final payment, when all principal is due at once. They are sometimes referred to as the 'last payment due', and have a concept that is the same as the bullet loan, but the due date for repaying principal may be five years or more in the future rather than the customary 90 days or 6 months for the bullet loan. In some cases a principal payment is made each time interest is paid, but because the principal payments do not amortise (pay off) the loan, a large sum is due at the loan maturity date.

- Amortised loans are a partial payment plan where part of the loan principal and interest on the unpaid principal are repaid each year. The standard plan of amortisation, used in many intermediate and long-term loans, calls for equal payments each period, with a larger proportion of each succeeding payment representing principal and a small amount representing interest.

  The constant annual payment feature of the amortised loan is similar to the 'add on' loan described above, but involves less interest because it is paid only on the outstanding loan balance, as with simple interest.

ACTIVITY 1

Distinguish between a bullet loan and a balloon loan.

For a suggested answer, see the 'Answers' section at the end of the book.

2.3 OVERDRAFTS

A bank loan is for a given period of time and for a given amount (the 'loan principal'). When a bank makes a loan to a customer, it opens a loan account, and the loan is eventually paid back when the balance on the loan account is reduced to 0.

With a bank overdraft, a bank allows a customer to pay more out of its current account than there is cash in the account. An overdraft is therefore a form of borrowing through the current account. The bank sets a limit to the size of the overdraft, and the customer can be overdrawn on the account up to the agreed limit. The size of the overdraft continually changes, with payments into and out of the account reducing and increasing the balance.

Interest on an overdraft is usually charged at a daily rate on the overdraft balance, and the rate is variable (usually subject to change whenever the bank alters its base rate). Overdrafts are repayable on demand. Unlike for private individuals, businesses pay an arrangement fee on an overdraft. This is in addition to the overdraft interest and is charged for setting up the overdraft facility.

There are two types of overdraft facility (overdraft arrangement):

- committed
- uncommitted.

With a committed facility, the bank agrees to allow the customer to be overdrawn up to the agreed limit, at any time during an agreed period of time. For example, a bank might allow a business to be overdrawn by up to $100,000 at any time for the next two years after the agreement is made.

With an uncommitted facility, the bank agrees to allow the customer to be overdrawn up to an agreed limit, but reserves the right to reduce the overdraft limit, or withdraw the overdraft facility completely, at any time and without notice. The customer therefore relies on the goodwill and support of the bank for any overdraft that it has.

A committed facility is more expensive to arrange, but an uncommitted facility exposes a business to the risk that the bank can demand repayment at any time, and effectively make the business insolvent.

2.4 LOAN TERMS AND CONDITIONS

The terms and conditions of a loan agreement or an overdraft agreement can vary considerably. Every agreement should specify:

- the term of the agreement
- the amount of the loan (the 'loan principal') or overdraft limit
- the interest rate payable, which is usually a variable rate and expressed as a margin above base rate or SOFR
- the frequency of interest payments.

For a loan, the agreement will specify whether the loan principal is to be repaid gradually over the term of the loan, or whether there will be no principal repayments until the end of the loan period.

Secured and unsecured loans

Loans and overdrafts can be either secured or unsecured. Borrowing is secured when the bank takes security for the money it lends. For companies that borrow, security is provided in the form of a charge over its assets. A charge can be either a fixed charge or a floating charge.

With a fixed charge, the borrower provides security in the form of a specified asset. If the borrower subsequently defaults and fails to make a scheduled interest payment or a scheduled repayment of loan principal, the lender can take the secured asset. This can then be sold to raise the money to pay off the loan. A fixed charge can be taken over an item of equipment or property. Until the loan is repaid in full, the borrower cannot sell off the secured asset, which must remain available to the lender as security for the loan.

With a floating charge, the borrower provides security in the form of assets such as its inventory and receivables. The bank allows the borrower to continue to trade, using up its inventory and buying new inventory, and using the money received from receivables but creating new receivables from new sales. However, if the borrower defaults, and fails to make a scheduled payment on the loan, the bank can call in its security. The floating charge will 'crystallise', and the bank will acquire the rights over the categories of assets that are subject to the floating charge that the business owns at that time. For example, if a bank has a floating charge over a borrower's receivables, if the borrower defaults and the bank calls on its security, the floating charge over the receivables will crystallise, and the bank will obtain the right to the money currently due from the receivables of the business.

The main difference between a fixed and floating charge is that a fixed charge relates to a specific asset, which the borrower cannot sell off or use until the loan is repaid. In contrast, a business can use assets subject to a floating charge. Even when there is a floating charge over receivables, the business can use the money from its receivables in whatever way that it wants, and does not have to use the money to pay interest or repay principal on the loan. Assets subject to a floating charge are therefore under the full control of the borrower unless and until the security is exercised and the floating charge crystallises.

With some loan agreements, a bank will take a fixed and floating charge from a company. The fixed charge might be a charge on a property owned by the company and the floating charge might be a charge on the 'undertaking' – in other words, all the other assets of the business.

For non-corporate borrowers, banks might take security in a form other than a charge, which will operate in a way similar to a fixed charge.

A bank might also ask for a personal guarantee from the business owner. For example, the owner of a business wanting to arrange a loan or overdraft facility might be required to provide a personal guarantee, whereby if the business defaults on its loan payment obligations, the bank can seek to recover the money from the individual's personal assets, such as his or her home.

Loans and overdrafts might be unsecured. When borrowing is unsecured, the bank relies on the borrower to pay the interest and repay the loan principal. If the borrower defaults, the bank does not have any security to call on, and cannot claim any assets of the business that it can sell off to raise money to repay the loan. Instead, the bank can take action through the courts to put the business into liquidation but would be one of the unsecured payables of the business in the 'winding up' of the business.

Other terms and conditions ('covenants')

A loan or overdraft agreement will also have other terms and conditions called covenants. Most of these relate to undertakings given by the borrower to the bank.

For example, if a loan is unsecured, the borrower might be required to give an undertaking that it will not subsequently take out any secured loans from any other lender.

The borrower might give an undertaking to provide the bank with regular information about its financial position, such as an statement of profit or loss every six months or a regular cash budget or cash forecast.

A borrower might also give undertakings to keep its financial position acceptable to the bank. For example, the borrower might undertake that its current assets (inventory, receivables and cash) will always be at least twice the amount of its current liabilities (short-term payables). Any such financial ratios in a loan agreement will be continually monitored by the bank.

If the borrower breaches any of the covenants on a loan, it will be in default, and the bank will have a right to call in the loan and exercise any security that it has.

Default

A borrower is in default if it breaches any condition of the loan. Typically, default occurs when the borrower is late with an interest payment.

Under the terms of a loan agreement, a breach of condition gives the bank the right to call in the loan immediately, and if the loan is secured the bank can sell off the secured asset or assets and use the proceeds to repay the loan. In practice, banks are often reluctant to take this action immediately. Instead, a bank will seek to discuss the problem with the borrower, and consider whether a solution can be found. Often, if the borrower is having short-term cash flow difficulties, the bank will be prepared to reschedule the loan repayments and give the borrower more time to pay.

Whenever a business thinks that it might be unable to make a scheduled payment on a loan, it should notify the bank immediately. If the borrower is open and honest with the bank, the bank will normally be prepared to discuss a solution.

In contrast, if a business exceeds its overdraft limit without notifying the bank, the bank's reaction is likely to be hostile. The bank could well insist on reducing the overdraft limit even if that effectively means putting the business into liquidation.

ACTIVITY 2

Your business is well-established and has a good relationship with its bank. It now wishes to arrange a loan of $500,000, and you have been asked to discuss terms with the bank.

What terms might you wish to negotiate, to try to obtain the 'best deal' possible for the loan?

For a suggested answer, see the 'Answers' section at the end of the book.

3 THE LEGAL RELATIONSHIP BETWEEN BANK AND CUSTOMER

3.1 TYPES OF RELATIONSHIP

The relationship arises between a banker and a customer with the opening of an account by the customer with a banker. The application for opening an account is considered as a letter of agreement for establishing the banker-customer relationship.

Because the customer must be an account holder, the basic relationship is that of 'receivable' and 'payable': the banker is the 'receivable' where the account holder deposits money, and the 'payable' where the individual borrows.

However, today the range of banking services is more extensive, and indeed is expanding all the time, so it must be expected that other relationships will arise besides that of 'receivable' and 'payable'. For instance:

- the relationship of principal and agent is present when the customer instructs the bank to buy or sell stocks on the customer's behalf
- when items are held in safe custody the relationship is that of bailor and bailee
- where the bank's executorship service takes on the administration of a deceased's estate the relationship is that of trustee and beneficiary

- duties akin to a trusteeship might also happen when a branch comes into possession of funds or property that belongs to a third party, as when the bank has sold property in mortgage, and has a surplus to pass to the subsequent mortgagee. Obviously the relationship with the customer in that situation is that of a mortgagor with a mortgagee. However, if the security had been given by a third party then another state of affairs would exist between the lender and its surety. There, duties and obligations would arise irrespective of the banker-customer relationship with the borrowing customer.

In English law a fiduciary relationship has been held to exist in relationships such as a bank and its clients, a lawyer and its clients, a doctor and a patient, a trustee and beneficiary, and a director and his or her company.

The primary aim of this equitable doctrine is to prevent those holding positions of power from abusing their authority.

3.2 RESPONSIBILITIES OF BANKERS TO CUSTOMERS

When you open an account with a bank you create a contract. This means that you and your bank have rights and obligations, which arise from the contract (although you should note that the contract is on their terms!). This guide is written with the customer in mind and will only cover the bank's rights where they have a direct impact on the customer.

Once a customer has deposited money with a bank, the bank has a legal right to use the customer's money for any (legal) purpose. Some banks advertise themselves as more ethical than their competitors in order to attract customers.

What can the customer expect from the bank?

- The bank should process cheques coming into and going out of the customer's account.

- If the bank wrongly dishonours a cheque, this may amount to defamation. If this is the case, the bank may have to pay damages.

- If the bank wrongly honours a cheque, they may have to refund the money paid. An example of this is where the customer has cancelled a cheque with due notice, but the bank has still honoured it. However, if the cheque is used to pay something that the customer would have had to pay anyway, such as an outstanding debt, the bank will not have to refund the money.

- The bank should give responsible financial advice. Should the bank give the customer advice they might be expected to act on it. If the bank gives the customer bad advice in this situation, which the customer acts on, the customer may be able to get some recourse. On the other hand, the law is unclear when the bank gives advice to someone who is not a customer.

- The bank must ask for permission from the customer if they have been approached for a credit reference. If the bank has been approached for a credit reference concerning the customer or the customer's company, the customer is entitled to see the reference they give. This reference can give rise to liability on the part of the bank if the customer relies on it to their detriment, and the reference given was overly optimistic. Because of this, banks usually give a reference disclaiming any liability.

- If the bank changes its interest rates on overdrafts they are allowed to notify the customers through newspapers. Customers should not be surprised if they find they are paying more interest on a long-standing overdraft, as the bank is under no obligation to notify the customers individually.

- However, if the customer is the recipient of a loan, depending on the terms of the agreement the bank may be able to change the rates. This would have to be notified individually.

3.3 RESPONSIBILITIES OF CUSTOMERS TO BANKERS

On the other hand, there are certain responsibilities of the customers. The customer must:

- ensure safety and security of the cheque book, ensuring that neither words nor figures can be altered

- take reasonable steps to provide documentation as to who is authorised to give instructions to the bank in order to prevent forgery and fraud

- keep authorisations current

- notify the bank of any suspected problem

- provide safeguards for electronic communications (including telephones, fax and computers).

3.4 TERMINATION OF BANKER-CUSTOMER RELATIONSHIP

As the banker-customer relationship can be established, so it can also be terminated. It arises between a banker and a customer with the opening of an account by the customer with a banker. So, the relationship terminates if the account is closed for any reason.

Banker-customer relationship may be terminated due to the following reasons:

- if a banker does not pay the cheque of a customer, which has been drawn duly on its account, notwithstanding the availability of deposited money in the account

- if the secrecy of the customer's account is not maintained legally and morally by the banker

- if the banker does not provide banking services to the customer properly. For example, if cheques, bills, etc. are not collected without informing the customer

- if the banker does not supply pass book or Statement of Account to the customer

- if any fraudulent cheque comes to the hand of a banker and if it makes payment without informing the customer)

- if the banker fraudulently embezzles the customer's money.

There are four recognised exceptions when a bank may disclose information about its customer's affairs:

- where the bank is required by law to disclose
- where there is a public duty to disclose e.g. if the bank is aware of some transactions that are damaging to the national interest
- where the interest of the bank requires disclosure e.g. the bank sues a customer to recover what it owes
- where the customer has given express or implied consent e.g. the customer might direct a third party to apply to the bank for a reference.

4 BANKS' CRITERIA FOR LENDING

4.1 CAMPARI

We have already determined that the bank-customer relationship is a contractual one, in which the bank is subject to an implied term that it will exercise due skill and care in and about executing the customer's orders. That duty is subsidiary to the bank's main contractual duty, to execute promptly a valid and proper order from the customer.
A bank will therefore be protected in acting upon a customer's order unless the bank:

- knows the order was given dishonestly
- shuts its eyes to the obvious dishonesty
- recklessly executed the order, having failed to make normal inquiries
- negligently executed the order, having failed to make normal inquiries.

To make sure the of this protection traditionally bankers have used the mnemonic **CAMPARI** to remind them of the main points which they have to consider every time they are making a lending decision. How would you measure up?

What does CAMPARI mean?

C=Character – the background and experience of the individuals or business can be a pointer to the potential for success. This includes integrity, past performance, and evidence of financial acumen. No business proposition can be viewed in isolation from the people who will put it into action, and the bank manager will scrutinize both closely.

A=Ability – the likelihood of the business being able to repay the money. This will often depend on the skills and abilities of the owners. On the personal side, intelligence, training and determination should all be considered. On the business front, the bank will look at profitability, capital requirements, and above all cash flow.

M=Means – the means and resources to run the business, and to do so in a way that allows the bank to see what is going on. You may be required to produce quarterly or monthly summaries of how the business is doing. Could you provide them?

P=Purpose – explain in detail why you wish to borrow money. The bank will want to know that you have thought it through, and that it seems sensible. The banker may comment on your purpose in general terms. Remember that you ought to know far more about your type of business than any banker, and treat any advice accordingly. Bankers can offer you knowledge of business theory but they have no practical experience of running their own businesses. However, the bank should tell you whether the form of finance you have asked for is the most suitable.

A=Amount – make sure that you establish the correct amount you need, allowing a margin for error in your forecasts. Be realistic: don't ask for too little or 'just enough to get by'. If you have to come back for an emergency second bite, the bank will really scrutinise the books to see what's gone wrong. The bank will look to the business to put some of its own money in. This shows the borrower's commitment.

R=Repayment – you will usually need to fill in the bank's cash flow forecast forms, to show that your business can afford repayments on the amount you wish to borrow.

I=Interest and Insurance – many lending schemes offer reducing loans over an agreed period and have a fixed rate of interest. If you are borrowing on overdraft, the bank will set the interest rate to reflect its view of the risk – and what it thinks it can get. Risk takes us to insurance. The bank may ask if security is available. They may also ask you to consider taking out insurance cover, against illness for instance. Illness of a key player can be a major risk to a new business.

4.2 ABILITY TO BORROW AND REPAY

'Legal capacity' concerns the borrower's power, in law, to undertake the proposed transaction. Some people, or entities, are unable to enter into certain kinds of contracts.

Those under 18 years old (known as 'minors') cannot enter into certain kinds of contract. These include taking out loans, including, mortgages and HP agreements. At one time minors could not contract at all, but nowadays they can enter into contracts for 'necessaries' – i.e. they can buy food, clothing and so on – but they would not have capacity to contract to buy a luxury holiday or expensive jewellery.

Similarly, undischarged bankrupts are limited in the types of contracts they can enter into.

Some people are incapable of understanding the consequences of entering into a transaction, because they are either temporarily mentally ill, or because they are more permanently disabled. They may be deemed to lack the capacity to contract.

A contract made with someone who is drunk may be 'voidable' (see below) if the other person knows he or she is not in a fit state to understand what he or she is doing or agreeing to.

Care must also be taken where the potential borrower is a company. The lender should examine the company's memorandum and articles of association to ensure that it will not be acting ultra vires in borrowing. You should not assume that the officer of a company approaching you for a loan is fully versed in the powers that the company has available to it.

Similarly, where the borrower is a partnership, care must be taken to examine the partnership terms to establish what borrowings can be raised and who is authorised to arrange them.

Where one party to a legal contract has no legal capacity, the contract will generally be 'void' or 'voidable', depending on the circumstances.

A void contract is one whose legal status is as if it had never been made: in effect, it never existed.

A voidable contact is one that remains in force, unless and until it is declared void by one of the contracting partners.

So, for example, where a child has bought non-necessary goods, the contract would generally be void. The seller could not enforce by suing (he could, however, recover the goods himself). More pertinently in the context of this course, if the contract is for a loan, the lender may have difficulty recovering the debt or enforcing security.

4.3 PURPOSE OF THE LOAN

(a) Does the loan fit in with the type of business that the bank carries on?

Not all banks carry on all types of lending business – indeed it is not so long ago that residential mortgages were almost entirely the province of building societies, with banks concentrating on shorter-term loans. Similarly, some institutions lend only on a fully-secured basis and simply do not make unsecured advances. Most lenders have a preferred area of activity – e.g. trade finance, residential mortgages, or personal loans. In some cases this is laid down by regulations, in others by the expertise and business profile of the institution. Loan proposals outside a lender's area of specialisation will generally be declined and, if possible, the borrower should be directed to a more suitable lender. In any event, a loan proposal that is clearly not in our normal sphere of business should alert our suspicions. Why has the applicant not approached a lender who fits the bill more naturally? Has the applicant in fact done so, and already been turned down? Is the applicant relying on our lack of expertise to cloud our judgement?

(b) Is the purpose of the loan legally and morally acceptable?

Banks are not expected to be their customers' moral guardians, but it is normally good business practice for them to ensure that they 'know their customer' and exercise some discretion over the people with whom they decide to do business.

An obvious example is where there are government controls on dealings with certain countries – e.g. if Britain were at war with another country, then in the interests of national security controls would most likely be introduced in respect of dealings with residents or citizens of that country. Less obviously, consider a prospective borrower looking to engage in dubious – albeit not illegal – activity. In this case the bank may decline, not because of commercial considerations (some dubious pursuits do very well, after all!), but because it wishes to protect its reputation and standing in the community.

(c) Is the purpose of the loan viable? There is little merit in a bank making advances for hare-brained schemes with little likelihood of success, even if it takes full security over the loan, Careful and courteous probing into the customer's plans not only shows a willingness to understand the customer's position, but may also highlight weaknesses in planning which can be remedied.

The loan amount should be considered from two perspectives: firstly, and most obviously, is it too high – so high that the borrower is unlikely to be able to repay it? Secondly, is it high enough? It is not uncommon for people to underestimate the resources they will need for a given project: for example they may have omitted to consider all the expenses they could incur. This may mean that they need to seek further funding later on, but the availability of this cannot be guaranteed, and failure to obtain it could endanger the viability of the entire project. It is much better to ensure that the full amount is ascertained at the outset.

A realistic assessment may also help the customer to focus on whether the project as a whole is really viable, and whether the proposed borrowings allow sufficient room to cope with unforeseen contingencies. Slightly larger borrowings properly scheduled and budgeted for at the outset, can place a customer under considerably less strain than 'emergency' funding arranged at a later date.

4.4 AMOUNT OF THE BORROWING

Of course, at least as important is an assessment of whether the borrowings are excessive – both in relation to the project itself, and to the borrower's ability to repay. We shall look at the latter in more detail in a moment, but proposed borrowings that are excessive for the planned purpose should also put us on the alert. Is the borrower seeking surplus funds because plans are imprecise and he or she is seeking a 'buffer' (as opposed to a properly planned contingency sum)? Is the borrower in fact having wider financing problems and seeking extra funds to support day-to-day living expenses, under the guise of funding a particular project?

As part of this assessment we should look at the proportion the customer is proposing to contribute from its own funds. A bank will be more comfortable with a large loan where the customer is proposing to provide 25% of the funding, with the bank lending the remaining 75% than it would be with a smaller loan where the bank funds 95% of the project. For one thing, the customer's 'stake' in the enterprise provides a buffer should things go badly, but as importantly, the fact that its own money is at risk ensures a measure of commitment which may mean that the customer behaves with greater financial discipline.

4.5 SECURITY FOR LENDING

Security should not be seen as a substitute for a thorough assessment of all the other factors we have considered above. If, for example, a customer seems to have little prospect of meeting repayments then no amount of security should encourage the lender to lend. Nonetheless, security can provide a lender with valuable comfort – in effect it provides a safety net in case things do not go to plan.

It is essential that the lender understands and is skilled in enforcing any security it takes. The exercise of some types of security can take time, be costly and involve administrative difficulties; it may also involve unhelpful adverse publicity.

Secured and unsecured lending

Secured lending – in general, to 'secure' lending means to give the lender some means of assurance – security – of repayment. It is achieved by making arrangements so that if the borrower defaults, the lender can claim certain assets or rights so as to enforce a recovery, or limit exposure to loss.

The benefits of taking security are therefore twofold: firstly, there is the obvious – it provides a safety net in the event that the borrower defaults and the lender has to take steps to recoup the money it has lent. There is, however, a second and very important benefit, and that is the effect on the borrower's attitude. Where the asset over which the lender has taken security represents something of value to the borrower, the prospect of potentially losing it may increase the borrower's financial self-discipline and therefore the likelihood of being able to keep up repayments.

Security can be taken over a variety of assets, the most typical being:

- land and property
- certain kinds of investment (stocks and bonds, equities, collective investment schemes, National Savings products and other investments)
- life assurance policies
- cash.

The asset over which security is taken may not belong to the borrower. Although it often does. As an alternative, loans can be secured by way of guarantees and third-party security (rights over assets owed by someone other than the borrower).

It is worth considering briefly the circumstance in which security may be taken.

Where there is some risk to the source of repayment. For example, consider a borrower planning to repay a loan from his or her salary. If the job is highly specialised, and he or she loses it, there may well be no other similar employment available locally; the lender may wish to take some security to protect itself.

Where the loan is to buy a specific asset, that asset may lend itself to being used as security for the loan. An example is a mortgage to fund a property purchase.

Where the loan is intended to be repaid from the proceeds of a specific asset, that asset may be used as security for the loan. An example is where a bank lends money to a client now against the security of an investment that will mature in the future, so that the eventual proceeds of the investment will repay the loan.

What value should be advanced against security?

Lenders need to consider a number of factors when making secured advances. The fact that it is there does not remove all risk entirely, and of course actually exercising it may entail administrative difficulties, costs, or other concerns that make it unattractive when 'push comes to shove'. For this reason, its true value needs to be objectively assessed at the outset.

This often means that rather than lending 100% of the value of the security, a lender will make a loan of a lesser amount – a sum adjusted down by an amount known as a 'margin'.

The main concerns to be borne in mind when considering what margin to apply will be:

- **Fluctuations in the asset's price**. Most asset classes – property, stocks and shares, etc. – can go down as well as up in price, and between the date the loan is made and the date the security is realised, that security could fall in value. Ultimately it may fail to cover the loan.

- **Expenses incurred in realising the asset** – stamp duties, estate agent's fees, legal fees – depending on the nature of the asset.

- **Time taken to realise the asset.** The point here is once the lender has decided to take legal action and enforce its security, it may be some time before it can actually realise (sell) the security. This is particularly so in the case of property, which can take a year or more to sell. During this period the capital amount of the loan may have been frozen, but interest will continue to roll up, and therefore the total amount owing may increase substantially before the sale proceeds of the security can be applied.

Where the lender does not take security as described above, the lending is described as 'unsecured'. In this case its risk is clearly rather higher: its prospects of repayment depend entirely on the borrower's ability and intention to repay. However, as we noted earlier, ideally a lender will not make a secured advance if it does not believe that it would have had a reasonable prospect of repayment on an unsecured basis: the taking of security merely adds a greater degree of comfort.

The consideration for lenders in connection with unsecured loans is essentially as set out above. It is usual (and very good discipline) for banks to use a structured approach when assessing propositions, to make sure that all these issues have been properly addressed. That is, the bank should have a standard format for loan assessments and there may well be some automated filter, such as computer-based assessment, statistical analysis or credit scoring (which we shall look at later) to remove the subjective element from the decision-making process.

It should be noted that the manner in which applications are handled these days is often very different from the personal approach which prevailed only a decade or so ago; volumes of lending have increased dramatically, and for many lenders the vast majority of applications for unsecured loans are processed and assessed automatically.

Where applications are individually assessed, either because that is the lender's policy or because the application is 'out of the normal run of things', it is vital to apply some sort of discipline to ensure that all of the relevant factors are considered.

The most common types of unsecured personal lending we shall encounter include overdrafts (both authorised and unauthorised) and personal loans of various types.

4.6 THE RELATIONSHIP BETWEEN SECURITY AND RISK-BASED LENDING

Where security is available, it clearly plays a role in reducing the lender's risk associated with a particular loan; so we may regard a secured loan as generally being less risky than an unsecured one. Security is not homogeneous, however, as we shall see in future chapters. Different forms of security can vary considerably both in terms of how robust their values are when we come to sell them, and how easy it is to actually gain control and possession of them (enforceability). This latter factor will be determined not only by the nature of the security itself, but also by whether the lender has the systems, procedures and knowledge to actually enforce the particular type of security in question.

For example, a lender may have the skills and systems to enforce security over bank deposits and portfolios of stocks and shares, but it may have no processes to facilitate security over property. In this case, a mortgage over a house would hold little appeal for it.

Lenders therefore take into account the availability and nature of any security when assessing loans. This assessment will determine not only whether they decide to proceed, but also, quite possibly, how much they charge for the loan (both in terms of interest rates and for any charges specifically relating to the security).

It should be clear to you at this stage that a lender may be inclined to regard an unsecured loan as riskier than a secured one, and to expect a greater reward for the risk taken in granting accordingly, if indeed it decides to proceed at all.

5 LEASING

The popularity of leasing has grown over recent years to be a particularly important source of finance. Leasing is now common for vehicles, office and production equipment etc.

A lease is a contract between a lessor and a lessee for the hire of a particular asset. The lessor retains **ownership** of the asset but conveys the right to the **use** of the asset to the lessee for an agreed period, in return for the payment of specified rentals.

There are many different types of lease arrangement. In particular, lease-purchases are the modern equivalent of hire purchase (HP).

5.1 CHARACTERISTICS OF LEASING

Leasing is a means of financing the use of capital equipment, the underlying principle being that use is more important than ownership. It is a medium-term financial arrangement, usually from one to ten years.

The lessee avoids the initial cost of buying an asset by leasing it and agreeing to pay a fixed annual charge to the lessor instead. This means that the lessee does not have to negotiate the finance separately from the asset investment, and it gives the lessee certainty of cash flows over the asset's life. Also, the lessee is not stuck with an obsolete asset at the end of the lease period.

From the lessor's perspective, leasing an asset out gives rise to a fixed stream of cash inflows. The asset is used as a cash generator. Also, if the value of the asset appreciates over the life of the lease, the lessor can benefit from this when the lease ends.

Leasing should be distinguished from short-term hire, contract hire and rental, which are all means of filling a temporary need. In the case of leasing, the firm intending to use the equipment selects its own supplier and then approaches the finance house which purchases the equipment and leases it to the user.

5.2 HIRE PURCHASE

Hire purchase finance is commonly associated with the purchase of durable goods by consumers. However hire purchase is also used by businesses as a means of finance for capital equipment. The initial transaction involves the hire purchase company, typically a subsidiary of a clearing bank, purchasing the equipment with the use then being transferred to the hirer, who after a series of regular payments, becomes the legal owner of the equipment. The title does not transfer to the hirer until the last payment has been made.

The fundamental distinction between the processes of hiring and leasing lies with the eventual title to the plant and equipment under consideration. With leases, legal ownership never transfers to the user.

The significance of hire purchase to the provider of the funds is that security for the loan is provided by the equipment until the final instalment has been paid. The benefit to the recipient lies with its ability to conserve perhaps scarce cash resources for other purposes within the organisation. No upfront payment is required other than providing the initial deposit, in order to acquire the use of the equipment. Many companies have made use of this method because of its ease of operation (no lengthy negotiations with the bank manager), and it could enable the firm to obtain financing that would not be available from other sources.

5.3 COMPARISON OF LEASING AND HIRE PURCHASE

Most types of equipment in normal use within the business environment may be obtained through leasing or hire purchase. Equipment can cost as little as a few hundred pounds, or more than $100 million in the case of some major industrial plant.

The fundamental characteristic of a lease is that ownership never passes to the customer. The leasing company claims the capital allowances and passes the benefit on to the customer, by way of reduced rental charges. The customer can generally deduct the full cost of lease rentals from taxable income, as a trading expense. This is not the case with hire purchase. After all the payments have been made, the customer becomes the owner of the equipment, either automatically or on payment of an option to purchase fee. For tax purposes, from the beginning of the agreement the customer is treated as the owner of the equipment and so can claim capital allowances. As with leasing, the customer will normally be responsible for maintenance of the equipment.

A hire purchase or leasing agreement is a medium-term facility, which cannot be withdrawn, provided the payments are made. The uncertainty that may be associated with facilities such as overdrafts, which are repayable on demand, is removed. However, both hire purchase and leasing agreements are long-term commitments and it may not be possible, or could prove costly, to terminate them early. The regular nature of the payments and their usually fixed amount helps a business to forecast cash flow. The business is able to compare the payments with the expected revenue and profits generated by the use of the asset. If, however, you wish to alter the payment frequency or amount, this will have to be agreed in advance with the finance company.

In most cases the payments are fixed throughout the hire purchase or lease agreement, so a business will know at the beginning of the agreement what their repayments will be. This can be beneficial in times of low, stable or rising interest rates but may appear expensive if interest rates are falling. On some agreements, such as those for a longer term, the finance company may offer the option of variable rate agreements. In such cases, rentals or instalments will vary with current interest rates; hence it may be more difficult to budget for the level of payment.

Under both hire purchase and leasing, the finance company retains legal ownership of the equipment, at least until the end of the agreement. This normally gives the finance company better security than lenders of other types of loan or overdraft facilities. The finance company may therefore be able to offer better terms.

Contract hire is a form of lease and it is often used for vehicles. The leasing company undertakes some responsibility for the management and maintenance of the vehicles. Services can include regular maintenance and repair costs, replacement of tyres and batteries, providing replacement vehicles, roadside assistance and recovery services and payment of the vehicle licences.

SELF-TEST QUESTIONS

		Paragraph
1	What are loan notes?	1.1
2	Why is the cost of debt lower than the cost of equity?	1.3
3	Briefly describe the various ways of classifying loans.	2.2
4	Distinguish between the two types of overdraft facility.	2.3
5	When is a borrower in 'default'?	2.4
6	When is the relationship of principal and agent present?	3.1
7	If your bank wrongly honours a cheque, what might happen?	3.2
8	What do the As stand for in CAMPARI?	4.1
9	List two assets that are typically used as security.	4.5

Chapter 12

LONG-TERM FINANCE

In this chapter we consider the long-term financing of the business. Because of the size of the investment and the length of time that it will be required, this type of financing is one of the most important decisions that the business will make. Equity share capital is a key method of financing for companies of all sizes and rights issues can be used by all types of companies to raise funds.

Either as an alternative to capital or as part of a mix of finance, there are long-term loans that businesses can obtain and we examine the criteria used to decide how much equity and how much loan finance a business should have. This is a popular topic for an exam.

This chapter covers Syllabus parts C3 and D3.

CONTENTS

LEARNING OUTCOMES

At the end of this chapter you should be able to:

- Discuss the nature and importance of internally generated funds
- Discuss situations where it may be appropriate to raise long-term finance
- Describe the key factors to be considered when deciding on an appropriate source of long-term finance (debt or equity)
- Calculate relative gearing and earnings per share under different financial structures
- Describe the way in which a stock market (both main and second tier) operates

- Discuss ways in which a company may obtain a stock market listing and the advantages and disadvantages of having a stock market listing
- Explain the purpose and main features of equity, preferred shares, debentures, unsecured loan stock, warrants, convertible and redeemable debt.

1 SOURCES OF FINANCE

1.1 THE NEED FOR LONG-TERM FINANCE

Long-term finance is needed to finance the long-term assets of the business and also some current assets. When a company wishes to increase its long-term capital, it has to consider the balance of its funding.

There should be a suitable balance between long-term and short-term funding. The optimal levels of short-term funding are influenced largely by the need for liquidity and the working capital cycle. The balance between debt and equity is partly a matter of judgement.

1.2 DEBT OR EQUITY?

The following factors should be taken into account when deciding upon the nature of long-term finance to be raised:

- **effect on cash flows** – returns on equity are paid in the form of dividends, which are more flexible than the (usually) fixed interest paid on debt.
- **effect on gearing levels** – equity finance will lower gearing levels, debt will increase them. The gearing ratio is commonly measured as either (value of debt/value of equity), or (value of debt/value of (debt plus equity)). A company with a high gearing ratio is perceived as risky, because high gearing implies high interest charges, which may cause the company to have cash flow problems. To assess whether the company's gearing seems too high, comparisons should be made with other, similar companies.
- **restrictions on gearing levels** – these may be imposed by the company's constitution (e.g. articles of association), terms of loan notes and other existing loan agreements, etc.
- **assets available for security** – debt finance often has to be secured on a company's assets. Therefore a company with high levels of tangible non-current assets will often find it relatively easy to raise debt finance.
- **control** – large new issues of shares will dilute control of existing shareholders.
- **earnings per share (EPS)** – this key ratio is commonly used by current and prospective investors to assess the performance of the company (calculations covered in Chapter 7 earlier). The impact of different types of finance on the EPS needs to be evaluated. For example, raising equity finance (increasing the number of shares in issue) will reduce EPS, and raising debt finance (hence paying more interest) will also reduce EPS.
- **share values** – these will depend upon (i) whether dividends are boosted by earnings less interest and tax (ii) the effect of debt raised on the cost of equity and (iii) market efficiency (i.e. whether the market 'sees' debt raised as being sustainable or is unaware of it, as in some forms of leasing.

- **the size of the company** – big companies (especially listed companies) usually have access to more financing sources than small companies. For example, a large company can borrow using debentures as well as bank loans, and can issue equity to the public as well as to private investors.
- the cost of the finance, including the impact of tax – see detail below.

1.3 THE COST OF DEBT AND EQUITY

Debt is regarded as a cheaper source of finance than equity. It is important to understand why.

Interest costs are an allowable expense for tax purposes, but dividends are not. The cost of debt capital to a company is therefore its after-tax cost. For example, suppose that a company has $1 million of 10% debt capital, and the rate of tax is 30%. The company will pay interest of $100,000 each year, but can claim a reduction in tax of $30,000 for this cost, leaving the net cost just $70,000 or 7%.

You might think that equity is even cheaper, because companies are not obliged to pay dividends in shares. If the directors decide there will be no dividend, you could argue that the cost of equity is zero. However, this is false logic. Shareholders put money into buying shares because they expect to receive dividends on them. If a company fails to pay a dividend, the shares will lose value. Shareholders will not use their money to buy new shares if they think that they might never get any dividends in the future. Equity therefore has a cost, which reflects the returns that shareholders expect to receive on their investment in the future. The returns required by equity shareholders are generally higher than the pre-tax cost of debt (and much higher than the after-tax cost of debt) because of this extra risk that the equity holders face.

1.4 LONG-TERM FINANCE – CAPITAL STRUCTURE

The capital structure of a company is the relationship between the different sources of its long-term finance. The major categories, excluding bank loans, are summarised below.

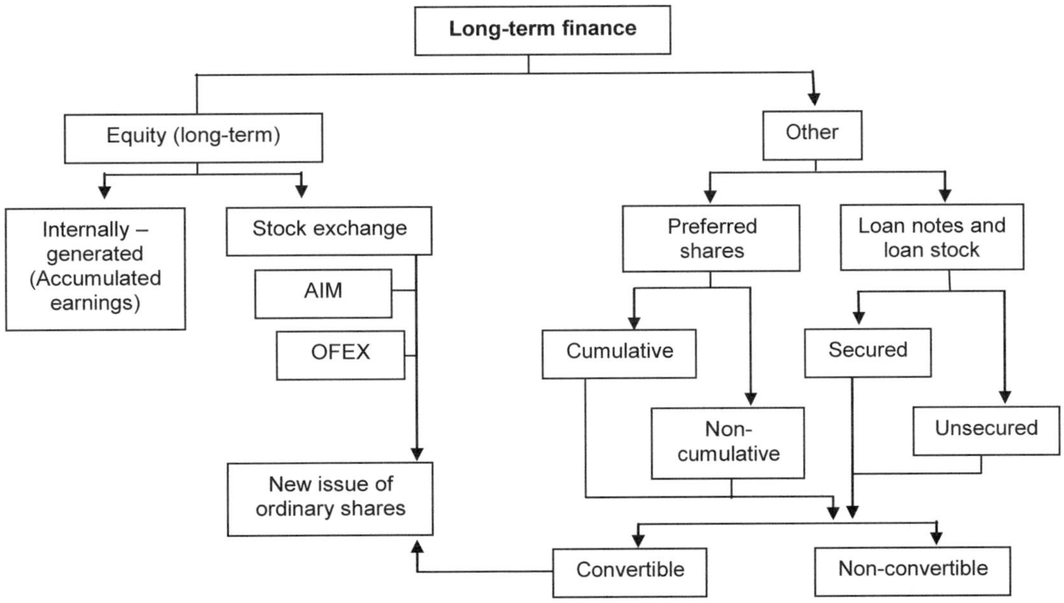

2 HOW A STOCK MARKET OPERATES

2.1 WHY DO COMPANIES LIST ON THE STOCK EXCHANGE?

The traditional answer is that private companies list on the Stock Exchange to raise capital and to provide a market in their shares. The owners give up part of their ownership in the company, and in return receive money to develop the business. But within that general explanation there are lots of subtleties:

A large family-controlled company may go public because its shares are split between hundreds of family members and there is internal pressure to provide a market which will allow them to cash in on their holdings.

A company whose shares are already quoted may decide to spin off a division and list it separately because the market is confused by having the two divisions together (e.g. AIG's decision to spin off its life insurance business).

A state-owned company may be privatised by the government because it has a political agenda to widen share ownership.

An entrepreneur with a City following may list on the Alternative Investment Market (AIM) with a view to using the new company's highly rated 'paper' (i.e. shares) as a currency for acquiring other companies.

An Internet company may list because the mere act of listing provides it with valuable free publicity (e.g. Internet companies found this useful in the early 2000s).

The common thread of all these is that listing does provide a company with a separate public identity, and its shares will have some kind of recognisable 'value' because their price will be quoted on the market.

In conclusion, gaining a public listing increases the marketability of the company's shares, and makes it easier to raise further equity finance from a large number of investors in the future. However, becoming a listed company is an expensive and time consuming process, and once listed, the company has to face a higher level of regulation and public scrutiny. Also, since the company's shares are likely to become widely distributed between many investors, the threat of takeover increases when a company becomes listed.

2.2 THE PROCESS OF LISTING

The process of listing for the first time is known as the 'primary market'. The most common way for a company to come to market is by an 'Offer for Sale'.

The company publishes a prospectus describing its business, who its directors are, what its financial position is, and what profits it thinks it is going to make. The prospectus announces the issue of new shares, sets an offer price for the shares, and invites subscriptions. Offer prices are often pitched low to make sure the issue is successful.

Low offer prices encourage investors to 'stag' an issue, applying for more shares than they want and selling them for an instant profit as soon as the market opens. Stagging was particularly good when companies only required payment after shares had been allocated. Now that they usually ask for money with your application, it's less attractive.

If an issue is oversubscribed, the company will usually allot each subscriber a percentage of the shares they wanted, and return a proportion of the subscription money. To avoid being under-subscribed most new issues are guaranteed by 'underwriters' i.e. merchant banks who promise to buy any shares not taken up by the public, in return for a fee from the company. This gives the company the comfort of knowing their listing will get off the ground.

Occasionally, the underwriters have to act – as they did when BP floated in 1987 at the time of the crash. The underwriters had to take up huge numbers of unsold shares, at fixed prices, then offload them onto the market at much lower prices and absorb the loss.

We have talked about companies 'coming to market' and the ways that they come to market. In fact there are two markets in the London Stock Exchange:

- The Official List – this is the top tier.
- Alternative Investment Market (AIM) – this is the second tier.

2.3 THE OFFICIAL LIST – TOP TIER

The Official List is the market for large companies which can meet stringent criteria of financial control, and which can afford to pay for the market's listing requirements. The companies will be followed by lots of analysts in the City, and most of the large pension funds and insurance funds will have substantial sums invested in them.

Trading volumes will be high, and the shares will have high levels of liquidity.

A company will wish to become listed on the stock exchange to increase its pool of potential investors. Only by being listed can a company offer its shares to the public.

The largest of the Official List companies (the FTSE 100 and some of the FTSE 250) will be traded on the Stock Exchange Electronic Trading Service (SETS) rather than through market makers, which theoretically means a narrower bid-offer spread.

The concepts of liquidity and spreads are very important for investors:

- Liquidity means 'How easy is it to buy and sell the shares?' A share that is highly liquid is one which your broker will always be able to buy and sell for you. The sell bit is particularly important. There is no point in owning a share if you cannot sell it.
- The 'spread' is the difference between the price at which a market maker offers to buy your shares in Company X (the 'bid price'), and the price at which it offers to sell your shares in Company X (the 'offer price'). The narrower the spread, the better for the investor.

2.4 ALTERNATIVE INVESTMENT MARKET (AIM) – SECOND TIER

This is the junior market of the London Stock Exchange, set up in 1995. The conditions for listing on AIM are much less demanding than for the main market, and the companies on AIM tend to be smaller and younger. There is an element of 'make or break' about many of them.

AIM companies are often too small for institutional funds to invest in, which is both good news and bad news for private investors.

- It's good because it means that the stocks are under-researched and you stand a chance of spotting a high growth stock at a good price before anybody else.

- It's bad because the liquidity of AIM stocks can be poor. AIM stocks often only have one market maker, and the spread can be wide.

There is a natural process of graduation by successful AIM companies to the main market. They do this because they want to attract a following among the large institutions, brokers and research houses, and because it is easier to raise large sums of capital from the main list than it is on AIM.

3 EQUITY

3.1 TYPES OF SHARE CAPITAL

The term equity relates to ordinary shares only. Equity finance is the investment in a company by the ordinary shareholders, represented by the issued ordinary share capital plus reserves. There are other types of share capital relating to various types of preferred share. These are not considered part of equity as their characteristics bear more resemblance to debt finance. The main types of share capital are summarised in the table below:

Type of share capital	**Security or voting rights**	**Income**	**Amount of capital**
Ordinary shares	Have voting rights in general meetings of the company. Rank after all payables and preferred shares in rights to assets on liquidation.	Dividends payable at the discretion of the directors (subject to sanction by share-holders) out of undistributed profits remaining after senior claims have been met. Amounts available for dividends but not paid out are retained in the company on behalf of the ordinary shareholders.	The right to all surplus funds after prior claims have been met.
Cumulative preferred shares	Right to vote at a general meeting only when dividend is in arrears or when it is proposed to change the legal rights of the shares. Rank after all payables but usually before ordinary shareholders in liquidation.	A fixed amount per year at the discretion of the directors, subject to sanction by shareholders and in accordance with rules regarding dividend payments. Arrears accumulate and must be paid before a dividend on ordinary shares may be paid. Note that unlike other forms of debt, the dividend paid on preferred shares is not tax deductible.	A fixed amount per share.
Non-cumulative preferred shares	Likely to have some voting rights at all times rather than in specified circumstances as in the case of cumulative. Rank as cumulative in liquidation.	A fixed amount per year, as above. Arrears do not accumulate.	A fixed amount per share.

3.2 RAISING EQUITY FINANCE

There are three main sources of equity finance:

- internally generated funds – cash from retained earnings
- new external share issues – placings, offers for sale, etc.
- rights issues.

3.3 INTERNALLY GENERATED FUNDS

Internally generated funds comprise the cash retained from accumulated profits (i.e. undistributed profits attributable to ordinary shareholders) plus non-cash charges against profits (e.g. depreciation). For an established company, internally generated funds can represent the single most important source of finance, for both short- and long-term purposes.

Such finance is cheap and quick to raise, requiring no transaction costs, professional assistance or time delay. However, it is essential that the company's dividend policy is taken into account when determining how much of each year's cash from earnings to retain.

Accumulated profits are also a continual source of new funds, provided that the company is profitable and cash generating and cash is not all paid out as dividends.

We shall explore this topic in more detail later. In general, however, shareholders of listed companies tend to prefer a stable growth dividend policy. Any unexpected cut in dividend, however potentially profitable, may lead to an adverse reaction in terms of a fall in share price.

Of course, for major investment projects, a greater amount of equity finance may be required than that available from internal sources. In this case some form of share issue will have to be made.

Internally generated funds are a cheap and immediate source of finance. However, the company's dividend policy must be taken into account when determining the level of usage.

3.4 NEW EXTERNAL SHARE ISSUES

There are several methods of issuing new shares according to the circumstances of the company.

New shares can be issued by private negotiation, placing, or offer for sale, or by a rights issue.

Type of company	Company requirement	Method of issue	Type of investor
Unquoted	Finance without an immediate stock market quotation.	Private negotiation or placing. Enterprise Investment Scheme (EIS).	Individuals, merchant banks, finance corporations.
Quoted or unquoted	Limited finance without offering shares to non-shareholders.	Rights issue.	Holders of existing shares.

Traditionally, unquoted companies obtained their funds from owner proprietors or rich patrons who were prepared to take a risk in order to show an above average return.

However, in the modern business environment, it can be difficult for small unquoted companies to raise equity finance from outside shareholders. A country's tax system may channel individual investors' money into institutions, and institutions are generally unenthusiastic about investing in unquoted companies for a number of reasons.

- The shares are not easily realisable.
- Costs can be kept down by investing in large parcels of shares rather than spreading investment over many small companies.
- Small firms are regarded as more risky (for example, they may lack proper financial control systems).

However, it is possible to arrange a placing of shares with an institution. Generally this is when there is at least a prospect of eventually obtaining a quotation on the Stock Exchange.

The small firm equity finance problem is dealt with in detail in the next chapter.

3.5 RIGHTS ISSUES

A rights issue is an offer to the existing shareholders to subscribe for more shares, in proportion to their existing holding, usually at a relatively cheap price. A rights issue can be made by a quoted or an unquoted company seeking limited finance without offering shares to non-shareholders.

In the UK, company legislation requires an offer to be made to existing shareholders before it can be made to the public. Any new shares issued by a UK public company to raise cash must therefore be offered to the existing shareholders in a rights issue, unless the existing shareholders have given their consent to new shares being issued by any method other than a rights issue.

When a rights issue is announced, the existing shareholders are given rights. A right is the right to buy a given number of new shares in the issue, at the issue price. For example, if a company announces a 1 for 4 rights issue at $3.25 per share, an ordinary shareholder with 50,000 shares will receive the right to buy 12,500 new shares at $3.25.

The price of the new shares should be below the current market price. For example, if a company announces a 1 for 4 rights issue at $3.25, the current share price will be higher than $3.25. Since the price of the new shares is lower than the current market price, it follows that the rights should have some value.

3.6 BONUS ISSUES, SCRIP DIVIDENDS

A bonus issue is a method of altering the share capital without raising cash. It is done by changing the company's reserves into share capital.

The rate of a bonus issue is normally expressed in terms of the number of new shares issued for each existing share held, e.g. one for two (one new share for each two shares currently held).

In the USA, capitalisation issues are usually expressed in terms of the number of shares held following the issue compared with the number previously held. Thus, a one for two scrip issue will be termed a **three for two split**. You need to be familiar with both UK and US terminology, as the majority of studies on this subject are to be found in American textbooks.

Example

UK terminology	Before	New	After	US terminology
1 for 2 scrip	2	1	3	3 for 2 split
2 for 5 scrip	5	2	7	7 for 5 split
3 for 10 scrip	10	3	13	13 for 10 split

A capitalisation issue does not change the shareholders' **proportionate** ownership of the company.

ACTIVITY 1

J Bloggs holds 1,000 shares in Deucalion Co which has a total issued capital of 4,000,000 shares. The directors decide to capitalise some of the revenue reserves by making a 1 for 4 scrip issue. Calculate J Bloggs' percentage share in the company before and after the scrip issue.

For a suggested answer, see the 'Answers' section at the end of the book.

Scrip dividends

A **scrip dividend** is where a company allows its shareholders to take their dividends in the form of new shares rather than cash.

Do not confuse a scrip issue (which is a bonus issue) with a scrip dividend.

The advantage **shareholders** of a scrip dividend is that they can painlessly increase their shareholding in the company without having to pay broker's commissions or stamp duty on a share purchase.

The advantage to the **company** is that it does not have to find the cash to pay a dividend and in certain circumstances it can save tax.

Bonus issues, the statement of financial position and investors' returns

The effect of a bonus issue on a company's statement of financial position and on investors' returns is shown in the following example.

Example

Pyrrha Co has issued share capital of one million shares of $0.10 each. It generally pays a total dividend of $12,000. The company decides to issue bonus shares in the ratio of one for every two held. Note that the market value of the company will not change.

	Before bonus issue	**After 1 for 2 bonus issue**
Number of shares	1,000,000	1,500,000
Nominal value	$0.10	$0.10
Issued capital	100,000	150,000
Reserves (change into share capital after bonus issue)	100,000	50,000
Net assets	200,000	200,000
Net assets per share	$0.20	$0.133
Market capitalisation	$150,000	$150,000
Market price (market capitalisation/ number of shares)	$0.15	$0.10
Dividend per share	$0.012	$0.08
Dividend yield	8.0%	8.0%

The purposes of a bonus issue are as follows:

- To increase marketability of the shares, since it will increase the number of shares in issue and hence reduce the market value of each share (in our example, from 15 cents to 10 cents each). This is the most common reason, and is peculiar to the UK. In the USA and Germany, for example, it is not uncommon to have single shares which are quoted at a price of the equivalent of several hundred pounds.

- To increase the amount of permanent capital of the business in line with growth in its assets. There is some merit in this argument, although it could also be argued that most shareholders would never expect the entire figure for 'accumulated profits' in a statement of financial position to be paid out by way of dividend.

Share splits

Like a bonus issue, a share split (also called a stock split) does not raise extra cash.

It simply makes the share capital more marketable, e.g. a company whose shares have a nominal value of $1 each but a market value of $10 each may decide to split each $1 share into 10 shares of 10 cents each. The market value of each share then becomes $1.

The reverse procedure might be appropriate where the market value of a company's share is very low. This procedure is known as a consolidation of shares.

ACTIVITY 2

What would be the difference in terms of impact on shareholder base between raising equity finance through accumulated profits and rights issues and raising equity finance via a new issue?

For a suggested answer, see the 'Answers' section at the end of the book.

4 CHOOSING BETWEEN SOURCES OF EQUITY FINANCE

Equity finance is not a single source of finance, but a group of alternative ways of raising risk-bearing funds e.g. rights issues and placings and issues to the general public.

When choosing between sources of equity finance, account must be taken of factors such as the accessibility of the finance, the amount of finance, costs of the issue procedure, pricing of the issue, control, taxation and dividend policy.

4.1 ABILITY OF COMPANY TO RAISE FINANCE BY THE MEANS INDICATED

The ability of a company to raise equity finance is restricted by its access to the general market for funds. Thus, whilst quoted companies are able to use any of the sources, an unquoted company is restricted to rights issues and private placings. Furthermore, there are statutory restrictions, for example those in the UK imposed by the Companies Act 1985. Only public limited companies may offer shares to the general public.

Obviously, the need to raise finance could be combined with a flotation (i.e. a private company going public and having its shares quoted on a recognised stock exchange). However, flotation will incur significant costs.

4.2 AMOUNT OF FINANCE REQUIRED

The amount of finance that can be raised by a rights issue from an unquoted company is limited by the number and resources of the existing shareholders. It is not possible to provide general estimates of the amounts that may be raised as the circumstances vary. For quoted companies, where rights may be sold, this is less problematic.

Larger sums can be raised by placings, but ultimately it is the offer of shares to the general public that opens up the full financial resources of the market.

4.3 COSTS AND COMPLEXITY OF ISSUE PROCEDURES

Use of internally generated funds is easily the cheapest and simplest method. We have seen that, for new issues, placings are the most attractive on cost grounds, followed by rights issues, with public offers being by far the most expensive.

However, the costs go beyond those incorporated in the above computation. All new share issues will take management and administrative time within the company. This will be much greater for an offer for sale than for the other two alternatives.

4.4 PRICING

One of the most difficult problems in making a new issue to the public is setting the price correctly. If it is too high, the issue will not be fully taken up and will be left with the underwriters, and if it is under-priced some of the benefits of the project for which the finance is being raised will accrue to the new shareholders and not to the old.

The same pricing problem exists with a placing as with a new issue. There will be no danger of under-subscription, of course, because the placing is agreed before the issue is made. However, the price will have been negotiated so as to be attractive to the subscribing institutions. Almost inevitably, it will be below the issue price that it would obtain in the market, because of the attractions of lower issue costs.

A rights issue, on the other hand, completely by-passes the price problem. Since the shares are offered to existing shareholders, it does not matter if the price is well below the traded price. Indeed, it would be normal for this to be so. Any gain on the new shares would, by the nature of a rights issue, go to the existing shareholders.

The pricing of new issues is even more complex when the company is unquoted. A company coming to the market for the first time would have no existing market price to refer to and would have to value the shares from scratch.

4.5 SHARE VALUATIONS AND INVESTOR RATIOS

A share price represents the amount that investors are currently prepared to pay to acquire a share in the company. Investors buy shares to obtain a return on investment. Clearly, there is a direct connection between a share's price and the value that investors put on the returns they expect to receive. We can even state that a share price equals the value of shareholders' expected future returns from the share.

Investor ratios can be used to measure the relationship of returns to share value. These ratios are based on historical returns, rather than expected future returns, but they are useful for monitoring and comparing the shares of different companies.

The main investment ratios relating to ordinary shares are:

Earnings per share (EPS). This is simply the total annual earnings of the company divided by the number of shares in issue. Although the detailed rules for calculating EPS are fairly complex, it is usually sufficient to assume that EPS is the total annual profit after interest, taxation and dividends on preferred shares, divided by the number of ordinary shares currently in issue. EPS is simply a measurement of the profit earned by the company for each share in issue.

P/E ratio. The price/earnings ratio is the ratio of the current share price to annual earnings per share. For example, if the EPS is $0.60 and the share price is $6, the P/E ratio is 10. Share valuations are sometimes expressed in terms of P/E; for example, we might say that a company's shares are valued on a P/E multiple of 12 when the average for companies in the industry is, say, 14.

Dividend yield. This is the dividend in cents expressed as a proportion of the current share price. For example, if the annual dividend per share is 15 cents and the share price is $4, the dividend yield is (15/400) × 100% = 3.75%.

$$\text{Dividend yield} = \frac{\text{Annual dividend in cents}}{\text{Share price}} \times 100\%$$

The dividend yield shows the annual cash return on a company's shares for an investor buying the shares at today's price.

5 PREFERRED SHARES

Preferred shares offer their owners preferences over ordinary shareholders. There are two major differences between ordinary and preferred shares:

- Holders of preferred shares are often entitled to a fixed dividend even when ordinary shareholders are not.
- Preferred shareholders cannot normally vote at general meetings.

The dividend on preferred shares is fixed in the sense that preferred shares are often issued with the rate of dividend fixed at the time of issue and you might see something like this: '4% preferred dividend $0.25'

Note that, if by any chance a company cannot pay its preferred share dividend, then it cannot pay any ordinary share dividend since the shareholders of preferred shares have the right to receive their dividend before the ordinary shareholders under all circumstances – hence the term 'preferred'.

Preferred shares are usually cumulative and this means that, if this year's dividend was not paid, then it will be carried forward to next year. So, if the $1,000 for 2004 was missed, then shareholders of preferred shares would receive $2,000 in 2005 (assuming the company is in a position to pay the dividend!).

A preferred share may be redeemable which means that, at some time in the future, the company will effectively buy it back. How do we know that a share is redeemable? Redeemable shares usually look like this: '4% cumulative preferred share of $0.25, 2007'.

This means that the $0.25 per share preferred share carries the right to a 4% dividend and it will be redeemed in 2007. Normally the date for redemption in 2007 will be agreed when it is issued so you will know well in advance when to expect your money back.

If a preferred share is a participating preferred share then the owner of such a share has the right to participate in, or receive, additional dividends over and above the fixed percentage dividend discussed above. The additional dividend is usually paid in proportion to any ordinary dividend declared.

Finally, preferred shares may be convertible. If the shares are convertible then the shareholders have the option at some stage of converting them into ordinary shares.

From the company's point of view, preferred shares have some attractive features:

- Dividends do not have to be paid in a year in which profits are poor, while this is not the case with interest payments on long-term debt (loans or loan notes).
- Since they do not carry voting rights, preferred shares avoid diluting the control of existing shareholders while an issue of equity shares would not.
- Unless they are redeemable, issuing preferred shares will lower the company's gearing. Redeemable preferred shares are normally treated as debt when gearing is calculated.
- The issue of preferred shares does not restrict the company's borrowing power, at least in the sense that preferred share capital is not secured against assets of the business.

- The non-payment of dividend does not give the shareholders with preferred shares the right to appoint a receiver, a right which is normally given to holders of loan notes.

- However, dividend payments on preferred shares are not tax deductible in the way that interest payments on debt are. Furthermore, for preferred shares to be attractive to investors, the level of payment needs to be higher than for interest on debt to compensate for the additional risks.

From the point of view of the investor, preferred shares are less attractive than loan stock because:

- they cannot be secured on the company's assets

- the dividend yield traditionally offered on preferred dividends has been much too low to provide an attractive investment compared with the interest yields on loan stock in view of the additional risk involved.

6 CORPORATE BONDS AND LOAN NOTES

Long-term debt (loan stock), usually in the form of loan notes or bonds, is frequently used as a source of long-term finance as an alternative to equity.

A loan note is a written acknowledgement of a debt by a company, normally containing provisions as to payment of interest and the terms or repayment of principal. It may also be referred to as a corporate bond or loan stock.

Loan notes are traded on stock markets in much the same way as shares, and may be secured or unsecured, and redeemable or irredeemable.

The term 'bond' is now used generally to mean any kind of long-term marketable debt security.

6.1 SECURED DEBT

Secured debt will carry a charge over:

- one or more specific assets, usually land and buildings, which are mortgaged in a **fixed charge**

- all assets – a floating charge.

On default, the holders of loan notes can appoint a receiver to administer the assets until the interest is paid. Alternatively the assets may be sold to repay the principal.

6.2 IRREDEEMABLE AND REDEEMABLE DEBT

Irredeemable debt is not repayable at any specified time in the future. Instead, interest is payable ad infinitum. As well as some loan notes, preferred shares are often irredeemable.

If the debt is **redeemable** the principal will be repayable at a future date.

For example, if a company has '5% 2025 Loan notes redeemable at par, quoted at $95 ex-int', this description refers to loan notes that:

- pay interest at 5% on nominal value, i.e. $5 per $100 (this is known as the **coupon rate**)
- are redeemable in the year 2025
- will be repaid at par value, i.e. each $100 nominal value will be repaid at $100
- currently have a market value of $95 per $100, without rights to the current year's interest payment.

6.3 CHARACTERISTICS OF LOAN NOTES AND OTHER LONG-TERM DEBT

Loan notes from the viewpoint of the investor

(a) Debt is viewed as low risk because:

- – it has a definite maturity and the holder has priority in interest payments and on liquidation
- – income is fixed, so the holder receives the same interest whatever the earnings of the company.

(b) Debt holders do not usually have voting rights. Only if interest is not paid will holders take control of the company.

Loan notes from the viewpoint of the company

(a) Advantages of debt:

- – Debt is cheap. Because it is less risky than equity for an investor, holders of loan notes will accept a lower rate of return than shareholders. Also, **debt interest is an allowable expense for tax**. So if the cost of borrowing for a company is 6%, say, and the rate of corporation tax is 30%, the company can set the cost of the interest against tax, and the effective 'after tax' cost of the debt would be just 4.2% (6% × 70%).
- – Cost is limited to the stipulated interest payment.
- – There is no dilution of control when debt is issued.

(b) Disadvantages of debt:

- – Interest must be paid whatever the earnings of the company, unlike dividends which can be paid in good years and not in bad. If interest is not paid, the trustees for the loan note holders can call in the receiver.
- – Shareholders may be concerned that a geared company cannot pay all its interest and still pay a dividend and will raise the rate of return that they require from the company to compensate for this increase in risk. This may effectively put a limit on the amount of debt that can be raised.
- – With fixed maturity dates, provision must be made for the repayment of debt.
- – Long-term debt, with its commitment to fixed interest payments, may prove a burden especially if the general level of interest rates falls.

Deep discounted bonds and zero coupon bonds

Deep discounted bonds are those where the coupon rate being offered is below the market rate at the time of issue. If there is no annual interest payment, they are referred to as **zero coupon bonds**.

The return to the investor of these bonds is mainly in the form of a high redemption value. The attractions of these bonds to the company are as follows:

- the initial financing cash outlays are small
- the discount element of the bond is amortised and allowed annually against tax.

From the investors' viewpoint, there are two other advantages:

- there is little chance of the bond being called early, as this would prove very expensive to the firm
- although the tax authorities amortise the discount element for tax purposes, the tax on this element of return to the investor is not normally payable until redemption.

7 HYBRIDS OF DEBT AND EQUITY

Convertible loan stock and convertible loan notes are issues of bonds that give the holder the right to convert to other securities, normally ordinary shares, at a pre-determined price/rate and time.

Convertible loan stock, convertible loan notes and **loan stock with warrants** represent forms of finance that are hybrids of debt and equity – they have elements of both.

7.1 CONVERTIBLE LOAN STOCK AND LOAN NOTES

The **conversion rights** on convertible loan stock or loan notes are either stated in terms of a **conversion ratio** (i.e. the number of ordinary shares into which $100 stock may be converted) or in terms of a **conversion price** (i.e. the right to convert into ordinary shares at a price of X cents) e.g.:

- '$100 of stock may be converted into 25 ordinary shares' is a conversion ratio
- 'stock may be converted into shares at a value of 400 cents per share' is the equivalent conversion price.

Sometimes, the conversion price increases during the convertibility – this is done to stimulate early conversion. Another variation is to issue partly convertible stocks whereby only a portion of the stock – usually 50% – may be converted. Conversion rights usually cater for an adjustment in the event of capitalisation, rights issues, etc. Convertible preferred shares are also possible.

A **conversion premium** exists when the market value of convertible stock exceeds the current market price of the shares into which they are or will become convertible. For example, suppose that $100 (nominal) of convertible stock is convertible into 10 shares of ABC Co. The stock has a market value of $102 and shares are currently priced at $9 each. The conversion premium for $100 of stock is therefore $12 ($102 – $90).

7.2 LOAN STOCK WITH WARRANTS

A warrant gives the holder the right to subscribe at fixed future dates for a certain number of ordinary shares at a predetermined price.

The difference between a loan stock with warrants and a convertible loan note is that with a warrant the loan stock itself is not converted into equity, but bond holders make a cash payment to acquire the shares and retain their loan stock. This means that the loan stock will continue in existence until it is redeemed.

Warrants have value when the market price of shares rises above the price specified in the warrant. They are commonly used as a 'sweetener' for debt issues, allowing the firm to place a low interest rate on the loan. The cost to the firm is the right given to holders to buy equity at a (possibly) reduced price at the conversion date.

7.3 ATTRACTIONS OF CONVERTIBLES AND WARRANTS AS A SOURCE OF FINANCE

A **warrant** is merely an option, not linked to an underlying security, whilst a **convertible** loan note combines an option with a loan note.

Advantages	**Comment**
Immediate finance at low cost	Because of the conversion option, the loans can be raised at below normal interest rates
Attractive, if share prices are depressed	Where companies wish to raise equity finance, but share prices are currently depressed, convertibles offer a 'back-door' share issue method
Self-liquidating	Where loans are converted into shares, the problem of repayment disappears
Exercise of warrants related to need for finance	Options would normally only be exercised where the share price has increased. If the options involve the payment of extra cash to the company, this creates extra funds when they are needed for expansion

Example

Raybeck Co issues 8% unsecured loan stock 20X1/X5 as part of the consideration for the acquisition of companies. With the loan stock are subscription rights (warrants) on the basis that holders of $100 loan stock could subscribe for up to 30 ordinary shares in Raybeck at a price of $8.75 per share. The option could be exercised any time between 20X2 and 20X5.

Associated Engineering Co issues 7% convertible loan stock 20X8/X9. The conversion option is 80 ordinary shares for each $100 loan stock, and is exercisable between 20X1 and 20X5. If the option is not exercised, the loan notes are redeemable at par between 20X8 and 20X9.

Describe the nature of these securities and comment on the exercise decisions that must be made by the investor.

Solution

Note the difference between these two issues. In the Raybeck case, the option is separate from the loan stock, which continues to exist whether or not the option is exercised. Also, the exercise of the option costs money. On the other hand, conversion of Associated Engineering loan stock is an actual replacement of the loan stock by shares, with no cash effect.

There are a number of variations on the theme of conversion rights including, for example, convertible preferred shares. There is no need for you to memorise all the possibilities.

The warrants issued by Raybeck Co are worth exercising if the share price of Raybeck is above $8.75. For example, if the share price rose to $10, then the value of the warrant would be:

Current market price – Exercise price = $10 – $8.75 = $1.25.

If share prices fell below $8.75 the warrant would be worthless. The above calculation is referred to as the **formula value of the warrant** or the **intrinsic value of the warrant**.

The conversion option on Associated Engineering's convertible is worth exercising if the share price rises above:

$$\frac{\text{Value of \$100 loan stock}}{\text{80 shares}}$$

Above this price, shareholders would receive equity of greater value than the $100 loan stock. Unlike a warrant, however, below this share price the value of the convertible does not fall to zero, but would settle at the market value of the security as a straight loan note.

The formula value of a convertible is the higher of its value as debt and its converted value.

7.4 THE EFFECT ON EPS OF CONVERSIONS AND OPTION RIGHTS

Earnings per share (EPS) is a widely used measure of a company's performance, particularly over a number of years, and is a component of the very important Stock Exchange yardstick – the price/earnings (P/E) ratio. A key objective in the financial management of a quoted company is to record an increase in EPS over successive accounting periods.

Earnings per share (in cents) =

$$\frac{\text{Net profit for the year after tax, minority interests, extraordinary items and preferred dividends}}{\text{Weighted average number of equity shares in issue}}$$

CONCLUSION

This chapter has extended our look at the sources of finance – concentrating on equity finance. While some companies rely solely on equity shareholders to provide their long-term finance needs, others obtain a mix of funds. The optimal mix – how much a company is geared – is an important decision.

SELF-TEST QUESTIONS

		Paragraph
1	Why is debt thought to be cheaper than equity?	1.3
2	Give two examples of the types of enterprise that might gain from joining the Stock Exchange.	2.1
3	Outline the procedures if a share issue is oversubscribed.	2.2
4	What are the three main sources of equity finance?	3.2
5	Which issue procedure is most expensive?	4.3
6	What is a warrant?	7.2

PRACTICE QUESTION

STOCK MARKETS

Explain briefly how stock markets work and assess their usefulness to business as a source of long-term capital. **(10 marks)**

For a suggested answer, see the 'Answers' section at the end of the book.

Chapter 13

SOURCES OF FINANCE FOR SMALL AND MEDIUM-SIZED ENTERPRISES

In this chapter we will be discussing why small and medium-sized enterprises (SMEs) have difficulty obtaining finance and how they can overcome the obstacles. Some of the sources of finance that are available have been devised especially to help this category of business, especially business angels and venture capital funds. Many Government initiatives have resulted in projects that are very useful for this group.

This chapter covers Syllabus parts D3 and D4.

CONTENTS

LEARNING OUTCOMES

The following study sessions are covered:

- Outline the major sources of government funds e.g. grants, regional and national schemes
- Outline the requirements for finance of SMEs (purpose, how much, how long)
- Describe the nature of the financing problem for SMEs in terms of the funding gap, maturity gap and inadequate security
- Discuss the contribution of lack of information in SMEs to help explain the problems of SME financing
- Describe and discuss the response of government agencies and financial institutions to the SME financing problem
- Describe the main features of venture capital

- Describe the key areas of concern to venture capitalists when evaluating an application for funding
- Explain how the use of such measures as credit suppliers, hire purchase, factoring and second-tier listing can help to ease the financial problems of SMEs
- Outline appropriate sources of finance for SMEs.

1 SMALL AND MEDIUM-SIZED ENTERPRISES (SMEs)

1.1 HOW DO WE DEFINE AN SME?

According to the UK Department for Trade and Industry (DTI):

A small enterprise has fewer than 50 employees, including the self-employed.

A medium-sized enterprise has between 50 and 249 employees.

McLaney (2000) identifies three characteristics of SMEs:

(i) firms are likely to be unquoted

(ii) ownership of the business is restricted to a few individuals, typically a family group

(iii) they are not micro businesses that are normally regarded as those very small businesses that act as a medium for self-employment of the owners. However, this too is an important sub-group.

1.2 UNDERLYING PROBLEMS

In the UK, the Wilson Committee on the provision of funds to industry and trade summarised the position as follows:

'Compared to large firms, small firms are at a considerable disadvantage in financial markets . . . External equity is more difficult to find and may only be available on relatively unfavourable terms. Venture capital is particularly hard to obtain . . . Proprietors of small firms do not always have the same financial expertise as their larger competitors and information and advice about finance may not be easily accessible.'

Equity finance provided by wealthy individuals once formed an important source of expansion funds for the small business. More recently, however, SMEs have found themselves cut off from this source of capital for two main reasons:

- the increasing expense and difficulty of obtaining a quotation on a stock market. The attractiveness of a speculative equity investment in a company is much increased if there is a reasonable chance of a quotation, which gives the opportunity of selling the shares
- in the UK the tax system has encouraged individuals to save with large institutions. These institutions prefer to invest in the shares of large companies rather than small ones or in non-corporate entities because of issues with marketability, risk and administrative costs.

Thus wealthy individuals, who once provided a major source of venture capital for SMEs, have been persuaded by the tax system to channel their funds indirectly into large companies.

2 THE PROBLEMS OF FINANCING SMEs

2.1 THE NATURE OF THE FUNDING PROBLEM

SMEs need finance to grow and develop. Unfortunately, most find it extremely difficult to obtain finance. The main reason is that, traditionally, small businesses have borrowed by means of loans and overdrafts from clearing banks. The main problems have always been the security required by the bank for granting the loan, and the risk averse attitude of banks when faced with a decision relating to a new and untested project. In the UK, the requirement for a personal guarantee from the proprietor to cover the loan or overdraft advance has inhibited the expansion of many small businesses and contributed towards the problem of British ideas being developed abroad.

Whilst the UK government has attempted to make debt investment in small businesses more attractive by the introduction of its Loan Guarantee Scheme, this has not proved very successful due to its relatively high interest rate.

Other reasons given for the funding problems are:

- the capital markets are not accessible to SMEs, only to large companies
- the owners are often not wealthy enough to provide additional finance when the business needs it
- SMEs are often young businesses, with relatively short trading histories. The lack of information available to potential investors regarding the past performance of the business makes it difficult for the investors to assess the likely creditworthiness of the SME
- SMEs can obtain some trade credit, but suppliers might be reluctant to give credit beyond a certain amount, because of the potential credit risk (bad debt risk)
- SMEs might also be able to lease capital equipment, but leasing and hire purchase finance is limited to the acquisition of certain types of non-current asset.

Medium-sized businesses might be able to obtain support from venture capital organisations, but it can be difficult to convince a venture capital organisation that the business would be a worthwhile investment. Similarly, it might be possible to obtain new finance from a private investor (a 'business angel'), but these individuals are not common and the amount of capital available from business angels is limited.

The problem is not about the size of investment required but the character of the business that is looking for funding. High-growth businesses are attractive to venture capitalists (and other equity investors) and asset-rich businesses are attractive to banks. Businesses that are neither high-growth nor asset-rich are not attractive to either so, although perfectly sound and profitable, find it difficult to raise any form of finance.

The obvious point to state is that directors and owner managers of SMEs often describe a situation of shortage of capital and consequential missed investment opportunities. At an economy wide level, if this is true, there is a reduction in the nation’s wealth through investment opportunities lost.

2.2 GOVERNMENT AID FOR SMEs

UK governments in recent years have recognised the importance of small firms to the economy and have introduced various forms of advisory services, e.g. Business Links which are government-funded agencies providing specialist advice in the fields of management skills, exporting, marketing, design, etc.

They have also tried to encourage the establishment of new small firms through various measures: (Note that £ value details will not be examined, but are shown for here for illustration.)

Advice – One of the most significant measures has been the creation of the Small Business Service (SBS). The SBS is designed to give small firms, or those thinking of setting up a small firm, easy access to advice and support. (Prior to the SBS, the large diversity of initiatives and regulations applying to small business meant that there was no clear point of reference for anyone seeking advice or guidance.) In addition to this, the SBS is designed to ensure that the interests and problems of small businesses are taken into account when the government formulates its economic policy.

Small firm markets – Perhaps **the** most important developments have been the creation of small firm markets, such as the Alternative Investment Market (AIM) in the UK.

In addition, in the UK, the Companies Act 1985 allows **companies to purchase their own shares**. This makes shares of small private companies more easily realisable and hence more attractive to the small investor. The position where a minority shareholder becomes trapped in such a company can be avoided.

Tax incentives – The Wilson Committee's recommendations led to the development of the current Enterprise Investment Scheme (EIS) which offers tax relief on investments in ordinary shares in qualifying unlisted trading companies, including those traded on the AIM. Individuals may invest up to £150,000 each tax year and qualify for 20% tax relief. Any gain on disposing of EIS shares after five years is exempt from capital gains tax. Income or capital gains tax relief is available on losses. The scheme applies to any company trading in the UK and enables companies to raise up to £1m a year. Participating investors can become paid directors of the company and still qualify for the relief.

Loans – under the Small Firms Loan Guarantee Scheme, the government guarantees 75% of loans of up to £100,000 by banks to small businesses against default. This therefore encourages banks to lend to businesses they might otherwise regard as too risky.

Finance is often available from central government or regional government to businesses that are willing to invest in a particular area or industry.

Tax concessions – can be lower tax rates (e.g. corporation tax) or tax relief for various purposes (e.g. investment or research and development). Also, tax credits are available to small companies for spending on research and development.

Venture Capital Trusts (VCTs) are quoted companies similar to investment trusts. At least 70% of the underlying investments must be held in a spread of small unquoted trading companies within three years of the date of launch. Income tax relief is available at 20% on new subscriptions by individuals for ordinary shares in VCTs, to a maximum of £100,000 per annum.

Share incentive schemes in the UK are designed to encourage employees to hold shares in companies by which they are employed. In the UK, such schemes require approval from HM Revenue & Customs.

2.3 SOURCES OF GOVERNMENT FUNDS

Here we shall concentrate on the financial aspects of government assistance. Whilst you are not expected to have a detailed knowledge of particular government schemes, you should have a general awareness of the type of assistance offered.

Regional Selective Assistance (RSA) is a discretionary scheme available in those parts of the UK designated as Assisted Areas. It takes the form of grants to encourage firms to locate or expand in these areas. Projects must either create new employment or safeguard existing jobs.

Enterprise grants are a selective scheme for firms employing less than 250 people. They are available for high quality projects in designated areas. Businesses may only receive one such grant.

Regional innovation grants are available in certain areas of the UK to encourage the development of new products and processes. They are available to individuals or businesses employing no more than 50 people. The scheme provides a fixed grant of up to 50% of eligible costs up to a maximum of £25,000.

Small firms training loans are available through the Department for Education and Employment and eight major banks in the UK. The scheme helps businesses with up to 50 employees to pay for vocational education or training, by offering loans on deferred repayment terms.

European Investment Bank (EIB) and European Investment Fund (EIF) schemes

The EIB provides loans to banks and leasing companies to help provide finance to small and medium-sized companies. The operators of EIB supported schemes include finance organisations such as Barclays Mercantile, Lombard Business Finance and Forward Trust.

The EIF provides loan guarantees in conjunction with some finance organisations' own environmental loan facilities. These facilities are designed to assist business to finance investments that produce a quantifiable environmental benefit (energy usage, raw material usage, etc).

2.4 GRANTS FOR RESEARCH, DEVELOPMENT AND INNOVATION

DTI Research and Development Grants provides grants to help individuals and small and medium-sized businesses research and develop technologically innovative products and processes. These were formerly known as the SMART award scheme and incorporate five different types of grant. The awards vary in size depending on the type of project, up to a maximum of £500,000.

Research Council Follow-on Fund is open to researchers in UK Universities and Research Council Institutes to take forward ideas generated by research funding from BBSRC, EPSRC and NERC. For applications to BBSRC and NERC this funding must be current or recently finished (previous six months). It is expected that 'typical' awards will be in the range of £25,000 to £50,000 up to a maximum of £100,000 over 12 to 24 months. Awards will be made in the form of a Research Grant.

Research and Development (R&D) Tax Credits for SMEs were introduced in 2000 to encourage small firms to invest in research and development. Under the scheme a company can increase the amount that it deducts for qualifying R&D spending when it computes its profits for tax purposes to 150%. Companies which are SMEs can, in certain circumstances, surrender this tax relief to claim payable tax credits in cash from HM Revenue & Customs.

3 SOURCES OF FINANCE FOR SMEs

Potential sources of financing for small and medium-sized companies include the following:

1. initial owner financing combined with grants, overdrafts and loans
2. business angel financing
3. trade credit – already covered in Chapter 6
4. leasing – covered in Chapter 11
5. factoring – covered in Chapter 8
6. venture capital
7. short- and medium-term bank loans
8. mezzanine finance
9. private placements
10. public equity
11. public debt.

This list is loosely structured along growth lines. Thus, very small organisations start at point 1 and work through to point 11. Not all of the financing is successive and a number will overlap. Furthermore, as businesses grow, more information becomes known as they develop a track record. Debt finance is an important early source, its availability depending on the security available. Thus the list is ordered as much in terms of information availability as it is in terms of growth.

3.1 OWNER FINANCING COMBINED WITH GRANTS, OVERDRAFTS AND LOANS

Most enterprises start with an injection of capital by the owner from personal savings, combined with spending on a credit card, or a loan from family or friends. It is very difficult to obtain external funding because the assets are intangible at this stage. When the business starts to make a profit then some of the surplus will be ploughed back and other potential sources of finance become available. To begin with, these will include overdrafts, loans, leasing and hire purchase.

Bank overdrafts are one of the most important sources of short-term finance for industry, even though the banks reserve the right to recall them on demand (e.g. in times of a credit squeeze or if the firm's financial position is deteriorating) and often exercise it.

Many technology start-up companies gain some of their first funding through various grants from government agencies, charitable foundations or private sector bodies. The Department of Trade and Industry (DTI) considers that:

- a grant is financial assistance, usually for a specific project, given to a business by an awarding body
- a grant provides financial assistance to allow a business to undertake a specific project that without financial assistance would not be able to proceed

- a grant is usually a one-off payment and will provide funding that covers a percentage of the costs of a specific project. Generally, a grant will meet up to 50% of the costs of a project, with the business meeting the remainder of the costs. This is known as 'matched funding'.

Banks will lend money to new businesses if they have a viable business plan and directors or proprietors are creditworthy. Security is required in the form of assets or other proof that the business can repay the amount borrowed. Loans to sole traders and partnerships are no longer subject to the Consumer Credit Act 1974 and can be quite flexible.

Most of the major banks have literature about different types of business loan. If a business requires money in the short term, perhaps to cover its start-up costs or the purchase of equipment, an overdraft is a way of obtaining the money quickly. However, a bank can demand instant repayment and will usually seek security in the form of personal assets, even if you have formed a limited company.

3.2 BUSINESS ANGELS

Business angels are a good source of equity or risk capital – investing their own funds. They can also offer the businesses the benefits of their own management expertise and may also have some knowledge of the type of business, hence their initial interest. In return for a share in the business, they will plough in money at their own risk. They operate very quickly, often making decisions in a few days based on little hard data after only a few meetings with the person seeking finance.

Angel networks operate throughout the world and, in some cases, these networks operate on the Internet. In the UK and the US, there are hundreds of networks with tens of thousands of business angels prepared to invest several billion pounds each year in new, small businesses. You need to understand their criteria to have the best chance of raising money in this way:

- 40% suffer partial or complete loss of their investment, which suggests they are prepared to take big risks.
- 50% do not conduct research into prospective investments and 55% do not take up personal references, compared with venture-capital providers who almost invariably do both.
- 90% have worked in a small firm or owned their own business before, so they know the small business world well.
- Business angels meet owners five times on average before investing, compared with venture capital providers who, in general, require ten meetings.
- 10% of business angel investment is for less than £10,000 and 45% is for over £50,000, but they often group together to make much more substantial investments.
- Business angels tend to want to invest within a 50-mile radius of their base.
- Business angels often flock together. Syndicated deals make up more than a quarter of all deals.
- Business angels are more likely to invest in early-stage investments, where relatively small amounts of money are needed. They are up to five times more likely to invest in start-ups and early-stage investments than venture-capital providers in general.

Benefits of business angels	Drawbacks of business angels
Most business angels are experienced and can be a useful addition to the business team	Close working relationships are vital and can cause problems
They provide low risk, long-term finance with no sudden demands for repayments or interest	Angels can determine when they receive financial rewards from your business and some require a salary
Unlike banks and corporate lenders, angels will consider non-financial rewards such as helping a new venture and often are a source of funds when others have failed	The arrangement must be clarified at the outset so that financial payments can be budgeted and personal involvement does not come as a surprise
	Most angels want involvement at board level and expect to be kept informed about business decisions and actions

3.3 TRADE CREDIT

Trade credit is the term used to describe the situation whereby a company is able to obtain goods (or services) from a supplier without immediate payment, the supplier accepting that the company will pay for the goods at a later date. For many businesses, trade credit is another major source of short-term finance. By allowing a customer time to pay for purchases, a supplier is effectively investing in the customer's business, and not receiving any return (other than the profit on its sales). Trade credit has already been explained in detail, and the point has been made that it is risky to take too much credit. Excessive trade credit can reduce liquidity and increases the risk of an eventual cash shortage.

3.4 VENTURE CAPITAL FUNDS

Definition **Venture capital** is risk capital, provided typically by specialist financiers, both private and institutional.

One of the central elements of government policy since 1979 has been to promote the growth of small businesses with the aim of encouraging enterprise, innovation and employment creation. As a result of this, venture capital funds have evolved to meet the capital needs of companies, often small and often new. Such companies require injections of equity on a small scale in addition to specialist advice on all aspects of business operation.

Early development of venture funds was concentrated in major institutions such as merchant banks, clearing banks, fund management groups and investment trusts. These organisations now provide most venture capital in the UK. The remainder comes from independent bodies including:

(a) private funds, usually backed by large institutions

(b) publicly listed investment companies.

Essentially the major providers of funds are the pension funds and insurance companies. Banks have declined in importance although they might be willing to provide loan capital when a venture capital organisation invests in the company's share capital.

Venture capitalists take a large risk when they invest in small companies and consequently expect a large return on their investment. They are not long-term investors, and look for an 'exit route' for their investment, whereby they will be able to sell their shares. Often they favour a 'trade sale' of the company to a corporate buyer.

There are quite a large number of venture capital funds and institutions. The largest in the UK is 3i Group. However, there is a limit to the amount of funds they have available to invest, and they will not invest in a company unless they believe that there is a good prospect of making a high return on their investments. The types of venture that apply to the group for help include:

- Business start-ups. When a business has been set up by someone who has already put time and money into getting it started, the group may be approached to provide finance to enable it to get off the ground.

- Business development. The group may be asked to provide development capital for a company that wants to invest in new products or new markets or to make a business acquisition.

- Management buyouts. A management buyout is the purchase of all or parts of a business from its owners by its managers.

- A company where one of its owners wants to realise all or part of his/her investment may ask the group to buy some of the company's equity.

The basic information required by a venture capital fund when assessing the viability of a new project can be classified as follows:

- business strategy outlined in the business plan, which should ensure that the prospects for the future profits compensate for the risk

- the level of expertise of the management and the know-how and support to fulfil the plan

- the market and competition – market research findings should indicate a market for the product or service as well as looking at the threat posed by current rivals and potential new entrants to the market

- assessing the commitment of the management by the amount of money that the owners themselves have invested in the project

- the feasibility of providing the goods or services proposed, judged by an analysis of the sales forecast and the cost estimates to ascertain their accuracy

- potential exit routes – venture capitalists will not invest in a share of the business unless they are confident that it can be sold at some point in the future.

If more in-depth information were required, it would include the following:

(a) Financial aspects:

- project viability – cash flow/profit projections, NPV calculations

- financing requirements in total, leaving the fund to decide the best package

- accounting system – to provide regular management accounting information

- availability of other sources of finance, including loans and grants from government bodies
- future policy as regards dividends and accumulation of profits – with high growth being preferred
- the intention of eventually obtaining a quotation – usually within seven to ten years
- the percentage stake which is offered in the firm – indicating the degree of control and risk.

(b) Additional information affecting the proposal

- For most venture funds, evaluating financial information comes second to evaluating the credibility of the firm's management. A view must be formed as to whether the existing team has sufficient expertise to manage a growing firm, or whether specialist talent needs to be added.
- The investor would then wish to see evidence that thorough studies of the firm's markets had been made, so that projected sales budgets were realistic. The single most common cause of failure in this sort of situation is over-optimism in sales projections. Relevant information includes market research, orders in hand, letters from potential customers and general projections of the market's prospects.
- Information on technical aspects of the firm's products would then be useful, especially new designs that have not yet been tested.
- The investor would also be interested in knowing how much influence it is envisaged it will have on the management decision making in the firm. The management of most venture funds will want a seat on the board.

ACTIVITY 1

Describe four circumstances in which a small business enterprise might seek venture capital finance.

For a suggested answer, see the 'Answers' section at the end of the book.

ACTIVITY 2

Put yourself in the position of being an entrepreneur requiring a loan of $1 million. Consider what information a potential lender would require before such an investment were offered.

For a suggested answer, see the 'Answers' section at the end of the book.

3.5 MEZZANINE FINANCE

Mezzanine finance is a hybrid form of risk capital, combining the main characteristics of ordinary bank debt and equity. It is a way of raising capital without losing control of the business. Depending on how it was structured, it may be in the form of an unsecured loan coupled with an equity stake (some companies call this an 'equity kicker'), such as redeemable preferred shares. In a legal sense it is debt and has all of the rights associated with debt, but in an economic sense it acts as 'quasi' equity.

CONCLUSION

Small and medium-sized enterprises (SMEs) need finance to grow and develop. Unfortunately, most find it extremely difficult to obtain finance. In this chapter we examined why this might be so and looked at some of the specialist products available to help finance such organisations. Whilst the UK government has attempted to make debt investment in small businesses more attractive by the introduction of its Loan Guarantee Scheme, this has not proved very successful due to its relatively high interest rate.

SELF-TEST QUESTIONS

		Paragraph
1	How many employees might a small enterprise have?	1.1
2	Explain why small enterprises find it difficult to raise finance.	2.1
3	What are VCTs?	2.2
4	Describe what an EIB is and what it does.	2.3
5	How does the DTI describe a 'grant'?	3.1
6	Give three drawbacks of a business angel.	3.2

Chapter 14

CAPITAL INVESTMENT PLANNING AND CONTROL

This chapter deals with the differences between capital and revenue expenditure. One of the differences is that non-current assets are often very expensive and therefore expenditure for the wrong reasons or the wrong amount can have a disastrous effect on the organisations effectiveness. This is why capital investment planning and control is so important.

This chapter covers Syllabus part E2.

CONTENTS

LEARNING OUTCOMES

The following study sessions are covered:

- Discuss the importance of capital investment planning and control
- Outline the issues to consider and the steps involved in the preparation of a capital expenditure budget
- Define and distinguish between capital and revenue expenditure
- Compare and contrast investment in non-current assets and investment in working capital
- Describe capital investment procedures (authorisation and monitoring).

---

1 CAPITAL AND REVENUE EXPENDITURE

1.1 CAPITAL EXPENDITURE COMPARED TO WORKING CAPITAL EXPENDITURE

Capital expenditure can be defined as expenditure on productive assets which are intended for use on a continuing basis in an enterprise's activities.

A non-current asset can be defined as an asset that is acquired and retained in the business with a view to earning profits and not merely turning into cash. Examples of non-current assets include buildings, water and sewerage installations, lifts, heating, ventilating and similar equipment forming an integral part of buildings and structures, land development and construction site development. Machinery, vehicles, electrical apparatus, office equipment, computers, furniture, fixtures and fittings not forming an integral part of buildings, durable containers, special tooling, etc.

Capital investment involves expenditure on non-current assets for use in a project which is intended to provide a return by way of interest, dividends or capital appreciation. There are various reasons why capital expenditure might be either necessary or desirable, and these can be categorised into the following types.

- **Maintenance** – this is spending on new non-current assets to replace worn-out assets or obsolete assets, or spending on existing non-current assets to improve safety and security features.
- **Profitability** – this is spending on non-current assets to improve the profitability of the existing business, to achieve cost savings, quality improvement, improved productivity, and so on.
- **Expansion** – this is spending to expand the business, to make new products, open new outlets, invest in research and development, etc.
- **Indirect** – this is spending on non-current assets that will not have a direct impact on the business operations or its profits. It includes spending on office buildings, or welfare facilities, etc. Capital spending of this nature is necessary, but a business should try to make sure that it gets good value for money from its spending.

Because of the large amounts of money involved, it is usual for decisions about capital expenditure to be taken at a senior level within an organisation.

In contrast to revenue expenditure, which is normally continual spending but in fairly small amounts, capital expenditure is irregular and often involves large amounts of spending.

However, there is always an exception and self-constructed assets are a little different. Where a business builds its own non-current assets, e.g. a programming engineer might build a computer system or a builder might construct an office, then all the costs associated with building the asset should be included in the recorded cost of the non-current asset. These costs will include raw materials and the cost of labour and related overhead costs. Assets that are self-constructed are treated in a similar way to purchased non-current assets. They result in being shown as a non-current asset in the statement of financial position of the business.

We must also distinguish between capital expenditure and working capital expenditure. Inventories are current assets that are a part of the working capital of the business, along with the amounts owed to the business by receivables.

1.2 REVENUE EXPENDITURE

Revenue expenditure is for ongoing spending. This includes salaries, bills for services such as telephone, gas, electricity, rent, stationery and other consumables.

It is incurred for the purpose of trade, i.e. for expenditure classified as selling and distribution expenses, administration expenses and fixed charges or to maintain the existing earning capacity of non-current assets.

Revenue expenditure results from the purchase of goods and services that will either be used fully in the accounting period in which they are purchased and so be a cost expense in the statement of profit or loss or result in a current asset as at the end of the accounting period because the goods or services have not yet been consumed or made use of. As a current asset this would be shown on the statement of financial position and not as an expense or cost in the statement of profit or loss.

It is impossible to list all the expenses that can be deducted but, generally speaking, allowable expenditure relates to day to day running costs of the business. It includes such items as wages, rent, lighting and heating of business premises, running costs of vehicles used in the business, purchase of goods for resale and the cost of replacing tools used in the business.

Where expenditure relates to both business and private use, only the part that relates to the business will be allowed, examples are lighting, heating, and telephone expenditure. If a vehicle is used for both business and private purposes then the capital allowances and the total running expenses will be split in proportion to the business and private mileage. A record would need to be kept of the total mileage and the number of miles travelled on business to calculate the correct split.

Depreciation – many assets lose value as a result of age, wear and tear or obsolescence. So the statement of financial position must reflect not only the cost of the assets but also their written down value. As a consequence the company has lost some value and has reduced its ability to repay its liabilities. This means that the annual depreciation is treated the same as revenue expenditure and deducted from profits as an expense.

ACTIVITY 1

Explain the significance of the distinction between capital and revenue expenditure.

For a suggested answer, see the 'Answers' section at the end of the book.

1.3 CAPITAL INCOME AND REVENUE INCOME

When non-current assets (for example, non-trading assets such as investments) are sold, the proceeds from the sale is capital income. The profits (or losses) as a result of the sale are included in the statement of profit or loss of the enterprise for the accounting period in which the sale takes place.

Revenue income can arise from the sale of trading assets or from interest and dividends received from investments held by the enterprise.

2 CONTROL OVER NON-CURRENT ASSETS

One of the most significant factors affecting the level of profitability in a business is the quality of management decisions relating to the commitment of the organisation's resources to the acquisition of non-current assets within the business. With these investments the organisation must maintain or develop its activities, and the importance to the future wellbeing of the concern cannot be stressed too highly. For example, consider the investment required in plant and buildings when a new motor vehicle model is introduced. If the decisions made are of poor quality, the losses to the organisation can be very great.

Coupled with this we must consider how effectively assets are used once they have been acquired. A profitable rate of return must be obtained to justify the continued use, and audits should be carried out to check that the anticipated benefits have, in fact, been realised.

Thus we can see that there is the need for efficient authorisation, control and post-audit techniques for the acquisition of new equipment. In addition we must recognise that strict control procedures are required for the maintenance of up-to-date records of the values, location and use of all non-current assets owned by an organisation. The investment in non-current assets can be very high and the stewardship function relating to the control of plant, equipment and buildings is therefore most important within any organisation.

2.1 ADDITIONS TO NON-CURRENT ASSETS

Additions to the non-current assets of an organisation may be required for one of the following reasons.

(a) Profit adding:

- expansion of existing operations
- new facilities.

(b) Profit maintaining:

- replacement
- repairs.

(c) Others not related directly to profit adding or maintaining.

When departments require additional equipment, or expansion is called for in the plans of the organisation, there should be a formalised procedure which must be followed.

The case for the expenditure should be summarised, preferably on a standard form, giving details of the equipment etc. required, the anticipated cost and estimates of any internal materials or labour required for installation. Details of the anticipated effect on profits through increased productivity, reduced costs, etc., should also be given.

2.2 EVALUATION OF CAPITAL EXPENDITURE

The data presented should then be evaluated by the accounts department following the approach adopted by the organisation. This approach may range from a simple payback assessment, i.e. how quickly will the investment be paid back from the profits arising, to more sophisticated procedures allowing for the time-value of money, i.e. discounted cash flow techniques.

2.3 AUTHORISATION OF CAPITAL EXPENDITURE AND DISPOSAL

Depending on the amount required for the investment the final figures will then be presented for authorisation by management. For example, for a factory which is part of a large group, levels of authority might be:

- up to $5,000 – works manager
- $5,001 – $10,000 – local director
- above $10,000 – group authority required.

In arriving at a decision various criteria will be considered. In addition to requiring that a target of payback within a given period or a specified rate of return be achievable, the degree of risk, the effect on the cash flows of the organisation and the comparability with competing projects will all be taken into account.

The disposal of an asset over a certain amount must also be authorised and the reason for its disposal documented.

2.4 CONTROL OF CAPITAL EXPENDITURE

When capital expenditure is authorised, for control of expenditure purposes it is recommended that a special code number be allocated to each project. This will then be quoted as each order is placed with suppliers or for internal work, and would be requested to be noted on suppliers' invoices or internal work tickets. By this means the work of building up each cost will be aided.

Whilst the progress of the work will be carefully maintained by engineering staff, the comparison of the actual expenditure against that authorised will at the same time be clearly scrutinised by the accounts department so that any over/under spending can be quickly identified.

Post-completion audit

Once new capital equipment is installed it is important that a post-completion audit is carried out. This aspect appears to have been neglected in many organisations, but a capital project cannot be said to be successful until management is assured that all the benefits promised at the evaluation stage can be shown to have been subsequently realised.

The audit should be conducted by staff experienced in appreciating the financial and/or production implications of the project and who are independent of the original commissioning team. Two purposes will be served:

(i) It checks whether benefits have been achieved and draws management's attention to unsuccessful projects.

(ii) It reduces the tendency in many organisations to be over-optimistic with the data when presenting projects for evaluation.

Asset register

As details of additions to non-current assets are received in the accounts department, in addition to recording in the appropriate ledger accounts, full information should be noted in a properly maintained asset register. This should have provision for the inclusion of a description, a build-up of the cost, the date of commission, the expected life, the annual depreciation and the written-down balance. In addition, space for details of any disposal should also be provided.

The reconciliation to the non-current assets recorded in the nominal ledger should be checked by a responsible official.

Asset disposal

Whenever any item of equipment is relocated or disposed of it is essential that details be prepared by the appropriate manager and forwarded to the accounts staff in charge of the asset register. This rule should be very strictly enforced to avoid the accuracy of the register very quickly becoming unreliable.

Some organisations have procedures to follow when an asset with a high residual value is no longer required. Its disposal will be discussed and perhaps the following points will be considered:

- timing of disposal
- disposal method preferred
- advertising necessary
- valuation and price sought
- selection of best offer
- replacement, if relevant.

ACTIVITY 2

What events might give rise to entries in the non-current asset register?

For a suggested answer, see the 'Answers' section at the end of the book.

2.5 ADVANTAGES OF NON-CURRENT ASSET CONTROL

If these procedures are properly carried out they will provide an effective contribution to financial management.

With properly conducted capital expenditure authorisation and appraisal techniques, only profitable additions to non-current assets will have a claim on the cash resources of the organisation. In addition, correct recording procedures are essential in order to provide the full information on capital expenditure when tax liabilities are being assessed.

The benefits from an up-to-date asset register are also great. The stewardship function will be greatly assisted and the calculation of the periodic depreciation charges will be achieved much more easily. This has proved of great importance due to the requirements of adjustments that have to be made to values and depreciation charges of non-current assets in connection with accounting for price-level changes. It is for this reason, and the greater availability of computer facilities, that many organisations have in recent years paid much more attention to this aspect of control that has in the past been neglected.

3 CAPITAL BUDGETING: PROJECT CONTROL, EVALUATION AND POST AUDIT

3.1 STEPS INVOLVED IN THE CAPITAL BUDGETING CYCLE

Businesses have to spend money on capital expenditures, equipment, and vehicles, etc. in anticipation of being able to earn, in the future, an income greater than the funds committed. In larger businesses, capital expenditure decisions are planned as part of a capital budgeting process.

The process can be divided into several stages to provide better management control. As shown in the diagram below, effort such as resource use is low at the start of the project, higher towards the end and then falls away rapidly as the project comes to the end.

Risk and uncertainty are highest at the start of the project, and the probability of successfully completing it is at its lowest. As the project progresses, the likelihood of successful completion increases.

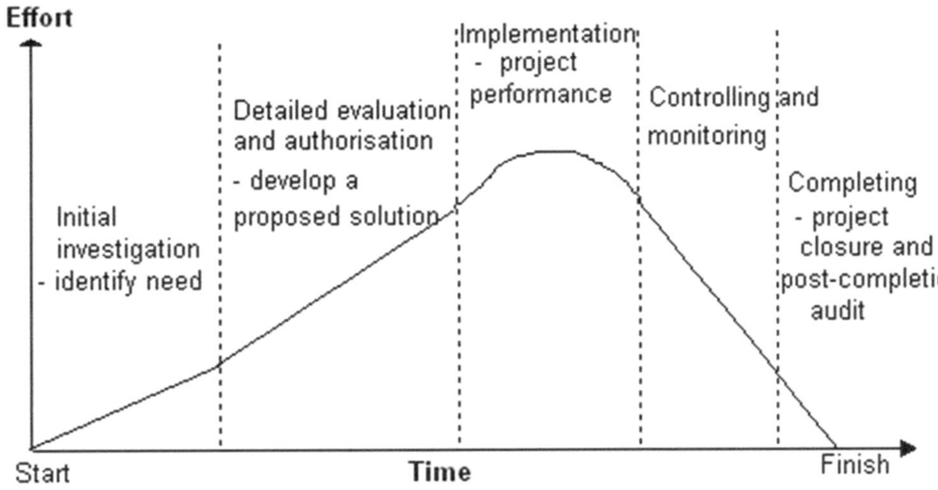

The stages for project appraisal include the following:

1 **Initial investigation of the proposal**

Firstly, a decision must be made as to whether the project is technically feasible and commercially viable. This involves assessing the risks and deciding whether the project is in line with the company's long-term strategic objectives.

2 **Detailed evaluation**

A detailed investigation will take place in order to examine the projected cash flows of the project. Sensitivity analysis is performed and sources of finance will be considered.

3 **Authorisation**

For significant projects, authorisation must be sought from the company's senior management and Board of Directors. This will only take place once such persons are satisfied that a detailed evaluation has been carried out, that the project will contribute to profitability and that the project is consistent with the company's strategy.

4 **Implementation**

At this stage, responsibility for the project is assigned to a project manager or other responsible person. The resources will be made available for implementation and specific targets will be set.

5 **Project monitoring**

Now the project has started, progress must be monitored and senior management must be kept informed of progress. Costs and benefits may have to be re-assessed if unforeseen events occur.

6 **Post-completion audit**

At the end of the project, an audit will be carried out so that lessons can be learned to help future project planning.

3.2 TYPES OF CAPITAL PROJECT

Reasons for capital expenditure vary widely. Projects may be classified into the following categories:

(a) **maintenance** – replacement of worn-out or obsolete assets, safety and security, etc.

(b) **profitability** – cost savings, quality improvement, productivity, relocation, etc.

(c) **expansion** – new products, new outlets, research and development, etc.

(d) **indirect** – office buildings, welfare facilities, etc.

A particular investment project, of course, could combine any number or all of the above classifications.

Even those projects which are not likely to earn profits must be subjected to investment appraisal, in order to choose the best way of achieving the project. For example, investment appraisal can be used to find the cheapest method for constructing a staff canteen, although such a project is unlikely to earn profits.

3.3 WORKING CAPITAL

In most industrial projects, investment is required, both in working capital and in fixed capital, although the risk attached to working capital is less than that for fixed capital. Values of land and buildings may appreciate and so present less risk, but money invested in machinery is a sunk cost, which is unlikely to be recovered, except for perhaps minimal scrap values.

In project appraisal, accurate estimates of working capital requirements are desirable, not only for assessment of project profitability, but also to facilitate forecasting of capital requirements.

3.4 CAPITAL EXPENDITURE FORECAST

In preparing budgets, it is necessary to consider how much money can or must be allocated to capital expenditure. Capital development schemes may be started because a surplus of cash resources is revealed by the long-term plan, but usually management decides on a capital development scheme and then seeks the means to finance it.

Initially, the budget will be an expression of management's intention to allocate funds for certain broad purposes. In the budget period, money will be required as follows:

(a) for previously authorised existing projects

(b) for new projects, full details of which may not yet be available.

The forecasts will indicate whether sufficient funds are available, and perhaps when additional funds will need to be obtained. It is advisable, therefore, for managers to submit long-term capital expenditure forecasts, say for two to five years ahead; consequently, the possibility of obsolescence (and the direction of the future development of the firm) must be borne in mind.

The capital budget is the outcome of a dual process:

(a) higher management allocating funds to various areas in relation to the corporate plan, i.e. according to the long-term objectives of the company, and

(b) individual managers seeking to utilise the funds for specific projects.

The importance of this aspect of planning cannot be over-emphasised, because present capital investment will determine the structure and profitability of the company in the near future. Errors made in forecasting and planning will, therefore, have serious results, and may prove difficult to rectify.

3.5 CAPITAL EXPENDITURE COMMITTEE

A capital expenditure committee may be formed, either as a sub-committee of the budget committee or as a separate meeting of the entire budget committee.

The functions of such a committee are to do the following:

(a) coordinate capital expenditure policy

(b) appraise and authorise capital expenditure on specific projects

(c) review actual expenditure on capital projects against the budget.

In many organisations, multi-disciplinary teams, or working parties, are set up to investigate individual proposals and report back to top management on their findings. Such a team might comprise the following members:

(a) project engineer

(b) production engineer

(c) management accountant

(d) relevant specialist e.g.:

  (i) personnel officer, for a project involving sports facilities or canteens

  (ii) safety officers, etc.

(e) economist.

3.6 CAPITAL EXPENDITURE DECISION

The seriousness of all decisions relating to capital expenditure must be stressed. Today's decisions will affect the direction and pace of the company's future growth or, indeed, its very survival. If a wrong decision is made, it will be difficult to correct, particularly where special purpose plant is involved.

It has frequently been reported that, in both the private and public sectors, investment decisions are made rather casually and that this laxity is one of the major causes of lack of growth within the UK economy. Of all the decisions taken by management, those concerned with investment are the most crucial: once made, they may fix the future of the company in terms of its technological role, cost structure and market effort required i.e. once the product has been selected and the plant built, the company is committed to the specific cost structure which accompanies that particular type of plant and the product made.

3.7 AUTHORISATION OF CAPITAL PROJECTS

The capital budget will not necessarily be based on a detailed analysis of required projects. It is likely that managers will be asked to forecast their capital expenditure requirements for inclusion in the budget but, even if such figures are included, it is still necessary for detailed proposals to be submitted to the committee before the projects may be started.

Many projects will incur fairly small expenditure and, in order not to involve the committee in unnecessary detail, broad guidelines ought to be laid down regarding the amounts of expenditure which may be committed by each level of management. Top management must see that the types of expenditure to be treated as capital are clearly defined, and that every subordinate or committee knows precisely the limits to which they can approve capital expenditure.

Capital expenditure requiring approval by the committee must be formulated by the managers. The amount of detail should be stipulated by the committee and would generally cover the following:

(a) outline of the project, including the budget classification and how it is linked, if at all, with other projects

(b) reason for the expenditure (if a new project) and the departments affected. An assessment of intangible benefits or disadvantages

(c) the amount of capital expenditure required (fixed and working capital), including a breakdown by budget periods, and an estimate of any internal work required

(d) a complete statement of incremental costs and revenue arising from the project, and the budget periods affected. An assessment of the effect of taxation ought to be made

(e) estimated life of the project

(f) assessment of risks to which the project is sensitive – political, economic, competitors, natural hazards, etc.

(g) projects which are feasible alternatives, and comparative data

(h) effect of postponement or rejection of project.

Major projects would probably be subjected to a comprehensive financial evaluation, as part of the committee's consideration; less important projects could be submitted, accompanied by an economic justification.

3.8 CAPITAL EXPENDITURE CONTROL

Strict control of large projects must be maintained and the accountant must submit periodic reports to top management on progress and cost. A typical report would include data such as the following:

(a) budgeted cost of the project, date started and scheduled completion date

(b) cost and over- or under-expenditure to date

(c) estimated cost to completion, and estimated final over- or under-expenditure

(d) estimated completion date and details of penalties, if any.

The capital expenditure committee will seek explanations for any overspending that may have arisen. Where projects are incomplete and actual expenditure exceeds the authorisation, additional authority must be sought to complete the project. In so doing, the committee must consider the value of the project as it then stands and the additional value that will be gained by completing it, compared with the additional expenditure to completion.

A vital consideration is the adequacy of funds available. Where existing projects are overspending their allocation, other perhaps more desirable projects may be delayed. When reviewing progress, therefore, the committee must consider the funds available, in the light of which it may become necessary to revise the order of priority in which funds are awarded to projects.

3.9 POST-PROJECT AUDIT

On completion of a project, an investigation should be undertaken to examine its profitability and compare it with the plan.

Definition **Post-completion audit** – an objective and independent appraisal of the measure of success of a capital expenditure project in progressing the business as planned. The appraisal should cover the implementation of the project from authorisation to commissioning and its technical and commercial performance after commissioning. The information provided is also used by management as feedback which aids the implementation and control of future projects. **(CIMA Official Terminology)**

There are three reasons for undertaking these reviews:

(a) to discourage managers from spending money on doubtful projects, because they may be called to account at a later date

(b) it may be possible over a period of years to discern a trend of reliability in the estimates of various managers

(c) a similar project may be undertaken in the future, and then the recently completed project will provide a useful basis for estimation.

CONCLUSION

In this chapter we reminded ourselves of the differences between capital and revenue expenditure and compared and contrasted investment in non-current (fixed) assets and investment in working capital. Because of the importance of capital investment we described the steps involved in preparing a capital expenditure budget.

SELF-TEST QUESTIONS

		Paragraph
1	Outline the reasons why capital investment might be necessary or desirable.	1.1
2	How is depreciation of the asset treated in the statement of financial position and statement of profit or loss?	1.2
3	Describe the procedures that might be followed when an asset with a high residual value is disposed of.	2.4
4	What are the basic stages in the capital budgeting cycle?	3.1
5	What information is likely to be included in the periodic reports submitted to management on the progress and cost of ongoing projects?	3.8
6	What are the aims of a post-project audit?	3.9

Chapter 15

CAPITAL INVESTMENT APPRAISAL

When making an investment appraisal the organisation must decide how to compare costs and benefits. Some approaches, such as the ARR and payback are quite simple, but the discounted cash flow approaches are probably more appropriate methods for a business to use when evaluating a proposed capital investment. This chapter explains the nature of compounding and discounting and the time value of money, and then goes on to show how the time value of money is recognised in discounted cash flows. It then explains and compares three DCF methods of appraisal: net present value, internal rate of return and payback.

This chapter covers Syllabus parts E1 and E3.

CONTENTS

LEARNING OUTCOMES

At the end of this chapter you should be able to:

- Calculate the payback and discounted payback of a project and assess its usefulness as a method of investment appraisal
- Calculate the accounting rate of return of a project and assess its usefulness as a method of investment appraisal

- Explain the differences between simple and compound interest
- Calculate future values
- Discuss the concept of time value of money
- Discuss the concept of discounting
- Calculate present values, making use of present value tables to establish discount factors
- Discuss the concept of relevant cash flows for decision making
- Identify and evaluate relevant cash flows for individual investment decisions
- Explain the concept of net present value and how it can be used for project appraisal
- Calculate net present value and interpret the results (Note: NPV calculations will not include adjustments for inflation, tax or working capital)
- Outline the concept of internal rate of return and how it can be used for project appraisal
- Calculate internal rate of return and interpret the results
- Discuss the relative merits of NPV and IRR, including mutually exclusive projects and multiple yields
- Calculate payback, discounted payback and accounting rate of return
- Explain the superiority of DCF methods over payback and accounting rate of return.

1 INVESTMENT APPRAISAL AND CASH FLOWS

1.1 THE FEATURES OF CAPITAL EXPENDITURE APPRAISAL

Before any capital expenditure is authorised, the proposed spending (or 'capital project') should be evaluated. Management should be satisfied that the spending would be beneficial.

If the purpose of a capital project is to improve profits, we need to be convinced that the expected profits are big enough to justify the spending. Will the investment provide a reasonable return?

If the capital expenditure is for an essential purpose, such as to replace a worn-out machine or to acquire a new office building, we need to be convinced that the spending decision is the best option available, and that there are no cheaper or more effective spending options.

When a proposed capital project is evaluated, the costs and benefits of the project should be evaluated over its foreseeable life. This is usually the expected useful life of the non-current asset to be purchased, which will be several years. This means that estimates of future costs and benefits call for long-term forecasting.

A 'typical' capital project involves an immediate purchase of a non-current asset. The asset is then used for a number of years, during which it is used to increase sales revenue or to achieve savings in operating costs. There will also be running costs for the asset. At the end of the asset's commercially useful life, it might have a 'residual value'. For example, it might be sold for scrap or in a second-hand market. (Items such as motor vehicles and printing machines often have a significant residual value.)

A problem with long-term forecasting of revenues, savings and costs is that forecasts can be inaccurate. However, although it is extremely difficult to produce reliable forecasts, every effort should be made to make them as reliable as possible.

- A business should try to avoid spending money on non-current assets on the basis of wildly optimistic and unrealistic forecasts.
- The assumptions on which the forecasts are based should be stated clearly. If the assumptions are clear, the forecasts can be assessed for reasonableness by the individuals who are asked to authorise the spending.

1.2 METHODS OF CAPITAL EXPENDITURE APPRAISAL

When forecasts of costs and benefits have been made for a capital project, the estimates must be analysed to establish whether the project should go ahead. Should the business spend money now in order to earn returns over a number of years into the future?

Capital investment appraisal is an analysis of the expected financial returns from a capital project over its expected life.

There are several methods of carrying out a capital expenditure appraisal. The methods that will be described in this chapter are:

1 the accounting rate of return (ARR)

2 payback

3 net present value method

4 internal rate of return method

5 discounted payback.

1.3 ACCOUNTING PROFITS AND CASH FLOWS

An investment involves the outlay of money 'now' in the expectation of getting more money back in the future. In capital investment appraisal, it is more appropriate to evaluate future cash flows – the money actually spent, saved and received – rather than accounting profits. Accounting profits do not properly reflect investment returns.

Suppose for example that a business is considering whether to buy a new non-current asset for $80,000 that is expected to increase profits before depreciation each year by $30,000 for four years. At the end of year 4, the asset will be worthless.

The business should assess whether the expected financial return from the asset is sufficiently high to justify buying it.

(a) If we looked at the accounting returns from this investment, we might decide that annual depreciation should be $20,000 each year ($80,000/4 years). Annual profits would then be $10,000. We could then assess the project on the basis that it will add $10,000 each year to profit for the next four years. (We could estimate an expected average return on capital employed, or 'accounting rate of return'. Since the average statement of financial position value of the asset over its useful life will be $40,000 after depreciation, we could say that the project will provide an average return on capital employed, in accounting terms, of 25% ($10,000/$40,000).

(b) If we looked at the investment cash flows, the analysis is different. Here we would say that to invest in the project, the business would spend $80,000 now and would expect a cash return of $30,000 each year for the next four years.

Capital investment appraisal should be based on cash flows, because it is realistic to do so. Capital spending involves spending cash and getting cash back in return, over time.

1.4 RELEVANT AND NON-RELEVANT COSTS

The concept of relevant cash flows for decision making is very important.

The only cash flows that should be taken into consideration in capital investment appraisal are:

- cash flows that will happen in the future, and
- cash flows that will arise only if the capital project goes ahead.

These cash flows are direct revenues from the project and relevant costs. Relevant costs are future costs that will be incurred or saved as a direct consequence of undertaking the investment.

Relevant costs are cash flows – only those future costs that are in the form of cash should be included. Therefore, costs that do not reflect cash spending should be ignored for the purpose of decision making. This means that depreciation charges should be ignored.

Relevant costs are future, incremental costs – a relevant cost is the increase in costs that results from making a particular decision. Any costs or benefits arising as a result of a past decision should be ignored. Costs that have already been incurred are not relevant to a current decision. Such past costs are called 'sunk costs'. For example, suppose a company makes a non-returnable deposit as a down payment for an item of equipment, and then re-considers whether it wants the equipment after all. The money that has already been spent and cannot be recovered and so is not relevant to the current decision about obtaining the equipment. Alternatively, if some material has already been purchased in preparation for a project, the cost of the material already bought is not relevant.

Opportunity costs – an opportunity cost is the value of a benefit foregone as a result of choosing a particular course of action. Such a cost will always be a relevant cost. Relevant costs may involve incurring a cost or losing a revenue which could be obtained from an alternative course of action. Opportunity cost can only arise when resources are limited or only one option can be selected. Otherwise an organisation will select all beneficial options. An example is when a material is in stock, but is in short supply. The relevant (opportunity) cost of using the material in a new project is the benefit foregone by not selling the material or using it in some other way.

Example

A company has been asked by a customer to carry out a job for which materials would have to be purchased, costing $600, and which would incur other additional expenses of $200. The labour time required to do the job would be 50 hours, and labour is paid $8 per hour. If the company does the job, the labour to do the work would have to be switched from other operations that earn a contribution of $5 per labour hour. Overhead costs are absorbed at the rate of $10 per direct labour hour. The customer is willing to pay $1,800 for the job.

Required:

Should the company accept the job?

Solution

Here, there is an opportunity cost of using the labour to do the job, costing $5 per labour hour. The labour cost of $8 per hour is also a relevant cost, even though the employees will be paid anyway. This is because the contribution of $5 per hour is calculated on the assumption that direct labour is a variable cost. The alternative work therefore earns a contribution of $5 per hour after covering labour costs of $8 per hour.

Absorbed production overhead is not a relevant cost, because it represents an allocation of overhead that doesn't change as a result of the decision. The only relevant overhead costs would be any change in actual overhead spending. For example, any variable overhead costs would be a relevant cost. In this example, there is no suggestion that the overhead costs are variable costs.

The relevant information is as follows.

	$
Relevant costs	
Direct materials	600
Other expenses	200
Direct labour (50 hours × $8)	400
Opportunity cost (50 hours × $5)	250
Total relevant costs	1,450
Price for the job	1,800
Net income	350

If the company wishes to maximise its return, it should agree to take on the job for $1,800.

Other non-relevant costs

Certain other costs will be irrelevant to decision making, such as 'committed costs'. A committed cost is a future cash outflow that will be incurred anyway, regardless of what decision will be taken. Fixed cost expenditures are an example of 'committed costs'. For the purpose of investment appraisal, a project should not be charged with an amount for a share of fixed costs that will be incurred anyway.

Non-cash items of cost can never be relevant to investment appraisal. In particular, the depreciation charges on a non-current asset are not relevant costs for analysis because depreciation is not a cash expenditure.

Other costs, such as interest costs, are also ignored. This is not because they do not meet the above criteria, but because they are taken into account in the discounting process. If these costs were included as relevant they would be double counted.

ACTIVITY 1

A company is evaluating a proposed expenditure on an item of equipment that would cost \$160,000. A technical feasibility study has been carried out by consultants, at a cost of \$15,000, into benefits from investing in the equipment. It has been estimated that the equipment would have a life of four years, and annual profits would be \$8,000. Profits are after deducting annual depreciation of \$40,000 and an annual charge of \$25,000 for a share of fixed costs that will be incurred anyway.

Required:

Identify the cash flows that should be evaluated for this project.

For a suggested answer, see the 'Answers' section at the end of the book.

2 ACCOUNTING RATE OF RETURN

2.1 DEFINITION

The accounting rate of return (ARR) which may also be called the return on capital employed (ROCE) expresses the profits from a project as a percentage of capital cost. However, the figures used for profits and capital costs may vary. The most common approach produces the following formula:

$$ARR = \frac{\text{Average annual (post depreciation) profits}}{\text{Initial capital costs}} \times 100\%$$

Example

A project involves the immediate purchase of an item of plant costing \$110,000. It would generate annual cash flows of \$24,400 for five years, starting in year 1. The plant purchased would have a scrap value of \$10,000 in five years, when the project terminates. Depreciation is on a straight-line basis.

Required:

Calculate the ARR of the project.

Solution

Annual cash flows are taken to be profit before depreciation.

Average annual depreciation = (\$110,000 – \$10,000) ÷ 5 = \$20,000

Average annual profit = \$24,400 – \$20,000 = \$4,400

$$ARR = \frac{\text{Average annual profits}}{\text{Initial capital costs}} \times 100\%$$

$$= \frac{\$4,400}{\$110,000} \times 100\% = 4\%$$

EXAMINER'S NOTE

The examiner has noted that you will need to be able to calculate the accounting rate of return (ARR) of a project. Since ARR is based on profits rather than cash flows, the calculations may involve reconciling cash flow to profit.

There are several ways of writing the ARR formula. Whichever you choose, be sure to use the same one throughout the calculation. It may be that the question specifically tells you to use a certain ARR formula. If this is the case, be sure to use the formula given or you will fail to gain maximum marks for that question. The most common formula is:

$$\frac{\text{Estimated average profit}}{\text{Estimated average investment}} \times 100\%$$

To calculate the value of the average investment you must first add the initial investment cost to the residual value. This gives the total amount of money tied up and it should be divided by two to find the average. Many candidates make the mistake of thinking that the average investment is calculated by taking the residual value from the initial cost. By doing this, candidates fail to gain easy marks. In an exam, you may also be required to discuss the usefulness of ARR as a method of project appraisal.

2.2 ADVANTAGES AND DISADVANTAGES OF THE ARR METHOD OF PROJECT APPRAISAL

The advantages and disadvantages are set out below:

Advantages of ARR for appraisal	**Disadvantages of ARR for appraisal**
Simplicity – it is easily understood and easily calculated.	It fails to take account of either the project life or the timing of cash flows (and time value of money) within that life.
Is widely used and the ARR is expressed in percentage terms with which managers and accountants are familiar.	The ARR method is based on accounting profits and statement of financial position values, and ignores cash flows entirely.
Links with other accounting measures.	

3 PAYBACK METHOD OF APPRAISAL

Definition **Payback** is the amount of time it is expected to take for the cash inflows from a capital investment project to equal the cash outflows.

It is the time that a project will take to pay back the money spent on it. It is based on expected cash flows from the project, not accounting profits.

The payback method of appraisal is used in one of two ways.

- A business might establish a rule for capital spending that no project should be undertaken unless it is expected to pay back the initial investment within a given length of time. For example, a rule might be established that capital expenditure should not be undertaken unless payback is expected within, say, five years.

- When two alternative capital projects are being compared, and the decision is to undertake one or the other but not both, preference might be given to the project that is expected to pay back sooner.

Payback is commonly used as an initial screening method, and projects that meet the payback requirement are then evaluated using another investment appraisal method.

3.1 CALCULATING PAYBACK: CONSTANT ANNUAL CASH FLOWS

The simple payback period is calculated by identifying the point at which cumulative net cash inflows equal the cost of the initial investment. The payback period is calculated by identifying the point at which cumulative net cash inflows equal the cost of the initial investment.

If the expected cash inflows from a project are an equal annual amount, the payback period is calculated simply as:

$$\text{Payback period} = \frac{\text{Initial payment}}{\text{Annual cash inflow}}$$

It is normally assumed that cash flows each year occur at an even rate throughout the year, although it might sometimes be more appropriate to assume that cash flows arise at the end of each year (this assumption is often made when evaluating projects using the NPV method – covered in detail below).

Example

An expenditure of $2 million is expected to generate cash inflows of $500,000 each year for the next seven years.

What is the payback period for the project?

Solution

$$\text{Payback period} = \frac{\$2{,}000{,}000}{\$500{,}000} = \textbf{4 years}$$

The payback method provides a rough measure of the liquidity of a project, in other words how much annual cash flow it earns. It is not a measure of the profitability of a project over its life. In the example above, the fact that the project pays back within four years ignores the total amount of cash flows it will provide over seven years. A project costing $2 million and earning cash flows of $500,000 for just five years would have exactly the same payback period, even though it would not be as profitable.

A payback period might not be an exact number of years.

Example

A project will involve spending $1.8 million now. Annual cash flows from the project would be $350,000.

What is the expected payback period?

Solution

Payback period = $\frac{\$1,800,000}{\$350,000}$ = **5.1429 years**

This can be stated in any of the following ways:

- payback will be in 5.1 years
- payback will be in just over 5 years (or between 5 and 6 years)
- payback will be in 5 years 2 months.

Payback in years and months is calculated by multiplying the decimal fraction of a year by 12 months. In this example, 0.1429 years = 1.7 months (0.1429 × 12 months), which is rounded to 2 months.

Alternatively, if we assume that the cash flows arise at the end of each year, payback will be in 6 years.

3.2 CALCULATING PAYBACK: NON-CONSTANT ANNUAL CASH FLOWS

If the cash flows from the project are not constant each year, the payback period is calculated by recalculating the cumulative cash position each year until the cumulative cash position becomes zero.

Example

A project requires an investment of $200,000 and the returns are expected to be:

Year 1	$60,000
Year 2	$100,000
Year 3	$100,000
Year 4	$80,000

The cumulative cash position is -$200,000 initially, and this changes to –$140,000 after one year (–200,000+60,000), then –$40,000 after 2 years (–140,000+100,000), and +$60,000 after three years (–40,000+100,000).

Although the cumulative position has never become zero, it has clearly changed from negative to positive.

The payback period in this case is between two and three years. In fact, it can be more accurately calculated as

2 years + (40,000/100,000) = 2.4 years or (approximately) 2 years and 5 months.

3.3 ADVANTAGES AND DISADVANTAGES OF THE PAYBACK PERIOD METHOD OF PROJECT APPRAISAL

The advantages and disadvantages of the payback period method of project appraisal are set out below.

Advantages of payback for appraisal	Disadvantages of payback for appraisal
Simplicity – it is easily understood and easily calculated.	Cash flows arising after the payback period are totally ignored. Short term, rather than long term focussed.
Widely used.	The time value of money is ignored.
It will tend to minimise the effects of risk by giving greater weight to earlier cash flows.	It does not take into account the overall profitability of the project.
	It is difficult to set a target. Any target is essentially arbitrary.

ACTIVITY 2

A project requires an initial investment of $800,000 and then earns net cash inflows of:

Year	1	2	3	4	5	6	7
Cash inflows ($000)	100	200	400	400	300	200	150

In addition, at the end of the seven-year project the assets initially purchased will be sold for $100,000.

You are required:

(a) to calculate the project's payback period

(b) to determine its accounting rate of return.

For a suggested answer, see the 'Answers' section at the end of the book.

ACTIVITY 3

An investment would cost $2.3 million and annual cash inflows from the project are expected to be $600,000.

Required:

Calculate the expected payback period in years and months.

State an assumption on which this estimate is based.

For a suggested answer, see the 'Answers' section at the end of the book.

ACTIVITY 4

A project requires an initial investment of $550,000 and will bring the following cash receipts:

Year	1	2	3	4	5	6
Receipts ($000)	100	200	200	100	75	25

Required:

Calculate the project's payback period.

For a suggested answer, see the 'Answers' section at the end of the book.

4 TIME VALUE OF MONEY

Money received now is worth more than money received at some point in the future. This is because of three issues:

- Investment opportunity. If I receive $100 today, I can invest it to earn interest. For example, if the interest rate is 5% per year I will have $105 in one year's time. This shows that $100 received today is worth more to me than $100 received in one year.
- Inflation. If I receive $100 today, I can use it to buy goods to the value of $100. However, if inflation is 3% per year, those same goods will cost $103 in one year's time. Therefore, $100 received in one year would be less valuable to me – it would have less purchasing power.
- Risk. Receiving money now is certain, whereas money I expect to receive in the future is not. Changes in circumstances might mean that future receipts will not materialise.

DCF is a capital expenditure appraisal technique that takes into account the time value of money.

5 DISCOUNTED CASH FLOW (DCF)

Discounted cash flow, or DCF, is an investment appraisal technique that takes into account both the timing of cash flows and also the total cash flows over a project's life.

- As with the payback method, DCF analysis is based on future cash flows, not accounting profits or losses.
- The timing of cash flows is taken into account by discounting them to a 'present value'. The effect of discounting is to give a higher value to each $1 of cash flow that occur earlier and a lower value to each $1 of cash flow occurring later in the project's life. $1 earned after one year will be worth more than $1 earned after two years, which in turn will be worth more than $1 earned after five years, and so on. Cash flows that occur in different years are re-stated on a common basis, at their present value.

5.1 COMPOUNDING AND DISCOUNTING

To understand discounting, it is helpful to start by looking at compounding or compound interest.

Suppose that a business has $100,000 to invest, and wants to earn a return of 10% (compound interest). If it could invest at 10% compound, the value of the investment with interest would build up as follows.

After 1 year	$100,000 × (1.10)	=	$110,000
After 2 years	$100,000 × $(1.10)^2$	=	$121,000
After 3 years	$100,000 × $(1.10)^3$	=	$133,100, and so on.

This is **compounding**. The formula for the future value of an investment plus accumulated interest after n years is:

$$FV = PV\,(1 + r)^n$$

where FV is the future value of the investment with interest

PV is the initial or 'present' value of the investment

r is the compound annual rate of return or rate of interest (the 'cost of capital'), expressed as a proportion (so 10% = 0.10, 5% = 0.05 and so on)

n is the number of years.

Discounting is compounding in reverse. It starts with a future amount of cash and converts it into a present value.

Definition A present value is the amount that would need to be invested now to earn the future cash flow, if the money is invested at the 'cost of capital'.

For example, if a business expects to earn a (compound) rate of return of 10% on its investments, how much would it need to invest now to build up an investment of:

(a) $110,000 after 1 year

(b) $121,000 after 2 years

(c) $133,100 after 3 years?

The answer is $100,000 in each case, and we can calculate it by discounting. The discounting formula to calculate the present value of a future sum of money at the end of n years is:

$$PV = FV\frac{1}{(1+r)^n}$$

(a) After 1 year, $110,000 × $\frac{1}{1.10}$ = $100,000

(b) After 2 years, $121,000 × $\frac{1}{1.10^2}$ = $100,000

(c) After 3 years, $133,100 × $\frac{1}{1.10^3}$ = $100,000

Both cash inflows and cash payments can be discounted to a present value. By discounting all payments and receipts from a capital investment to a present value, they can be compared on a like-for-like basis.

ACTIVITY 5

(a) How much would you need to invest now to earn $2,000 after 4 years at a compound interest rate of 8% a year?

(b) What is the present value of $5,000 receivable at the end of year 3 at a cost of capital of 7% per annum?

For a suggested answer, see the 'Answers' section at the end of the book.

5.2 DISCOUNT FACTORS AND DISCOUNT TABLES

A present value for a future cash flow is calculated by multiplying the future cash flow by a factor:

$$\frac{1}{(1+r)^n}$$

Check that you know how to do this on your calculator.

For example:

$$\frac{1}{1.10} = 0.909$$

$$\frac{1}{1.10^2} = 0.826$$

$$\frac{1}{1.10^3} = 0.751$$

However, there are tables that give you a list of these 'discount factors' without you having to do the calculation yourself. A copy of these tables is included in the introductory pages to this text.

To calculate a present value for a future cash flow, you simply multiply the future cash flow by the appropriate discount factor.

Any cash flows that take place 'now' (at the start of the project) take place in Year 0. The discount factor for Year 0 is 1.0, regardless of what the cost of capital is. Cash flows 'now' therefore do not need to be discounted to a present value equivalent, because they are already at present value.

ACTIVITY 6

The cash flows for a project have been estimated as follows:

Year	$
0	(25,000)
1	6,000
2	10,000
3	8,000
4	7,000

The cost of capital is 6%. Discount factors at a cost of capital of 6% are:

Year	Discount factor at 6%
1	0.943
2	0.890
3	0.840
4	0.792

Required:

Convert these cash flows to a present value.

Add up the total of the present values for each of the years.

For a suggested answer, see the 'Answers' section at the end of the book.

5.3 THE COST OF CAPITAL

The cost of capital has used by a business in DCF analysis is the cost of funds for the business. It is therefore the minimum return that the business should make from its own investments, to earn the cash flows out of which it can pay interest or profits to its own providers of funds.

For the purpose of this text, the cost of capital is assumed to be a known figure.

6 NET PRESENT VALUE METHOD (NPV)

EXAMINER'S NOTE

In the exam, you may be asked to calculate the NPV of a project and interpret the result. Alternatively, you may need to explain this method of project appraisal. When performing NPV calculations, the following approach should be taken:

- identify the relevant cash inflows and outflows of the project, not forgetting the initial investment
- set up a table and discount each of the cash flows to its present value, using the company's required rate of return – discount tables will be provided on the day to facilitate calculations
- calculate the net present value of the project by taking the outflows away from the inflows
- decide whether or not the project should be accepted on the basis of whether or not it has a positive NPV.

The **net present value (NPV)** method of DCF analysis is to calculate a net present value for a proposed investment project. The NPV is the value obtained by discounting all the cash outflows and inflows for the project capital at the cost of capital, and adding them up. Cash outflows are negative values and inflows are positive values. The sum of the present value of all the cash flows from the project is the 'net' present value amount.

The NPV is the sum of the present value (PV) of all the cash inflows from a project minus the PV of all the cash outflows.

- **If the NPV is positive**, it means that the cash inflows from a capital investment will yield a return in excess of the cost of capital. The project therefore seems financially attractive.
- **If the NPV is negative**, it means that the cash inflows from a capital investment will yield a return below the cost of capital. From a financial perspective, the project is therefore unattractive.
- **If the NPV is exactly zero**, the cash inflows from a capital investment will yield a return exactly equal to the cost of capital. The project is therefore just about financially attractive.

Example

Rug is considering a capital investment in new equipment. The estimated cash flows are as follows:

Year	**Cash flow**
	$
0	(240,000)
1	80,000
2	120,000
3	70,000
4	40,000
5	20,000

The company's cost of capital is 9%.

Required:

Calculate the NPV of the project to assess whether it should be undertaken.

The following are discount factors for a 9% cost of capital.

Year	**Discount factor at 9%**
1	0.917
2	0.842
3	0.772
4	0.708
5	0.650

Solution

Year	Cash flow	Discount factor at 9%	Present value
	$		$
0	(240,000)	1.000	(240,000)
1	80,000	0.917	73,360
2	120,000	0.842	101,040
3	70,000	0.772	54,040
4	40,000	0.708	28,320
5	20,000	0.650	13,000
Net present value			+ 29,760

The PV of cash inflows exceeds the PV of cash outflows by $29,760, which means that the project will earn a DCF return in excess of 9%. It should therefore be undertaken.

The advantages and disadvantages of NPV as a method of project appraisal are set out below:

Advantages of NPV for appraisal	Disadvantages of NPV for appraisal
Shareholder wealth is maximised.	It can be difficult to identify an appropriate discount rate.
It takes into account the time value of money.	Some managers are unfamiliar with the concept of NPV.
It is based on cash flows, which are less subjective than profits.	Cash flows are usually assumed to occur at the end of a year, but in practice this is over simplistic.
All cash flows are considered (unlike payback). Long term rather than short term focussed.	

ACTIVITY 7

Fylingdales Fabrication is considering investing in a new delivery vehicle which will make savings over the current out-sourced service.

The cost of the vehicle is $35,000 and it will have a five-year life.

The savings it will make over the period are:

Cash flow:

Year	$
1	8,000
2	9,000
3	12,000
4	9,500
5	9,000

The firm currently has a return of 12% and this is considered to be its cost of capital.

Discount factors at 12%.

Year	
1	0.893
2	0.797
3	0.712
4	0.636
5	0.567

Required:

Calculate the NPV of the investment.

On the basis of the NPV you have calculated, recommend whether or not the investment should go ahead.

For a suggested answer, see the 'Answers' section at the end of the book.

6.1 ASSUMPTIONS IN DCF ABOUT THE TIMING OF CASH FLOWS

In DCF, certain assumptions are made about the timing of cash flows in each year of a project.

- A cash outlay at the beginning of an investment project ('now') occurs in Year 0.
- A cash flow that occurs **during the course of a year** is assumed to occur all at once at the end of the year. For example, profits of $30,000 in Year 3 would be assumed to occur at the end of Year 3.
- If a cash flow occurs **at the beginning of a year**, it is assumed that the cash flow happens at the end of the previous year. For example, a cash outlay of $10,000 at the beginning of Year 2 would be treated as a cash flow in Year 1, occurring at the end of Year 1.

6.2 INVESTMENT IN WORKING CAPITAL

Some capital projects involve an investment in working capital as well as non-current assets. Working capital should be considered to consist of investments in inventory and receivables, minus trade payables.

An investment in working capital slows up the receipt of cash. For example, suppose that a business buys an item for $10 for cash and resells it for $16. It has made a cash profit of $6 on the deal. However, if the item is sold for $16 on credit, the cash flow is different. Although the profit is $6, the business is actually $10 worse off for cash. This is because it has invested $16 in receivables (working capital).

An increase in working capital reduces cash flows and a reduction in working capital improves the cash flow in the year that it happens.

By convention, in DCF analysis, if a project will require an investment in working capital, the investment is treated as a cash outflow at the beginning of the year in which it occurs. The working capital is eventually released at the end of the project, when it becomes a cash inflow. (It is treated as a cash inflow because actual cash flows will exceed cash profits in the year by the amount of the reduction in working capital.)

Note: Working capital in an NPV analysis is specifically excluded from the syllabus, but this short example has been included in the text for illustration only.

Example

A company is considering whether to invest in a project to buy an item of equipment for $40,000. The project would require an investment of $8,000 in working capital. The cash profits from the project would be:

Year	Cash profit
	$
1	15,000
2	20,000
3	12,000
4	7,000

The equipment would have a resale value of $5,000 at the end of Year 4.

The cost of capital is 10%. Discount factors at 10% are:

Year	
1	0.909
2	0.826
3	0.751
4	0.683

Required:

Calculate the NPV of the project and recommend whether or not, on financial grounds, you would recommend that the project should be undertaken.

Solution

Year	Equipt	Working capital	Cash profit	Total cash flow	Discount factor at 10%	Present value
	$	$	$	$		$
0	(40,000)	(8,000)		(48,000)	1.000	(48,000)
1			15,000	15,000	0.909	13,635
2			20,000	20,000	0.826	16,520
3			12,000	12,000	0.751	9,012
4	5,000	8,000	7,000	20,000	0.683	13,660
						+ 4,827

The NPV is positive, and from a financial perspective should therefore be undertaken.

6.3 ALTERNATIVE LAYOUT OF AN NPV QUESTION

You may sometimes see NPV calculations laid out as follows:

Time	0	1	2	3	4
Cash flows	x	x	x	x	x
	x	x	x	x	x
Net cash flow	x	x	x	x	x
Discount factor	1	x	x	x	X
Present value	x	x	x	x	x

Net present value $XX,XXX

This method can be used to save time in an exam if there are lots of different cash flows each year.

7 ANNUITIES AND CUMULATIVE PRESENT VALUES

7.1 ANNUITIES

Definition An **annuity** is a fixed periodic payment which continues either for a specified time, or until the occurrence of a specified event.

A ground rent is an example of an annuity, the holder of the freehold receiving an annual payment for the number of years specified in the lease.

Annuities and ground rent are constantly being bought and sold and the method of present values can be used to calculate a fair price for the transaction.

Example

Find the present value of an annuity of $300 for five years, reckoning compound interest at 4% pa, the first receipt being in one year's time.

This can be tackled using the simple discount factor identified in the previous section using the tabular approach; the factors can either be calculated directly or taken from the tables:

Time	Cash flow $	Discount factor			PV $
1	300	$\frac{1}{(1.04)^1}$	=	0.962	289
2	300	$\frac{1}{(1.04)^2}$	=	0.925	277
3	300	$\frac{1}{(1.04)^3}$	=	0.889	267
4	300	$\frac{1}{(1.04)^4}$	=	0.855	256
5	300	$\frac{1}{(1.04)^5}$	=	0.822	247
Total present value					1,336

This means that if $1,336 were invested now at a compound rate of 4%, the investor would be able to withdraw $300 a year for five years (at the end of which the investment would be down to nil). You can check this for yourself.

This type of calculation can get quite time-consuming, especially if the annuity continues for a lifetime! A quicker way is by the use of **annuity factors or cumulative discount factors**, which can again be obtained from a formula or from tables.

7.2 ANNUITY FACTOR FORMULA

The calculation in the table above could be written as:

$$PV = \frac{300}{1.04} + \frac{300}{(1.04)^2} + \frac{300}{(1.04)^3} + \ldots + \frac{300}{(1.04)^5}$$

These terms form a geometric progression with $A = \frac{300}{1.04}$, $R = \frac{1}{1.04}$ and $n = 5$

Using $S_n \quad = \quad \frac{A\left(1-R^n\right)}{1-R}$

$$= \frac{\frac{300}{1.04}\left(1-\left(\frac{1}{1.04}\right)^5\right)}{\left(1-\frac{1}{1.04}\right)}$$

This can be shown to rearrange to:

$$\$300\left[\frac{1}{0.04}-\frac{1}{(0.04)(1.04)^5}\right]$$

The expression in the square brackets is known as the cumulative (or annuity) discount factor for an annuity receivable over 5 years at a 4% discount rate. It evaluates to 4.4518.

Thus the PV of the annuity can be calculated as $300 × 4.4518 = $1,336 as before.

The general equation for the cumulative discount factor for an annuity payable over n years at a rate of r can be seen to be:

$$\frac{1}{r}-\frac{1}{r(1+r)^n}$$

This is supplied in Mathematical Tables (where t is used instead of n).

7.3 THE USE OF CUMULATIVE PRESENT VALUE TABLES (ANNUITY TABLES)

The values of the above formula have been tabulated for n= 1 to 15 and r = 1% to 20% (see the table at the front of this text).

Cumulative PV factor of $1 for five years at 4% pa = 4.452

Hence: PV = $300 × 4.452

= $1,336 (as before)

The cumulative present values of $1 are also called 'annuity factors' and are denoted by the symbol $a_{\overline{n|}\,r}$ where a stands for annuity, n = number of years and r = rate of interest.

Thus $a_{\overline{5|}\,0.04} = 4.452$

ACTIVITY 8

Calculate the amount to be invested now at 6% pa to provide an annuity of $5,000 p.a. for ten years commencing in five years' time.

For a suggested answer, see the 'Answers' section at the end of the book.

7.4 PRESENT VALUE AND ANNUITY FACTORS COMPARED

Note that the annuity factors are simply the cumulative present value factors, e.g.:

Year	10% discount factors from Present Value Tables
1	0.909
2	0.826
3	0.751
	2.486

$a_{\overline{3|}\,0.10}$ from Cumulative Present Value Table = 2.487

7.5 ANNUITY FACTORS WHEN ANNUITIES DO NOT START IN 1 YEAR

Note that the calculations above have all assumed that the first cash flow in the annuity is likely to arise in one year's time. This will not always be the case, but the figures taken from the cumulative present value tables can easily be adjusted if necessary.

For example, if an annuity starts immediately, simply add 1 to the figure from the cumulative present value table.

Example

Find the present value of an annuity of $300 for five years, reckoning compound interest at 4% pa, the first receipt being immediately.

Solution

In this case, we have a single cash flow immediately, followed by a four year annuity starting in one year.

Hence, the present value is $300 × (1 + 3.630) = $1,389

Delayed annuities

On the other hand, the first cash flow in the annuity might be later than in one year's time. In this case, the relevant annuity factor is found by subtracting the factor for the period before the annuity starts from the annuity factor that runs up until the end of the annuity.

Example

Find the present value of an annuity of $300 for five years, reckoning compound interest at 4% pa, the first receipt being in four years' time.

Solution

In this case, we have an annuity of five cash flows starting in four years' time and ending in eight years' time.

Hence, the present value is:

$300 × (6.733 – 2.775) = $1,187

(where 6.733 is the eight year annuity factor and 2.775 is the three year annuity factor – so it relates to the period before our annuity starts in four years' time).

7.6 PERPETUITIES

Definition A **perpetuity** is a periodic payment continuing for a limitless period.

The present value of a perpetuity where:

the annual amount receivable = a

the discount rate = r

is given by $PV = \frac{a}{r}$

Example

An investment will yield future cash flows of $5,000 in perpetuity. What is the present value of this income stream at a discount rate of 20%?

Solution

Using the formula above

$$\text{Present value} = \frac{\text{Annual perpetuity}}{\text{Discount rate}}$$

$$= \frac{\$5{,}000}{0.20} = \$25{,}000$$

7.7 PERPETUITY FACTORS WHEN PERPETUITIES DO NOT START IN 1 YEAR

As with annuities earlier, the perpetuity calculations above have all assumed that the first cash flow in the perpetuity is likely to arise in one year's time. This will not always be the case, but the calculations can easily be adjusted if necessary.

For example, if a perpetuity starts immediately, simply add 1 to the (1/r) factor from the formula.

Example

An investment will yield future cash flows of $5,000 in perpetuity, starting immediately. What is the present value of this income stream at a discount rate of 20%?

Solution

In this case, we have a single cash flow immediately, followed by a 'normal' perpetuity.

Hence, the present value is $5,000 × (1 + (1/0.20)) = $30,000

Delayed annuities

On the other hand, the first cash flow in the perpetuity might be later than in one year's time. In this case, the relevant perpetuity factor is found by subtracting the annuity factor for the period before the perpetuity starts from the (1/r) perpetuity factor.

Example

An investment will yield future cash flows of $5,000 in perpetuity, starting in six years' time. What is the present value of this income stream at a discount rate of 20%?

Solution

In this case, we have a perpetuity, but only after five years of no income (the perpetuity starts in six years' time)

Hence, the present value is:

$5,000 × ((1/0.20) – 2.991) = $10,045

(where 2.991 is the five year annuity factor – so it relates to the period before our perpetuity starts in six years' time).

ACTIVITY 9

A project requires an initial outlay of $10,000 and will then generate $2,000 annually. Should the project be accepted at a discount rate of 16%?

For a suggested answer, see the 'answers' section at the end of the book.

8 INTERNAL RATE OF RETURN (IRR) METHOD

EXAMINER'S NOTE

The examiner has noted that you may be asked to calculate the internal rate of return and interpret the results, or discuss its uses as a method of investment appraisal. The internal rate of return tells us the rate at which the NPV of a project is neither positive nor negative. There are four steps to an IRR calculation:

Calculate the project's NPV at any reasonable discount rate (this may be given to you in the exam).

If the above NPV is positive, choose a higher discount rate (again this may be given in the exam) and calculate the NPV again. If the above NPV was negative, choose a lower discount rate.

Hopefully, you will end up with one positive and one negative NPV.

N.B. If your two NPVs are both positive or both negative, don't waste time recomputing NPVs. The following formula will still give you an estimate of IRR, albeit a less accurate one.

You must now calculate the IRR by using the following formula:

$$\text{IRR} = \text{A} + \left[\frac{\text{a}}{\text{a} - \text{b}} \times (\text{B} - \text{A})\right]$$

Where A is the lower discount rate and B is the higher rate, a is the NPV at the lower rate and b is the NPV at the higher rate. It is vital that you learn this formula.

The IRR must then be compared to the company's required rate of return. If it is higher than the required rate of return, the project should be accepted. If it is lower than the required rate of return, the project should be rejected.

Please note that all workings should be shown when performing NPV calculations. Even if you are using a sophisticated calculator to help you, you won't gain full marks unless your workings are clearly set out. Such calculators are really not that useful, and will not give you a competitive advantage.

8.1 THE INTERNAL RATE OF RETURN

Using the NPV method of discounted cash flow, present values are calculated by discounting cash flows at a given cost of capital, and the difference between the PV of costs and the PV of benefits is the NPV. In contrast, the **internal rate of return (IRR)** method of DCF analysis is to calculate the exact DCF rate of return that the project is expected to achieve. This is the cost of capital at which the NPV is zero.

If the expected rate of return (known as the internal rate of return or IRR, and also as the DCF yield) is higher than a target rate of return, the project is financially worth undertaking.

Calculating the IRR of a project can be done with a programmed calculator. Otherwise, it has to be estimated using a rather laborious technique called the interpolation method. The interpolation method produces an estimate of the IRR, although it is not arithmetically exact.

The steps in this method are as follows.

Step 1 Calculate two net present values for the project at two different costs of capital. You should decide which costs of capital to use. However, you want to find two costs of capital for which the NPV is close to 0, because the IRR will be a value close to them. Ideally, you should use one cost of capital where the NPV is positive and the other cost of capital where the NPV is negative, although this is not essential.

Step 2 Having found two costs of capital where the NPV is close to 0, we can then estimate the cost of capital at which the NPV is 0. In other words, we can estimate the IRR. This estimating technique is illustrated in the example below.

Example

A company is trying to decide whether to buy a machine for $13,500. The machine will create annual cash savings as follows.

Year	$
1	5,000
2	8,000
3	3,000

Required:

Calculate the project's IRR.

Solution

Step 1 The first step is to calculate the NPV of the project at two different costs of capital. Ideally the NPV should be positive at one cost of capital and negative at the other.

So what costs of capital should we try?

One way of making a guess is to look at the profits from the project over its life. These are $16,000 over the three years. After deducting the capital expenditure of $13,500, this gives us a net return of $2,500, or an average of $833 each year of the project. $833 is about 6% of the capital outlay. The IRR is actually likely to be a bit higher than this, so we could start by trying 7%, 8% or 9%.

Here, 8% is used.

Year	Cash flow	Discount factor at 8%	PV
	$		$
0	(13,500)	1.000	(13,500)
1	5,000	0.926	4,630
2	8,000	0.857	6,856
3	3,000	0.794	2,382
			+ 368

The NPV is positive at 8%, so the IRR is higher than this. We need to find the NPV at a higher cost of capital. Let's try 11%.

Year	Cash flow	Discount factor at 11%	PV
	$		$
0	(13,500)	1.000	(13,500)
1	5,000	0.901	4,505
2	8,000	0.812	6,496
3	3,000	0.731	2,193
			(306)

The NPV is negative at 11%, so the IRR lies somewhere between 8% and 11%.

Step 2 The next step is to use the two NPV figures we have calculated to estimate the IRR.

We know that the NPV is +368 at 8% and that it is –306 at 11%.

Therefore:

a = 368

b = −306

A = 8%

B = 11%

If we assume that the decline in NPV occurs in a straight line, we can estimate the IRR as follows:

$$\text{IRR} = \text{A} + \left[\frac{\text{a}}{\text{a}-\text{b}} \times (\text{B}-\text{A})\right]$$

$$= 8\% + \left[\frac{368}{(368 - -306)} \times (11-8)\%\right]$$

$$= 8\% + \left[\frac{368}{674} \times 3\%\right]$$

$$= 8\% + 1.6\% = 9.6\%.$$

An estimated IRR is therefore 9.6%.

Alternative formula for calculating IRR

You might find the following formula for calculating the IRR easier to remember.

If the NPV at A% is positive, +$P

and if the NPV at B% is negative, –$N

then

$$IRR = A\%\left[\frac{P}{(P+N)}\times(B+A)\%\right]$$

Ignore the minus sign for the negative NPV. For example, if P = +60 and N = –50, then P + N = 110.

Another example

A business undertakes high-risk investments and requires a minimum expected rate of return of 17% on its investments. A proposed capital investment has the following expected cash flows:

Year	$
0	(50,000)
1	18,000
2	25,000
3	20,000
4	10,000

Required:

(a) Calculate the NPV of the project if the cost of capital is 15%.

(b) Calculate the NPV of the project if the cost of capital is 20%.

(c) Use the NPVs you have calculated to estimate the IRR of the project.

(d) Recommend, on financial grounds alone, whether this project should go ahead.

Discount factors:

Year	Discount factor at	
	15%	**20%**
1	0.870	0.833
2	0.756	0.694
3	0.658	0.579
4	0.572	0.482

Solution

Year	**Cash flow**	**Discount factor at 15%**	**Present value at 15%**	**Discount factor at 20%**	**Present value at 20%**
	$		$		$
0	(50,000)	1.000	(50,000)	1.000	(50,000)
1	18,000	0.870	15,660	0.833	14,994
2	25,000	0.756	18,900	0.694	17,350
3	20,000	0.658	13,160	0.579	11,580
4	10,000	0.572	5,720	0.482	4,820
NPV			+ 3,440		(1,256)

The IRR is above 15% but below 20%.

Using the interpolation method:

The NPV is +3,440 at 15%.

The NPV is –1,256 at 20%.

Therefore we can estimate the IRR as follows:

$$IRR = A + \left[\frac{a}{a-b} \times (B-A)\right]$$

Where:

a = 3,440

b = −1,256

A = 15%

B = 20%

$$IRR = 15\% + \left[\frac{3{,}440}{(3{,}440 - 1{,}256)} \times (20 - 15)\%\right]$$

= 15% + 3.7%

= 18.7%

Recommendation

The project is expected to earn a DCF return in excess of the target rate of 17%, so (ignoring risk) on financial grounds it is a worthwhile investment.

8.2 ADVANTAGES AND DISADVANTAGES OF IRR AS A METHOD OF PROJECT APPRAISAL

The advantages and disadvantages of IRR as a method of project appraisal are set out below:

Advantages of IRR for appraisal	Disadvantages of IRR for appraisal
It takes into account the time value of money, which is a good basis for decision making.	Projects with unconventional cash flows can have either negative or multiple IRRs (see example below) – this can be confusing to the user.
Results are expressed as a simple percentage, and are more easily understood than some other methods.	IRR can be confused with ARR or Return on Capital Employed since all methods give answers in percentage terms – hence, a cash-based method can be confused with a profit-based method.
It indicates how sensitive decisions are to a change in interest rates.	It may give conflicting recommendations to NPV.
	Some managers are unfamiliar with the IRR method.
	IRR cannot accommodate changes in interest rates over the life of a project.
	It assumes funds are re-invested at a rate equivalent to the IRR itself, which may be unrealistically high.

8.3 MULTIPLE IRRS

A standard investment project comprises an outflow of cash initially and then inflows of cash thereafter. Such a project will have (at most) one IRR.

However, if a project consists of alternating cash inflows and outflows, it may have more than one IRR.

For example, the following project has IRRs of 37% and –27% (check this by discounting at these rates to give zero NPVs):

Year	$
0	(100)
1	210
2	(100)

Evaluating a project with multiple IRRs is difficult, because it is hard to compare this project with another project with a single IRR.

8.4 MUTUALLY EXCLUSIVE INVESTMENTS

Organisations may often face decisions in which only one of two or more investments can be undertaken; these are called mutually exclusive investment decisions.

Example

Barlow is considering two short-term investment opportunities, which they have called Project A and Project B, and which have the following cash flows:

Time	**0**	**1**
Project A ($000)	(200)	240
Project B ($000)	(100)	125

Barlow has a cost of capital of 10%. Find the NPVs and IRRs of the two projects.

Solution

		NPV	IRR
		$000	%
Project A:	(240 ÷ 1.10) – 200	18.18	20
Project B:	(125 ÷ 1.10) – 100	13.64	25

The IRRs could be found either by trial and error or by using the formula. It would be easier to notice that Project A, over 1 year, earns $40,000 on an investment of $200,000 (a 20% return) whilst Project B earns $25,000 on $100,000 (25%).

It can be seen that A has the higher NPV whilst B has the higher IRR – a conflict. How can we explain this?

Which method should be used to decide?

The golden rule for deciding between mutually exclusive projects is to **accept the project with the higher NPV**:

To **maximise shareholder wealth**, i.e. the market value of their shares, we wish to maximise **absolute** return, i.e. NPV. Whilst Project B shows a higher **relative** return, it is on a smaller investment, yielding a lower absolute benefit. (It is assumed that you cannot do B twice – for example, A and B may be two different uses of an existing building).

Project B will give a higher NPV for all discount rates **above 15%** – but this is **irrelevant** to an investor with a 10% discount rate.

The higher IRR of Project B indicates that Project B will yield a positive NPV over a wider range of discount rates (0–25%) than A (0–0%) and this is therefore useful for sensitivity analysis where the discount rate is uncertain.

9 COMPARING THE NPV AND IRR

9.1 CALCULATING THE NPV OR IRR OF A PROJECT: SUMMARY

To calculate the NPV or the IRR of a capital project, we recommend the following steps.

1 Identify the relevant cash flows for each year of the project. You might need to do some workings to calculate what the cash flows are.

(a) There is normally a cash outlay on a capital expenditure item in Year 0.

(b) Ignore sunk costs (historical costs that have already been incurred and costs that will be incurred anyway, regardless of the investment decision). Exclude non-cash expenses such as depreciation, because these are not cash flows.

(c) If there is an investment in working capital at the start of the project, this will reduce cash flows early in Year 1, and so is usually treated as a cash outflow in Year 0. At the end of the project, the working capital will reduce to zero, and the reduction in working capital is treated as a cash inflow in that year.

2 Having worked out what the cash flows are for each item in each year, it helps to present them in a table of cash flows, and to calculate the net cash flow each year.

An example of a layout is shown below, with illustrative figures included.

Year	Capital equipment	Working capital	Cash flows from gross profits	Other running costs	Net cash flow
	$	$	$	$	$
0	(100,000)	(5,000)			(105,000)
1			40,000	(18,000)	22,000
2			50,000	(18,000)	32,000
3			60,000	(18,000)	42,000
4	20,000	5,000	40,000	(18,000)	47,000

3 Having established the net cash flow each year, you can then apply the appropriate discount factors to calculate present values and the net present value of the project, as follows. (Again, illustrative figures are used, with a 9% cost of capital applied.)

Year	Net cash flow	Discount factor at 9%	Present value
	$		$
0	(105,000)	1.000	(105,000)
1	22,000	0.917	20,174
2	32,000	0.842	26,944
3	42,000	0.772	32,424
4	47,000	0.708	33,276
NPV			+ 7,818

Here, the NPV is positive and so the project is financially worthwhile if the cost of capital is 9%.

4 If you are required to calculate an IRR, you can add another two columns to the above table, for the second cost of capital you use. For example, suppose that in the above example, we are asked to calculate the IRR, using 12% as a second cost of capital. The table can be enlarged as follows.

Year	Net cash flow	Discount factor at 9%	Present value at 9%	Discount factor at 12%	Present value at 12%
	$		$		$
0	(105,000)	1.000	(105,000)	1.000	(105,000)
1	22,000	0.917	20,174	0.893	19,646
2	32,000	0.842	26,944	0.797	25,504
3	42,000	0.772	32,424	0.712	29,904
4	47,000	0.708	33,276	0.636	29,892
NPV			+ 7,818		(54)

The approximate IRR can now be calculated by the interpolation method, although in the illustrative example shown here, it should be clear that the IRR is very close to 12%.

9.2 WHY THE NPV AND IRR SOMETIMES SELECT DIFFERENT PROJECTS

When comparing two projects, the use of the NPV and the IRR methods may give different results. A project selected according to the NPV may be rejected if the IRR method is used.

Suppose there are two alternative projects, X and Y. The initial investment in each project is $2,500. Project X will provide annual cash flows of $500 for the next 10 years. Project Y has annual cash flows of $100, $200, $300, $400, $500, $600, $700, $800, $900, and $1,000 in the same period.

Using the trial and error method explained before, you find that the IRR of Project X is 17% and the IRR of Project Y is around 13%. If you use the IRR, Project X should be preferred because its IRR is 4% more than the IRR of Project Y. But what happens to your decision if the NPV method is used? The answer is that the decision will change depending on the discount rate you use. For instance, at a 5% discount rate, Project Y has a higher NPV than X does. But at a discount rate of 8%, Project X is preferred because of a higher NPV.

The purpose of this numerical example is to illustrate an important distinction: The use of the IRR always leads to the selection of the same project, whereas project selection using the NPV method depends on the discount rate chosen.

There are reasons why the NPV and the IRR are sometimes in conflict: the size and life of the project being studied are the most common ones. A ten-year project with an initial investment of $100,000 can hardly be compared with a small three-year project costing $10,000. Actually, the large project could be thought of as ten small projects. So if you insist on using the IRR and the NPV methods to compare a big, long-term project with a small, short-term project, don't be surprised if you get different selection results.

Different cash flows

Furthermore, even two projects of the same length may have different patterns of cash flow. The cash flows of one project may continuously increase over time, while the cash flows of the other project may increase, decrease, stop, or become negative. These two projects have completely different forms of cash flow, and if the discount rate is changed when using the NPV approach, the result will probably be different orders of ranking. For example, at 10% the NPV of Project A may be higher than that of Project B. As soon as you change the discount rate to 15%, Project B may be more attractive.

When are the NPV and IRR reliable?

Generally speaking, you can use and rely on both the NPV and the IRR if two conditions are met. First, if projects are compared using the NPV, a discount rate that fairly reflects the risk of each project should be chosen. There is no problem if two projects are discounted at two different rates because one project is riskier than the other. Remember that the result of the NPV is as reliable as the discount rate that is chosen. If the discount rate is unrealistic, the decision to accept or reject the project is baseless and unreliable. Second, if the IRR method is used, the project must not be accepted only because its IRR is very high. Management must ask whether such an impressive IRR is possible to maintain.

In other words, management should look into past records, and existing and future business, to see whether an opportunity to reinvest cash flows at such a high IRR really exists. If the firm is convinced that such an IRR is realistic, the project is acceptable. Otherwise, the project must be re-evaluated by the NPV method, using a more realistic discount rate.

10 DISCOUNTED PAYBACK

Simple payback is the length of time before a project is expected to pay back the original capital outlay from its cash inflows. Payback is calculated without discounting any of the cash flows. A company might have a policy of rejecting capital expenditure proposals if the payback takes longer than a given number of years.

Definition **Discounted payback** is similar to simple payback, except that all the cash flows are discounted at the company's cost of capital. The discounted payback period is therefore the time it will take before the project's cumulative NPV becomes positive.

A company might have a policy of rejecting capital expenditure proposals unless the discounted payback is less than a target maximum length of time. This means that the project must have a positive NPV and this must be achieved within a given period of time.

To calculate a discounted payback period, you should calculate the cumulative NPV each year. In other respects, the calculation of discounted payback is the same as for simple payback.

Example

A company is considering a capital expenditure proposal that will involve spending $75,000 at the start of the five-year project. Annual cash flows from the project are expected to be:

Year	$
1	25,000
2	30,000
3	24,000
4	18,000
5	10,000

The cost of capital is 10%.

Required:

(a) Calculate the discounted payback period.

(b) If it is company policy that projects should not be undertaken unless they are expected to achieve a discounted payback within four years, would this project be undertaken?

Solution

The cumulative NPV is shown in the right hand column of the following table.

Year	**Cash flow**	**Discount factor at 10%**	**Present value**	**Cumulative NPV**
	$		$	$
0	(75,000)	1.000	(75,000)	(75,000)
1	25,000	0.909	22,725	(52,275)
2	30,000	0.826	24,780	(27,495)
3	24,000	0.751	18,024	(9,471)
4	18,000	0.683	12,294	2,823
5	10,000	0.621	6,210	9,033
			+ 9,033	

Discounted payback occurs between the end of Year 3 and the end of Year 4. A more exact estimate might be:

$$3\text{ years} + \frac{(9{,}471)}{(9{,}471 + 2{,}823)} \times 12\text{ months}$$

= 3 years 9 months.

This is within the maximum discounted payback period allowed, so the project would be undertaken, on the basis of the information available.

10.1 ADVANTAGES AND DISADVANTAGES OF USING THE DISCOUNTED PAYBACK METHOD

The advantages of using the discounted payback method are as follows.

- Projects that are expected to take a long time to achieve a positive NPV are rejected, on the grounds that long-term estimates of cash inflows are likely to be unreliable and over-optimistic.
- It is a crude way of allocating money between projects when there is only a limited amount of money available.
- Payback is an easy concept to understand.
- Unlike simple payback, discounted payback prevents any project from being accepted unless it is expected to have a positive NPV.

The disadvantages of discounted payback are similar to those of simple payback.

- The choice of a maximum acceptable payback period is arbitrary.
- The method ignores the size of the expected NPV. For example, suppose that a company sets a maximum discounted payback period of five years. Project A might have an expected discounted payback period of 4.5 years, and an expected net present value of $3,000. Project B might have an expected discounted payback period of 5.5 years, and an expected net present value of $300,000. Applying only the discounted payback decision rule, Project A would be undertaken and Project B would be rejected, despite the much greater potential value of Project B.

CONCLUSION

Discounted cash flow analysis is based on the idea that there is a time value of money, and that $1 today is worth more than $1 in one year's time, which in turn is worth more than $1 in two years' time, and so on. For investors, the time value of money reflects return on investment required to make investing in a particular company or capital project worthwhile.

The cash flows for an investment can all be expressed at a present value, and cash flows at different periods of time can be compared on an equal basis. This provides a basis for evaluating proposed capital expenditure projects.

Of the three methods of discounted cash flow analysis, the most widely used is net present value, because the net present value of a project shows the expected money value that the project will add to a business if it is undertaken.

KEY TERMS

Accounting rate of return (ARR) – also called the return on capital employed (ROCE). The ARR expresses the profits from a project as a percentage of capital cost.

Payback – the amount of time it is expected to take for the cash inflows from a capital investment project to equal the cash outflows.

Discounting – compounding in reverse. It starts with a future amount of cash and converts it into a present value.

Present value – the amount that would need to be invested now to earn the future cash flow, if the money is invested at the 'cost of capital'.

Net present value (NPV) method of DCF analysis – involves calculating a net present value for a proposed investment project. The NPV is the value obtained by discounting all the cash outflows and inflows for the project capital at the cost of capital, and adding them up. Cash outflows are negative values and inflows are positive values. The sum of the present value of all the cash flows from the project is the 'net' present value amount.

Annuity – a fixed periodic payment which continues either for a specified time, or until the occurrence of a specified event.

Perpetuity – a periodic payment continuing for a limitless period.

Internal rate of return (IRR) method of DCF analysis – involves calculating the exact DCF rate of return that a project is expected to achieve. The IRR is the cost of capital at which the NPV is zero.

Discounted payback – similar to simple payback, except that all the cash flows are discounted at the company's cost of capital. The discounted payback period is therefore the time it will take before the project's cumulative NPV becomes positive.

PRACTICE QUESTION – NOTE THAT THIS QUESTION IS LONGER THAN A TYPICAL EXAM QUESTION BUT IS INCLUDED HERE TO COVER SEVERAL KEY TOPICS

TOYSRME

ToysRme produces a wide range of toys. Recently, it has developed a new product and the directors of the company are now considering whether this product should be put into production.

The following information has been produced to help evaluate the commercial viability of the new product.

(i) The cost of developing the new product was $130,000. In addition, market research was carried out by a firm of marketing consultants at a cost of $90,000. The development costs have all been paid and the market research costs are due for payment next month.

(ii) The company expects to sell 10,000 units of the new product per year for each of the next five years. The selling price of each unit will be $65.

(iii) Machinery which originally cost $1,500,000 and which has a written down value of $950,000 will be required.

If production does not go ahead, the machinery will be sold immediately for $790,000. If, however, production goes ahead, the machinery will be sold at the end of five years for $70,000.

(iv) Additional working capital of $150,000 will be required immediately in order to support production of the new product. This can be released at the end of the production period.

(v) To produce the new product, two types of material will be required.

- Type A material is used throughout the product range of the business and 20,000 kilos are already held in inventory at a purchase cost of $14 per kilo. Recently, however, the supplier of this material has raised the price to $15 per kilo.

- Type B material is also held in inventory although there is no further use for this material except for use in the production of new product. There are 12,000 kilos currently held in inventory at a purchase cost of $2 per kilo, however, the replacement cost is $2.50 per kilo. If production does not go ahead, the existing material will be sold immediately for $1.50 per kilo. Each product requires one kilo of Type A material and three kilos of Type B material.

(vi) Labour costs are estimated at $12 per unit of product. If the new product is not produced, some existing employees will be made redundant immediately at a cost of $50,000 to the company. If, however, the new product is produced, these employees will be used to produce the new product and will be made redundant at the end of the production period at a cost of $80,000 to the company.

(vii) Total fixed costs apportioned to the new product will be $200,000 per annum of which $60,000 per annum is estimated to arise as a direct result of the decision to produce the new product.

The company has a cost of capital of 12 per cent.

Present value of $1 receivable in n years at:

n	**12%**	**18%**
0	1.00	1.00
1	0.89	0.85
2	0.80	0.72
3	0.71	0.61
4	0.64	0.52
5	0.57	0.44

Required:

(a) Explain the treatment of the various item of costs, discuss if they are relevant or non-relevant in project evaluation. **(8 marks)**

(b) Calculate the incremental cash flows arising from a decision to produce the new product. **(15 marks)**

(c) Calculate:

(i) the net present value (NPV), and

(ii) the approximate internal rate of return (IRR) of the product and state whether or not ToysRme should produce this product. **(10 marks)**

(d) State which of the two methods of investment appraisal mentioned in (c) above you prefer and why. **(7 marks)**

(Total: 40 marks)

For a suggested answer, see the 'Answers' section at the end of the book.

Chapter 16

EMPLOYABILITY AND TECHNOLOGY SKILLS

A professional accountant needs technical knowledge and skills, but also employability and technology skills related to using information technology.

This chapter contains an overview of the employability and technology skills syllabus area, which is relevant for all ACCA exams.

This chapter covers Syllabus part G.

CONTENTS

LEARNING OUTCOMES

At the end of this chapter you should be able to:

- Use computer technology to efficiently access and manipulate relevant information
- Work on relevant response options, using available functions and technology as would be required in the workplace
- Navigate windows and computer screens to create and amend responses to exam requirements, using the appropriate tools
- Present data and information effectively, using the appropriate tools.

1 THE PURPOSE OF THIS CHAPTER

This chapter explains the content included within the employability and technology skills syllabus area. A similar syllabus area is included in all ACCA exam syllabi.

ACCA exams utilise software and technology similar to those used in the modern workplace. By studying ACCA exams, candidates will be equipped with not only technical syllabus knowledge and professional skills, but also practical, applied software skills. The employability and technology skills syllabus area is included within the syllabus to acknowledge this acquired skillset.

2 CONTENT OF THE EMPLOYABILITY AND TECHNOLOGY SKILLS SYLLABUS AREA

The employability and technology skills syllabus area is outlined in the syllabus and study guide. It consists of the following:

- Use computer technology to efficiently access and manipulate relevant information.
- Work on relevant response options, using available functions and technology, as would be required in the workplace.
- Navigate windows and computer screens to create and amend responses to exam requirements, using the appropriate tools.
- Present data and information effectively, using the appropriate tools.

By using a computer-based examination (CBE), the ACCA has enabled the use of word processing, spreadsheet, screen navigation and data processing functionalities to become part of their assessment range. This replicates the skills used in the modern workplace, whether in accounting practice, in industry or outside of accountancy altogether.

Whilst sitting an exam, candidates will be using the functionality of the CBE software in a variety of ways e.g. to prioritise information within the question data provided, to organise and present their answers in a manageable fashion, to use shortcuts and software functionality to increase efficiency. Skills garnered in the workplace can be used in the examination and vice versa.

This reflects that ACCA exams are designed to be relevant and accessible to all students. The delivery mode and assessment types require students to demonstrate similar skills to those required in the modern workplace. Offering computer-based exams (CBE) at all levels gives students the opportunity to focus on the application of knowledge to scenarios, using a range of tools – spreadsheets, word processing and presentations. This not only allows students to demonstrate their technical and professional skills, but also their use of the technology relevant to the modern workplace. CBEs, therefore, offer candidates an examination delivery method that allows them to demonstrate their knowledge and skills with the technology they are most familiar with, in the classroom or at work.

3 CBE SUPPORT ON THE ACCA WEBSITE

It is imperative that candidates are familiar with the CBE software before attempting the real exam.

Support, access to past exam papers, examining team guidance and CBE advice can be found on the ACCA website:

https://www.accaglobal.com/uk/en/student/exam-support-resources/foundation-level-study-resources/ffm.html

4 CBE RESPONSE OPTIONS

4.1 RESPONSE OPTIONS

The **Response Options** are where the candidate will attempt their answers.

There are three types of response options in the ACCA exams. Not every option will appear in each exam. Check the past exam papers on the ACCA website for examples of the responses that are commonplace within your exam.

The response options are:

- word processor,
- spreadsheet, and
- slides.

These replicate the functionality of widely used software packages. The ACCA has developed this software, for use during home question practice and under exam conditions, to replicate the practical skill sets and work-based behaviours adopted by various industries throughout the world. By studying the ACCA qualification, candidates will improve, not only on their technical knowledge and understanding, but also on skills applied on a daily basis within their work environments. Candidates should practise questions using the CBE software to ensure they are familiar with the various functions available within their specific examination.

4.2 WORD PROCESSOR

The word processor response option, when relevant, will appear as follows:

This resource has the following advantages and disadvantages:

Advantages	**Disadvantages**
It is easier to continue typing without entering new cells or becoming concerned about cell width	It cannot automatically perform calculations
Answers can be more easily split into paragraphs to make them more visually appealing and easier to mark	Numerical tables can be difficult to label and align
Bullet points can be used to present lists	
Text can be easily aligned and justified	
Superscript and subscript can be easily added to express terms such as 42, for example	

It is, therefore, best suited to discursive answers where candidates are asked, for example, to list points, or discuss issues.

The word processing software application could be used in the workplace within the writing of meeting agendas, meeting minutes, external letters, marketing output, briefings, audit reports, textbooks and instructional documentation.

4.3 SPREADSHEET

The spreadsheet response option, when relevant, will appear as follows:

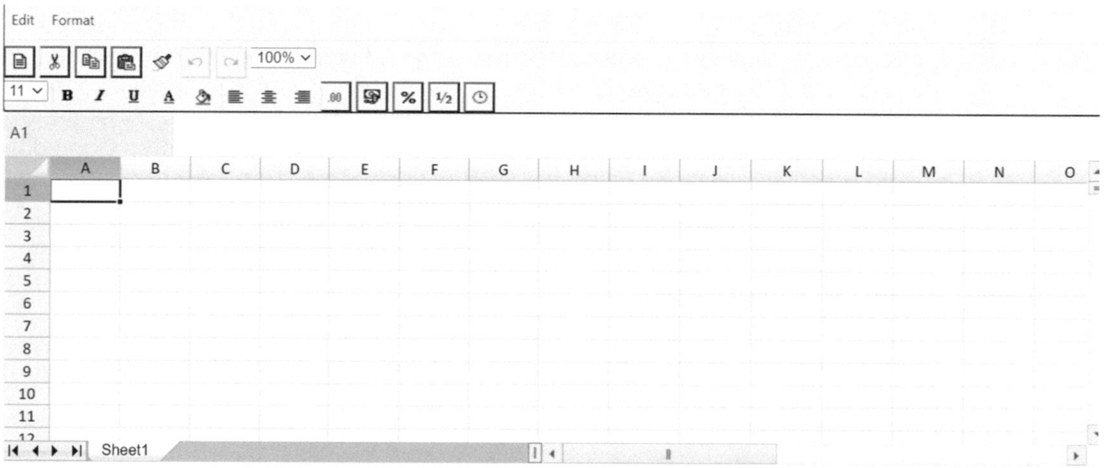

The spreadsheet software uses the same functionality as other commonly used spreadsheet software. Basic formulae functionality, such as SUM, power functions (e.g. SQRT) and the use of brackets are all reproduced within the ACCA software. Candidates are advised to practise questions using the software so that they are familiar with the functions available and how they can be utilised to the candidate's advantage through improved efficiency.

The spreadsheet resource has the following advantages and disadvantages:

Advantages	**Disadvantages**
This can quickly and easily perform calculations (e.g. using sums for totals or formulae for calculations)	Text will carry over beyond one cell and may go across and beyond the page width making answers difficult to follow (and mark)
Data within tables can be easily aligned	Bullet points are difficult to use
Shortcut icons can be used to quickly round figures, change numbers to percentages etc.	
Tables can easily and quickly be copied when calculations need to be reperformed (e.g. for sensitivity analysis, tax calculations for more than one person, financial statements for more than one company etc.)	
Column width can be adjusted to label length	

It is, therefore, best suited for performing calculations within the examination e.g. NPVs.

Spreadsheet software is ubiquitous in the modern workplace. It has the capacity to record, store and organise huge amounts of data and information relating to all aspects of a business. Examples of only a few of its possible practical applications include the preparation of management and financial accounts, operational controls and record-keeping e.g. expense claims, data analytics, project appraisals, sample size selection and tax computations.

4.4 SLIDES

NOTE: The slides response option will not appear in FFM. This section has been included to give you an overview of the response options across the whole ACCA syllabus right up to the Strategic Professional level.

The slides response option, when relevant, will appear as follows:

This resource has the following advantages and disadvantages:

Advantages	Disadvantages
Key messages are easier to see	There is limited space and ability to contain detail outside of the speaker notes
Tables can be easily added	It cannot automatically perform calculations
Speaker notes can be added for the detail	
Bullet points can be used to provide lists	
Titles can be given more prominence	

This is best suited for requirements that ask for presentations. This is not a common response option and is not applicable to most papers. Don't expect to see it within FFM.

The simple, aesthetically pleasing visual information provided by slide software is effectively used in the workplace when material is required to be shared with a wider audience. Slide software will be used during sales pitches, job interviews, presentations, keynote speeches and product launches.

CONCLUSION

This chapter provided an introduction to the employability and technology skills that you will need to demonstrate in your exam.

ANSWERS TO ACTIVITIES AND PRACTICE QUESTIONS

CHAPTER 1

ACTIVITY 1

The three different meanings of the word 'capital' are:

1 Capital (the noun) – the money invested in a business by its owner(s).

2 Capital (the adjective) – used in phrases like capital expenditure and capital items; it indicates that the items in question are for permanent use in the business.

3 Working capital – the excess of current assets over current liabilities. This is the only money in the business, which is not either tied up in non-current assets or needed for paying payables.

ACTIVITY 2

	Profit	Operating cash flow
	$	$
Sales	240,000	240,000
Opening receivables (cash received in year)		18,000
Closing receivables (cash outstanding)		(28,800)
Cash in		229,200
Cost of sales	204,000	204,000
Closing inventory (bought but not used)		25,200
Opening inventory (used but not bought)		(14,400)
Purchases in year		214,800
Opening payables (paid during year)		13,200
Closing payables (outstanding at year end)		(16,800)
Cash out		211,200
Profit/operational cash flow	36,000	18,000

ACTIVITY 3

If you have a lot of sales, you still may not have cash, since you will always have some outstanding accounts receivable to be collected. If you put that together with the purchase of inventory and equipment, payments to suppliers for items purchased prior to the actual payment and payments on debt, you will likely have less cash – or less access to it – than you think.

ACTIVITY 4

	$
Operating profit	X
Add: Depreciation charges	25,000
Deduct profit on sale of non-current assets	(15,000)
Add: Decrease in inventory	4,500
Add: Decrease in trade receivables	5,000
Deduct decrease in trade payables	(3,500)
Net cash inflow from operating activities	44,500

Therefore, working backwards, the profit must have been $28,500

CHAPTER 2

ACTIVITY 1

Workings: Receipts from credit sales

			Cash receipts	
Sales month	**Credit sales**	**July**	**August**	**September**
	$	$	$	$
April	60,000	6,000	–	–
May	64,000	19,200	6,400	–
June	50,000	30,000	15,000	5,000
July	60,000		36,000	18,000
August	65,000	–		39,000
September	75,000	–	–	–
Total receipts		55,200	57,400	62,000

	Cash receipts budget, July to September		
	July	**August**	**September**
	$	$	$
Receipts from cash sales	4,500	4,500	5,000
Receipts from credit sales	55,200	57,400	62,000
Total receipts	59,700	61,900	67,000

ACTIVITY 2

		January units	February units	March units
Sales quantity		400	450	420
Less: Opening inventory		(100)	(150)	(120)
Add: Closing inventory		150	120	180
Production in units = units purchased		450	420	480
Cost of purchases at $2 per unit		$900	$840	$960
Payment in March		$		
For January purchases	(60% of $900)	540		
For March purchases	(40% of $960)	384		
Total payments for materials		924		

ACTIVITY 3

(a) **Tutorial note:** Inventory is used up by material usage, and by closing inventory. This usage is made up partly from opening inventory. The balance must be made up from purchases. This situation is shown in the solution following.

	June	July	August
	$	$	$
Material usage	8,000	9,000	10,000
Closing inventory	3,500	6,000	4,000
	11,500	15,000	14,000
Less: Opening inventory	5,000	3,500	6,000
Purchases	6,500	11,500	8,000

(b) **Tutorial note:** The main points to watch out for are sales receipts and overheads. Tackle sales receipts by calculating separate figures for cash sales (10% of total sales, received in the month of sale) and credit sales (90% of **last month's** sales). For overheads, remember that depreciation is not a cash expense and must therefore be stripped out of the overheads cash cost.

Cash budgets, June – August

	June	July	August
	$	$	$
Receipts of cash			
Cash sales	4,500	5,000	6,000
Credit sales	29,500	40,500	45,000
	34,000	45,500	51,000
Cash payments			
Wages	12,000	13,000	14,500
Overheads	6,500	7,000	8,000
Direct materials	6,500	11,500	8,000
Taxation	–	25,000	–
	25,000	56,500	30,500
Surplus/(deficit) for month	9,000	(11,000)	20,500
Opening balance	11,750	20,750	9,750
Closing balance	20,750	9,750	30,250

ACTIVITY 4

Simple price index = $\frac{p_1}{p_0}$ × 100 where p_1 is the price in 20X1 and p_0 is the price in 20X0:

$$= \frac{13.65}{12.50} \times 100$$

= 1.092 × 100

= 109.20

This means that the price has increased by 9.2% on its base year price of $12.50.

ACTIVITY 5

Let's start by preparing a table of all the information required to answer the question:

Item	**p_0 20X1**	**p_1 20X2**	**q**	**Quantity weight only W_A(= q)**	**Value weight W_B(= p_0 × q)**
Product A	6.5	6.9	10	10	65
Product B	2.2	2.5	30	30	66
Σ				40	131

Item	$\frac{p_1}{p_0} \times 100$	$W_A\left(\frac{P_1}{P_0} \times 100\right)$	$W_B\left(\frac{P_1}{P_0} \times 100\right)$
Product A	106.2	1,062	6,903.0
Product B	113.6	3,408	7,497.6
Σ		4,470	14,400.6

(a) To calculate the index using quantity weights, we need to insert the data into the formula:

$$\frac{\Sigma\left[W_A \times \frac{P_1}{P_0} \times 100\right]}{\Sigma W_A} = \frac{4,470}{40} = 111.75$$

(b) To calculate the index using value weights, we need to insert the data into the formula:

$$\frac{\Sigma\left[W_B \times \frac{P_1}{P_0} \times 100\right]}{\Sigma W_B} = \frac{14,400.6}{131} = 109.93$$

ACTIVITY 6

	18/6	19/6	20/6	21/6
	$	$	$	$
Receipts				
Owen Co	10,000			
Betjeman Co	7,000			
Hughes Co				12,000
	17,000	**0**	**0**	**12,000**
Payments				
Hooting Co	10,000			
Howling Co				10,000
Wages		25,000		
Salaries			88,000	
Petty cash			800	
Machine				14,000
	10,000	**25,000**	**88,800**	**24,000**
Cleared excess receipts over payments	7,000	(25,000)	(88,800)	(12,000)
Cleared balance b/f	226,000	233,000	208,000	119,200
Cleared balance c/f	233,000	208,000	119,200	107,200
Uncleared funds float				
Receipts	12,000	12,000	12,000	0
Payments	(24,000)	(24,000)	(24,000)	0
Net	(12,000)	(12,000)	(12,000)	0
Total book balance c/f	221,000	196,000	107,200	107,200

ACTIVITY 7

(a) To: Tom Harris

From: Assistant accountant

Date: XXXXXX

Subject: Draft cash budget.

I have been asked to submit my comments about the draft cash budget.

1 The sales budget shows an increase in sales of $1,000 each month. This could be reasonable, but it would be appropriate to ask the sales manager to confirm that this rate of monthly sales growth is reasonable.

2 Although sales increase each month, direct costs do not increase at the same rate. For example, sales in April are 20% higher than in December, but direct materials and direct labour costs are only 10% higher. The accuracy of this prediction should be checked with the managers responsible for materials purchasing and direct labour costs. These managers should also be asked to confirm that any expected increases in labour costs or material purchase costs have been allowed for in the budget.

3 From January, customers will take longer to pay, with only 50% paying in the month after sale instead of 100% as previously. The sales manager and manager responsible for collections should be consulted to find out why this change in payment pattern is predicted.

4 The cash budget does not include any exceptional items of receipt or payment. In particular, no capital expenditures are planned. Senior management should be asked to confirm that this is correct, and that no planned payments (or receipts) have been overlooked.

I hope these comments are helpful. If you would like me to consult with anyone about the assumptions and forecasts in the draft budget, please let me know.

(b) There are two ways of dealing with the cash deficit in February, if the company does not yet have an overdraft facility.

1 The company could approach its bank and ask for an overdraft facility to cover the expected cash deficit.

2 The expected deficit is due to the slower payments from customers. If all customers continue to pay in the month following sale, the cash shortage could be avoided. The sales manager and manager responsible for debt collections should be consulted to ask whether this will be possible.

PRACTICE QUESTION 1

ANN DREW

MEMO

To: Ann Drew

From: Assistant accountant

Re: Cash flow report

The cash flow report for January to March shows that actual cash flows have not been as good as expected, and at the end of March there was a cash deficit of $3,300 instead of the budgeted surplus of $8,000.

There appear to be three reasons for this, which should be investigated.

Cash receipts have been lower than budgeted. It seems likely that sales volume is lower than budget, but this should be checked.

Although cash receipts are lower than budgeted, payments for variable cost items (direct materials and direct labour) do not seem to be proportionately lower. It is possible that spending is higher than it should be. This too should be checked.

Only $2,000 of capital expenditure was budgeted but actual capital expenditure was $5,400. The reasons for this additional capital expenditure should be investigated.

The cash deficit is close to the overdraft limit of $5,000. As a matter of urgency, I recommend that we prepare a revised cash forecast, to establish what the future cash position could be. If necessary, we might have to approach the bank to discuss an increase in the overdraft limit.

Measures might also be needed to bring spending on materials and labour under better control, and to defer any further capital expenditures.

PRACTICE QUESTION 2

CHASE

(a) Workings: Cash from sales

		Receipts					
Month	**Total**	**Jan**	**Feb**	**March**	**April**	**May**	**June**
Sales	$	$	$	$	$	$	$
Opening receivables	80,000	60,000	18,400				
January	70,000	14,000	35,000	21,000			
February	70,000		14,000	35,000	21,000		
March	70,000			14,000	35,000	21,000	
April	80,000				16,000	40,000	24,000
May	80,000					16,000	40,000
June	80,000	–	–	–	–	–	16,000
Total	450,000	74,000	67,400	70,000	72,000	77,000	80,000

Cost of sales: 75% of $450,000 = $337,500

Workings: Payments to suppliers

Purchases are 75% of sales value.

- Purchases in December and January, for sales in February and March, will be 75% of $70,000 = $52,500 each month.
- Purchases each month in February to April, for sales in April to June, will be 75% of $80,000 = $60,000 each month.
- Purchases each month in May and June, for sales in July and August, will be 75% of $75,000 = $56,250 each month.

Purchases are paid for one month in arrears.

Workings: Administration and distribution expenses

It is assumed that these exclude the advertisement cost of $1,500.

Cash expenses are $8,500 each month less $500 depreciation = $8,000 each month.

These include rental costs of $2,000 each month, which are payable in June.

Cash expenditures are therefore $8,000 – $2,000 = $6,000 each month in January to May, and $6,000 + $12,000 = $18,000 in June.

Cash budget for the six months January to June 20X5

	Jan	Feb	March	April	May	June
	$	$	$	$	$	$
Receipts						
Share issue					80,000	
Cash from sales	74,000	67,400	70,000	72,000	77,000	80,000
Total receipts	74,000	67,400	70,000	72,000	157,000	80,000
Payments						
To suppliers	52,500	52,500	60,000	60,000	60,000	56,250
Admin and distribution	6,000	6,000	6,000	6,000	6,000	18,000
Total payments	58,500	58,500	66,000	66,000	66,000	74,250
Receipts less payments	15,500	8,900	4,000	6,000	91,000	5,750
Opening cash balance	(108,000)	(93,580)	(85,616)	(82,472)	(77,297)	12,930
Interest charge	(1,080)	(936)	(856)	(825)	(773)	–
Closing cash balance	(93,580)	(85,616)	(82,472)	(77,297)	12,930	18,680

(b) Workings: Interest charges

Interest is charged each month on the closing overdraft balance, and paid in the following month. The interest payment in January therefore relates to the previous six-month period, since it is a December charge.

Interest costs for the period January to June are therefore 936 + 856 + 825 + 773 = $3,390.

Workings: Purchases

Sales in the six-month period are $450,000. The gross profit is 25% of sales, so cost of sales = 75% of sales = $450,000 × 75% = $337,500.

Budgeted statement of profit or loss for the period January to June 20X5

	$	$
Sales		450,000
Cost of sales		337,500
Gross profit		112,500
Admin and distribution costs		
(6 × $8,500)	51,000	
Advertisement	1,500	
Irrecoverable debt (2% × $80,000)	1,600	
Interest charges	3,390	
		57,490
Net profit (before tax)		55,010

(c) Workings:

	$	$
Opening balance – payables		
Purchases	52,500	
Interest charges	1,080	
		53,580
Closing balance – payables		
Purchases	56,250	
Advertisement	1,500	
		57,750
Increase in payables		4,170

	$	$
Opening balance – receivables		80,000
Closing balance – receivables		
May sales	24,000	
June sales	64,000	
		88,000
Increase in receivables		8,000

Reconciliation of profit to cash flow

	$	$
Profit after interest		55,010
Depreciation charges		3,000
Increase in inventory (112,500 – 105,000)	(7,500)	
Increase in receivables	(8,000)	
Increase in payables	4,170	
		(11,330)
		46,680
Cash from share issue		80,000
		126,680
Opening bank overdraft	108,000	
Closing cash balance	18,680	
Improvement in cash position		126,680

CHAPTER 3

ACTIVITY 1

$69,594,521 × 4 × .06 = $16,702,685

ACTIVITY 2

Note: This is a fairly challenging task, because there is no single 'correct' answer. Your memo should, however, address the issues set out in the memo below, even if your final recommendations are different.

MEMO

To: Chief accountant

From: Assistant accountant

Date: XXXXXX

Subject: Bank borrowing

The business is expecting a cash shortfall of $52,000 in August, but we currently have an overdraft facility for just $25,000. We therefore urgently need to take steps to improve liquidity. Since actual cash flows could turn out to be worse than forecast, we should plan for a liquidity requirement of at least $55,000.

A large part of the cash shortfall ($20,000) will be caused by spending on capital equipment in August. Even if this spending is cancelled or deferred, we will still exceed our current overdraft limit in August.

We must therefore arrange to increase our borrowing.

1 South Bank has offered an overdraft limit of $50,000 if we switch our account. However, unless we cut back on payments or improve receipts, this will not be enough to cover the shortfall in August.

2 We have not yet made any approach to North Bank. In view of our established relationship with North Bank, it would be advisable to discuss with the bank whether it would agree to provide extra funding, perhaps as a combination of a $20,000 loan to finance the capital spending (possibly secured) and an increase in the overdraft limit to, say, $35,000 or $40,000. This request will test the strength of our relationship with North Bank.

3 We should also consider ways of improving cash flows, by improving receipts from collections or reducing payments.

4 If we cannot arrange more borrowing through North Bank, reaching an arrangement with South Bank could be essential, although some of the planned capital spending might have to be deferred.

ACTIVITY 3

MEMO

To: Accounts supervisor

From: Accountant

Date: XXXXXX

Subject: Cash management

The cash budget for the next six months shows that there will be a positive cash balance in every month except March.

An overdraft of up to $27,000 is forecast for March. We need to check and confirm that the business has a sufficient overdraft limit and can allow its account to be overdrawn by this amount. Since actual cash flows could be worse than budgeted, I suggest that an overdraft limit of at least $35,000 could be required.

If the business does not have a sufficient overdraft facility, we must consider ways of maintaining adequate liquidity. It might be possible to negotiate a higher overdraft limit. Alternatively, it might be possible to defer some planned payments until April, when the cash position should improve.

Some of the cash surpluses in the other months could be invested for a short time. We should try to avoid investing too much, so that we face an unexpected cash deficit and it becomes necessary to cash in the investments much sooner than planned.

However, it might be appropriate to invest about $20,000 in January and February and about $80,000 or so in April to June. This money would then be expected to earn a return in the form of interest. If the cash is left in the current account, it will not earn any interest at all.

The situation should be kept under continual review, because the cash forecast is likely to change as the year progresses.

PRACTICE QUESTION

CASH MANAGEMENT

Tutorial note: Part (a) requires a fairly standard discussion of the motives for, and costs of, holding cash. In part (b), speeding up banking will effectively reduce the firm's overdraft requirement. In this question there are no extra costs given for banking daily but they can exist and should be mentioned in your discussion.

(a) The reasons for holding cash are as follows:

The transaction motive – cash will be required for the day-to-day operations of the business, e.g. to pay suppliers, to buy inventory or to make dividend payments.

The speculative motive – the company will need cash to finance risky business ventures, e.g. the purchase of a machine to carry out a speculative project.

The precautionary motive – contingent losses may materialise, e.g. legal claims against the company. Cash will need to be held to satisfy such contingencies as they arise. The company must, therefore, maintain a sufficient level of cash to satisfy the above three requirements. Any cash in excess of this level will result in lower profits. It is true that surplus cash can be invested in the short term to earn interest, and in this respect cash is different from other assets, but such returns will nearly always be less than the return that can be earned on the business's other assets. Thus, in general, cash is really the same as any other working capital asset and should be subject to similar management and control. Surplus cash that can only be invested at low short-term interest rates or, worse still, which is lying idle, is not being properly utilised and will result in decreased profitability.

On the other hand, if the company is holding too little cash it may encounter liquidity problems. Such a shortage of cash could mean that the company is forced to reject certain worthwhile investment opportunities owing to lack of funds, or that its very survival is threatened. Many profitable companies have been forced into liquidation or sale purely as a consequence of cash flow problems.

Proper cash budgeting and planning procedures should ensure that a company does not fall into the trap of holding too little or too much cash.

(b) AB Credit Collection Company

Annual collections = $5,200,000

$$\therefore \text{ Weekly collections (average)} = \frac{\$5,200,000}{52} = \$100,000 \text{ per week}$$

$$\therefore \text{ Average daily collections} = \frac{\$100,000}{5} = \$20,000 \text{ per day}$$

Annual overdraft rate = 9%

$$\therefore \text{ Daily overdraft rate} = \frac{9\%}{365} = 0.0246\%$$

Cost of not banking daily = sums not banked × days not banked × daily overdraft rate

		$
Monday	$20,000 × 4 days × 0.0246%	19.68
Tuesday	$20,000 × 3 days × 0.0246%	14.76
Wednesday	$20,000 × 2 days × 0.0246%	9.84
Thursday	$20,000 × 1 day × 0.0246%	4.92
Friday	No change to banking pattern	–
Total weekly cost of not banking daily		49.20

Annual cost = $49.20 × 52 = $2,558.40

Assumptions

There are 52 weeks in a year, five days each week, and collections are made on each of these days.

Takings are evenly spread daily and weekly.

Bankings are used to reduce the overdraft and thus the overdraft rate is suitable for calculating the annual cost of weekly banking. If the company were able to make use of the funds released in other ways then a different rate may be appropriate. For example, if the company had available investment opportunities, then the cost of capital should be used.

It appears that a daily remitting system would save the company $2,558 pa. However, this must be assessed in the light of the possible effects on agents and costs. At present agents may be earning interest prior to remitting collections to head office and might resent the change in company policy. Also, what effect will the new system have on the number of agent defaults?

CHAPTER 4

ACTIVITY 1

Risk	**Systematic risk**	**Unsystematic risk**
Inflation risk	Yes	
Interest rate risk	Yes	
Price risk	Yes	
Reinvestment risk	Yes	
Default (credit) risk		Yes
Tax rate risk	Yes	
Call (prepayment) risk		Yes
Liquidity (market) risk		Yes
Currency risk		Yes
Political risk		Yes

ACTIVITY 2

(a) **Interest yield** $=\frac{4}{94.00}\times 100\% = 4.25\%$

(b) **Approximate redemption yield**

If an investor buys the stock now at $94.00 and holds it for three years until maturity, the investor will make a capital gain of 100 – 94 = 6 at redemption. In other words, there will be a capital gain of $6 for every $100 of stock, or for every $94 invested. This gives an average annual gain on redemption of $2 for each $94 invested, which is about 2% per annum.

The approximate redemption yield is therefore the interest yield of 4.25% plus 2%, which is about 6.25%.

ACTIVITY 3

MEMO

To: Manager

From: Accountant

Date XXXXXX

Subject: Investing in bills

We have $5 million to invest for 50 days. We want to invest at a fairly low risk.

There are two risks with investing in bills.

1 **Credit risk.** This is the risk of non-payment of the bill at maturity. This is non-existent for Treasury bills and very low for bank bills. We can invest in either of these types of bill, through our bank.

2 **Risk of falling market prices.** The market value of bills in the discount market will fall if interest rates go up in the next 50 days. This risk only exists if we intend to re-sell the bills before their maturity. To overcome this problem, we can ask our bank to purchase 'second-hand' bills in the discount market with a maturity of 50 days. In this way, the return on our investment will come from the payment of the bills at maturity, and we will not have to sell them in the discount market to cash in our investment.

CHAPTER 5

ACTIVITY 1

Cash operating cycle = 4 + 1 + 3 + 2 – 6 weeks

= 4 weeks.

ACTIVITY 2

Step 1 Calculate annual cost of sales, using the cost structure.

	%	$m
Sales	160	8
Cost of sales	100	5
Gross profit	60	3

Step 2 Calculate payables, receivables and inventory.

Payables $= \frac{2}{12} \times$ annual COS $= \frac{2}{12} \times \$5m = \$0.833m$

Receivables $= \frac{1.5}{12} \times$ annual sales $= \frac{1.5}{12} \times \$8m = \$1m$

Inventory $= \frac{1}{12} \times$ annual COS $= \frac{1}{12} \times \$5m = \$0.417m$

Step 3 Calculate the ratios.

$$\text{Current ratio} = \frac{\text{Inventory} + \text{receivables} + \text{cash}}{\text{Payables}} = \frac{0.417 + 1 + 1.25}{0.833} = 3.2$$

$$\text{Quick ratio} = \frac{\text{Receivables} + \text{cash}}{\text{Payables}} = \frac{1 + 1.25}{0.833} = 2.7$$

ACTIVITY 3

1 Payables:

Average payment period

$$= \left(365 \times \frac{\text{Payables}}{\text{Purchases}}\right) = 365 \times \frac{21}{140} = \text{(55 days)}$$

2 Receivables:

Average collection period

$$= \left(365 \times \frac{\text{Receivables}}{\text{Sales}}\right) = 365 \times \frac{31.25}{250} = \text{46 days}$$

3 Inventory turnover:

$$= 365 \times \frac{\text{Inventory}}{\text{Cost of goods sold}} = 365 \times \frac{92.5}{210} = \text{161 days}$$

Length of cash operating cycle 152 days

ACTIVITY 4

'Overtrading' refers to the situation where a company is **over reliant** on **short-term finance** to support its operations. This is risky because short-term finance may be withdrawn relatively quickly if providers of short-term finance lose confidence in the business, or if there is a general tightening of credit in the economy, and this may result in a liquidity crisis and even bankruptcy, even though the firm is profitable. The fundamental solution to overtrading is to replace short-term finance with longer-term finance such as term loans or equity funds.

The term overtrading is used because the condition commonly arises when a company is **expanding** rapidly. In this situation, because of increasing volumes, more cash is frequently needed to pay input costs such as wages or purchases than is currently being collected from customers. The result is that the company runs up its overdraft to the limit and sometimes there is insufficient time to arrange an increase in facilities to pay other payables on the due dates.

These problems are often compounded by a general lack of attention to cost control and working capital management, such as debt collection, because most management time is spent organising selling or production. The result is an unnecessary drop in profit margins.

When the overdraft limit is reached the company frequently raises funds from other expensive short-term sources, such as debt factoring or receivables' prompt payment discounts, and delays payment to payables, instead of underpinning its financial position with equity funds or a longer-term loan. The consequent under-capitalisation delays investment in non-current assets and staff and can further harm the quality of the firm's operations.

PRACTICE QUESTION

EWDEN

Report on Ewden's financial position

(a) Reasons for Ewden's fall in liquidity

1. Comparison of the two statements of financial position reveals that Ewden has suffered a significant fall in liquidity – cash balances have fallen sharply from $1.5m (probably an unnecessarily high level) in 20X2 to just $0.1m in 20X3 while an overdraft of $0.2m has appeared, reflecting a reduction in net cash resources of $1.6m. However, company profitability remains satisfactory, indicating that the run-down in liquidity was required to finance the acquisition of assets.

2. Analysis of the financial statements reveals that Ewden has been able to reinvest $3.0m of retained earnings (plus an unspecified amount of depreciation provisions) in order to fund a substantial net increase in non-current assets of $3.0m, presumably to support an output expansion. It is possible that this significant capacity increase might have been obtained via the acquisition of another company. Such a large increase implies that during the past recession, Ewden had cut back its capacity in order to reduce costs.

3. As well as an increase in non-current assets, Ewden has invested $0.8m in stocks and $1.0m in receivables. This substantial investment in working capital is partially offset by an increase in trade and other payables of $0.2m making a total increase in operating capital of $1.6m.

4 No additional external long-term finance has been raised, so the increased investment in non-current assets and working capital has had to be financed by a significant reduction in cash balances and the opening-up of a bank overdraft, resulting in a heavy net outflow of liquid resources of $1.6m.

(b) Is Ewden overtrading?

1 Overtrading is the term applied to a company which rapidly increases its sales revenue without having sufficient capital backing, hence the alternative term 'under-capitalisation'. Output increases are often obtained by more intensive utilisation of existing non-current assets, and growth tends to be financed by more intensive use of working capital. Overtrading companies are often unable or unwilling to raise long-term capital and thus tend to rely more heavily on short-term sources such as payables and bank overdrafts. Receivables usually increase sharply as the company follows a more generous trade credit policy in order to win sales. Overtrading is thus characterised by increased gearing and a declining liquidity position, usually in terms of both the quick ratio and the current ratio.

2 The accounts indicate some of the signs of overtrading, although the case is not proven. Checking the ratios against the common symptoms of overtrading:

(i) Fall in the liquidity ratios. The current ratio falls from 2.25 to 2.04, which does not seem to indicate a serious decline in liquidity, although the extent of the decline in the quick ratio (i.e. excluding inventory), from 1.55 to 1.13, might give more cause for concern, especially as the bulk of its quick assets (96%) are now in the form of receivables.

(ii) Rapid increase in sales revenue – 33%.

(iii) Sharp increase in the sales revenue-to-non-current assets ratio. For Ewden, this has remained steady at 1.33 because the increase in sales revenue has been supported by an increase in non-current assets, suggesting that the output increase was well-planned.

(iv) Increase in inventory in relation to sales revenue. The increase is from 11.7% (43 days) to 13.8% (50 days), which is marked but hardly dramatic.

(v) Increase in receivables. Accounts receivable rise as a percentage of sales revenue from 13.3% (49 days) to 16.3% (59 days), which indicates a significant loosening of control over receivables.

(vi) Increase in the trade credit period. The ratio of trade receivables to cost of goods sold rises slightly from 21.4% (78 days) to 22.2% (81 days). The trade payables payment period is considerably longer (81 days versus 59 days) than the receivables collection period, suggesting it is exploiting the generosity of suppliers in order to enhance sales.

(vii) Increase in short-term borrowing and a decline in cash balances. Clearly, this has happened.

(viii) Increase in gearing. Taking the ratio of long and short-term debt-to-equity as the appropriate measure, gearing has actually fallen (from a relatively low level of 21% to 18%) despite the opening of the overdraft, primarily due to the increase in equity via retentions.

(ix) Fall in the profit margin. In terms of its gross profit margin (operating profit-to-sales), Ewden actually achieves an increase from 42% to 44%, although there is a marginal fall in the ratio of profit after tax-to-sales from 31.7% to 31.3%. This does not suggest aggressive price discounting in an attempt to increase sales.

3 It seems that Ewden's liquidity is under pressure but it displays by no means all the classic signs of overtrading. The company might consider issuing further long-term securities if it wishes to support a further sales surge. If sales are expected to stabilise, the recent increase in capacity should be sufficient to produce the desired output, enabling the liquidity position to be repaired via cash flow, which was substantial in 20X3, before allowing for financing of the capital investment.

CHAPTER 6

ACTIVITY 1

$$\sqrt{\frac{2 \times \$150 \times 5{,}000}{\$2}}$$

= 866 units (to nearest unit).

ACTIVITY 2

(a) Annual demand is 30,000. The original EOQ is 3,162. The company will therefore place an order once every 30,000/3,162 = 9.49 orders per year. 9.49 orders per year is equivalent to placing an order every 365 days/9.49 orders = every 38 days approximately.

(b) The company must be sure that there is sufficient stock on hand when it places an order to last the two weeks' lead-time. It must therefore place an order when there is two weeks' worth of demand in inventory:

i.e. $\frac{2}{52} \times 30{,}000 \approx 1{,}154$ units.

ACTIVITY 3

(a)	$(100 \times 30) \times 120\%$	=	3,600 units
(b)	$\sqrt{\frac{2 \times \$400 \times (100 \times 48 \times 5)}{0.1 \times \$10}}$	=	4,382 units
(c)	$3{,}600 + 4{,}382 - (100 \times 20)$	=	5,982 units
(d)	$3{,}600 - (100 \times 30)$	=	600 units

ACTIVITY 4

Introducing JIT/lean manufacturing might bring the following benefits:

- a lower level of investment in working capital
- reduced inventory holding costs
- reduced manufacturing lead times
- improved labour productivity
- reduced scrap work, rework and warranty costs
- price reductions on purchased materials
- reductions in the number of accounting transactions.

ACTIVITY 5

Simple interest cost = $\frac{200}{9{,}800} \times \frac{365}{45} \times 100\% = 16.6\%$

Compound interest cost = $\left(1+\frac{200}{9{,}800}\right)^{365/45} - 1 = 16.7\%$

PRACTICE QUESTION 1

COMPUTER BUREAU ORDER QUANTITY

(a) Calculation of cost associated with particular order quantities

Order quantity x	Delivery cost $\frac{1{,}000}{x} \times 15$	Storage cost $\frac{x}{2} \times 2.70$	Ordering cost Delivery cost + Storage cost
	\$	\$	\$
50	$\frac{1{,}000}{50} \times 15 = 300$	$\frac{50}{2} \times 2.70 = 67.50$	367.50
100	$\frac{1{,}000}{100} \times 15 = 150$	$\frac{100}{2} \times 2.70 = 135.00$	285.00
150	$\frac{1{,}000}{150} \times 15 = 100$	$\frac{150}{2} \times 2.70 = 202.50$	302.50
200	$\frac{1{,}000}{200} \times 15 = 75$	$\frac{200}{2} \times 2.70 = 270.00$	345.00
250	$\frac{1{,}000}{250} \times 15 = 60$	$\frac{250}{2} \times 2.70 = 337.50$	397.50

(b) From the figures calculated in (a) we can see that the order quantity of 100 units results in the lowest cost.

PRACTICE QUESTION 2

K & L GAMES

(a) Annual demand = 40 × 250 = 10,000 boxes = D

Order cost = $64 = C_o

Holding cost per year per unit = 25% of $2 = $0.50 = C_h

$$\text{EOQ} = \sqrt{\frac{2C_oD}{C_h}} \quad \sqrt{\frac{2 \times 64 \times 10{,}000}{0.5}}$$

= 1,600 boxes

$$\text{Number of orders per year} = \frac{\text{Annual demand}}{\text{order quantity}}$$

$$= \frac{10{,}000}{1{,}600}$$

= 6.25

$$\text{Re-order interval} = \frac{250 \text{ days}}{\text{No. of orders}}$$

$$= \frac{250}{6.25} \text{ days}$$

= 40 days

Tutorial note: 'Frequency of replenishment' is a somewhat ambiguous term, so both the re-order interval and the number of orders per year have been given.

Cost per annum when ordering 1,600:

				$
Holding cost	=	Average inventory × Holding cost/unit		
	=	$\frac{1{,}600 \times \$0.5}{2}$	=	400
Order cost	=	No. of orders × Cost/order		
	=	6.25 × $64	=	400
Total holding and order cost			=	800

Cost per annum when ordering 200:

Holding cost	=	$\frac{200 \times \$0.5}{2}$	=	50
Order cost	=	50 × $64	=	3,200
Total holding and ordering cost =				3,250

Annual saving by ordering 1,600 = $(3,250 – 800)

= $2,450

(b) With the new discount scheme, if 1,600 boxes are ordered, the first discount will be automatically obtained, so that the EOQ must be re-calculated.

C_h becomes 0.25 × 0.95 × \$2 = \$0.475

The EOQ becomes $\sqrt{\frac{2 \times 64 \times 10{,}000}{0.475}}$

= 1,642

The choice is therefore between ordering 1,642 and 5,000.

(i) Order 1,642:

				\$
Holding cost	=	$\frac{1{,}642 \times \$0.475}{2}$	=	390
No of orders	=	$\frac{10{,}000}{1{,}642}$		
	=	6.09		
Order cost	=	6.09 × \$64	=	390
Purchase costs	=	10,000 × \$1.9	=	19,000
Total cost per annum			=	19,780

(ii) Order 5,000:

The holding cost per unit becomes 0.25 × 0.9 × \$2 = \$0.45

Number of orders/year = $\frac{10{,}000}{5{,}000}$ = 2

				\$
Holding cost	=	$\frac{5{,}000 \times 0\$.45}{2}$	=	1,125
Order cost	=	2 × \$64	=	128
Purchase cost	=	10,000 × \$1.8	=	18,000
Total cost per annum				19,253

Hence it is worthwhile to order 5,000.

Tutorial note: Always work to the minimum discount quantity. If more than the minimum is ordered, costs will increase until a further discount (if any) is obtained.

PRACTICE QUESTION 3

DOCUMENTARY CHECKS

Before a company/organisation pays an invoice for goods or services which it has received on credit, it must check the **validity** of the invoice. This involves setting up a **pass for payments system** which establishes and verifies that the invoice details are correct and that the goods and services to which it relates have in fact been delivered/supplied. The following diagram provides an overview of such a system:

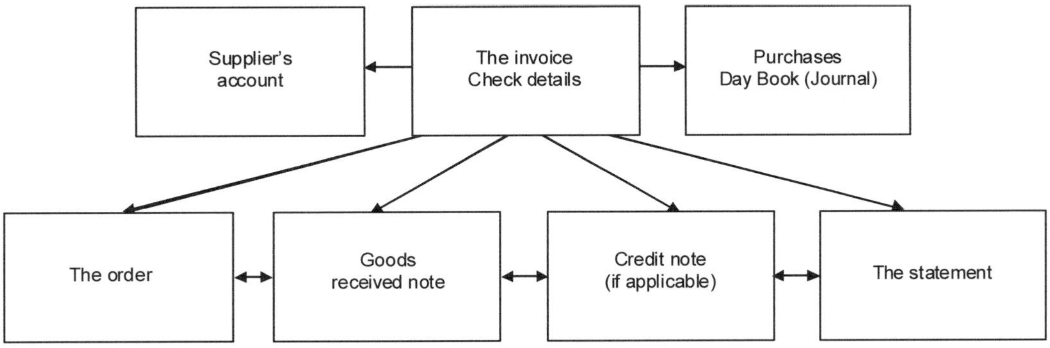

A pass for payments system of checks

The invoice

The details on the invoice will need to be checked and looked at very carefully to ensure:

(a) that it is addressed to the company

(b) that the amounts for the goods/services, calculation of discounts and sales tax being charged are correct. Errors can occur due to **denomination of quantity problems** e.g. the price per batch of 100 boxes being applied to the price of each box!

(c) it has been correctly entered in the **recording system** i.e. on the supplier's account and in the day book (journal) system.

The order

The goods/services described on the invoice should be checked against the order (plus any quotations received, if applicable) via the order number reference. This should verify that the invoice relates to the goods/services which were actually ordered.

The goods received note

The invoice should also be matched against the goods received note or other documentation to verify that the goods/services have in fact been received. For goods received but then returned, a good returned note would be matched against the credit note. Any balance payable on an invoice which needs to be adjusted by a credit note would not be paid until the credit note was received.

The statement

The statements which are sent out by the suppliers at or around the month end show the opening and closing balances outstanding and list invoices, credit notes and payments etc. The invoice would be cross checked with the statement.

At each stage of the checking process the delegated authority would be verified e.g. to ensure that an approved person had authorised the order or goods received note etc. More in depth checks could also be test checked e.g. checking that goods received have been booked into the stores/recorded and are physically held in inventory.

Finally, having been processed and each checking stage being in effect ticked off, as having been done e.g. ticked/initialled/dated the invoice would then be authorised for payment.

CHAPTER 7

ACTIVITY 1

We need to calculate the increase in average receivables in order to calculate the interest cost of the extra receivables.

	Category W	Category Y	Category Z
Extra sales	\$500,000	\$500,000	\$1,500,000
Average collection period	20 days	30 days	60 days
Extra receivables	\$500,000 × 20/365 = \$27,397	\$500,000 × 30/365 = \$41,096	\$1,500,000 × 60/365 =\$ 246,575
Annual interest cost at 7.5%	\$2,055	\$3,082	\$18,493

	Category W	Category Y	Category Z	Total
	\$	\$	\$	\$
Additional sales	500,000	500,000	1,500,000	2,500,000
Additional contribution (40%)	200,000	200,000	600,000	1,000,000
Additional irrecoverable debts:				
2% of \$500,000	10,000			10,000
5% of \$500,000		25,000		25,000
8% of \$1,500,000			120,000	120,000
Interest cost	2,055	3,082	18,493	23,630
Total additional cost	12,055	28,082	138,493	178,630
Net benefit	187,945	171,918	461,507	821,370

ACTIVITY 2

	$
Current annual sales revenue	80,000,000
Increase in annual sales revenue with new credit policy (7%)	5,600,000
Total annual sales revenue with new credit policy	85,600,000
Total receivables with new policy [(3/12) × $85.6m]	21,400,000
Total receivables with current policy [(2/12) × $80m]	13,333,333
Increase in total receivables	8,066,667
Increase in inventory levels	4,000,000
Increase in trade payables	(1,000,000)
Increase in working capital investment	11,066,667
Required return on this investment (15%)	1,660,000

ACTIVITY 3

(a) Effective interest rate = $\frac{\$1.50}{\$98.50} \times 100\% = 1.52\%$

(b) Simple annual interest rate = 1.52% × $\frac{365\text{days}}{(60-14)\text{days}} = 12.1\%$

(c) Compound annual interest rate = $(1.052^{365/46} - 1) = 12.7\%$

ACTIVITY 4

(a) Jane cannot reclaim her money. The implied condition as to satisfactory quality in SGA 1979 only applies where a business sells to a consumer. Stan is not selling in the course of a business.

(b) Regardless of the notice, Sarah will be able to claim a refund for the coat, as the clause excluding liability is not valid.

You may have seen notices on products which you have bought which set out the rights of the buyer and seller, for example to a 'full refund within 21 days if not completely satisfied'. Such notices are almost always accompanied by the phrase 'This does not affect your statutory rights'. This means that your rights under the implied terms of the Sale of Goods Act are protected, even if they seem to be contradicted by the additional terms set out by the seller.

(c) Mark is entitled to a refund. The shop is in breach of the implied terms of fitness for purpose, as it is reasonable to assume that all-weather boots are for the purpose of standing in water. This term cannot be excluded in a consumer sale, so Outdoor Outfitters' exclusion clause is not valid.

PRACTICE QUESTION

CRUST CO

	Current year	Previous year
Working capital	$90,000	$45,000
Total assets	$477,000	$527,000
Working capital: total assets	**0.19**	**0.09**
Receivables, cash and short-term investments	$105,000	$94,000
Daily cash operating expenses (to nearest $100, assuming 365 day year)	$2,400,000/365 = $6,600	$2,700,000/365 = $7,400
No credit interval (in days)	**16 days**	**13 days**
Retained earnings	$35,000	$22,000
Total assets	$477,000	$527,000
Retained earnings: total assets	**0.07**	**0.04**
Earnings before interest and taxation (EBIT)	$105,000	$53,000
Interest charges	$4,000	$3,000
Loan repayments (40,000 – 30,000)	$10,000	$10,000 (given)
EBIT: interest charges and loan repayments	**7.5**	**4.1**
Borrowings (assuming just long term loans should be included)	$40,000	$30,000
Shareholders' funds (equity)	$360,000	$382,000
Total capital employed	$400,000	$412,000
Gearing (borrowings/capital employed)	**10%**	**7.3%**

Note: You might be able to see that all five ratios have deteriorated in the current year compared with the previous year. This will give the credit controller a problem. If credit is granted to this customer, the account should be kept under close watch to monitor the customer's payments.

CHAPTER 8

ACTIVITY 1

Number of weeks after the due payment date	Action
1	Reminder letter
2	Telephone call
3	Second reminder letter
4	Telephone call
6	Final reminder letter
6½	Telephone call. Report to supervisor
8	Stop order. Letter to customer or telephone call to notify customer. Notify individuals within the business who need to be informed, such as sales staff.
9	Senior management decision. Solicitor's letter? Debt collection agency?

These responses could be varied, depending on the customer's response to any letter or telephone call. In addition, if the business has a field sales force, the sales representative responsible for the customer could be involved in trying to collect a debt, for example by visiting the customer and discussing the debt during the visit.

ACTIVITY 2

	$	$
Annual cost of using the factor:		
Fee: 2% × [($125,000 × 12/3) – $30,000]		(9,400)
Loss of profits (50% × $30,000)		(15,000)
		(24,400)
Annual benefits of using the factor:		
Administration savings	20,000	
Reduction in irrecoverable debts: 3% × [($125,000 × 12/3) – $30,000]	14,100	
		34,100
Net savings		9,700

The net annual saving from using the factor is $9,700 (although this solution ignores interest costs).

ACTIVITY 3

		Costs of factoring	Savings
		$	$
Receivables ledger administration	2% × $200,000 × 12	48,000	
Administration cost savings			30,000
Credit protection insurance	1.5% × $200,000 × 12	36,000	
Reduction in irrecoverable debt losses	2.5% × $200,000 × 12		60,000
Cost of factor finance	7.75% × 80% × $200,000 × 2 months	24,800	
Overdraft interest saved	8% × 80% × $200,000 × 2 months		25,600
Total		108,800	115,600
Net benefit from factoring	$(115,600 – 108,800)		6,800

ACTIVITY 4

1 Factoring and invoice discounting are two ways in which a company can obtain speedier payment in respect of sales made to customers. Finance from a factor or invoice discounter means an earlier receipt of cash and improved liquidity. Finance obtained in this way is often easier to arrange and more flexible than a bank loan or overdraft.

2 A factor will lend the firm up to around 80% of the value of its receivables. The factor then administers the receivables ledger accounts and collects the debts. The remaining 20% or so of the value of receivables is paid over to the client company when the invoices are paid, net of administration fees and interest charges.

3 There is a distinction between 'non-recourse' factoring, whereby irrecoverable debts are the responsibility of the factor, as opposed to 'with recourse' factoring under which irrecoverable debts remain the liability of the client company.

4 Sometimes, a company wants better cash flow but also wants to retain control over its receivables ledger administration. If so, it can use invoice discounting, whereby an invoice discounter provides finance against selected invoices. The administration of the customer accounts remains with the company, which settles the debt to the invoice discounter when payment is eventually received from its customers.

5 The main additional benefit provided by full service-and-finance factoring, compared with invoice discounting, is the saving in administrative costs from not having to operate the credit management function. The factor, perhaps by utilising information about customers obtained from operating the sales accounts of other firms, may also be a more efficient collector of debt than the client company, although there may be adverse goodwill implications.

ACTIVITY 5

	Sales in month	Cumulative	
	$	$	
December	103,000	103,000	
November	210,000	313,000	
October	112,000	425,000	(balance)

DSO = 2 months + (112,000/503,000) × 30 days

= 60 + 7 days, i.e. 67 days.

ACTIVITY 6

Step 1 Match the payments and credit notes received to the invoices. Brandeth is more complicated to analyse because cash discounts are taken. However, as most of the cash payments have a discount shown on the same date, it should be reasonably clear that the cash payment and the discount should together be equal to the invoice value.

Gilde & Co

		$				$	
20 Dec	Inv 2946	118.38		30 Jan	Credit note	172.48	✓
28 Dec	Inv 2983	72.03	✓	15 Feb	Cash	228.36	✓
17 Jan	Inv 3029	228.36	✓	28 Feb	Cash	72.03	✓
25 Jan	Inv 3046	172.48	✓	12 March	Cash	48.30	✓
2 Feb	Inv 3103	48.30	✓	14 March	Credit note	49.20	✓
11 Feb	Inv 3135	69.02					
26 Feb	Inv 3157	159.27					
12 March	Inv 3204	49.20	✓				
15 March	Inv 3221	49.20					
28 March	Inv 3252	169.39		31 March	Balance c/d	565.26	
		1,135.63				1,135.63	

Brandreth

		$				$	
3 Jan	Inv 2999	378.29	✓	12 Jan	Cash	363.16	✓
12 Jan	Inv 3012	115.29	✓	12 Jan	Discount	15.13	✓
26 Jan	Inv 3047	39.20	✓	25 Feb	Cash	398.59	✓
13 Feb	Inv 3140	415.20	✓	25 Feb	Discount	16.61	✓
18 Feb	Inv 3145	415.20	✓	28 Feb	Credit note	162.41	✓
25 Feb	Inv 3156	162.41	✓	28 Feb	Cash	115.29	✓
4 March	Inv 3178	441.79	✓	4 March	Credit note	39.20	✓
18 March	Inv 3229	150.39		16 March	Cash	424.12	✓
20 March	Inv 3237	66.20		16 March	Discount	17.67	✓
27 March	Inv 3250	551.29		30 March	Cash	415.20	✓
				31 March	Balance c/d	767.88	
		2,735.26				2,735.26	

Step 2 Next, analyse the remaining unpaid invoices according to their date. Today's date is 31 March. If we assume a 30-day month:

- < 30 days = invoices with a March date
- 30–60 days = invoices with a February date
- 60–90 days = invoices with an January date
- > 90 days = invoices with a December date (or earlier).

	Date	Amount
Gilde & Co		$
> 90 days	20 December	118.38
60–90 days	–	
30–60 days	11 February	69.02
	26 February	159.27
		228.29
< 30 days	15 March	49.20
	28 March	169.39
		218.59

	Date	Amount
Brandreth		$
< 30 days	18 March	150.39
	20 March	66.20
	27 March	551.29
		767.88

Step 3 We can now prepare an aged analysis report for these customers and in total.

Customer	**Total owing**	**Outstanding for**			
		< 30 days	**30–60 days**	**60–90 days**	**> 90 days**
	$	$	$	$	$
Gilde & Co	565.26	218.59	228.29	–	118.38
Brandreth Co	767.88	767.88	–	–	–
	1,333.14	986.47	228.29	–	118.38
Percentage	100%	74%	17%	–	9%

PRACTICE QUESTION

NITTON CO

To: Supervisor

From: Accountant

Date XXXXXX

Subject: Aged receivables report

As at 30 June, outstanding receivables were $353,000. Of these, $172,000 or 49% were not yet due for payment, and 51% were overdue.

Smith. This customer's debts have now been outstanding for more than 60 days, and the customer is taking longer to pay than the standard 30 days. However, there are no seriously overdue payments, and I recommend that we continue to chase for payment of the overdue amounts, by letter or telephone call, according to standard procedures.

Brown. This customer has a payment pattern worse than Smith's. It is taking up to 90 days to pay, which is too long. I recommend that a sales representative should visit this customer and discuss the problem of late payments, in an effort to improve the customer's payment record.

Jones. This customer is a regular buyer but appears to ignore our credit terms. Some payments have been outstanding for over 90 days. I recommend that we check the credit limit, to establish how much credit the customer is allowed. The account should be put under close scrutiny. As with Brown, I also recommend that a sales representative should visit this customer and discuss the problem of late payments, in an effort to improve the customer's payment record. If the customer continues to be slow with payments, the matter should perhaps be referred to a senior manager with a view to issuing a stop order on further sales.

Shah. Most of the outstanding debts of this customer are under 30 days and so not yet due. However, there is a payment of $8,000 that has been outstanding for over 90 days. I recommend that we contact the customer to ask whether there is a problem with this invoice. It might be that the customer has an unresolved complaint that we should try to resolve quickly.

West. This customer has no payments that are overdue. At this stage, no action is required, although if the customer maintains a good payment record, this will be a factor to consider if it asks for more credit in the future.

CHAPTER 9

ACTIVITY 1

Financial intermediaries are organisations that bring together potential borrowers and potential lenders. A lender does not need to find an individual borrower but can deposit his/her money with a bank, building society, investment trust or other financial intermediary. An intermediary can act as a broker, handling a transaction on behalf of others or as a principal holding money balances of lenders for lending on to borrowers.

ACTIVITY 2

REPOS (sale and purchase agreements) are a means whereby banks obtain liquidity for short periods of time, by selling gilts or other securities, on the condition that they repurchase them at an agreed date in the near future. The Bank of England operates in these two markets. By buying (rediscounting) bills and through gilt repos, it provides liquidity to the banks. It is always prepared to lend in this way in order to ensure adequate liquidity in the economy.

CHAPTER 10

ACTIVITY 1

The cost of overdraft interest will fall. Kitchens are often bought on credit and so people may buy more on the cheaper credit available. Lower interest rates mean cheaper mortgages and so people will be encouraged to move to larger houses and more first time buyers will enter the market. More house sales mean more people will want to replace kitchens. The company's sales should hopefully increase.

ACTIVITY 2

Companies will need to keep their pricing policies under regular review to ensure that their selling prices are keeping pace with inflation. If inflation is at high levels, prices may need to be reviewed more frequently than usual. Companies that fail to keep their prices in step with inflation will ultimately find that their costs are rising faster than their revenues and profits will suffer.

The general level of inflation is of course only one factor influencing the pricing decision. The specific competitive position in which the company finds itself will often be more important. A company that exports goods will need to take account of conditions in its overseas markets. An overseas customer will not pay a significant extra percentage because there is inflation in the producer's own country. Companies operating in markets where prices are fixed for a period may have difficulties in keeping their revenues in pace with inflation.

CHAPTER 11

ACTIVITY 1

A balloon loan and a bullet loan each involve a large final payment to repay a loan. The difference is the amount. A bullet is the full principal amount of the loan; no principal is paid off prior to the date of the bullet. By contrast, a balloon payment is normally less than the full loan amount and some of the loan principal is paid back prior to the date of the balloon payment.

ACTIVITY 2

The following terms could be negotiated.

1 **The term (period) of the loan.** You should try to make sure that the term of the loan is appropriate for its purpose, so that the business will be able to repay the money on time from its expected future income.

2 **The interest rate.** This is likely to be a variable rate. The main point of negotiation should be the margin above base rate or SOFR that the bank will charge. Negotiating a reduction of just 0.5% in the interest rate would save $2,500 in interest each year on a loan of $500,000.

3 **The repayment schedule.** You should try to make sure that the repayment schedule suits the requirements of the business. The business might want to repay the loan principal in a single payment at the end of the loan term. If so, you should resist any suggestions from the bank for gradual repayment of the principal over the term of the loan. You might also be able to negotiate a frequency of interest payment to suit the business requirements, such as six-monthly interest rather than monthly interest.

4 **Security.** The bank might insist on taking security for the loan. Your business would prefer the loan to be unsecured, but this might be an unrealistic expectation. The nature of the security should be negotiated. You should not agree to give more security than the amount of the loan would justify.

5 **Other terms and conditions.** You should check the other terms and conditions proposed by the bank, to make sure that these are acceptable. If they are reasonable, you should probably agree to them. If any seem unreasonable, you should explain why you think they are unacceptable, and negotiate an amendment.

The key objective should be to raise the required amount of money for a suitable term and at a suitable interest rate, without giving excessive security.

CHAPTER 12

ACTIVITY 1

Before		After
J Bloggs' shareholding	1,000 shares	1,250 shares
Total issued capital	4,000,000 shares	5,000,000 shares
J Bloggs' percentage holding	0.025%	0.025%

ACTIVITY 2

Equity finance raised through accumulated profits and rights issues will principally be provided by existing shareholders; new issues will result in a wider shareholder base.

PRACTICE QUESTION

STOCK MARKETS

A stock market is a financial intermediary which brings together individuals with different financial requirements. One of its functions is to enable those who need funds to be matched with those who have a surplus of funds. One example of this might be when a private company goes public, the owner realising some cash by selling off part or all of the interest in the company. Alternatively, companies needing money to carry out investment projects can raise the funds by issuing securities in the primary market.

The secondary market is the other most important role carried out by the London Stock Market. This refers to the purchase and sale of second-hand shares and bonds, those which are already held by investors, rather than newly-issued securities.

Long-term capital can be defined in a number of ways, but the usual period over which long-term funds are lent is ten years or more. There are very many types of long-term capital which a company may issue, but essentially it has a choice of three basic categories: ordinary shares, preferred shares or loan stock.

Ordinary shares, or equity, are held by the owners of the company. Each share represents a share in the assets of the company and entitles its owner to a dividend, paid out of the profits of the company. The dividend is variable both upwards and downwards although, in practice, dividends per share tend to rise slowly over time. In general, ordinary shares also confer the right to vote on their owner.

Preferred shares do not represent ownership of the company, nor do they carry votes. They are entitled to a fixed dividend, which must be paid before the ordinary shareholders receive a dividend. If profits are not high enough to pay the dividend, it remains unpaid, although if the shares are cumulative, all unpaid dividends must be paid as soon as the company makes sufficient profits. Preferred shares are more akin to loan stock than they are to equity.

Loan stock has many different names, the most familiar ones being loan notes or bonds. This is debt capital, normally carrying fixed rate interest. The loan is usually made for a specific number of years, after which it is repaid (although a company may issue irredeemable loan stock, which is never repaid). This is different from ordinary and preferred shares, which are usually not redeemed by the company; investors wishing to realise their investment sell their shares on to other investors.

The main advantage of raising long-term funds on the stock market is the fact that it provides a regulated and ordered way of finding individuals or organisations with money they want to lend. In addition to this function, the secondary market gives assurance to investors that they will be able to realise their investments when they need to. As large volumes of securities are traded on the stock market every day, people are relatively safe in tying up their money for apparently long periods of time. Should they need funds, they can liquidate their investments by selling the securities on to somebody else. This means that companies do not have to find investors who are willing to lend money indefinitely or for many years at a time.

Raising equity or debt both have advantages and disadvantages. Equity is useful as the dividends paid depend on profits, so can be reduced or cancelled in times of difficulty. On the other hand, bringing in new shareholders dilutes the control of the company and subjects the original owners to controls and regulations which they may find onerous.

Debt receives a fixed interest payment which is tax deductible, unlike dividends. This makes debt a fairly cheap form of finance, as the payment of interest is offset to a certain extent by the saving of tax. However, debt agreements usually carry with them the right of the debt holders to force the company into liquidation if interest payments are not met.

One of the main criticisms levelled at the stock market and those who provide funds through it, is the short termism. Share ownership, although perhaps wider than it once was, is concentrated in the hands of a few large institutions, such as pension funds, insurance companies and investment and unit trusts. These institutions are often accused of being interested only in short-term gains, concentrating on dividend pay-outs and fast capital growth. This means that companies are forced into making short-term decisions to satisfy the institutions, rather than considering the longer term and, for example, carrying out research and development, which may use up cash in the present, but will increase future profits.

Another area of complaint which was noted many years ago, but which is less of a problem today, is the lack of funds available for risky or small ventures. The big institutions are reluctant to make such investments, and the cost of raising money on the stock market makes it prohibitive for all but the largest companies. Other sources of capital, in particular venture capital companies, have stepped in to fill this need.

CHAPTER 13

ACTIVITY 1

Expansion

A private company might want to invest more capital in an expansion programme, but be unable to raise the funds internally or from a bank loan. It might therefore seek venture capital.

Management buy-out

A business might need capital for a management buy-out. The management team buying out the business is unlikely to have enough capital of its own to buy the entire business.

Research and development

A business might want capital to invest in research and development, which would be regarded as a high-risk venture. Other sources of finance might therefore be unavailable.

Start-ups

Venture capital is sometimes available for company start-ups.

ACTIVITY 2

The following information would be required, though the actual amount and composition might vary depending on the specific potential financier involved:

(a) presentation of the business plan indicating the goals and directions of the firm

(b) the history of the firm and the type and nature of its production

(c) list of directors and their present and past positions

(d) amount and types of funding required

(e) possible exit routes for the investors

(f) degree of involvement of the investors with the decision making of the firm.

CHAPTER 14

ACTIVITY 1

Revenue expenditure is expenditure incurred either for the purpose of the trade of the business (for example, selling and distribution expenses, administration expenses and finance charges), or is incurred to maintain the existing capacity of non-current assets.

Revenue expenditure is charged to the statement of profit or loss of a period, provided that it relates to the trading activity and sales of that particular period.

Non-current assets, which are the result of capital expenditure, should be distinguished from inventories which are the result of revenue expenditure and which the entity buys and sells as part of its working capital.

Whether expenditure relates to capital or revenue items depends on the type of industry that the entity is in. For example, the purchase of cars for a motor trader is revenue expenditure as these are purchased for resale. However, for an estate agency, company cars are non-current assets.

The distinction between capital and revenue expenditure is important since revenue and capital items are accounted for in different ways. The correct and consistent calculation of profit for any accounting period depends on the correct and consistent classification of items as revenue or capital.

ACTIVITY 2

The events that might give rise to entries in the non-current asset register include:

- purchase of asset
- sale of asset
- loss or destruction of asset
- transfer of assets between departments
- revision of estimated useful life of asset
- scrapping of asset.

CHAPTER 15

ACTIVITY 1

The $15,000 already spent on the feasibility study is not relevant, because it has already been spent. (It is a 'sunk cost'.) Depreciation and apportioned fixed overheads are not relevant. Depreciation is not a cash flow and apportioned fixed overheads represent costs that will be incurred anyway.

	$
Estimated profit	8,000
Add back depreciation	40,000
Add back apportioned fixed costs	25,000
Annual cash flows	73,000

The project's cash flows to be evaluated are:

Year		$
Now (Year 0)	Purchase equipment	(160,000)
1 – 4	Cash flow from profits	73,000 each year

ACTIVITY 2

(a) Payback period

Cumulative cash flows are tabulated below.

Year	0	1	2	3	4	5	6	7
Cumulative ($000)	(800)	(700)	(500)	(100)	300	600	800	950

The payback period appears during the fourth year in which $400,000 arises. Since $100,000 still has to be paid off at the start of the fourth year, the payback period is:

$$3 \text{ years} + \frac{100}{(100+300)} \times 12 \text{ months}$$

= 3 years 3 months

(b) Accounting rate of return

This uses **profits** rather than cash flows.

Average annual inflows	=	$1,750,000 ÷ 7	=	$250,000
Average annual depreciation	=	($800,000 – $100,000) ÷ 7	=	$100,000

(A net $700,000 is being written off as depreciation over 7 years.)

Average annual profit	=	$250,000 – $100,000	=	$150,000

$$\text{ARR} = \frac{\text{Average annual profit}}{\text{Initial investment}} \times 100\% = \frac{\$150{,}000}{\$800{,}000} \times 100\%$$

= **18.75%**

Note: If ARR had been based on the average book value of assets, $150,000 would have been divided by the average of initial capital cost, $800,000, and final scrap value, $100,000 i.e. $450,000, to give an accounting rate of return of $33^1/_3$%.

ACTIVITY 3

$$\text{Payback period} = \frac{\$2{,}300{,}000}{\$600{,}000} = 3.8333 \text{ years}$$

0.8333 years = 10 months (0.8333 ×12)

Payback is therefore after 3 years 10 months.

It is assumed that the cash flows each year occur at an even rate throughout the year.

ACTIVITY 4

The payback period could be found by inspection or by tabulating cumulative cash flows.

Year	0	1	2	3	4	5	6
Cumulative cash flows ($000)	(550)	(450)	(250)	(50)	50	125	150

After 3 years $50,000 is still 'outstanding'; the inflow over the fourth year is $100,000. If cash inflows accrue evenly over the year, the payback period is:

$$3 \text{ years} + \frac{50}{(50+50)} \times 12 \text{ months}$$

= 3 years 6 months

ACTIVITY 5

(a) $\$2,000 \times \frac{1}{1.08^4} = \$1,470$

(b) $\$5,000 \times \frac{1}{1.07^3} = \$4,081$

ACTIVITY 6

Year	Cash flow $	Discount factor at 6%	Present value $
0	(25,000)	1.000	(25,000)
1	6,000	0.943	5,658
2	10,000	0.890	8,900
3	8,000	0.840	6,720
4	7,000	0.792	5,544
			+ 1,822

+ $1,822 is in fact the net present value of the project.

ACTIVITY 7

DCF Schedule (NPV method)

Discount rate 12%

Year	Outflow	Inflow	Discount factor at 12%	NPV
	$	$		$
0	(35,000)		1.000	(35,000)
1		8,000	0.893	7,144
2		9,000	0.797	7,173
3		12,000	0.712	8,544
4		9,500	0.636	6,042
5		9,000	0.567	5,103
			NPV	(994)

Recommendation

At the cost of capital of 12%, the NPV is negative, showing that the investment would earn a return below 12% per annum. On financial considerations, the recommendation is that the project should not be undertaken.

ACTIVITY 8

The first income payment will be received at the end of five years from now and has a present value of

$$\frac{\$5{,}000}{(1.06)^5}$$

The second payment has a present value of $\frac{\$5{,}000}{(1.06)^6}$, etc.

The total PV of the ten payments will therefore be:

$$PV = \$5{,}000\left[\frac{1}{(1.06)^5} + \frac{1}{(1.06)^8} + \frac{1}{(1.06)^7} + \quad + \frac{1}{(1.06)^{14}}\right]$$

The terms inside the square brackets can be regarded as the cumulative PV of $1 for the first 14 years minus the cumulative PV of $1 for the **first four** years. It is worthwhile checking that years 5 to 14 inclusive correspond to years 1 to 14 less years 1 to 4. Thus:

PV = $5,000 × [9.295 – 3.465] (from the tables)

= $29,150

ACTIVITY 9

NPV of project = PV of initial outlay + PV of perpetual receipts

$$= (10,000) + \frac{2,000}{0.16} = (10,000) + 12,500$$

= $2,500

The NPV is positive therefore the project should be accepted.

PRACTICE QUESTION

TOYSRME

(a) The cash flows to consider are only those future cash flows arising as a direct consequence of deciding to manufacture the product. Sunk costs (costs already committed or future spending already committed) and costs not involving any cash spending (such as depreciation charges) must be ignored for decision-making purposes.

(i) Development costs are irrelevant because they have already been incurred, and future marketing costs are irrelevant because they have already been committed.

(ii) The only relevant costs of machinery are the amount it could be sold for now ($790,000) which is a benefit forgone of going into production, and what it could be sold for in five years' time, which would be a cash benefit of going into production.

(iii) The relevant cost of Type A material is its replacement cost, $15 per unit.

(iv) The relevant cost of the first 12,000 kilos of Type B material (4,000 units of product) is $1.50 per kilo or $18,000 in total. This is a benefit that would be forgone immediately, i.e. in Year 0. Further costs of Type B material for units after the first 4,000 are $2.50 per kilo, or $7.50 per unit. Cost are therefore $75,000 per annum except in year 1, when Type B materials for only 6,000 units will be purchased (cost $45,000).

(v) If the project goes ahead, labour costs will be $12 per unit, with a redundancy cost of $80,000 at the end of year 5. However, there would be a saving in current redundancy costs of $50,000.

(vi) The only relevant fixed costs are those relating to incremental expenditure as a consequence of going into production, $60,000 per annum.

(b) Cash flows

Year	0	1	2	3	4	5
	$000	$000	$000	$000	$000	$000
Sales		650	650	650	650	650
Machinery	(790)					70
Working capital	(150)					150
Type A material		(150)	(150)	(150)	(150)	(150)
Type B material	(18)	(45)	(75)	(75)	(75)	(75)
Labour costs	50	(120)	(120)	(120)	(120)	(200)
Fixed costs		(60)	(60)	(60)	(60)	(60)
Net cash flow	(908)	275	245	245	245	385

(c) The NPV and the IRR

Year	Cash flow $000	Discount factor at 12%	Present value $000	Discount factor at 18%	Present value $000
0	(908.0)	1.00	(908.0)	1.00	(908.0)
1	275	0.89	244.8	0.85	233.8
2	245	0.80	196.0	0.72	176.4
3	245	0.71	174.0	0.61	149.5
4	245	0.64	156.8	0.52	127.4
5	385	0.57	219.5	0.44	169.4
		NPV	83.1		–51.5

Approximate IRR

$$IRR = 12\% + \left[\frac{83.1}{(83.1 - -51.5)} \times (18-12) \right] \%$$

= 15.7%

The NPV is $83,100 at the company's cost of capital and the IRR is 15.7%.

Since the NPV is positive at the company's cost of capital and the IRR exceeds the company's cost of capital, ToysRme should make the product, subject to the view being taken that the risk is not excessive. Some sensitivity analysis might be carried out on the estimates of cash flows, to assess the sensitivity of the NPV and IRR to realistic potential variations in the estimates.

(d) Both the NPV and IRR methods of DCF analysis take into account both the incremental cash flows arising from a project and the line value of the money. This makes them superior to other methods of capital expenditure appraisal, such as accounting rate of return and payback. In most cases, the NPV and IRR methods would point to the same recommendation as to whether or not to undertake the project. However, the two methods might point to differing recommendations when there are two projects under consideration and only one of them can be undertaken (i.e. the projects are mutually exclusive). In such cases, it is possible for one project to have a higher NPV but a lower IRR than the other.

When the NPV method and IRR method give conflicting recommendations, the recommendation of the NPV method should be preferred. An underlying assumption is that cash flows received from a project can be reinvested in other projects at the cost of capital. This is more sensible than the underlying assumption of the IRR method, which is that cash flows can be reinvested on other projects to yield a return equal to the project's IRR.

The NPV method gives a money value to a project (whereas the IRR method gives a percentage annual yield). In theory, this is the amount by which the equity value of the company should increase if the project is undertaken. Since a major objective of a company should be to increase shareholder wealth, the NPV method has the added advantage over the IRR method that it gives an indication of the increase in shareholder wealth that ought to be expected as a consequence of making the investment.

INDEX

N

O

P

Q

R